Distributed Computer Systems

Distributed Computer Systems
Theory and practice

H. S. M. Zedan, BSc, PhD
Department of Computer Science
University of York,
York, UK

Butterworths
London   Boston   Singapore   Sydney   Toronto   Wellington

First published 1990

© Butterworth & Co (Publishers) Ltd, 1990, excepting Chapter 2, copyright 1983,
Association for Computing Machinery, Inc., reprinted by permission

British Library Cataloguing in Publication Data

Zedan, H. S. M.
  Distributed computer systems: theory and practice.
  1. Distributed computer systems
  I. Title
  004.36

  ISBN 0-408-02938-2

Library of Congress Cataloging in Publication Data

Distributed computer systems: theory and practice / [edited by]
  H. S. M. Zedan.
       p.   cm.
  Includes bibliographical references.
  ISBN 0-408-02938-2:
  1. Electronic data processing—Distributed processing.
  I. Zedan, H. S. M.
  QA76.9.D5D4858   1990
  004'.36—dc20

Filmset by Bath Typesetting Ltd., London Road, Bath, Avon
Printed and bound by Hartnolls Ltd, Bodmin, Cornwall

Preface

Distributed computing systems have increasingly become, for the past two decades or so, an active area of research and development. This, however, was an inevitable consequence as the cost of processing elements has continually fallen which was a contributing factor in attracting and encouraging many of such systems to be built, cost-effectively, and be experimented with. The overall poor performance of centralized computer systems and the diversity in the user's required facilities have also made the design of such systems a viable alternative.

With the advent of this new technology, new challenging problems have emerged that motivated and stimulated many theoreticians and practitioners. But what really is a distributed system? and why do we need them? Many authors have expressed their views about what constitutes a distributed system and presented models for such a system. Enslow's model* has provided a global model for distributed computing systems. The model is considered by some authors to be an extreme and to others as a unification view of the system.

Nevertheless, the term 'Distributed system' itself has been used by many designers of both multicomputer and multiprocessor computer systems. Several classifications have been proposed to identify the differences between the different computing system designs which are often referred to as 'distributed'. Among these classifications are the *loosely-coupled distributed systems, tightly-coupled multiprocessor systems, array processors* and other *parallel* and *pipeline* architectures (such as *dataflow* and *systolic* machines).

Distributed systems are now in use in a wide range of computer applications and are being considered as a 'first candidate' whenever a new application emerges. Although some of the design and implementation principles of such systems have been widely understood and accepted there are still some issues which are subject to current research and likely to influence the next generation of distributed computing systems. Multi-media systems, reliability and fault-tolerance, real-time distributed systems, and language support are among many issues that are under current investigations.

Programming languages which exhibit some form of parallel composition of commands have also become more prominent as distributed processing moved to a more mature state of art. **CSP**, **CCS**, **SCCS**, **ada** and **occam** are just a few examples of the several parallel languages which have been

* Enslow, P. H., What is a 'distributed' system? *Computer*, 1978, pp. 13–21.

developed. It is well known that allowing concurrent execution may very well lead to undesirable pathological behaviour, such as deadlock and starvation. Reasoning effectively about programs which are written in these languages is vitally important as it helps in proving properties about the programs such as absence of deadlock and starvation. To be able to do so, formal models need to be developed as a basis for the required formal proofs and reasoning. Interests in specifying and reasoning about properties of concurrent systems have grown and several semantic models for concurrency have been proposed. Much work has been carried out on proofs of equivalency between the different semantics. In Brookes, et al.,* some of these models have been reported and other research areas on concurrency have also been represented.

The idea behind compiling this book was borne from a workshop which was held in July 1987 at Teesside Polytechnic. The workshop aimed to bring together both theoreticians and practitioners in the field of distributed computing systems. It was decided however to present the book as a reference book rather than merely a workshop proceedings. Hence the book is intended for those who are already working in the distributed computing field and for those who have just started, for example MSc and PhD students.

Besides some selected papers from the workshop, which address some rather important areas in distributed systems, the book contains a 'survey' part and a references and annotated bibliography part which we hope will give the reader an easy and quick access to references of previous work.

The book begins with the surveys part which consists of three state-of-the-art surveys covering three major and important topics in distributed computer systems.

Jonathan Bowen and Tim Gleeson's survey on *Distributed operating systems* considers some of the forces and the nature of distributed systems. The survey concentrates on some of the issues relevant to the design and implementation of distributed (operating) systems. The authors then present an overview of some of the distributed systems which are either under development or are commercially available. These case studies include the **amoeba** system, **argus**, **andrew** and **grapevine**. The survey ends with a discussion of the current practice and future trends in distributed systems research.

The second survey paper is *Concepts and notations for concurrent programming* by Gregory R. Andrews and Fred B. Schneider. This important survey identifies the major concepts of concurrent programming and describes some of the more important language notations for writing concurrent programs. Language notations for expressing concurrent execution and for specifying process interaction are surveyed. Synchronization primitives based on shared variables and on message passing are also described. The survey ends by identifying three general classes of concurrent programming languages and then compares them. (I should mention here that in a book of the nature and objectives such as this, one ought to devote a large section to address the topic of concepts and notations of concurrency in programming languages. However, I feel impelled to say that in every attempt to write on such a topic

---

* Brookes, S. D., Roscoe, A. W. and Winskel, G. *Seminar on Concurrency* LNCS **197**, 1985.

it was found to be rather difficult to do better than this excellent survey by professors Andrews and Schneider. Therefore I decided to include it in the book.)

The third and last survey deals with an important aspect of distributed operating systems; that is of load balancing which attempts to improve system performance by redistributing the workload submitted to the system by its users. *Load balancing algorithms in loosely-coupled distributed systems: a Survey* by A. J. Harget and Ian D. Johnson discusses in detail the problem of load balancing and presents an account of previously studied approaches of the two main categories: static and adaptive load balancing.

The second part of the book is devoted to a few selected papers from the above mentioned workshop. The papers present recent research and development of important topics in distributed systems.

The paper by Andy Wellings and D. Snowden: *Debugging distributed real-time applications: a case study in* **ada** discusses the considerations involved in the design of a debugger for distributed **ada** programs. The system presented in the paper facilitates a wide range of debugging approaches: For any given program, the user can select the particular approach which provides the maximum of debugging assistance without significantly disturbing the behaviour of the program. A brief survey of related work in the area of multiprocess debugging is also given.

In his paper, *Reliable systems in* **occam**, H. Zedan proposed a scheme to support error recovery in the programming language **occam**. The scheme is based on structuring the concurrent **occam** program into a set of communication-closed layers which are then run sequentially. Each layer is in fact a 'basic' atomic action and to achieve consistency, each layer is made recoverable. A recovery scheme is then proposed and incorporated into the layered structure of the system.

Real-time database is an important research area in computer network. In *The architecture of real-time distributed database for computer network monitoring*, C. H. C. Leung and J. Z. Lu have described an architecture of a real-time distributed database system used for computer network management. This architecture is able to provide a high degree of resilience and reliability. This is achieved by the use of a novel crash recovery mechanism which is superior to conventional ones; it makes use of network status monitoring information to detect in advance any network failures before the instigation of database transactions.

The paper by Andy Cheese, *A distributed model of computation for combinatory code*, presents a model to exploit the implicit parallelism present in a functional program. The model is based upon a parallel packet based graph reduction scheme which allows code to be treated in exactly the same manner as data.

The final contribution in this section is by J. Mead. In his paper, **isaac**: *a high-level distributed language* he describes the design of the distributed language **isaac**. It is a high-level language for writing distributed programs with communication structure as its central design point. Aspects of implementing **isaac** on a network of SUN workstations are also considered.

The final part of the book is devoted to references and annotated bibliographies. In this part, over 1600 references on distributed/concurrent languages, systems and related topics covering the period from 1959 to 1989 are compiled. In addition, an annotated bibliography to the 'key' papers in the field is also given. These 'key' contributions are considered to be the milestones of the subject concerned. The bibliography deals with the following topics: models for concurrent programming, formal treatment of concurrency, and concurrent programming languages.

H. S. M. Zedan
July 1989
York University, UK

Acknowledgements

I would like to express my gratitude to both professors Gregory Andrews and Fred Schneider and to the editors of *ACM Computing Surveys* for granting us permission to reproduce the article 'Concepts and notations for concurrent programming', (**15**(1), March 1983). I would also like to acknowledge D. S. Simpson for the help in organizing the July Workshop. Finally, I should like to thank Danica, Nadia and Camillia who put up with my merciless moods and still love me (I hope!).

Contributors

Gregory R. Andrews
Professor and Head, Department of Computer Science, The University of Arizona, Tucson, USA

Jonathan P. Bowen MA (Oxon)
Programming Research Group, Oxford University Computing Laboratory, Oxford, UK

Andy Cheese BSc, MSc
European Computer-Industry Research Centre GmbH, Munich, West Germany

Tim J. Gleeson
Cambridge University Computer Laboratory, Cambridge, UK

A. J. Harget BSc, PhD, MBCS
Lecturer, Department of Computer Science and Applied Mathematics, Aston University, Birmingham, UK

I. D. Johnson BSc, PhD
Department of Computer Science and Applied Mathematics, Aston University, Birmingham, UK

C. H. C. Leung PhD
Professor, Department of Computer Science, Birkbeck College, London University, London, UK

J. Z. Lu BSc
Software Engineer, Cellnet Centre, London, UK

Jerud J. Mead PhD
Associate Professor, Computer Science Department, Bucknell University, Lewisburg, Pennsylvania, USA

Fred B. Schneider BSc, PhD
Associate Professor, Department of Computer Science, Cornell University, Ithaca, USA

D. S. Snowden BSc, D.Phil
Research Associate, Department of Computer Science, University of York, York, UK

A. J. Wellings BA, D.Phil
Lecturer, Department of Computer Science, University of York, York, UK

H. S. M. Zedan BSc, PhD
Lecturer, Department of Computer Science, University of York, York, UK

Contents

Part 1

Surveys

Chapter 1

Distributed operating systems

Jonathan P. Bowen and Tim J. Gleeson

The last decade has seen the creation and rapid expansion of the field of distributed computing systems. This has been driven by both technical and social forces and it seems likely that the pressure from both will continue for some time yet.

Initially we will consider some of those forces and the nature of the distributed systems which have resulted. In particular, throughout this chapter, we will look at the form of distributed operating systems (DOS) which represent, technically, the leading edge of the field.

In later sections we will examine some of the issues relevant to the design and implementation of distributed systems and present a number of case studies. Finally we will look at current practices and future trends and provide some pointers to other work.

Reasons for distribution

The two major forces behind the rapid adoption of distributed systems are *technical* and *social* ones.

Technical reasons

The two major forces here are *communication* and *computation*.

Long haul, relatively slow communication paths between computers have existed for a long time, but only recently has the technology for fast, cheap and reliable *local area networks* (LAN) emerged. These LANs allow the connection of large numbers of computing elements with a high degree of information sharing. These typically run at 1–10 M bits per second. These have become relatively cheap and plentiful with the advances of microelectronics and microprocessor technology. In response, the *wide area networks* (WAN) are becoming faster and more reliable.

Social reasons

Many enterprises are cooperative in nature, e.g. offices, multinational companies, university campuses etc., requiring sharing of resources and information. Distributed systems can provide this either by integrating pre-existing systems, or building new systems which inherently reflect sharing patterns in their structure. A further, and somewhat contrary, motivation is the desire for autonomy of resources seen by individuals in an enterprise.

Discussion

That the new technology can meet these immediate social pressures is one thing, but it can provide far more, and in turn increase social expectations.

Distributed systems can offer greater *adaptability*. Their nature forces them to be designed in a modular way and this can be used to advantage to allow incremental (and possibly dynamic) changes in performance and functionality by the addition or removal of elements.

The *performance* of distributed systems can be made much better than that of centralized systems and with the fall in the price of microprocessors can also be very much cheaper. However, this performance gain is usually manifested in the form of greater *capacity* rather than *response*. Increasing the latter is currently limited by our ability to make use of parallelism, which is mainly a software problem, and will probably see more progress in the area of *tightly coupled systems*. These are multiprocessor systems with very fast communications, such as is provided by shared memory systems and **transputer** systems. This is in contrast to the *loosely coupled systems* which we consider here, typified by asynchronous, autonomous computers on a LAN.

Availability can be increased because the adaptability of distributed systems allows for the easy addition of redundant elements. This is a potential benefit which has only been realized in a few systems. In many, the system as a whole becomes less available because it is made dependent on the availability of all of (the large number of) its components. This again is largely a software problem.

Design issues in distributed systems

Before we can examine the issues and problems in designing distributed systems we need to define their fundamental properties. For this we rely on the analysis of LeLann (1981) who lists the following characteristics:

1. They contain an arbitrary number of processes.
2. They have a modular architecture and possibly dynamic composition.
3. The basic method of communication is message passing between processes.
4. There is some system-wide control.
5. There are variable (non-zero) message delays.

The existence of the last item means that centralized control techniques cannot be used, because there may never be a globally consistent state to observe and from which decisions can be made. Distributed systems carry over most of the problems of centralized systems, but it is this problem which gives them their unique flavour and characteristics.

Distributed operating systems

DOSs have been the subject of much research activity in the field of distributed systems and thus provide a suitable vehicle for the discussion of design issues in general.

Operating systems (OS) control the bare resources of a computing system to provide users with a more convenient abstraction for computation. Thus the user's view of a system is mostly determined by the OS. A DOS is an OS built on distributed resources. There is much argument over what abstraction for computation a DOS should provide for its users. We will cover these issues as we proceed.

The term *network operating system* (NOS) is now fading in its usage, but requires some mention. Like many terms it means different things to different people. For many, a NOS is a 'guest level extension' applied to a number of existing centralized operating systems which are then interconnected via a network. These systems are characterized by the high degree of autonomy of the nodes, the lack of system-wide control and the non-transparency of the network. On the other hand, DOSs are normally systems designed from scratch to be integrated and exercise much system-wide control. Others distinguish the two, not on the lines of implementation but on the lines of the view of computation provided to users: in a DOS it is generally transparent but in a NOS it is not; special utilities are needed to use network facilities.

We will take the view that the provision of transparency of distribution of computation is one that DOSs are free to make, whilst they must use system-wide control. We will not discuss NOSs further.

A distributed computing system (or any computing system) is normally built in a hierarchical manner using a number of layers. Each layer provides a set of facilities to the level above, and uses the facilities of the level below. We propose to look at the issues of the provision of functions in one particular layer, the DOS *kernel*; we must look both at *what* functions are going to be provided and *how* they are going to be implemented. Many of the issues that arise are not peculiar to this layer but occur elsewhere, maybe in higher, service and application layers, or maybe lower, within the layers of the implementation of the kernel.

Model of computation

We must choose a convenient model of computation in which to discuss these issues. Two popular models are the 'object–action' model and the 'process–message' model. In the former, a system consists of a set of objects (e.g. files) on which a number of operations (e.g. read and write) are defined; these operations can be invoked by users to change the state of the objects to get work done. In the latter model, a system is a set of processes (e.g. clients and file servers) prepared to exchange messages (e.g. read file request, write file request); receipt of messages causes processes to change state and thus get work done.

The terminology in this area is in some state of confusion but 'object–actions' systems roughly correspond to 'monitor-based' and 'abstract data type' systems while 'process–message' systems correspond to 'client–server' systems. Lauer and Needham (1979) have shown these models to be duals of each other.

Most systems can be placed in one of these categories; e.g. **argus** (Liskov and Scheifler, 1983) and **eden** (Almes *et al.*, 1985) are object–action systems and **amoeba** (Mullender, 1987), **accent/mach-1** (Rashid and Robertson, 1981;

Baron *et al.*, 1985) and the **V-kernel** (Cheriton, 1984) are process–message systems.

This characterization should not be applied too zealously. Both models essentially provide a way of performing computations and it is relatively straightforward to transform one type of system to the other. As already mentioned, because of the nature of the hardware, the basic method of communication in distributed systems is message passing between processes but in many cases the two models can be found at different layers within a system.

Naming

Objects and processes have to be named so that they can be accessed and manipulated. Since there are many sorts of objects in a system it is tempting to adopt many sorts of names. This must be tempered by a desire for conceptual simplicity. An important property of names is their scope of applicability; e.g. 'the value at location (with name) 7000' is only unique within a particular machine. As examples of such contexts, we can imagine the names of different sorts of objects which reside in a WAN, on a single LAN, in a service, on a server or somewhere in the memory of a particular machine.

Transforming names from one form to another is a very important function, even in centralized systems. One example is transforming a string name for a **UNIX*** file to an *inode* number. Because distributed systems are so much more dynamic it is even more important to delay the binding of 'logical' and 'physical' names. Some sort of *mapping* or *name service* is required. Since this is such an important function, availability and reliability are vital. The domains and ranges of the mapping are often wide but sparse so in many systems names are structured to allow more efficient searches for entries.

Names can also be used, implicitly or explicitly for protection purposes, as we will discuss later.

Processes and inter-process communication (IPC)

We have defined the exchange of messages between processes to be the basic form of communication in distributed systems but also note that it is easy to build the actions of object–action systems on top of this mechanism. For these, the idea of *remote procedure call* (RPC) forms a useful extension from the world of single machine local procedure calls (Nelson, 1981; Birrell and Nelson, 1983). How transparent these should be from issues of location and errors is a matter of some debate. Whether RPCs or messages are used, the destination has to be located, using the mapping facilities already sketched. The use of RPCs has become popular because they represent an easy to use, familiar communication concept. They do not, however, solve all problems (Tanenbaum and van Renesse, 1988).

The structure of units of activity is very important. Work in recent years (in centralized as well as distributed systems) has led to the realization that a

---

* **UNIX** is a trademark of AT & T Bell Laboratories.

single kind of activity is inadequate in system design. Many have adopted a two level structuring. The outer level, called *heavy-weight processes* (HWP), represent complete address spaces, are relatively well protected and accounted for, but switching between them is slow because of the large amount of state involved. Distribution is performed at the level of HWPs. They are typified by **UNIX** processes. Within these a number of *light-weight processes* (LWP) operate; these have much less state associated with them, are unprotected, share the address space of the containing HWP but it is possible to switch between these relatively rapidly. For example, there may be a number of HWPs on each node. One of these may represent a server. The server may be structured as a number of LWPs, one dedicated to the service of each client request.

Consistency

The abnormal (e.g. crashes) and normal (e.g. concurrent sharing) activity of a system may threaten its consistency.

The problem of concurrency control is well known in multiprocessing systems. The problem and its solutions become harder when the degree of sharing and the amount of concurrency increase in distributed systems. In particular, the lack of global state first of all makes the solutions more difficult and also introduces the need for replication which causes more consistency problems. Maintaining consistency requires the imposition of some ordering of the events within a system. The substantial insight of Lamport (1978) is that the events in a distributed system only define a *partial order* rather than a *total order*. Required orderings can be achieved by extending existing centralized mechanisms, such as *locking*, or using *time-stamp* based algorithms.

Making systems resilient to faults in order to increase their reliability is an often quoted, rarely achieved feature of distributed systems. Both of these issues have been tackled with the notion of *atomic actions*. Their semantics are a conceptually simple 'all or nothing', but their implementation is rather harder, requiring essentially images of 'before' states should things prove sufficiently difficult that the only option is to roll back. This gets much harder when many objects are involved. Much work from the database world, particularly the notions of *transactions* and *two-phase commit* protocols have been adapted and extended to a distributed world. Atomic actions match quite well to RPC systems that provide 'at-most-once' semantics.

Another source of problems for consistency is dynamic reconfiguration of the system itself, adding or perhaps removing elements for maintenance whilst the system is still running.

Heterogeneity and transparency

Heterogeneity must often be handled by OSs and particularly by DOSs. Examples of possible heterogeneity occur in network hardware, communication mechanisms, processor architectures (including multiprocessors), data representations, location etc. In order that such disparate resources should not increase system complexity too much, they need to be accommodated in a coherent way. Notkin *et al.* (1986) consider some of the issues and means involved. The key issue of such systems is *transparency*. How much of the heterogeneity is made visible to the user and how much is hidden depends very much on the nature of the heterogeneity. Other factors apart from heterogeneity can be made transparent to users, such as plurality of homogeneous processors in, for example, a processor pool.

The choice to be made is generally one of providing users with conceptually simpler interfaces, or more complicated ones which allow for the possibility of higher performance. For example, if location of processes is not transparent and can be manipulated, users can co-locate frequently communicating elements of their applications. If location is transparent the system will have to infer patterns of communication before it can consider migrating processes.

Issues of transparency cut across most of the other issues we will cover (e.g. naming, IPC and security) and need to be considered along with them.

Security and protection

A *security policy* governs who may obtain, and how they may modify, information. A *protection mechanism* is used to reliably enforce a chosen security policy (Jones, 1979). The need to identify users and resources thus arises.

The distribution of a system into disjoint components increases the independence of those components and eases some security problems. On the other hand, a network connecting these components is open to attack, allowing information to be tapped or altered (whether maliciously or accidentally), thus subverting the *privacy* and *integrity* of their communication. In such a situation each component must assume much more responsibility for its own security. Claims about identity must be *authenticated*, either using a local mechanism or with some external agency, to prevent impersonation. The total security of a system cannot rely on all the kernels being secure since there may be many types of these (for all the different processors) and a variable number of instances of them. It would be easy to subvert an existing instance or to insert a new one. Thus authentication functions should be moved out of kernels.

Access control is a particular security model. There exists a conceptual matrix which identifies the *rights* that *subjects* (e.g. users, processes, process groups) have over all *objects* (e.g. data, peripherals, processes). Two popular realizations of this are *access control lists* (ACL) and *capabilities*. In the former, an ACL is associated with each object, listing the subjects and their rights over it. In the latter, each subject possesses a set of capabilities each of which identifies an object and the rights that the subject has over it. Each realization has its own merits and drawbacks, but capability based distributed systems seem to be more numerous.

Capabilities must identify objects and rights, so it is natural to extend a naming scheme to incorporate this mechanism. They must also be difficult to forge, which is harder to achieve without a trusted kernel. Drawing them from a sparse space and validating them before use allows them to be employed in distributed systems.

Cryptographic techniques can be used to tackle a number of these problems including ensuring privacy and integrity of communications, authentication of parties and digital signatures as proof of origins, (Needham and Schroeder, 1978). Eventually, VLSI technology will make their use, at least at network interfaces, standard, though they can be used at different levels in the communications hierarchy for different purposes.

Many of these techniques centre on the knowledge that parties have about encryption *keys* and thus *key distribution* becomes a new problem which needs to be solved. Use of *public key* systems can ease this, but many systems rely on some (more or less) trusted registry of keys, or an authentication server. The parallels with name servers again show the interdependence of naming and security.

Language support

The trend has been for generally useful concepts to find themselves expressed in programming languages, and the features of distributed systems are no exception (Feldman, 1979).

There are many languages that incorporate the notions of processes and messages, or light-weight processes and RPCs. Others are object oriented and can be used for dealing with objects in a distributed environment and in others still the notion of atomic actions is supported.

The problem of separately compiled, linked and executed cooperating programs are to some extent a superset of those already found in programs with separately compiled modules in centralized systems. The notion of a server managing a set of objects of a particular abstract data type and its implementation as a module allows module interfaces to be used as the unit of binding before services are used.

As an example, the **eden** system (Black, 1985) is based on the ideas of capabilities and invocations. The language **EPL** provides direct support for these, and for LWPs.

Evolution of DOSs

DOSs have not appeared from nowhere; they are strongly influenced both in their form and development by existing systems. In fact Gray (1986) cites the integration of pre-existing systems to provide common services to be one of the main organizational reasons for decentralized computing. In general, this leads to NOSs, but there are examples of where existing functionality, rather than particular systems, are decentralized. **UNIX** is one example of this; the software base is so great that there is very strong pressure to build distributed systems which are either object code, or at least source code, compatible with it.

locus (Walker *et al.*, 1983; Popek and Walker, 1985) is a version of **UNIX** which runs on a collection of networked, heterogeneous machines, providing a 'centralized system' view to application programs. A replicated file system and the plurality of machines allow for greater reliability, availability and performance.

amoeba is an entirely different system from **UNIX** yet sees the utility in first providing a mechanism for the handling of **UNIX** system calls to allow **UNIX** programs to be run on *amoeba* systems and secondly by providing a mechanism for **amoeba** calls to be used on connected **UNIX** systems (van Renesse, 1986).

The proliferation of **UNIX** systems has naturally made it an attractive vehicle on which to develop and prototype distributed systems. However, there are sometimes drawbacks; for example, implementing objects under **UNIX** is difficult (Black, 1985). The most obvious approach is a light-weight process for each object, but **UNIX** processes are very heavy-weight.

Review of some current systems

The case studies included here are each selected to represent examples of a class of systems. Rather than cover a large number of different systems in little depth, a small number of representative systems are presented so that a fuller account of each of their features can be conveyed. A final subsection lists a number of other important systems, together with references, for those interested in investigating this diverse field further.

amoeba

The **amoeba** distributed system is being developed at the Vrije Universiteit and the Centre for Mathematics and Computer Science (CWI), both in Amsterdam, the Netherlands. As previously mentioned, it is an example of a process–message based system.

The system consists of a minimal kernel which runs on a number of machines on a LAN; the machines can be roughly classed as workstations, processor-pool machines, specialized servers and gateways. The kernel has been implemented on a variety of hardware including a multiprocessor. There are several widely available papers on aspects of **amoeba**, but many of these can be found in the collection (Mullender, 1987).

The units of activity are *clusters* and *tasks* (or *processes* and *threads* in the latest version) which match our notion of HWPs and LWPs. Threads synchronize using semaphores. Segments are manipulated by mapping them in and out of the address space of clusters. Mechanisms exist to migrate clusters between nodes.

One name space in the system is that of *ports*. Processes send and receive messages on these using an unreliable, bounded length datagram facility. Protection in the system rests on the fact that it is only possible to communicate with a process if the port on which it is listening is known.

On top of these are the concept of *servers*; these support *transactions* (operations) on *objects*. Servers are object managers and are associated with the ports on which they handle transactions on those objects. In a transaction, a client transmits a request for an operation on an object to the appropriate server. While the client blocks, the server process carries out the request and eventually returns a reply. This request–reply pair is called a transaction. The transaction layer is built on the port layer datagram facility but uses timers and acknowledgements to achieve reliable delivery. The messages are again of bounded length. A great deal of effort has been invested to make transactions fast, both in terms of latency and throughput.

Another name space is that of *capabilities*; these name objects. A capability for an object has the port of the server that created the object bound in (thus preventing the movement of objects between servers) along with a rights field and a field to identify individual objects within a server. Transactions are in fact applied to capabilities for objects, and are implemented by extracting the port field from the capability. The kernel locates processes listening on ports using a *broadcast* message on the LAN. Each node maintains a cache of known port/host address pairs to speed up location.

Protection is provided by the capabilities themselves. These are made secure against modification or fabrication by effectively signing them using an encryption method.

Most functionality in the system has been moved out of the kernel and into services. Those designed or built include several different file services (including a very sophisticated one using optimistic concurrency control), a directory service, loader and boot services for process manipulation and a bank service for accounting and gateways. The kernel itself only offers primitives for the creation and management of clusters, tasks and their associated segments (which are all, of course, named by capabilities), as well as the transaction facility.

In contrast to these relatively long-lived and well publicized public services, users can create their own private services to manage any type of objects they see fit. Unless the user publishes the port on which these services listen, by handing out capabilities for the objects created, no one else will be able to access or interfere with them. These services can be as short-lived as desired.

The system already provides support for running existing **UNIX** applications. Work is under way to adapt **amoeba** for use in WANs. This involves the construction of gateways, new wide-area transaction protocols and locate mechanisms.

argus

argus (Liskov and Scheifler, 1983) is an object-oriented distributed operating system developed at Massachusetts Institute of Technology (MIT). It was designed with a number of requirements in mind:

- The system should provide continuous service.
- Dynamic reconfiguration should be possible.
- Nodes may be owned by different individuals and organizations.
- Placement of modules should be under programmer control for efficiency reasons.
- Advantage should be made of concurrency using distribution where possible.
- Consistency must be maintained.

The last item is particularly hard to meet in a distributed system.

The **argus** programming language was derived from an object-oriented language called **CLU** (Liskov *et al.*, 1981), also developed at MIT. Extra linguistic support was added for the construction of reliable distributed programs.

An object in **argus** is known as a '*guardian*'. Each guardian executes on a single processor node in its own address space. A program consists of a number of guardians and thus may be distributed across a number of nodes. Only guardians have global names. Each guardian has an external interface and a number of processes for handling this interface and for internal maintenance as required. The state of a guardian is held in *data objects*. Some of these may be updated by *atomic* transactions. Some objects are *stable* as well as being atomic; this makes them resilient to hardware faults. New data types may be defined if desired. A data object may only be passed by value between guardians. Guardians are the only means of data storage provided by **argus**. Thus for example, there is no concept of a file in the normal sense.

Guardians are created dynamically. They are positioned at a particular node under programmer control. The name of a guardian may be passed to another guardian and can subsequently be used to perform operations on that guardian. It is not necessary to know the location of a guardian to access it. Indeed a guardian may change its position and continue to work; this allows easy dynamic reconfiguration.

There is no guardian hierarchy in terms of types, composition, naming, etc. Any guardian that knows the name of another guardian can communicate with it. Hence there is only limited support for capabilities.

Objects within a guardian can be manipulated transparently. Several guardians may be present on the same processor node but this is not visible to application programs under normal circumstances. However, data within a guardian is handled differently from data stored on remote guardians. This impresses on the programmer the difference in efficiency in accessing local and remote data objects.

argus provides *at-most-once* semantics. Each action can either succeed or fail; in the case of failure, it is guaranteed that the original request has not been carried out. Actions may be nested. Nested actions, or subactions, are a means of introducing concurrency and sequencing into an action. The overall action is still performed atomically. Subactions can commit or abort independently. If a subaction aborts, the parent need not necessarily abort. However, if the parent does abort, then even committed subactions will be aborted. Nested actions aid modularization and allows existing actions to be combined into a new action. The **argus** nested transaction facility was based on work done by Moss, see Moss (1985).

A two phase locking mechanism is used: in the first phase locks are gradually acquired and changes made on temporary versions of objects; in the second phase the updates are made permanent and locks are released. A two phase commit mechanism is also used; in the first phase temporary versions of objects are written to stable storage; if successful a commit decision is made and in the second phase locks and old versions of objects can be discarded.

Locks and temporary versions of data are held in (volatile) memory and are thus lost if a node crashes. This causes any transaction affected to abort. Deadlocks can occur as in any system with locking, and it is up to the programmer to avoid this problem. However, the programmer is freed from the low-level task of supplying explicit time-outs, etc. This is provided by **argus**, but the programmer must be prepared to take avoiding action if they do occur.

argus provides two levels of fault tolerance. The atomicity of transactions is achieved by holding multiple versions of objects in memory. Recovery from hardware faults is provided using stable objects. This is implemented as a log which can be used to restore objects back into memory. Management of stable and atomic objects is automatically handled by **argus**. Replicated objects are not provided but may be easily implemented using atomic transactions.

Nodes may be heterogeneous and the network may be a LAN or a WAN in principle; neither need be reliable. There is a canonical form for each data type for transmission over the network. Encoding and decoding routines must be supplied by the programmer at each node. Type checking is provided at compile-time rather than run-time.

argus has a number of disadvantages and omissions. It does not easily interface to other network-based systems. No authorization or encryption mechanisms are supplied. This could be a major disadvantage in, say, a distributed office system, and would require a considerable amount of work to incorporate. Thus **argus** is an interesting research tool, but is unlikely to be exploited commercially in its current form.

Experience in the use of **argus** (Grief *et al.*, 1986) has suggested that the mechanisms provided do help in building reliable distributed programs. There were, however, problems, one being the existence of two separate, but very different abstraction mechanisms, namely **argus** guardians and **CLU** clusters. The choice of which to use is sometimes difficult to make. This contrasts with the **emerald** system which tried to tackle this problem by providing a uniform object model to the programmer (Black *et al.*, 1987).

The two most important concepts in **argus** are *guardians* and *actions*. Data within a guardian is local to that guardian; it cannot be directly accessed by other guardians. Actions are the means by which distributed computation is achieved. A top-level action can invoke nested subactions. Thus **argus** presents a good example of the object–action model of distributed computation.

NFS

NFS (Network File System) (SUN, 1986a) is a commercially available system originally designed by SUN Microsystems Inc. It provides a facility for sharing files in a heterogeneous environment of networks and computer systems. Servers make resources available to clients. Machines may be clients, servers, or both. However, intermediate servers are not allowed. Remote file systems may be mounted and then accessed in place, without the necessity to copy the file from the remote server to the local machine.

The system is not a complete distributed operating system in that it only addresses one aspect of an operating system, namely providing permanent read/write storage in the form of files. However, it is widely and commercially available and as such provides an interesting comparison with some of the more research-oriented systems described elsewhere in this chapter. It is an example of a self-sufficient system – i.e. in principle, each node is capable of stand-alone operation. **NFS** does not depend on **UNIX**, but in practice it is normally used to mount remote file systems onto (often diskless) client **UNIX** workstations. SUN have made details of the **NFS** protocols widely available (SUN, 1986b) so a number of manufacturers now support it.

NFS attempts to address a number of design goals:

- Transparent information access for users.
- Operation under different machines and operating systems.
- Easy extension by providing network services rather than a network operating system.
- Simple network administration which is no more difficult than that for a centralized system.
- Reliable robust file system in the event of network failures.
- Flexible configuration.
- Competitive cost/performance trade-offs.

NFS provides access to different files systems using a Virtual File System (VFS). For example, the UNIX, MS-DOS and VMS operating systems can all make use of NFS if required. In NFS, the concept of the UNIX *inode* is reimplemented as a '*vnode*' (virtual node) to structure files. The VFS is accessed using Remote Procedure Calls (RPC) and a network representation of data which is machine independent. This is known as the eXternal Data Representation (XDR). A separate database service (the Yellow Pages) is used for the initialization and administration of NFS.

An NFS server exports a complete file system. The file system is organized in a hierarchical tree structure. Directories may include other directories as well as normal files. A client may mount any subtree of an exported remote file system onto a local directory. Each client will typically mount a number of file systems. The same file system may be mounted on more than one local directory if required. However, file servers cannot mount other file servers. Once mounted, the location and access of remote files is transparent.

All communication between clients and servers is accomplished using RPCs. This is normally synchronous and designed to be transport independent. Thus new transport protocols (e.g. ISO) can be used as they become available. Currently UDP/IP is supported. As well as standard RPCs from the client to the server, a call-back procedure is provided whereby the server and client swap rolls. This is useful when doing remote debugging, for example.

There is no support for remote file locking. Instead, this facility can be provided at a higher level if required. Thus there is no support for atomic updates of files. There are no replicated or recoverable files for users. However, the Yellow Pages provide a replicated database service for the registration of users, etc., for use by system administrators.

It is possible to use the authentication provided by UNIX on NFS files. This allows *user*, *group* and *world* access rights to be assigned to each file or directory.

NFS servers do not maintain information about clients. This provides robustness at the loss of some compatibility with UNIX. However, NFS attempts to maintain UNIX compatibility where possible.

Performance is enhanced by a number of optimizations such as caching and read-ahead on both the client and the server.

NFS is available on a wide range of different hardware and under a number of major operating systems. Under UNIX, the client side is implemented within the kernel. This means application programs need not be changed normally. **NFS** RPCs are designed to be transport independent, thus allowing the possibility of using **NFS** on different networks.

andrew

andrew (Satyanarayanan, 1984; Satyanarayanan *et al.*, 1985; Rosenthal and Donelson-Smith, 1986; Howard, 1988) is a distributed operating system developed at the Information Technology Center (established in 1982) at Carnegie-Mellon University (CMU) with the support of IBM. It is designed to operate with a large number of nodes; it is hoped that the system will cover much of the campus at Carnegie-Mellon with at least 7,000 nodes. **andrew** is an example of a system with partitioned functionality; the servers do not maintain client state between calls.

The goal of the project was to advance the state of the art in distributed computing by establishing a new model of computer usage with high accessibility and functionality. For example, a major component of **andrew** is its distributed file system, which allows users to access their files from any node.

The **andrew** system is made up of two parts, *Vice* and *Virtue*. *Vice* consists of the network and remote computing and storage facilities. *Virtues* are the individual workstations which can make use of these resources. *Vice* is designed to support a very large number of users. Each workstation has a local file system, for booting and temporary files. Files on the network are transparently cached into the local disc space as required.

Vice includes a number of cluster servers on a very fast backbone network. Each user is associated with a particular cluster known as the user's 'custodian'. This cluster manages the files of the user and helps to locate files on other clusters. It is possible to replicate important files across all the servers. *Vice* supports a hierarchical filing system, along the lines of the **UNIX** file system. Authorization and accounting services are also provided.

A workstation's file name space is separated into local and shared files. Most files are shared and thus a user can move between workstations and still see virtually the same file system. Each user has a 'volume' allocated for personal use; this consists of a subtree of shared files. The location of files is stored in a volume database which is replicated on all servers. Thus the location and access of files is transparent to the user.

Communication between *Vice* and *Virtue* is based on the client–server model using a high level RPC package. Retransmission of calls, low-level error detection and multiplexing are performed by the package. Files are transferred as a side effect of the appropriate RPCs.

Shared files are fetched from clusters and cached locally as required by software on each workstation. If a cached file is accessed, the local copy is used if it is up to date. Otherwise a new copy is fetched from the appropriate server. Read and write operations are directed to the cached copy. On closing the file, it is written back to the server if it has been updated. All this is totally transparent to the application program which is accessing the file.

Many users may read a file simultaneously; read locks are optional. However, write locks are mandatory and only one user may write a file at any one time. Locking is done by the caching software rather than application programs. If a workstation crashes then all associated locks on *Vice* are removed automatically. However, there is no support for atomic update of files.

andrew supports replicated data in workstation caches. Additionally, often used but rarely updated files such as system programs can be replicated as read-only files on a number of servers. This enhances the availability of such files across the network and also helps to distribute the load between servers.

Support for the representation of data types on the network has been introduced into **andrew** part way through its development. However, the application programmer must translate any data to be transmitted into a standard form using the basic types provided.

When a user starts a session on a workstation, the user's copy of *Virtue* authenticates itself to *Vice*. Encrypted authentication using a three way handshake is possible. Access to shared files is controlled by an access list consisting of users and groups. Groups may contain users and other groups. The user's access rights are determined by any group in which he or she is directly or indirectly a member. Access lists only apply to directories, although individual files may be protected on a global basis. Thus **andrew** provides simpler access control than **UNIX** using directory access, but with more flexibility through access lists.

The **andrew** file system provides high compatibility with **UNIX**, allowing application programs to run unmodified. A user normally uses a workstation connected directly to the corresponding custodian for increased efficiency. However, because of the backbone network, it is possible to access files from any point on the network, allowing mobility when required, although with some loss of efficiency.

andrew is expected to scale up to large configurations well because of its high-speed backbone network. Carnegie-Mellon University are planning to use standard telephone wiring and a token-ring network in the expanded version of the system across the entire campus. In its final form, it will be an order of magnitude larger than the more typical departmental networks currently in widespread use in universities.

grapevine

grapevine (Birrell *et al.*, 1982) is a distributed system which provides facilities for the handling of electronic mail. It runs on the Xerox 'internet' and provides services to thousands of machines over several countries. We will not look too deeply at the issues of electronic mail that **grapevine** tackles, but more about how it tackles some of the issues of distributed systems we have discussed.

Apart from internet addresses, objects in the system are given '*RNames*'. These have a two level structure of the form *subname.registryname*. Registry names are globally unique whilst subnames are unique within registries. The partitioning is basically an administrative one; registries can correspond to organizational, geographic or other arbitrary partitions that suit the situation. Objects are either *individuals* or *groups*.

grapevine provides a *registration service* which provides primitives for authentication, access control and resource location. There is also a *delivery service* which allows messages to be sent to a number of recipients, either individuals or groups. Messages are buffered in *'inboxes'* on particular message servers for clients. Individuals must poll for their messages. The designers considered in retrospect that a facility to allow clients to be notified when certain entries are changed would have been useful. The registration and delivery services are clients of each other.

The registration service is implemented by a number of *registration servers*. They provide the service's functions by maintaining a *registration database*. It is essentially a naming database, providing name to value mappings and the ability to alter them. Groups are lists of other names, thus forming a naming network with no structural constraints. Individual entries have a password, ordered list of *inbox* sites, connect site etc. associated with them. Though the **grapevine** system itself uses and interprets the database in its own way, e.g. the message service interprets group names as distribution lists, it is open to clients to use and interpret database entries in any way they please.

The database is distributed and replicated over servers at the granularity of registries. Servers will not in general hold all registries, but each registry will be held by at least two different servers. Servers can only provide registration functions for names in the registries that they hold. They can, however, help in locating other servers to allow functions on any name to be performed.

The registry named *'GV'* is maintained on every registration server, this being the only globally replicated entity. Every server appears in this as an individual of the form *regServer.GV*. For these individuals the *connect site* holds the internet address of the named server. Every registry of the database appears as a group entry of the form *registry.GV*. The members of each group are the *RNames* of the servers which hold that registry.

There is an *authentication service* in the registration service which allows clients to determine the authenticity of individual/password pairs which they possess. A primitive *access control service* (again part of the registration service) exists in that anyone can test whether a particular name is a member of a particular group. This is basically an ACL mechanism. **grapevine** encourages external services to use its facilities, and the authentication service is used by a file service.

Values in the database are represented by sets of time-stamped operations. This allows a change to a value in a particular registry to be started at one server and then sent to all other servers holding that registry. The reliable delivery service is used for this. These update messages can be reordered or delayed in crashed machines, but the mechanism allows **grapevine** to guarantee that copies of the registry will eventually get the new value. While an update is converging, clients may detect different values at different servers. This weaker than usual consistency guarantee allowed the designers to provide a very available system in a relatively straightforward way.

grapevine made extensive use of the notions of *caches* and *hints* to provide safe shortcuts for potentially expensive actions involving its distributed, replicated database containing many indirections. Caches provide quickly accessible records of previous (possibly expensive) calculations. Hints are values which are highly likely to be correct and which can be checked much faster than they can be recalculated.

grapevine has survived an enormous increase in its size and a consequent change in usage patterns which its designers could hardly be expected to have anticipated (Schroeder *et al.*, 1984). There is much to be learnt about building distributed systems from this exercise.

Other systems

There are many important distributed operating system research projects which have not been covered or only mentioned in passing so far. This section lists some of these, together with references and a very brief description, to allow the interested reader to investigate them further if desired. The list should not be considered complete, but is rather a selection of systems which are interesting and/or have been influential on the state of the art in this area.

accent and mach

References   Baron *et al.* (1987); Rashid and Robertson (1981); Tevanian and Rashid (1987); Walmer and Thompson (1987); Young *et al.* (1987).

Place   Carnegie-Mellon University, Pittsburgh, USA.

Note   These are process–message systems. In **accent** only one process may reside in each virtual address space. Communication is via ports, which have associated capabilities. The IPC primitives are asynchronous. Virtual memory management is included in the kernel and is efficiently integrated with the IPC mechanism. A separate network server process is used for communication to other machines. **mach** is the successor to **accent** which is **UNIX** compatible and provides support for multiple processes ('threads') in a single address space. It is used as a base for **andrew**.

archons

Reference   Jensen and Pleszoch (1984).

Place   Carnegie-Mellon University, Pittsburgh, USA.

Note   **archOS** is a decentralized **OS** designed by the **archons** project; it is oriented towards real-time applications. Other issues include team and consensus decision making, transaction management and probabilistic algorithms.

athena

References   Cohen (1987); Lerman (1984).

Place   Massachusetts Institute of Technology, USA.

Note   Supported by DEC. This is a large distributed system project designed for educational use.

Cambridge Distributed Computing System

References   Needham and Herbert (1982); Wilkes and Needham (1980).

Place   University of Cambrige, UK.

Note   This is based on the Cambridge Ring LAN and a processor bank model of computing. It includes the concepts of servers, protection and authentication.

chorus

References   Armand *et al.* (1986); Banino (1983); Guillemont (1982); Zimmermann *et al.* (1981).

Place   INRIA Chorus systèmes, France

Note   A **UNIX** compatible distributed operating system.

clouds

References   Ahamad *et al.* (1987); Allchin and McKendry (1983); LeBlanc and Wilkes (1985); LeBlanc *et al.* (1985).

Place   Georgia Institute of Technology, Atlanta, USA.

Note   An object based DOS. Its features include fault tolerance, transactions, and the fact that it is *not* based on **UNIX**. The associated applications programming language is called **aeolus**.

demos/mp

References   Baskett *et al.* (1977); Miller *et al.* (1987).

Note   A tightly coupled DOS – originally on a Cray but now based on a number of Z8000 microprocessors.

eden and emerald

References   Almes *et al.* (1985); Black (1985); Black *et al.* (1986a); Black *et al.* (1986b); Black *et al.* (1987); Jul *et al.* (1987a); Jul *et al.* (1987b); Lazowska *et al.* (1981).

Place   University of Washington, USA.

Note   An example of an object–action system. A program in **eden** (programmed in **EPL**) consists of a number of distributed objects (or '*Ejects*'). An *Eject* is an instance of a particular **eden** type, referenced by a capability. This does not contain any location information, so objects are mobile. **emerald** is a more recent project. Its main innovation is that it presents a unified view of objects regardless of their size.

gothix

Reference   Kermarrec (1988).

Place   IRISA, Rennes-Cedex, France.

Note   A distributed system based on **UNIX**. The system supports the concept of 'multi-functions', which are a distributed generalization of a standard programming language function or procedure. **gothix** provides three basic objects (directories, files or segments, and fragmented files) from which all other objects are built.

hydra/starOS/medusa

References   Jones (1977); Jones *et al.* (1979); Levin *et al.* (1975); Ousterhout *et al.* (1980); Ousterhout (1981); Wulf *et al.* (1974); Wulf *et al.* (1981).

Place   Carnegie-Mellon University, Pittsburgh, USA.

Note   These were early experimental tightly coupled distributed operating systems. **hydra** was a multiprocessor OS. **CM*** was a multiprocessor based system on which the **starOS** and **medusa** operating systems were implemented.

isis

References   Birman (1985); Birman (1986).

Place   Cornell University, USA.

Note   This is a project which is investigating fault-resilient distributed computing. The essential premiss is that building fault-tolerant distributed systems is hard so high-level support and automatic generation from fault-intolerant systems are needed.

locus

References   Kline (1986); Popek *et al.* (1981); Popek and Walker (1985); Walker *et al.* (1983).

Place   UCLA/Locus Corp., Los Angeles, USA.

Note   A commercially available distributed version of **UNIX**. There is network transparency allowing remote forking, data replication and IPC between remote sites. There is also locking for files and transactions.

MOS

Reference   Barak and Litman (1985).

Place   Hebrew University of Jerusalem, Israel.

Note   **MOS** is an integrated, homogeneous **UNIX** compatible DOS. It is network transparent and all nodes have a complete copy of the kernel so they can run autonomously. The system allows for dynamic reconfiguration and process migration.

Newcastle Connection

Reference   Brownbridge *et al.* (1982).

Place   University of Newcastle, UK

Note   This system provides a distributed **UNIX** filing system by extending the root directory of each machine upwards and then downwards again to other machines to form a global hierarchy of files.

pulse

Reference   Keefe *et al.* (1985).

Place   University of York, UK.

Note   This presents a functional behaviour which is very similar to the **UNIX** interface; however, the **ada** task is used as the process model. There are two main parts, the kernel and the storage system.

roscoe

Reference   Solomon and Finkel (1979).

Place   University of Wisconsin, USA.

Note   **roscoe** was an operating system for a connected set of processors. All the processors are identical, there is no shared memory and no assumptions are made about the connection topology. Communication is by message passing along *links*, there being no notion of a process address.

soda

Reference   Kepecs and Solomon (1985).

Note   Simplified Operating system for Distributed Applications. This is a small but interesting system; it lies somewhere between a smart communications front-end and a dumb OS kernel.

taos

References   Birrell *et al.* (1987); McJones and Swart (1987); Thacker *et al.* (1987).

Place   DEC Systems Research Center (SRC), Palo Alto, USA.

Note   This is a **UNIX** compatible OS for the **Firefly** multiprocessor workstation. The concept of multiple *threads* of control is supported. The formal specification language **larch** was used to specify the synchronization primitives. SRC have also developed an associated software environment **topaz**, for research into multiprocessing and distributed personal computing.

time warp

References   Jefferson (1985); Jefferson *et al.* (1987); West *et al.* (1987).

Place   Jet Propulsion Laboratory, Los Angeles, USA.

Note   This system totally decouples real-time from system-time and uses a radical 'rollback' scheme to ensure correct ordering. It is intended for simulations on relatively tightly coupled systems.

V kernel

References   Cheriton (1984); Cheriton and Mann (1984); Cheriton (1985); Cheriton and Roy (1985); Lantz *et al.* (1985).

Place   Stanford University, Palo Alto, USA.

| Note | This system is of the process–message type. It uses very light-weight processes to construct programs. Several processes in a single address space may be combined to form a 'team'. Message passing is synchronous. There is no concept of capabilities. |

xerox

References	Brown *et al.* (1984); Gifford *et al.* (1987); Hagmann (1987); Oppen and Dalal (1983); Schroeder *et al.* (1985); Swinehart *et al.* (1985); Swinehart *et al.* (1986); Teitelman (1984).
Place	Xerox Corp., Palo Alto, USA.
Note	Xerox Palo Alto Research Center (PARC) pioneered many early distributed systems including work on RPCs, several filing systems (**alpine**, **cedar** caching file system and **XDFS**) and the **grapevine** system (see earlier). The ideas from **grapevine** have been incorporated in **clearinghouse**, a Xerox product.

Current practice and future trends

Some ideas for the design and implementation of distributed systems have crystallized and become accepted practice. For example:

- A clear separation of policy from mechanism, e.g. separate the mechanism for migrating processes from the policy that decides when it is best done.
- The use of *lean* kernels; they are easier to understand and more likely to be correct. Additional functionality can be provided at higher levels, giving greater flexibility.
- RPC and the use of light-weight processes for constructing services is standard in many systems.

Other issues which are the subject of current research but are likely to be influential include the following:

- The use of atomic actions and nested transactions to build large, reliable concurrent systems is being investigated.
- Language support will become more important, aiding particular distributed design methodologies.
- Multi-media (e.g. voice, video, hypertext) systems will increase the functionality of distributed systems, but will introduce many new problems.
- The more transparent integration of WANs with current LAN technology will enable greater information sharing.

The problems involved with the design of distributed operating systems are significantly more complex than those concerned with traditional centralized operating systems since issues of concurrency and communication must also be considered. To design 'correct' systems, the use of sound software engineering principles such as formal methods will become more important and widespread. For example, a set of network services which form the basis of a distributed operating system have been designed and documented using the formal specification language **Z** (Bowen *et al.*, 1987; Gimson and Morgan, 1984; Hayes, 1987).

Other work

We have only been able to scratch the surface of distributed systems in this short survey, but the area is a very active one and there is a great deal of other literature of interest.

Tanenbaum and van Renesse, (1985), provide an introduction to distributed operating systems and review a number of current research projects.

The book Lampson *et al.* (1981) is a collection of papers from an advanced course on distributed systems. Though getting a little old in some areas it is an invaluable reference to just about every aspect of distributed systems. It contains a very large bibliography.

ANSA is the Alvey funded Advanced Networked Systems Architecture project which aims to describe an architecture that exploits distributed computing concepts. The project has already published a number of papers but their main technical output is the **ANSA** Reference Manual (ANSA, 1987).

OSI provides a document describing service conventions suitable for distributed systems (OSI, 1985). This also lists a number of other relevant standards.

Svobodova has produced an excellent article (Svobodova, 1984), which examines the issues in the construction of file services, a very important component of many distributed systems. It also reviews and contrasts a number of them.

There are several symposia that contain many of the most important articles in the field of distributed computing. These include the ACM Symposia on Principles of Distributed Computing, the International Conferences on Distributed Computing Systems, and the ACM Symposia on Operating System Principles (published as special issues of ACM (SIGOPS) Operating Systems Review).

References

ANSA (1987) *ANSA Reference Manual*, Advanced Networked Systems Architecture Project, 24 Hills Road, Cambridge, UK

Ahamad, M., Dasgupta, D., LeBlanc, R. J. and Wilkes, C. T. (1987) Fault tolerant computing in object based distributed operating systems. *Proceedings of the Sixth IEEE Symposium on Reliability in Distributed Software and Database Systems*, pp. 115–125

Allchin, J. E. and McKendry, M. S. (1983) Synchronization and recovery of actions. *Proceedings of the Second Annual ACM Symposium on Principles of Distributed Computing*, August, pp. 31–44

Almes, G. T., Black, A. P., Lazowska, E. D. and Noe, J. D. (1985). The Eden system: a technical review. *IEEE Transactions on Software Engineering*, **11**(1)

Armand, F., Gien, M., Guillemont, M. and Leonard, P. (1986) Towards a distributed **UNIX** system—the Chorus approach. *Proceedings of the EUUG Autumn 1986 Conference*, September, pp. 413–431

Banino, J. S. (1983) Architecture of the Chorus distributed system. In *Distributed Computing Systems: Synchronization, Control and Communication*, (eds Y. Parker and J. P. Verjus) Academic Press, London, pp. 251–264

Barak, A. and Litman, A. (1985) MOS: a multicomputer distributed operating system. *Software Practice and Experience*, **15**(8), 725–737

Baron, R., Rashid, R., Siegel, E., Tevanian, A. and Young, M. (1985) MACH-1: an operating system environment for large scale multiprocessor applications. *IEEE Software*, July

Baron, R. V., Black, D., Bolosky, W., Chew, J., Golub, D. B., Rashid, R. F., Tevanian, A. Jr. and Young, M. W. (1987) *MACH kernel interface manual*. Technical Report, Department of Computer Science, Carnegie-Mellon University, Pittsburgh, USA, October

Baskett, F., Howard, J. H. and Mantague, J. T. (1977) Task communications in DEMOS. *Operating Systems Review*, **11**(5), 23–32

Birman, K. P. (1985) Replication and fault tolerance in the ISIS system. *Operating Systems Review*, **19**(5), 79–86

Birman, K. P. (1986) ISIS: a system for fault-tolerant distributed computing. Technical Report 86–744 Department of Computer Science, Cornell University, Ithaca, USA, April

Birrell, A. D., Levin, R., Needham, R. M. and Schroeder, M. D. (1982) Grapevine: an exercise in distributed computing. *Communications of the ACM*, **25**(4), 260–274

Birrell, A. D. and Nelson, B. J. (1983) Implementing remote procedure calls Report. CSL-83-7, December, Xerox PARC, USA

Birrell, A. D., Guttag, J. V., Horning, J. J. and Levin, R. (1987) Synchronization primitives for a multiprocessor: a formal specification. *Proceedings of the Eleventh ACM Symposium on Operating Systems Principles*, November, pp. 94–102

Black, A. P. (1985) Supporting distributed applications: experience with Eden. *Proceedings of the Tenth ACM Symposium on Operating Systems Principles*, pp. 181–193

Black, A. P., Hutchinson, N., Jul, E. and Levy, H. M. (1986a) Object structure in the Emerald system. *Proceedings of the Conference on Object Oriented Programming Systems, Languages and Applications*, pp. 78–86

Black, A. P., Lazowska, E. D., Noe, J. D. and Sanislo, J. (1986b) The Eden project: a final report. Technical Report 86-11-01, Department of Computer Science, University of Washington, Seattle, USA

Black, A. P., Hutchinson, N., Jul, E., Levy, H. M. and Carter, L. (1987) Distribution and abstract types in Emerald. *IEEE Transactions on Software Engineering*, **13**(1), 65–76

Bowen, J. P., Gimson, R. B. and Topp-Jørgensen, S. (1987) The specification of network services. Technical Monograph PRG-61, August, Programming Research Group, Oxford University, UK

Brown, M. R., Kolling, K. and Taft, E. A. (1984) The Alpine File System. Technical Report CSL-84-4, October, Xerox PARC, USA

Brownbridge, D. R., Marshall, L. F. and Randell, B. (1982) The Newcastle Connection or UNIXes of the world unite! *Software Practice and Experience*, **12**, 1147–1162

Cheriton, D. R. (1984) The V kernel: a software base for distributed systems. *Software*, **1**(2), 19–42

Cheriton, D. R. and Mann, T. P. (1984) Uniform access to distributed name interpretation in the V-system. *Proceedings of the Fourth International Conference on Distributed Computing Systems*, May

Cheriton, D. R. (1985) Distributed process groups in the V kernel. *ACM Transactions on Computer Systems*, **3**(2), May 77–107

Cheriton, D. R. and Roy, P. J. (1985) Performance of the V storage server. *Proceedings of the ACM Thirteenth National Computer Science Conference*, ACM, pp. 302–308

Cohen, K. C. (1987) Project Athena: assessing the educational results. *Proceedings of the ASEE Annual Conference*, June, pp. 1279–1282

Dasgupta, P. and LeBlanc, R. J. (1986) Clouds: a support architecture for fault-tolerant distributed systems. *Proceedings of the Workshop on Future Directions in Computer Architectures and Software*, May, pp. 122–129

Feldman, J. A. (1979) High level programming for distributed computing. *Communications of the ACM*, **22**(6), 353–368

Gifford, D. K., Needham, R. M. and Schroeder, M. D. (1987) The Cedar File System, Xerox PARC, USA

Gimson, R. B. and Morgan, C. C. (1984) Ease of Use Through Proper Specification. In *Distributed Computing Systems Programme*, (ed. D. A. Duce), Peter Peregrinus, Stevenage, on behalf of IEE, London

Gray, J. N. (1986) An approach to decentralized computer systems. *IEEE Transactions on Software Engineering*, **12**(6)

Grief, I., Seliger, R. and Weihl, W. (1986) Atomic data abstractions in a distributed collaborative editing system (extended abstract). *Conference Record Thirteenth Annual ACM Symposium on Principles of Programming Languages*, January, pp. 160–161

Guillemont, M. (1982) The Chorus distributed operating system: design and implementation. *Proceedings of the ACM International Symposium on Local Computer Networks*, April

Hagmann, R. (1987) Reimplementing the Cedar File System using logging and group commit. Technical Report CSL-87-7, August, Xerox PARC, USA

Hayes, I. (ed.) (1987) Specification Case Studies, Prentice-Hall International, Hemel Hempstead

Howard, J. H. (1988) An overview of the Andrew file system. *Proceedings of the USENIX 1988 Conference*, February, pp. 23–26

Hydra (1976) Hydra: kernel reference manual. Technical Report, November, Department of Computer Science, CMU, Pittsburgh, USA

Jefferson, D. R. (1985) Virtual time. *ACM Transactions on Programming Languages and Systems*, **7**(3), 404–425

Jefferson, D., Beckman, B., Wieland, F., Blume, L., DiLoreto, M., Hontalas, P., Laroche, P., Sturdevant, K., Tupman, J., Van Warren, Wedel, J., Younger, H. and Bellenot, S. (1987) Distributed simulation and the Time Warp operating system. *Proceedings of the Eleventh ACM Symposium on Operating Systems Principles*, November, pp. 77–93

Jensen, E. D. and Pleszoch, N. (1984) ArchOS: a physically dispersed operating system. *IEEE Distributed Processing Technical Committee Newsletter, Special Issue on Distributed Operating Systems*, June

Jones, A. K. (1977) CM* – a distributed multiprocessor. *Proceedings of the AFIPS 46*, AFIPS Press, Montvale, New Jersey

Jones, A. K. (1977) Protection mechanisms and the enforcement of security policies. In *Operating Systems – an Advanced Course*, Springer-Verlag, Berlin, pp. 228–251

Jones, A. K., Chansler, R. J., Durham, I., Schwans, K. and Vegdahl, S. R. (1979) StarOS, a multiprocessor operating system for the support of task forces. In *Proceedings of the Seventh ACM Symposium on Operating Systems Principles*, December, pp. 117–127

Jul, E., Levy, H., Hutchinson, N. and Black, A. (1987a) Fine-Grained Mobility in the Emerald System. Technical Report TR-87-02-03, February, Department of Computer Science, University of Washington, Seattle, USA

Jul, E., Levy, H., Hutchinson, N. and Black, A. (1987b) Fine-grained mobility in the Emerald system (extended abstract). *Proceedings of the Eleventh ACM Symposium on Operating Systems Principles*, November, pp. 105–106

Keefe, D., Thomlinson, G. M., Wand, I. C. and Wellings, A. J. (1985) Pulse: an Ada-based Distributed Operating System, APIC Studies in Data Processing Series, Academic Press, London

Kepecs, J. H. and Solomon, M. H. (1985) SODA; a simplified operating system for distributed applications. *Proceedings of the Third Annual ACM Symposium on Principles of Distributed Computing*, October, pp. 45–56

Kermarrec, A. (1988) An overview of the Gothix distributed system. *Proceedings of the EUUG Spring 1988 Conference*, April, pp. 69–78

Kline, C. (1986) Complete vs. partial transparency in LOCUS. *Proceedings of the EUUG Autumn 1986 Conference*, September, pp. 5–13

Lamport, L. (1978) Time, clocks and the ordering of events in a distributed system. *Communications of the ACM*, **21**(7), 558–565

Lampson, B. W., M. Paul, and H. J. Siegert (eds) (1981) *Distributed Systems – Architecture and Implementation*, Springer-Verlag, Berlin

Lantz, K. A., Nowicki, W. I. and Theimer, M. M. (1985) An empirical study of distributed application performance. *IEEE Transactions on Software Engineering*, **11**(10)

Lauer, H. C. and Needham, R. M. (1979) On the duality of operating system structures. *Operating Systems Review*, **13**(2), 3–19

Lazowska, E. D., Levy, H. M., Almes, G. T., Fischer, M. J., Fowler, R. J. and Vestal, S. C. (1981) The architecture of the Eden system. In *Proceedings of the Eighth ACM Symposium on Operating Systems Principles*, December, pp. 148–159

LeBlanc, R. (1985) The Clouds Projects. Technical Report TR85-01, Georgia Institute of Technology, Atlanta, USA, January

LeBlanc, R. and Wilkes, T. (1985) Systems programming with objects and actions. *Proceedings of the Fifth International Conference on Distributed Computing Systems*, July

LeLann, G. (1981) Motivations, objectives and characterization of distributed systems. In *Distributed Systems – Architecture and Implementation*. (eds B. W. Lampson, M. Paul and H. J. Siegert), Springer-Verlag, Berlin, pp. 1–9

Lerman, S. (1984) Project Athena at MIT. *EDUCOM Bulletin*, **19**(4), 5–7

Levin, R., Cohen, E., Corwin, W., Pollack, F. and Wulf, W. (1975) Policy/mechanisms separation in Hydra. *Proceedings of the Fifth ACM Symposium on Operating Systems Principles*, November, pp. 132–140

Liskov, B. (1979) Primitives for distributed computing. *Proceedings of the Seventh ACM Symposium on Operating Systems Principles*, December, pp. 33–41

Liskov, B., Atkinson, R., Bloom, T., Moss, E., Schaffert, J. C., Scheifler, R. and Snyder, A. (1981) *CLU Reference Manual*. Springer-Verlag, Berlin

Liskov, B. and Scheifler, R. (1983) Guardians and actions: linguistic support for robust, distributed programs. *ACM Transactions on Programming Languages and Systems*, **5**(3), 381–404

Liskov, B. (1985) The Argus language and system. In *Lecture Notes in Computer Science*, **190**, Springer-Verlag, Berlin pp. 343–431

Liskov, B., Curtis, D., Johnson, P. and Scheifler, R. (1987) Implementation of Argus. *Proceedings of the Eleventh ACM Symposium on Operating Systems Principles*, November, pp. 111–122

McJones, P. R. and Swart, G. F. (1987) *Evolving the UNIX System Interface to Support Multithreaded Programs*. SRC Report 21, September, DEC Systems Research Center, Palo Alto, USA

Miller, B. P., Presotto, D. L. and Powell, M. L. (1987) DEMOS/MP: the development of a distributed operating system. *Software Practice and Experience*, **17**(4), 277–290

Moss, J. Eliot B. (1985) *Nested Transactions: An Approach to Reliable Distributed Computing*, MIT Press, Cambridge, Massachusetts, USA

Mullender, S. J. (ed.) (1987) *The Amoeba Distributed Operating System: Selected Papers 1984– 1987*, Centruum voor Wiskunde en Informatica, Amsterdam, The Netherlands

Needham, R. M. and Schroeder, M. D. (1978) Using encryption for authentication in large networks of computers. *Communications of the ACM*, **21**(12), 993–999

Needham, R. M. and Herbert, A. J. (1982) *The Cambridge Distributed Computing System*, Addison-Wesley, London

Nelson, B. J. (1981) Remote Procedure Call. Technical Report CSL-81-9, May, Xerox PARC, USA

Notkin, D., Hutchinson, N., Sanislo, J. and Schwartz, M. (1986) Report on the ACM SIGOPS workshop on accommodating heterogeneity. *Operating Systems Review*, **20**(2), 9–24

Oppen, D. C. and Dalal, Y. K. (1983) The Clearinghouse: a decentralized agent for locating named objects in a decentralized environment. *ACM Transactions on Office Information Systems*, **1**(3)

OSI (1985) *Open Systems Interconnection: service conventions (ISO/DP 8509)*, British Standards Institution, Milton Keynes, UK

Ousterhout, J. K., Scelza, D. A. and Sindhu, P. S. (1980) Medusa: an experiment in distributed operating system structure. *Communications of the ACM*, **23**(2), 92–105

Ousterhout, J. (1981) *Medusa: a distributed operating systems*, UMI Research Press

Popek, G. J., Walker, B., Chow, J., Edwards, D., Kline, C., Rudisin, G. and Thiel, G. (1981) LOCUS: a network transparent, high reliability distributed system. *Proceedings of the Eighth ACM Symposium on Operating Systems Principles*, **15**(5), 169–177

Popek G. J. and Walker, B. J. (1985) *The LOCUS Distributed System Architecture*, MIT Press, Cambridge, Massachusetts, USA

Rashid, R. F. and Robertson, G. G. (1981) Accent: a communications oriented NOS kernel. *Proceedings of the Eighth ACM Symposium on Operating Systems Principles*, December, pp. 64–75

Rosenthal, D. and Donelson-Smith, F. (1986) Andrew: a distributed personal computing environment. *Communications of the ACM*, **29**(3), 184–210

Sandberg, R., Goldberg, D., Kleiman, S., Walsh, D. and Lyon, B. (1985) Design and implementation of the SUN Network File System. *Proceedings of the USENIX Summer Conference*, June, pp. 119–130

Satyanarayanan, M. (1984) The ITC project: a large-scale experiment in distributed personal computing. In *Proceedings of the Networks 84 Conference, Indian Institute of Technology, Madras*, October, North-Holland, Amsterdam

Satyanarayanan, M., Howard, J. H., Nichols, D. A., Sidebotham, R. N., Spector, A. Z. and West, M. J. (1985) The ITC distributed file system: principles and design. *Proceedings of the Tenth ACM Symposium on Operating Systems Principles*, December, pp. 35–50

Schroeder, M. D., Birrell, A. D. and Needham, R. M. (1984) Experience with Grapevine: the growth of a distributed system. *ACM Transactions on Computer Systems*, **2**(1), 3–23

Schroeder, M. D., Gifford, D. K. and Needham, R. M. (1985) A caching file system for a programmer's workstation. *Proceedings of the Tenth ACM Symposium on Operating Systems Principles*, December, pp. 25–34

Solomon, M. H. and Finkel, R. A. (1979) The Roscoe distributed operating system. *Proceedings of the Seventh ACM Symposium on Operating Systems Principles*, December, pp. 108–114

SUN (1986a) Network services guide. In *Networking on the SUN Workstation*, February, SUN Microsystems Inc., Mountain View, California, USA

SUN (1986b) Network file system protocol specification. In *Networking on the SUN Workstation*, February, SUN Microsystems Inc., Mountain View, California, USA

Svobodova, L. (1984) File servers for network-based distributed systems. *ACM Computing Surveys*, **16**(4), 353–398

Swinehart, D., Zellweger, P. and Hagmann, R. (1985) The structure of Cedar. *SIGPLAN Notices*, **20**(7), 230–244

Swinehart, D., Zellweger, P., Beach, R. and Hagmann, R. (1986) A structural view of the Cedar programming environment. *ACM Transactions on Programming Languages and Systems*, **8**(4), 419–490

Tanenbaum, A. S. and van Renesse, R. (1985) Distributed operating systems. *ACM Computing Surveys*, **17**(4), 419–470

Tanenbaum, A. S. and van Renesse, R. (1988) A critique of the remote procedure call paradigm. In *Research into Networks and Distributed Applications – EUTECO 1988*, (ed. R. Speth), Elsevier, Amsterdam, pp. 775–783

Teitelman, W. (1984) A tour through Cedar. *Proceedings of the Seventh International Conference on Software Engineering*, March

Tevanian, A. and Rashid, R. F. (1987) MACH: a basis for future UNIX development. Technical Report CMU-CS-87-139, June, Department of Computer Science, Carnegie-Mellon University, Pittsburgh, USA

Thacker, C. P., Stewart, L. C. and Satterthwaite, E. H. Jr. (1987) Firefly: a multiprocessor workstation. SRC Report 23, DEC Systems Research Center, Palo Alto, USA, December

van Renesse, R. (1986) From UNIX to a usable distributed operating system. *Proceedings of the EUUG Autumn 1986 Conference*, September, pp. 15–21

Walker, B., Popek, G., English, R., Kline, C. and Thiel, G. (1983) The LOCUS distributed operating system. *Proceedings of the Ninth ACM Symposium on Operating Systems Principles*, October, pp. 49–70

Walmer, L. R. and Thompson, M. R. (1987) A MACH tutorial. Technical Report, August. Department of Computer Science, Carnegie-Mellon University, Pittsburgh, USA

West, D., Lomow, G. and Unger, B. (1987) Optimizing Time Warp using the semantics of abstract data types. In *Proceedings of the Conference 'Simulation and AI'*, (eds P. A. Luker and G. Birtwistle), January, pp. 3–8

Wilkes, M. V. and Needham, R. M. (1980) The Cambridge model distributed system. *Operating Systems Review*, **14**(1), 21–29

Wulf, W. A., Cohen, E. S., Corwin, W. M., Jones, A. K., Levin, R., Pierson, C. and Pollack, F. J. (1974) HYDRA: the kernal of a multiprocessor operating system. *Communications of the ACM*, **17**(6), 337–345

Wulf, W. A., Levin, R. and Harbison, S. P. (1981) *HYDRA/C.mmp: an Experimental Computer System*. McGraw-Hill, New York

Young, M., Tevanian, A., Rashid, R., Golub, D., Eppinger, J., Chew, J., Bolosky, W., Black, D. and Baron, R. (1987) The duality of memory and communication in the implementation of a multiprocessor operating system. *Proceedings of the Eleventh ACM Symposium on Operating Systems Principles*, November, pp. 63–76

Zimmermann, H., Banino, J.-S., Caristan, A., Guillemont, M. and Morisset, G. (1981) Basic concepts for the support of distributed systems: the Chorus approach. *Proceedings of the Second International Conference on Distributed Computing Systems*, pp. 60–66

Chapter 2

Concepts and notations for concurrent programming*

Gregory R. Andrews and Fred B. Schneider

Much has been learned in the last decade about concurrent programming. This paper identifies the major concepts of concurrent programming and describes some of the more important language notations for writing concurrent programs. The roles of processes, communication and synchronization are discussed. Language notations for expressing concurrent execution and for specifying process interaction are surveyed. Synchronization primitives based on shared variables and on message passing are described. Finally, three general classes of concurrent programming languages are identified and compared.

Introduction

The complexion of concurrent programming has changed substantially in the past ten years. First, theoretical advances have prompted the definition of new programming notations that express concurrent computations simply, make synchronization requirements explicit, and facilitate formal correctness proofs. Second, the availability of inexpensive processors has made possible the construction of distributed systems and multiprocessors that were previously economically infeasible. Because of these two developments, concurrent programming no longer is the sole province of those who design and implement operating systems; it has become important to programmers of all kinds of applications, including database management systems, large-scale parallel scientific computations, and real-time, embedded control systems. In fact, the discipline has matured to the point that there are now undergraduate-level text books devoted solely to the topic (Holt *et al.*, 1978; Ben-Ari, 1982). In light of this growing range of applicability, it seems appropriate to survey the state of the art.

This paper describes the concepts central to the design and construction of concurrent programs and explores notations for describing concurrent computations. Although this description requires detailed discussions of some concurrent programming languages, we restrict attention to those whose designs we believe to be influential or conceptually innovative. Not all the languages we discuss enjoy widespread use. Many are experimental efforts that focus on understanding the interactions of a given collection of

* Reprinted from: *ACM Computing Surveys*, **15**(1), March 1983 with permission of the Association for Computing Machinery Inc.

constructs. Some have not even been implemented; others have been, but with little concern for efficiency, access control, data types, and other important (though nonconcurrency) issues.

We proceed as follows. In Section 1 we discuss the three issues that underlie all concurrent programming notations: how to express concurrent execution, how processes communicate, and how processes synchronize. These issues are treated in detail in the remainder of the paper. In Section 2 we take a closer look at various ways to specify concurrent execution: coroutines, **fork** and **cobegin** statements, and **process** declarations. In Section 3 we discuss synchronization primitives that are used when communication uses shared variables. Two general types of synchronization are considered—exclusion and condition synchronization—and a variety of ways to implement them are described: busy-waiting, semaphores, conditional critical regions, monitors, and path expressions. In Section 4 we discuss message-passing primitives. We describe methods for specifying channels of communication and synchronization, and higher level constructs for performing remote procedure calls and atomic transactions. In Section 5 we identify and compare three general classes of concurrent programming languages. Finally, in Section 6, we summarize the major topics and identify directions in which the field is headed.

1. Concurrent programs: processes and process interaction

Processes

A *sequential program* specifies sequential execution of a list of statements; its execution is called a *process*. A *concurrent program* specifies two or more sequential programs that may be executed concurrently as *parallel processes*. For example, an airline reservation system that involves processing transactions from many terminals has a natural specification as a concurrent program in which each terminal is controlled by its own sequential process. Even when processes are not executed simultaneously, it is often easier to structure a system as a collection of cooperating sequential processes rather than as a single sequential program. A simple batch operating system can be viewed as three processes: a *reader* process, an *executer* process, and a *printer* process. The *reader* process reads cards from a card reader and places card images in an input buffer. The *executer* process reads card images from the input buffer, performs the specified computation (perhaps generating line images), and stores the results in an output buffer. The *printer* process retrieves line images from the output buffer and writes them to a printer.

A concurrent program can be executed either by allowing processes to share one or more processors or by running each process on its own processor. The first approach is referred to as *multiprogramming*; it is supported by an operating system kernel (Dijkstra, 1968a) that multiplexes the processes on the processor(s). The second approach is referred to as *multiprocessing* if the processors share a common memory (as in a multiprocessor (Jones and Schwarz, 1980)), or as *distributed processing* if the processors are connected by a communications network.[1] Hybrid approaches

---

[1] A concurrent program that is executed in this way is often called a *distributed program*.

also exist – for example, processors in a distributed system are often multi-programmed.

The rate at which processes are executed depends on which approach is used. When each process is executed on its own processor, each is executed at a fixed, but perhaps unknown, rate; when processes share a processor, it is as if each is executed on a variable-speed processor. Because we would like to be able to understand a concurrent program in terms of its component sequential processes and their interaction, without regard for how they are executed, we make no assumption about execution rates of concurrently executing processes, except that they all are positive. This is called the *finite progress assumption*. The correctness of a program for which only finite progress is assumed is thus independent of whether that program is executed on multiple processors or on a single multiprogrammed processor.

Process interaction

In order to cooperate, concurrently executing processes must communicate and synchronize. Communication allows execution of one process to influence execution of another. Interprocess communication is based on the use of shared variables (variables that can be referenced by more than one process) or on message passing.

Synchronization is often necessary when processes communicate. Processes are executed with unpredictable speeds. Yet, to communicate, one process must perform some action that the other detects – an action such as setting the value of a variable or sending a message. This only works if the events 'perform an action' and 'detect an action' are constrained to happen in that order. Thus one can view synchronization as a set of constraints on the ordering of events. The programmer employs a *synchronization mechanism* to delay execution of a process in order to satisfy such constraints.

To make the concept of synchronization a bit more concrete, consider the batch operating system described above. A shared buffer is used for communication between the *reader* process and the *executer* process. These processes must be synchronized so that, for example, the *executer* process never attempts to read a card image from the input if the buffer is empty.

This view of synchronization follows from taking an *operational approach* to program semantics. An execution of a concurrent program can be viewed as a sequence of *atomic actions*, each resulting from the execution of an indivisible operation.[2] This sequence will comprise some interleaving of the sequences of atomic actions generated by the individual component processes. Rarely do all execution interleavings result in acceptable program behaviour, as is illustrated in the following. Suppose initially that $x = 0$, that process $P1$ increments x by 1, and that process $P2$ increments x by 2:

$$P1: x := x + 1 \qquad P2: x := x + 2$$

It would seem reasonable to expect the final value of x, after $P1$ and $P2$ have executed concurrently, to be 3. Unfortunately, this will not always be the case, because assignment statements are not generally implemented as

---

[2] We assume that a single memory reference is indivisible; if two processes attempt to reference the same memory cell at the same time, the result is as if the references were made serially. This is a reasonable assumption in light of the way memory is constructed. See Lamport (1980b) for a discussion of some of the implications of relaxing this assumption.

indivisible operations. For example, the above assignments might be implemented as a sequence of three indivisible operations: (i) load a register with the value of x; (ii) add 1 or 2 to it; and (iii) store the result in x. Thus, in the program above, the final value of x might be 1, 2 or 3. This anomalous behaviour can be avoided by preventing interleaved execution of the two assignment statements – that is, by controlling the ordering of the events corresponding to the atomic actions. (If ordering were thus controlled, each assignment statement would be an indivisible operation.) In other words, execution of $P1$ and $P2$ must be synchronized by enforcing restrictions on possible interleavings.

The *axiomatic approach* (Floyd, 1967; Hoare, 1969; Dijkstra, 1976) provides a second framework in which to view the role of synchronization.[3] In this approach, the semantics of statements are defined by axioms and inference rules. This results in a formal logical system, called a 'programming logic.' Theorems in the logic have the form

$$\{P\}\,S\,\{Q\}$$

and specify a relation between statements (S) and two predicates, a *precondition* P and a *postcondition* Q. The axioms and inference rules are chosen so that theorems have the interpretation that if execution of S is started in any state that satisfies the precondition, and if execution terminates, then the postcondition will be true of the resulting state. This allows statements to be viewed as relations between predicates.

A *proof outline*[4] provides one way to present a program and its proof. It consists of the program text interleaved with assertions so that for each statement S, the triple (formed from (1) the assertion that textually precedes S in the proof outline, (2) the statement S, and (3) the assertion that textually follows S in the proof outline) is a theorem in the programming logic. Thus the appearance of an assertion R in the proof outline signifies that R is true of the program state when control reaches that point.

When concurrent execution is possible, the proof of a sequential process is valid only if concurrent execution of other processes cannot invalidate assertions that appear in the proof (Ashcroft, 1975; Keller, 1976; Owicki and Gries, 1976a, 1976b; Lamport, 1977, 1980a; Lamport and Schneider, 1982). One way to establish this is to assume that the code between any two assertions in a proof outline is executed atomically[5] and then to prove a series of theorems showing that no statement in one process invalidates any assertion in the proof of another. These additional theorems constitute a proof of *noninterference*. To illustrate this, consider the following excerpt from a proof outline of two concurrent processes $P1$ and $P2$:

$P1$:	...	$P2$:	...
	$\{x > 0\}$		$\{x < 0\}$
	$S1: x := 16$		$S2: x := -2$
	$\{x = 16\}$		...
	...		

---

[3] We include brief discussions of axiomatic semantics here and elsewhere in the paper because of its importance in helping to explain concepts. However, a full discussion of the semantics of concurrent computation is beyond the scope of this paper.

[4] This sometimes is called an asserted program.

[5] This should be construed as specifying what assertions must be included in the proof rather than as a restriction on how statements are actually executed.

In order to prove that execution of *P2* does not interfere with the proof of *P1*, part of what we must show is that execution of *S2* does not invalidate assertions $\{x > 0\}$ and $\{x = 16\}$ in the proof of *P1*. This is done by proving

$$\{x < 0 \text{ and } x > 0\}\ x := -2\ \{x > 0\}$$

and

$$\{x < 0 \text{ and } x > 0\}\ x := -2\ \{x = 16\}$$

Both of these are theorems because the precondition of each, $\{x < 0$ **and** $x > 0\}$, is false. What we have shown is that execution of *S2* is not possible when either the precondition or postcondition of *S1* holds (and thus *S1* and *S2* are mutually exclusive). Hence, *S2* cannot invalidate either of these assertions.

Synchronization mechanisms control interference in two ways. First, they can delay execution of a process until a given condition (assertion) is true. By doing so, they ensure that the precondition of the subsequent statement is guaranteed to be true (provided that the assertion is not interfered with). Second, a synchronization mechanism can be used to ensure that a block of statements is an indivisible operation. This eliminates the possibility of statements in other processes interfering with assertions appearing within the proof of that block of statements.

Both views of programs, operational and axiomatic, are useful. The operational approach – viewing synchronization as an ordering of events – is well suited to explaining how synchronization mechanisms work. For that reason, the operational approach is used rather extensively in this survey. It also constitutes the philosophical basis for a family of synchronization mechanisms called *path expressions* (Campbell and Habermann, 1974) which are described on page 56.

Unfortunately, the operational approach does not really help one understand the behaviour of a concurrent program or argue convincingly about its correctness. Although it has borne fruit for simple concurrent programs – such as transactions processed concurrently in a database system (Bernstein and Goodman, 1981) – the operational approach has only limited utility when applied to more complex concurrent programs (Akkoyunlu *et al.*, 1978; Bernstein and Schneider, 1978). This limitation exists because the number of interleavings that must be considered grows exponentially with the size of the component sequential processes. Human minds are not good at such extensive case analysis. The axiomatic approach usually does not have this difficulty. It is perhaps the most promising technique for understanding concurrent programs. Some familiarity with formal logic is required for its use, however, and this has slowed its acceptance.

To summarize, there are three main issues underlying the design of a notation for expressing a concurrent computation:

(i) how to indicate concurrent execution;
(ii) which mode of interprocess communication to use;
(iii) which synchronization mechanism to use.

Also, synchronization mechanisms can be viewed either as constraining the ordering of events or as controlling interference. We consider all these topics in depth in the remainder of the paper.

2. Specifying concurrent execution

Various notations have been proposed for specifying concurrent execution. Early proposals, such as the **fork** statement, are marred by a failure to separate process definition from process synchronization. Later proposals separate these distinct concepts and characteristically possess syntactic restrictions that impose some structure on a concurrent program. This structure allows easy identification of those program segments that can be executed concurrently. Consequently, such proposals are well suited for use with the axiomatic approach, because the structure of the program itself clarifies the proof obligations for establishing noninterference.

Below, we describe some representative constructs for expressing concurrent execution. Each can be used to specify computations having a *static* (fixed) number of processes, or can be used in combination with process-creation mechanisms to specify computations having a *dynamic* (variable) number of processes.

Coroutines

Coroutines are like subroutines, but allow transfer of control in a symmetric rather than strictly hierarchical way (Conway, 1963a). Control is transferred between coroutines by means of the **resume** statement. Execution of **resume** is like execution of procedure **call**: it transfers control to the named routine, saving enough state information for control to return later to the instruction following the **resume**. (When a routine is first resumed, control is transferred to the beginning of that routine.) However, control is returned to the original routine by executing another **resume** rather than by executing a procedure **return**. Moreover, any other coroutine can potentially transfer control back to the original routine. (For example, coroutine *C1* could **resume** *C2*, which could **resume** *C3*, which could **resume** *C1*.) Thus **resume** serves as the only way to transfer control between coroutines, and one coroutine can transfer control to any other coroutine that it chooses.

A use of coroutines appears in Figure 2.1. Note that **resume** is used to transfer control between coroutines *A* and *B*, a **call** is used to initiate the coroutine computation, and **return** is used to transfer control back to the caller *P*. The arrows in Figure 1 indicate the transfers of control.

Each coroutine can be viewed as implementing a process. Execution of **resume** causes process synchronization. When used with care, coroutines are an acceptable way to organize concurrent programs that share a single processor. In fact, multiprogramming can also be implemented using coroutines. Coroutines are not adequate for true parallel processing, however, because their semantics allow for execution of only one routine at a time. In essence, coroutines are concurrent processes in which process switching has been completely specified, rather than left to the discretion of the implementation.

Statements to implement coroutines have been included in discrete event simulation languages such as SIMULA I (Nygaard and Dahl, 1978) and its successors; the string-processing language SL5 (Hanson and Griswold, 1978); and systems implementation languages including BLISS (Wulf *et al.*, 1971) and most recently Modula-2 (Wirth, 1982).

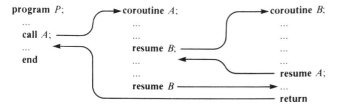

Figure 2.1 A use of coroutines

The fork and join statements

The **fork** statement (Dennis and Van Horn, 1966; Conway, 1963b), like a **call** or **resume**, specifies that a designated routine should start executing. However, the invoking routine and the invoked routine proceed concurrently. To synchronize with completion of the invoked routine, the invoking routine can execute a **join** statement. Executing **join** delays the invoking routine until the designated invoked routine has terminated. (The latter routine is often designated by a value returned from execution of a prior **fork**.) A use of **fork** and **join** follows:

program *P1*;	program *P2*;
...	...
fork *P2*;	...
...	...
join *P2*;	**end**
...	

Execution of *P2* is initiated when the **fork** in *P1* is executed; *P1* and *P2* then execute concurrently until either *P1* executes the **join** statement or *P2* terminates. After *P1* reaches the **join** and *P2* terminates, *P1* executes the statements following the **join**.

Because **fork** and **join** can appear in conditionals and loops, a detailed understanding of program execution is necessary to understand which routines will be executed concurrently. Nevertheless, when used in a disciplined manner, the statements are practical and powerful. For example, **fork** provides a direct mechanism for dynamic process creation, including multiple activations of the same program text. The UNIX[6] operating system (Ritchie and Thompson, 1974) makes extensive use of variants of **fork** and **join**. Similar statements have also been included in PL/I and Mesa (Mitchell *et al.*, 1979).

The cobegin statement

The **cobegin** statement[7] is a structured way of denoting concurrent execution of a set of statements. Execution of

cobegin $S_1 \parallel S_2 \parallel \cdots \parallel S_n$ **coend**

causes concurrent execution of $S_1, S_2, \ldots, S_n$. Each of the S_i's may be any

[6] UNIX is a trademark of Bell Laboratories.
[7] This was first called **parbegin** by Dijkstra (1968b).

statement, including a **cobegin** or a block with local declarations. Execution of a **cobegin** statement terminates only when execution of all the S_i's have terminated.

Although **cobegin** is not as powerful as **fork/join**,[8] it is sufficient for specifying most concurrent computations. Furthermore, the syntax of the **cobegin** statement makes explicit which routines are executed concurrently, and provides a single-entry, single-exit control structure. This allows the state transformation implemented by a **cobegin** to be understood by itself, and then to be used to understand the program in which it appears.

Variants of **cobegin** have been included in ALGOL68 (van Wijngaarden *et al.*, 1975), Communicating Sequential Processes (Hoare, 1978), Edison (Brinch Hansen, 1981), and Argus (Liskov and Scheifler, 1982).

Process declarations

Large programs are often structured as a collection of sequential routines, which are executed concurrently. Although such routines could be declared as procedures and activated by means of **cobegin** or **fork**, the structure of a concurrent program is much clearer if the declaration of a routine states whether it will be executed concurrently. The *process declaration* provides such a facility.

Use of process declarations to structure a concurrent program is illustrated in Figure 2, which outlines the batch operating system described earlier. We shall use this notation for process declarations in the remainder of this paper to denote collections of routines that are executed concurrently.

In some concurrent programming languages (e.g., Distributed Processes (Brinch Hansen, 1978) and SR (Andrews, 1981), a collection of process declarations is equivalent to a single **cobegin**, where each of the declared processes is a component of the **cobegin**. This means there is exactly one instance of each declared process. Alternatively, some languages provide an explicit mechanism – **fork** or something similar – for activating instances of process declarations. This explicit activation mechanism can only be used during program initialization in some languages (e.g., Concurrent PASCAL (Brinch Hansen, 1975) and Modula (Wirth, 1977a)). This leads to a fixed number of processes but allows multiple instances of each declared process to be created. By contrast, in other languages (e.g., PLITS (Feldman, 1979) and Ada (U.S. Department of Defense, 1981)) processes can be created at any time during execution, which makes possible computations having a variable number of processes.

---

[8] Execution of a concurrent program can be represented by a *process flow graph*: an acyclic, directed graph having one node for each process and an arc from one node to another if the second cannot execute until the first has terminated (Shaw, 1974). Without introducing extra processes or idle time, **cobegin** and sequencing can only represent series-parallel (properly nested) process flow graphs. Using **fork** and **join**, the computation represented by any process flow graph can be specified directly. Furthermore, **fork** can be used to create an arbitrary number of concurrent processes, whereas **cobegin** as defined in any existing language, can be used only to activate a fixed number of processes.

```
program OPSYS;

    var input_buffer : array [0..N−1] of cardimage;
        output_buffer : array [0..N−1] of lineimage;

    process reader;
      var card : cardimage;
      loop
        read card from cardreader;
        deposit card in input_buffer
        end
      end;

    process executer;
      var card : cardimage;
          line : lineimage;
      loop
        fetch card from input_buffer;
        process card and generate line;
        deposit line in output_buffer
        end
      end;

    process printer;
      var line : lineimage;
      loop
        fetch line from output_buffer;
        print line on lineprinter
        end
      end

    end.
```

Figure 2.2 Outline of batch operating system

3. Synchronization primitives based on shared variables

When shared variables are used for interprocess communication, two types of synchronization are useful: mutual exclusion and condition synchronization. *Mutual exclusion* ensures that a sequence of statements is treated as an indivisible operation. Consider, for example, a complex data structure manipulated by means of operations implemented as sequences of statements. If processes concurrently perform operations on the same shared data object, then unintended results might occur. (This was illustrated earlier where the statement $x := x + 1$ had to be executed indivisibly for a meaningful computation to result.) A sequence of statements that must appear to be executed as an indivisible operation is called a *critical section*. The term 'mutual exclusion' refers to mutually exclusive execution of critical sections. Notice that the effects of execution interleavings are visible only if two computations access shared variables. If such is the case, one computation can see intermediate results produced by incomplete execution of the other. If two routines have no variables in common, then their execution need not be mutually exclusive.

Another situation in which it is necessary to coordinate execution of concurrent processes occurs when a shared date object is in a state inappropriate for executing a particular operation. Any process attempting such an operation should be delayed until the state of the data object (i.e., the values of the variables that comprise the object) changes as a result of other processes executing operations. We shall call this type of synchronization *condition synchronization*.[9] Examples of condition synchronization appear in the simple batch operating system discussed above. A process attempting to execute a 'deposit' operation on a buffer (the buffer being a shared data object) should be delayed if the buffer has no space. Similarly, a process attempting to 'fetch' from a buffer should be delayed if there is nothing in the buffer to remove.

Below, we survey various mechanisms for implementing these two types of synchronization.

Busy-waiting

One way to implement synchronization is to have processes set and test shared variables. This approach works reasonably well for implementing condition synchronization, but not for implementing mutual exclusion, as will be seen. To signal a condition, a process sets the value of a shared variable; to wait for that condition, a process repeatedly tests the variable until it is found to have a desired value. Because a process waiting for a condition must repeatedly test the shared variable, this technique to delay a process is called *busy-waiting* and the process is said to be *spinning*. Variables that are used in this way are sometimes called *spin locks*.

To implement mutual exclusion using busy-waiting, statements that signal and wait for conditions are combined into carefully constructed protocols. Below, we present Peterson's solution to the two-process mutual exclusion problem (Peterson, 1981). (This solution is simpler than the solution proposed by Dekker (Shaw, 1974).) The solution involves an *entry protocol*, which a process executes before entering its critical section, and an *exit protocol*, which a process executes after finishing its critical section:

process *P1*;
  loop
      Entry Protocol;
      Critical Section;
      Exit Protocol;
      Noncritical Section
      end
  end

process *P2*;
  loop
      Entry Protocol;
      Critical Section;
      Exit Protocol;
      Noncritical Section
      end
  end

[9] Unfortunately, there is no commonly agreed upon term for this.

Three shared variables are used as follows to realize the desired synchronization. Boolean variable *enteri* ($i = 1$ or 2) is true when process *Pi* is executing its entry protocol or its critical section. Variable *turn* records the name of the next process to be granted entry into its own critical section; *turn* is used when both processes execute their respective entry protocols at about the same time. The solution is

```
program Mutex_Example;

  var enter1, enter2 : Boolean initial (false,false);
      turn : integer initial ("P1");    { or "P2" }

  process P1;
    loop

      Entry_Protocol:
        enter1 := true;    { announce intent to enter }
        turn := "P2";      { set priority to other process }
        while enter2 and turn = "P2"
          do skip; { wait if other process is in and it is his turn }

      Critical Section;

      Exit_Protocol:
        enter1 := false;    { renounce intent to enter }

      Noncritical Section
      end
    end;

  process P2;
    loop

      Entry_Protocol:
        enter2 := true;    { announce intent to enter }
        turn := "P1";      { set priority to other process }
        while enter1 and turn = "P1"
          do skip; { wait if other process is in and it is his turn }

      Critical Section;

      Exit_Protocol:
        enter1 := false;    { renounce intent to enter }

      Noncritical Section
      end
    end

  end.
```

In addition to implementing mutual exclusion, this solution has two other desirable properties. First, it is *deadlock free*. *Deadlock* is a state of affairs in which two or more processes are waiting for events that will never occur. Above, deadlock could occur if each process could spin forever in its entry protocol; using *turn* precludes deadlock. The second desirable property is *fairness*:[10] if a process is trying to enter its critical section, it will eventually be able to do so, provided that the other process exits its critical section. Fairness is a desirable property for a synchronization mechanism because its presence ensures that the finite progress assumption is not invalidated by delays due to synchronization. In general, a synchronization mechanism is *fair* if no process is delayed forever, waiting for a condition that occurs infinitely often; it is *bounded fair* if there exists an upper bound on how long a process will be delayed waiting for a condition that occurs infinitely often. The above protocol is bounded fair, since a process waiting to enter its

---

[10] A more complete discussion of fairness appears in Lehmann *et al.* (1981).

critical section is delayed for at most one execution of the other process' critical section; the variable *turn* ensures this. Peterson (1981) gives operational proofs of mutual exclusion, deadlock freedom, and fairness; Dijkstra (1981a) gives axiomatic ones.

Synchronization protocols that use only busy-waiting are difficult to design, understand, and prove correct. First, although instructions that make two memory references part of a single indivisible operation (e.g., the TS (test-and-set) instruction on the IBM 360/370 processors) help, such instructions do not significantly simplify the task of designing synchronization protocols. Second, busy-waiting wastes processor cycles. A processor executing a spinning process could usually be employed more productively by running other processes until the awaited condition occurs. Last, the busy-waiting approach to synchronization burdens the programmer with deciding both what synchronization is required and how to provide it. In reading a program that uses busy-waiting, it may not be clear to the reader which program variables are used for implementing synchronization and which are used for, say, interprocess communication.

Semaphores

Dijkstra was one of the first to appreciate the difficulties of using low-level mechanisms for process synchronization, and this prompted his development of semaphores (Dijkstra, 1968a, 1968b). A *semaphore* is a nonnegative integer-valued variable on which two operations are defined: **P** and **V**. Given a semaphore s, **P**(s) delays until $s > 0$ and then executes $s := s - 1$; the test and decrement are executed as an indivisible operation. **V**(s) executes $s := s + 1$ as an indivisible operation.[11] Most semaphore implementations are assumed to exhibit fairness: no process delayed while executing **P**(s) will remain delayed for ever if **V**(s) operations are performed infinitely often. The need for fairness arises when a number of processes are simultaneously delayed, all attempting to execute a **P** operation on the same semaphore. Clearly, the implementation must choose which one will be allowed to proceed when a **V** is ultimately performed. A simple way to ensure fairness is to awaken processes in the order in which they were delayed.

Semaphores are a very general tool for solving synchronization problems. To implement a solution to the mutual exclusion problem, each critical section is preceded by a **P** operation and followed by a **V** operation on the same semaphore. All mutually exclusive critical sections use the same semaphore, which is initialized to one. Because such a semaphore only takes on the values zero and one, it is often called a *binary* semaphore.

To implement condition synchronization, shared variables are used to represent the condition, and a semaphore associated with the condition is used to accomplish the synchronization. After a process has made the condition true, it signals that it has done so by executing a **V** operation; a

[11] P is the first letter of the Dutch word 'passeren,' which means 'to pass'; V is the first letter of 'vrygeven,' the Dutch word for 'to release' (Dijkstra, 1981b). Reflecting on the definitions of **P** and **V**, Dijkstra and his group observed the P might better stand for 'prolagen' formed from the Dutch words 'proberen' (meaning 'to try') and 'verlagen' (meaning 'to decrease') and V for the Dutch word 'verhogen' meaning 'to increase.' Some authors use **wait** for **P** and **signal** for **V**.

process delays until a condition is true by executing a **P** operation. A semaphore that can take any nonnegative value is called a *general* or *counting* semaphore. General semaphores are often used for condition synchronization when controlling resource allocation. Such a semaphore has as its initial value the initial number of units of the resource; a **P** is used to delay a process until a free resource unit is available; **V** is executed when a unit of the resource is returned. Binary semaphores are sufficient for some types of condition synchronization, notably those in which a resource has only one unit.

A few examples will illustrate uses of semaphores. We show a solution to the two-process mutual exclusion problem in terms of semaphores in the following:

```
program Mutex_Example;

  var mutex : semaphore initial (1);

  process P1;
    loop
      P(mutex);        { Entry Protocol }
      Critical Section;
      V(mutex);        { Exit Protocol }
      Noncritical Section
      end
    end;

  process P2;
    loop
      P(mutex);        { Entry Protocol }
      Critical Section;
      V(mutex);        { Exit Protocol }
      Noncritical Section
      end
    end

  end.
```

Notice how simple and symmetric the entry and exit protocols are in this solution to the mutual exclusion problem. In particular, this use of **P** and **V** ensures both mutual exclusion and absence of deadlock. Also, if the semaphore implementation is fair and both processes always exit their critical sections, each process eventually gets to enter its critical section.

Semaphores can also be used to solve *selective mutual exclusion* problems. In the latter, shared variables are partitioned into disjoint sets. A semaphore is associated with each set and used in the same way as *mutex* above to control access to the variables in that set. Critical sections that reference variables in the same set execute with mutual exclusion, but critical sections that reference variables in different sets execute concurrently. However, if two or more processes require simultaneous access to variables in two or more sets, the programmer must take care or deadlock could result. Suppose that two processes, *P1* and *P2*, each require simultaneous accesss to sets of shared variables *A* and *B*. Then, *P1* and *P2* will deadlock if, for example, *P1* acquires access to set *A*, *P2* acquires access to set *B*, and then both processes try to acquire access to the set that they do not yet have. Deadlock is avoided here (and in general) if processes first try to acquire access to the same set (e.g., *A*), and then try to acquire access to the other (e.g., *B*).

Figure 3 shows how semaphores can be used for selective mutual exclusion and condition synchronization in an implementation of our simple example operating system. Semaphore *in__mutex* is used to implement mutually exclusive access to *input__buffer* and *out__mutex* is used to implement mutually exclusive access to *output__buffer*.[12] Because the buffers are disjoint, it is possible for operations on *input__buffer* and *output__buffer* to proceed concurrently. Sempahores *num__cards*, *num__lines*, *free__cards*, and *free__lines* are used for condition synchronization: *num__cards* (*num__ lines*) is the number of card images (line images) that have been deposited but not yet fetched from *input__buffer* (*output__buffer*); *free__cards* (*free__ lines*) is the number of free slots in *input__buffer* (*output__buffer*). Executing **P**(*num__cards*) delays a process until there is a card in *input__buffer*; **P**(*free__cards*) delays its invoker until there is space to insert a card in *input__buffer*. Semaphores *num__lines* and *free__lines* play corresponding roles with respect to *output__buffer*. Note that before accessing a buffer, each process first waits for the condition required for access and then acquires exclusive access to the buffer. If this were not the case, deadlock could result. (The order in which **V** operations are performed after the buffer is accessed is not critical.)

Semaphores can be implemented by using busy-waiting. More commonly, however, they are implemented by system calls to a kernel. A *kernel* (sometimes called a *supervisor* or *nucleus*) implements processes on a processor (Dijkstra, 1968a; Shaw, 1974). At all times, each process is either *ready* to execute on the processor or is *blocked*, waiting to complete a **P** operation. The kernel maintains a *ready list* – a queue of descriptors for ready processes – and multiplexes the processor among these processes, running each process for some period of time. Descriptors for processes that are blocked on a semaphore are stored on a queue associated with that semaphore; they are not stored on the ready list, and hence the processes will not be executed. Execution of a **P** or **V** operation causes a trap to a kernel routine. For a **P** operation, if the semaphore is positive, it is decremented; otherwise the descriptor for the executing process is moved to the semaphore's queue. For a **V** operation, if the semaphore's queue is not empty, one descriptor is moved from that queue to the ready list; otherwise the semaphore is incremented.

This approach to implementing synchronization mechanisms is quite general and is applicable to the other mechanisms that we shall discuss. Since the kernel is responsible for allocating processor cycles to processes, it can implement a synchronization mechanism without using busy-waiting. It does this by not running processes that are blocked. Of course, the names and details of the kernel calls will differ for each synchronization mechanism, but the net effects of these calls will be similar: to move processes on and off a ready list.

---

[12] In this solution, careful implementation of the operations on the buffers obviates the need for semaphores *in__mutex* and *out__mutex*. The semaphores that implement condition synchronization are sufficient to ensure mutually exclusive access to individual buffer slots.

```
program OPSYS;

    var in_mutex, out_mutex : semaphore initial (1,1);
        num_cards, num_lines : semaphore initial (0,0);
        free_cards, free_lines : semaphore initial (N,N);
        input_buffer : array [0..N−1] of cardimage;
        output_buffer : array [0..N−1] of lineimage;

    process reader;
        var card : cardimage;
        loop
            read card from cardreader;
            P(free_cards);  P(in_mutex);
                deposit card in input_buffer;
            V(in_mutex);  V(num_cards)
            end
        end;

    process executer;
        var card : cardimage;
            line : lineimage;
        loop
            P(num_cards);  P(in_mutex);
                fetch card from input_buffer;
            V(in_mutex);  V(free_cards);
            process card and generate line;
            P(free_lines);  P(out_mutex);
                deposit line in output_buffer;
            V(out_mutex);   V(num_lines)
            end
        end;

    process printer;
        var line : lineimage;
        loop
            P(num_lines);  P(out_mutex);
                fetch line from output_buffer;
            V(out_mutex);  V(free_lines);
            print line on lineprinter
            end
        end

    end.
```

Figure 2.3 Batch operating system with semaphores

Things are somewhat more complex when writing a kernel for a multi-processor or distributed system. In a multiprocessor, either a single processor is responsible for maintaining the ready list and assigning processes to the other processors, or the ready list is shared (Jones and Schwarz, 1980). If the ready list is shared, it is subject to concurrent access, which requires that mutual exclusion be ensured. Usually, busy-waiting is used to ensure this mutual exclusion because operations on the ready list are fast and a processor cannot execute any process until it is able to access the ready list. In a distributed system, although one processor could maintain the ready list, it is more common for each processor to have its own kernel and hence its own ready list. Each kernel manages those processes residing at one processor; if a process migrates from one processor to another, it comes under the control of the other's kernel.

Conditional critical regions

Although semaphores can be used to program almost any kind of synchronization, **P** and **V** are rather unstructured primitives, and so it is easy to err when using them. Execution of each critical section must begin with a **P** and end with a **V** (on the same semaphore). Omitting a **P** or **V**, or accidentally coding a **P** on one semaphore and a **V** on another can have disastrous effects, since mutually exclusive execution would no longer be ensured. Also, when using semaphores, a programmer can forget to include in critical sections all statements that reference shared objects. This, too, could destroy the mutual exclusion required within critical sections. A second difficulty with using semaphores is that both condition synchronization and mutual exclusion are programmed using the same pair of primitives. This makes it difficult to identify the purpose of a given **P** or **V** operation without looking at the other operations on the corresponding semaphore. Since mutual exclusion and condition synchronization are distinct concepts, they should have distinct notations.

The *conditional critical region* proposal (Hoare, 1972; Brinch Hansen 1972, 1973b) overcomes these difficulties by providing a structured notation for specifying synchronization. Shared variables are explicitly placed into groups, called *resources*. Each shared variable may be in at most one resource and may be accessed only in conditional critical region (CCR) statements that name the resource. Mutual exclusion is provided by guaranteeing that execution of different CCR statements, each naming the same resource, is not overlapped. Condition synchronization is provided by explicit Boolean conditions in CCR statements.

A resource r containing variables $v1, v2, \ldots, vN$ is declared as[13]

resource $r: v1, v2, \ldots, vN$

The variables in r may only be accessed within CCR statements that name r. Such statements have the form.

region r **when** B **do** S

where B is a Boolean expression and S is a statement list. (Variables local to the executing process may also appear in the CCR statement.) A CCR statement delays the executing process until B is true; S is then executed. The evaluation of B and execution of S are uninterruptible by other CCR statements that name the same resource. Thus B is guaranteed to be true when execution of S begins. The delay mechanism is usually assumed to be fair: a process awaiting a condition B that is repeatedly true will eventually be allowed to continue.

One use of conditional critical regions is shown in Figure 2.4, which contains another implementation of our batch operating system example. Note how condition synchronization has been separated from mutual

---

[13] Our notation combines aspects of those proposed by Hoare (1972) and by Brinch Hansen (1972, 1973b).

exclusion. The Boolean expressions in those CCR statements that access the buffers explicitly specify the conditions required for access; thus mutual exclusion of different CCR statements that access the same buffer is implicit.

```
program OPSYS;

  type buffer(T) = record
                slots : array [0..N−1] of T;
                head, tail : 0..N−1 initial (0, 0);
                size : 0..N initial (0)
                end;
  var inp_buff : buffer(cardimage);
      out_buff : buffer(lineimage);

  resource ib : inp_buff;  ob : out_buff;

  process reader;
    var card : cardimage;
    loop
      read card from cardreader;
      region ib when inp_buff.size < N do
        inp_buff.slots[inp_buff.tail] := card;
        inp_buff.size := inp_buff.size + 1;
        inp_buff.tail := (inp_buff.tail + 1) mod N
        end
      end
    end;

  process executer;
    var card : cardimage;
        line : lineimage;
    loop
      region ib when inp_buff.size > 0 do
        card := inp_buff.slots[inp_buff.head]
        inp_buff.size := inp_buff.size − 1;
        inp_buff.head := (inp_buff.head + 1) mod N
        end;
      process card and generate line;
      region ob when out_buff.size < N do
        out_buff.slots[out_buff.tail] := line;
        out_buff.size := out_buff.size + 1;
        out_buff.tail := (out_buff.tail + 1) mod N
        end
      end
    end;

  process printer;
    var line : lineimage;
    loop
      region ob when out_buff.size > 0 do
        line := out_buff.slots[out_buff.head];
        out_buff.size := out_buff.size − 1;
        out_buff.head := (out_buff.head + 1) mod N
        end;
      print line on lineprinter
      end
    end

  end.
```

Figure 2.4 Batch operating system with CCR statements

Programs written in terms of conditional critical regions can be understood quite simply by using the axiomatic approach. Each CCR statement implements an operation on the resource that it names. Associated with each resource r is an *invariant relation* I_r: a predicate that is true of the resource's state after the resource is intialized and after execution of any operation on the resource. For example, in OPSYS of Figure 4, the operations insert and remove items from bounded buffers and the buffers *inp__buff* and *out__buff* both satisfy the invariant

IB:

$0 \leqslant head, tail \leqslant N - 1$ **and**
$0 \leqslant size \leqslant N$ **and**
$tail = (head + size)$ **mod** N **and**
$slots[head]$ through $slots[(tail - 1)$ **mod** $N]$
   in the circular buffer contain
   the most recently inserted items
   in chronological order

The Boolean expression B in each CCR statement is chosen so that execution of the statement list, when started in any state that satisfies I_r **and** B, will terminate in a state that satisfies I_r. Therefore the invariant is true as long as no process is in the midst of executing an operation (i.e., executing in a conditional critical region associated with the resource). Recall that execution of conditional critical regions associated with a given shared data object does not overlap. Hence the proofs of processes are interference free as long as (1) variables local to a process appear only in the proof of that process and (2) variables of a resource appear only in assertions within conditional critical regions for that resource. Thus, once appropriate resource invariants have been defined, a concurrent program can be understood in terms of its component sequential processes.

Although conditional critical regions have many virtues, they can be expensive to implement. Because conditions in CCR statements can contain references to local variables, each process must evaluate its own conditions.[14] On a multiprogrammed processor, this evaluation results in numerous context switches (frequent saving and restoring of process states), many of which may be unproductive because the activated process may still find the condition false. If each process is executed on its own processor and memory is shared, however, CCR statements can be implemented quite cheaply by using busy-waiting.

CCR statements provide the synchronization mechanism in the Edison language (Brinch Hansen, 1981), which is designed specifically for multiprocessor systems. Variants have also been used in Distributed Processes (Brinch Hansen, 1978) and Argus (Liskov and Scheifler, 1982).

Monitors

Conditional critical regions are costly to implement on single processors. Also, CCR statements performing operations on resource variables are

---

[14] When delayed, a process could instead place condition evaluating code in an area of memory accessible to other processes, but this too is costly.

dispersed throughout the processes. This means that one has to study an entire concurrent program to see all the ways in which a resource is used. Monitors alleviate both these deficiencies. A *monitor* is formed by encapsulating both a resource definition and operations that manipulate it (Dijkstra, 1968b; Brinch Hansen, 1973a; Hoare, 1974). This allows a resource subject to concurrent access to be viewed as a module (Parnas, 1972). Consequently, a programmer can ignore the implementation details of the resource when using it, and can ignore how it is used when programming the monitor that implements it.

Definition

A monitor consists of a collection of *permanent variables*, used to store the resource's state, and some procedures, which implement operations on the resource. A monitor also has permanent-variable initialization code, which is executed once before any procedure body is executed. The values of the permanent variables are retained between activations of monitor procedures and may be accessed only from within the monitor. Monitor procedures can have parameters and local variables, each of which takes on new values for each procedure activation. The structure of a monitor with name *mname* and procedures *op1, . . . , opN* is shown in Figure 2.5.

```
mname : monitor;

    var declarations of permanent variables;

    procedure op1(parameters);
      var declarations of variables local to op1;
      begin
        code to implement op1
      end;

      ...

    procedure opN(parameters);
      var declarations of variables local to opN;
      begin
        code to implement opN
      end;

    begin
      code to initialize permanent variables
    end
```

Figure 2.5 Monitor structure

Procedure *opJ* within monitor *mname* is invoked by executing

call *mname.opJ*(arguments).

The invocation has the usual semantics associated with a procedure call. In addition, execution of the procedures in a given monitor is guaranteed to be mutually exclusive. This ensures that the permanent variables are never accessed concurrently.

A variety of constructs have been proposed for realizing condition synchronization in monitors. We first describe the proposal made by Hoare (1974) and then consider other proposals. A *condition variable* is used to delay processes executing in a monitor; it may be declared only within a monitor. Two operations are defined on condition variables; **signal** and **wait**. If *cond* is a condition variable, then execution of

cond.**wait**

causes the invoker to be blocked on *cond* and to relinquish its mutually exclusive control of the monitor. Execution of

cond.**signal**

works as follows: if no process is blocked on *cond*, the invoker continues; otherwise, the invoker is temporarily suspended and one process blocked on *cond* is reactivated. A process suspended due to a **signal** operation continues when there is no other process executing in the monitor. Moreover, signalers are given priority over processes trying to commence execution of a monitor procedure. Condition variables are assumed to be fair in the sense that a process will not for ever remain suspended on a condition variable that is signaled infinitely often. Note that the introduction of condition variables allows more than one process to be in the same monitor, although all but one will be delayed at **wait** or **signal** operations.

An example of a monitor that defines a bounded buffer type is given in Figure 2.6. Our batch operating system can be programmed using two instances of the bounded buffer in Figure 2.6; these are shared by three processes, as shown in Figure 2.7.

```
type buffer(T) = monitor;

    var { the variables satisfy invariant IB — see p. 66 }
        slots : array [0..N−1] of T;
        head, tail : 0..N−1;
        size : 0..N;
        notfull, notempty : condition;

    procedure deposit(p : T);
      begin
        if size = N  then notfull.wait;
        slots[tail] := p;
        size := size + 1;
        tail := (tail + 1) mod N;
        notempty.signal
      end;

    procedure fetch(var it : T);
      begin
        if size = 0  then notempty.wait;
        it := slots[head];
        size := size − 1;
        head := (head + 1) mod N;
        notfull.signal
      end;

    begin
      size := 0;  head := 0;  tail := 0
    end
```

Figure 2.6 Bounded buffer monitor

```
program OPSYS;

  type buffer(T) = ...;  { see Figure 2.5 }

  var inp_buff : buffer(cardimage);
      out_buff : buffer(lineimage);

  process reader;
    var card : cardimage;
    loop
      read card from cardreader;
      call inp_buff.deposit(card)
      end
    end;

  process executer;
    var card : cardimage;
        line : lineimage;
    loop
      call inp_buff.fetch(card);
      process card and generate line;
      call out_buff.deposit(line)
      end
    end;

  process printer;
    var line : lineimage;
    loop
      call out_buff.fetch(line);
      print line on lineprinter
      end
    end

  end.
```

Figure 2.7 Batch operating system with monitors

At times, a programmer requires more control over the order in which delayed processes are awakened. To implement such *medium-term scheduling*,[15] the *priority* **wait** statement can be used. This statement

cond.**wait**(*p*)

has the same semantics as *cond*.**wait**, except that in the former processes blocked on condition variable *cond* are awakened in ascending order of *p*. (Consequently, condition variables used in this way are not necessarily fair.)

A common problem involving medium-term scheduling is 'shortest-job-next' resource allocation. A resource is to be allocated to at most one user at a time; if more than one user is waiting for the resource when it is released, it is allocated to the user who will use it for the shortest amount of time. A monitor to implement such an allocator is shown below. The monitor has two procedures: (1) *request*(*time* : *integer*), which is called by users to request access to the resource for *time* units; and (2) *release*, which is called by users to relinquish access to the resource:

---

[15] This is in contrast to *short-term scheduling*, which is concerned with how processors are assigned to ready processes, and *long-term scheduling*, which refers to how jobs are selected to be processed.

```
shortest_next_allocator : monitor;

    var free : Boolean;
        turn : condition;

    procedure request(time : integer);
        begin
            if not free then  turn.wait(time);
            free := false
        end;

    procedure release;
        begin
            free := true;
            turn.signal
        end;

    begin
        free := true
    end
```

Other approaches to condition synchronization

Queues and delay/continue. In Concurrent PASCAL (Brinch Hansen, 1975), a slightly simpler mechanism is provided for implementing condition synchronization and medium-term scheduling. Variables of type *queue* can be defined and manipulated with the operations **delay** (analogous to **wait**) and **continue** (analogous to **signal**). In contrast to condition variables, at most one process can be suspended on a given *queue* at any time. This allows medium-term scheduling to be implemented by (1) defining an array of queues and (2) performing a **continue** operation on that queue on which the next-process-to-be-awakened has been delayed. The semantics of **continue** are also slightly different from **signal**. Executing **continue** causes the invoker to return from its monitor call, whereas **signal** does not. As before, a process blocked on the selected queue resumes execution of the monitor procedure within which it was delayed.

It is both cheaper and easier to implement **continue** than **signal** because **signal** requires code to ensure that processes suspended by **signal** operations reacquire control of the monitor before other, newer processes attempting to begin execution in that monitor. With both **signal** and **continue**, the objective is to ensure that a condition is not invalidated between the time it is signaled and the time that the awakened process actually resumes execution. Although **continue** has speed and cost advantages, it is less powerful than **signal**. A monitor written using condition variables cannot always be translated directly into one that uses queues without also adding monitor procedures (Howard, 1976b). Clearly, these additional procedures complicate the interface provided by the monitor. Fortunately, most synchronization problems that arise in practice can be coded using either discipline.

Conditional wait and automatic signal. In contrast to semaphores, **signals** on condition variables are not saved: a process always delays after executing

wait, even if a previous **signal** did not awaken any process.[16] This can make **signal** and **wait** difficult to use correctly, because other variables must be used to record that a **signal** was executed. These variables must also be tested by a process, before executing **wait**, to guard against waiting if the event corresponding to a **signal** has already occurred.

Another difficulty is that, in contrast to conditional critical regions, a Boolean expression is not syntactically associated with **signal** and **wait**, or with the condition variable itself. Thus, it is not easy to determine why a process was delayed on a condition variable, unless **signal** and **wait** are used in a very disciplined manner. It helps if (1) each **wait** on a condition variable is contained in an **if** statement in which the Boolean expression is the negation of the desired condition synchronization, and (2) each **signal** statement on the same condition variable is contained in an **if** statement in which the Boolean expression gives the desired condition synchronization. Even so, syntactically identical Boolean expressions may have different values if they contain references to local variables, which they often do. Thus there is no guarantee that an awakened process will actually see the condition for which it was waiting. A final difficulty with **wait** and **signal** is that, because **signal** is preemptive, the state of permanent variables seen by a signaler can change between the time a **signal** is executed and the time that the signaling process resumes execution.

To mitigate these difficulties, Hoare (1974) proposed the *conditional wait* statement

wait (B)

where B is a Boolean expression involving the permanent or local variables of the monitor. Execution of **wait**(B) delays the invoker until B becomes true; no **signal** is required to reactivate processes delayed by a conditional wait statement. This synchronization facility is expensive because it is necessary to evaluate B every time any process exits the monitor or becomes blocked at a conditional wait and because a context switch could be required for each evaluation (due to the presence of local variables in the condition). However, the construct is unquestionably a very clean one with which to program.

An efficient variant of the conditional wait was proposed by Kessels (1977) for use when only permanent variables appear in B. The buffer monitor in Figure 2.6 satisfies this requirement. In Kessels' proposal, one declares *conditions* of the form

cname : **condition** B

Executing the statement *cname*.**wait** causes B, a Boolean expression, to be evaluated. If B is true, the process continues; otherwise the process relinquishes control of the monitor and is delayed on *cname*. Whenever a process relinquishes control of the monitor, the system evaluates those Boolean expressions associated with all conditions for which there are waiting processes. If one of these Boolean expressions is found to be true, one of the waiting processes is granted control of the monitor. If none is found to be true, a new invocation of one of the monitor's procedures is permitted.

---

[16] The limitations of condition variables discussed in this section also apply to queue variables.

Using Kessels' proposal, the buffer monitor in Figure 2.6 could be recoded as follows. First, the declarations of *not_full* and *not_empty* are changed to

not_full : **condition** *size* < *N*;
not_empty : **condition** *size* > *O*

Second, the first statement in *deposit* is replaced by

not_full.**wait**

and the first statement in *fetch* is replaced by

not_empty.**wait**

Finally, the **signal** statements are deleted.

The absence of a **signal** primitive is noteworthy. The implementation provides an *automatic signal*, which, though somewhat more costly, is less error prone than explicitly programmed **signal** operations. The **signal** operation cannot be accidentally omitted and never signals the wrong condition. Furthermore, the programmer explicitly specifies the conditions being awaited. The primary limitation of the proposal is that it cannot be used to solve most scheduling problems, because operation parameters, which are not permanent variables, may not appear in conditions.

Signals as hints. Mesa (Mitchell *et al.*, 1979; Lampson and Redell, 1980) employs yet another approach to condition synchronization. Condition variables are provided, but only as a way for a process to relinquish control of a monitor. In Mesa, execution of

cond.**notify**

causes a process waiting on condition variable *cond* to resume at some time in the future. This is called *signal and continue* because the process performing the **notify** immediately continues execution rather than being suspended. Performing a **notify** merely gives a *hint* to a waiting process that it might be able to proceed.[17] Therefore, in Mesa one writes

while not *B* **do wait** *cond* **endloop**

instead of

if not *B* **then** *cond*.**wait**

as would be done using Hoare's condition variables. Boolean condition *B* is guaranteed to be true upon termination of the loop, as it was in the two conditional-wait/automatic-signal proposals. Moreover, the (possible) repeated evaluation of the Boolean expression appears in the actual monitor code – there are no hidden implementation costs.

The **notify** primitive is especially useful if the executing process has higher priority than the waiting processes. It also allows the following extensions to condition variables, which are often useful when doing systems programming:

---

[17] Of course, it is prudent to perform **notify** operations only when there is reason to believe that the awakened process will actually be able to proceed; but the burden of checking the condition is on the waiting process.

(i) A time-out interval *t* can be associated with each condition variable. If a process is ever suspended on this condition variable for longer than *t* time units, a **notify** is automatically performed by the system. The awakened process can then decide whether to perform another **wait** or to take other action.

(ii) A **broadcast** primitive can be defined. Its execution causes all processes waiting on a condition variable to resume at some time in the future (subject to the mutual exclusion constraints associated with execution in a monitor). This primitive is useful if more than one process could proceed when a condition becomes true. The broadcast primitive is also useful when a condition involves local variables because in this case the signaler cannot evaluate the condition (*B* above) for which a process is waiting. Such a primitive is, in fact, used in UNIX (Ritchie and Thompson, 1974).

An axiomatic view
The valid states of a resource protected by a monitor can be characterized by an assertion called the *monitor invariant*. This predicate should be true of the monitor's permanent variables whenever no process is executing in the monitor. Thus a process must reestablish the monitor invariant before the process exits the monitor or performs a **wait(delay)** or **signal(continue)**. The monitor invariant can be assumed to be true of the permanent variables whenever a process acquires control of the monitor, regardless of whether it acquires control by calling a monitor procedure or by being reactivated following a **wait** or **signal**.

The fact that monitor procedures are mutually exclusive simplifies non-interference proofs. One need not consider interleaved execution of monitor procedures. However, interference can arise when programming condition synchronization. Recall that a process will delay its progress in order to implement medium-term scheduling, or to await some condition. Mechanisms that delay a process cause its execution to be suspended and control of the monitor to be relinquished; the process resumes execution with the understanding that both some condition *B* and the monitor invariant will be true. The truth of *B* when the process awakens can be ensured by checking for it automatically or by requiring that the programmer build these tests into the program. If programmed checks are used, they can appear either in the process that establishes the condition (for condition variables and queues) or in the process that performed the **wait** (the Mesa model).

If the signaler checks for the condition, we must ensure that the condition is not invalidated between the time that the **signal** occurs and the time that the blocked process actually executes. That is, we must ensure that other execution in the monitor does not interfere with the condition. If the signaler does not immediately relinquish control of the monitor (e.g., if **notify** is used), interference might be caused by the process that established the condition in the first place. Also, if the signaled process does not get reactivated before new calls of monitor procedures are allowed, interference might be caused by some process that executes after the condition has been signaled (this can happen in Modula (Wirth, 1977a)). Proof rules for monitors and the various signaling disciplines are discussed by Howard (1976a, 1976b).

Nested monitor calls

When structuring a system as a hierarchical collection of monitors, it is likely that monitor procedures will be called from within other monitors. Such nested monitor calls have caused much discussion (Haddon, 1977; Lister, 1977; Parnas, 1978; Wettstein, 1978). The controversy is over what (if anything) should be done if a process having made a nested monitor call is suspended in another monitor. The mutual exclusion in the last monitor called will be relinquished by the process, due to the semantics of **wait** and equivalent operations. However, mutual exclusion will not be relinquished by processes in monitors from which nested calls have been made. Processes that attempt to invoke procedures in these monitors will become blocked. This has performance implications, since blockage will decrease the amount of concurrency exhibited by the system.

The nested monitor call problem can be approached in a number of ways. One approach is to prohibit nested monitor calls, as was done in SIMONE (Kaubisch *et al.*, 1976), or to prohibit nested calls to monitors that are not lexically nested, as was done in Modula (Wirth, 1977a). A second approach is to release the mutual exclusion on all monitors along the call chain when a nested call is made and that process becomes blocked.[18] This release-and-reacquire approach would require that the monitor invariant be established before any monitor call will block a process, the monitor invariant would have to be established before every call. A third approach is the definition of special-purpose constructs that can be used for particular situations in which nested calls often arise. The *manager* construct (Silberschatz *et al.*, 1977) for handling dynamic resource allocation problems and the *scheduler monitor* (Schneider and Bernstein, 1978) for scheduling access to shared resources are both based on this line of thought.

The last approach to the nested monitor call problem, and probably the most reasonable, is one that appreciates that monitors are only a structuring tool for resources that are subject to concurrent access (Andrews and McGraw, 1977; Parnas, 1978). Mutual exclusion of monitor procedures is only one way to preserve the integrity of the permanent variables that make up a resource. There are cases in which the operations provided by a given monitor can be executed concurrently without adverse effects, and even cases in which more than one instance of the same monitor procedure can be executed in parallel (e.g., several activations of a read procedure, in a monitor that encapsulates a database). Monitor procedures can be executed concurrently, provided that they do not interfere with each other. Also, there are cases in which the monitor invariant can be easily established before a nested monitor call is made, and so mutual exclusion for the monitor can be released. Based on such reasoning, Andrews and McGraw (1977) defines a monitor-like construct that allows the programmer to specify that certain monitor procedures be executed concurrently and that mutual exclusion be released for certain calls. The Mesa language (Mitchell *et al.*, 1979) also provides mechanisms that give programmer control over the granularity of exclusion.

---

[18] Once signaled, the process will need to reacquire exclusive access to all monitors along the call chain before resuming execution. However, if permanent monitor variables were not passed as reference parameters in any of the calls, the process could reacquire exclusive access incrementally, as it returns to each monitor.

Programming notations based on monitors

Numerous programming languages have been proposed and implemented that use monitors for synchronizing access to shared variables. Below, we very briefly discuss two of the most important: Concurrent PASCAL and Modula. These languages have received widespread use, introduced novel constructs to handle machine-dependent systems-programming issues, and inspired other language designs, such as Mesa (Mitchell *et al.*, 1979) and PASCAL-Plus (Welsh and Bustard, 1979).

Concurrent PASCAL. Concurrent PASCAL (Brinch Hansen, 1975, 1977) was the first programming language to support monitors. Consequently, it provided a vehicle for evaluating monitors as a system-structuring device. The language has been used to write several operating systems, including Solo, a single-user operating system (Brinch Hansen, 1976a, 1976b), Job Stream, a batch operating system for processing PASCAL programs, and a real-time process control system (Brinch Hansen, 1977).

One of the major goals of Concurrent PASCAL was to ensure that programs exhibited reproducible behaviour (Brinch Hansen, 1977). Monitors ensured that pathological interleavings of concurrently executed routines that shared data were no longer possible (the compiler generates code to provide the necessary mutual exclusion). Concurrent execution in other modules (called *classes*) was not possible due to compile-time restrictions on the dissemination of class names and scope rules for class declarations.

Concurrent PASCAL also succeeded in providing the programmer with a clean abstract machine, thereby eliminating the need for coding at the assembly language level. A systems programming language must have facilities to allow access to I/O devices and other hardware resources. In Concurrent PASCAL I/O devices and the like are viewed as monitors implemented directly in hardware. To perform an I/O operation, the corresponding 'monitor' is called; the call returns when the I/O has completed. Thus the Concurrent PASCAL run-time system implements synchronous I/O and 'abstracts out' the notion of an interrupt.

Various aspects of Concurrent PASCAL, including its approach to I/O have been analyzed by Loehr (1977), Silberschatz (1977) and Keedy (1979).

Modula. Modula was developed for programming small, dedicated computer systems, including process control applications (Wirth, 1977a, 1977b, 1977c, 1977d). The language is largely based on PASCAL and includes processes, *interface modules*, which are like monitors, and *device modules*, which are special interface modules for programming device drivers.

The run-time support system for Modula is small and efficient. The kernel for a PDP-11/45 requires only 98 words of storage and is extremely fast (Wirth, 1977c). It does not time slice the processor among processes, as Concurrent PASCAL does. Rather certain kernel-supported operations – **wait**, for example – always cause the processor to be switched. (The programmer must be aware of this and design programs accordingly.) This turns out to be both a strength and weakness of Modula. A small and efficient kernel, where the programmer has some control over processor switching allows Modula to be used for process control applications, as intended. Unfortunately, in order to be able to construct such a kernel some of the constructs in the language – notably those concerning multiprogramming – have associated restrictions that can only be understood in terms of the kernel's implementation. A variety of subtle interactions between the various synchronization constructs must be understood in order to program in Modula without experiencing unpleasant surprises. Some of these pathological interactions are described by Bernstein and Ensor (1981).

Modula implements an abstract machine that is well suited for dealing with interrupts and I/O devices on PDP-11 processors. Unlike Concurrent PASCAL, in which the run-time kernel handles interrupts and I/O, Modula leaves support for devices in the programmer's domain. Thus new devices can be added without modifying the kernel. An I/O device is considered to be a process that is implemented in hardware. A software process can start an I/O operation and then execute a **doio** statement (which is like a **wait** except that it delays the invoker until the kernel receives an interrupt from the corresponding device). Thus interrupts are viewed as **signal** (**send** in Modula) operations generated by the hardware. Device modules are interface modules that control I/O devices. Each contains, in addition to some procedures, a *device process*, which starts I/O operations and executes **doio** statements to relinquish control of the processor (pending receipt of the corresponding I/O interrupt). The address of the interrupt vector for the device is declared in the heading of the device module, so that the compiler can do the necessary binding. Modula also has provisions for controlling the processor priority register, thus allowing a programmer to exploit the priority interrupt architecture of the processor when structuring programs.

A third novel aspect of Modula is that variables declared in interface modules can be exported. Exported variables can be referenced (but not modified) from outside the scope of their defining interface module. This allows concurrent access to these variables, which, of course, can lead to difficulty unless the programmer ensures that interference cannot occur. However, when used selectively, this feature increases the efficiency of programs that access such variables.

In summary, Modula is less constraining than Concurrent PASCAL but requires the programmer to be more careful. Its specific strengths and weaknesses have been evaluated by Andrews (1979), Holden and Wand (1980) and Bernstein and Ensor (1981). Wirth, Modula's designer, has gone on to develop Modula-2 (Wirth, 1982). Modula-2 retains the basic modular structure of Modula, but provides more flexible facilities for concurrent programming and these facilities have less subtle semantics. In particular, Modula-2 provides coroutines and hence explicit transfer of control between processes. Using these, the programmer builds support for exclusion and condition synchronization, as required. In particular, the programmer can construct monitor-like modules.

Path expressions

Operations defined by a monitor are executed with mutual exclusion. Other synchronization of monitor procedures is realized by explicitly performing **wait** and **signal** operations on condition variables (or by some similar mechanism). Consequently, synchronization of monitor operations is realised by code scattered throughout the monitor. Some of this code, such as **wait** and **signal**, is visible to the programmer. Other code, such as the code ensuring mutual exclusion of monitor procedures, is not.

Another approach to defining a module subject to concurrent access is to provide a mechanism with which a programmer specifies, in *one* place in each module, all constraints on the execution of operations defined by that module. Implementation of the operations is separated from the specification of the constraints. Moreover, code to enforce the constraints is generated by a compiler. This is the approach taken in a class of synchronization mechanisms called *path expressions*.

Path expressions were first defined by Campbell and Habermann (1974). Subsequent extensions and variations have also been proposed (Habermann, 1975; Lauer and Campbell, 1975; Campbell, 1976; Flon and Habermann, 1976; Lauer and Shields, 1978; Andler, 1979). Below, we describe one specific proposal (Campbell, 1976) that has been incorporated into Path PASCAL, an implemented systems programming language (Campbell and Kolstad, 1979).

When the path expressions are used, a module that implements a resource has a structure like that of a monitor. It contains permanent variables, which store the state of the resource, and procedures, which realize operations on the resource. Path expressions in the header of each resource define constraints on the order in which operations are executed. No synchronization code is programmed in the procedures.

The syntax of a path expression is

path *path__list* **end**

A *path__list* contains operation names and *path operators*. Path operators include ',' for concurrency, ';' for sequencing, '*n*: (*path__list*)' to specify up to *n* concurrent activations of *path__list*, and '[*path__list*]' to specify an unbounded number of concurrent activations of *path__list*.

For example, the path expression

path *deposit, fetch* **end**

places no constraints on the order of execution of *deposit* and *fetch* and no constraints on the number of activations of either operation. This absence of synchronization is equivalent to that specified by the path expressions

path [*deposit*], [*fetch*] **end**

or

path [*deposit, fetch*] **end**

(A useful application of the '[. . .]' operator will be shown later.) In contrast,

path *deposit*; *fetch* **end**

specifies that each *fetch* be preceded by a *deposit*; multiple activations of each operation can execute concurrently as long as the number of active or completed *fetch* operations never exceeds the number of completed *deposit* operations. A module implementing a bounded buffer of size one might well contain the path

path 1 : (*deposit*; *fetch*) **end**

to specify that the first invoked operation be a *deposit*, that each *deposit* be followed by a *fetch*, and that at most one instance of the path '*deposit*; *fetch*' be active – in short, that *deposit* and *fetch* alternate and are mutually exclusive. Synchronization constraints for a bounded buffer of size N are specified by

path $N : (1 : (deposit); 1 : (fetch))$ **end**

This ensures that (i) activations of *deposit* are mutually exclusive, (ii) activations of *fetch* are mutually exclusive, (iii) each activation of *fetch* is preceded by a completed *deposit*, and (iv) the number of completed *deposit* operations is never more than N greater than the number of completed *fetch* operations. The bounded buffers we have been using for *OPSYS*, our batch operating system, would be defined by

```
module buffer(T);

    path N:( 1:(deposit); 1:(fetch) ) end;

    var { the variables satisfy the invariant IB (see p. 66)
            with size equal to the number of executions of
            deposit minus the number of executions of fetch }
        slots : array [0..N−1] of T;
        head, tail : 0..N−1;

    procedure deposit(p : T);
        begin
            slots[tail] := p;
            tail := (tail + 1) mod N
        end;

    procedure fetch(var it : T);
        begin
            it := slots[head];
            head := (head + 1) mod N
        end;

        begin
            head := 0;  tail := 0
        end.
```

Note that one *deposit* and one *fetch* can proceed concurrently, which was not possible in the *buffer* monitor given in Figure 2.6. For this reason, there is no variable *size* because it would have been subject to concurrent access.

As a last example, consider the readers/writers problem (Courtois *et al.*, 1971). In this problem, processes read or write records in a shared data base. To ensure that processes read consistent data, either an unbounded number of concurrent *reads* or a single *write* may be executed at any time.
The path expression

path $1 : ([read], write)$ **end**

specifies this constraint. (Actually, this specifies the 'weak reader's preference' solution to the readers/writers problem: readers can prevent writers from accessing the database.)

Path expressions are strongly motivated by, and based on, the operational approach to program semantics. A path expression defines all legal sequences of the operation executions for a resource. This set of sequences can be viewed as a formal language, in which each sentence is a sequence of operation names. In light of this, the resemblance between path expressions and regular expressions should not be surprising.

While path expressions provide an elegant notation for expressing synchronization constraints described operationally, they are poorly suited for specifying condition synchronization (Bloom 1979). Whether an operation can be executed might depend on the state of a resource in a way not directly related to the history of operations already performed. Certain variants of the readers/writers problem (e.g., writers preference, fair access for readers and writers) require access to the state of the resource – in this case, the number of waiting readers and waiting writers–in order to implement the desired synchronization. The *shortest_next_allocator* monitor shown on page 50 is an example of a resource in which a parameter's value determines whether execution of an operation (*request*) should be permitted to continue. In fact, most resources that involve scheduling require access to parameters and/or to state information when making synchronization decisions. In order to use path expressions to specify solutions to such problems, additional mechanisms must be introduced. In some cases, definition of additional operations on the resource is sufficient; in other cases 'queue' resources, which allow a process to suspend itself and be reactivated by a 'scheduler' must be added. The desire to realize condition synchronization using path expressions has motivated many of the proposed extensions. Regrettably, none of these extensions has solved the entire problem in a way consistent with the elegance and simplicity of the original proposal. However, path expressions have proved useful for specifying the semantics of concurrent computations (Shields, 1979; Shaw, 1980, Best, 1982).

4. Synchronization primitives based on message passing

Critical regions, monitors, and path expressions are one outgrowth of semaphores; they all provide structured ways to control access to shared variables. A different outgrowth is *message passing*, which can be viewed as extending semaphores to convey data as well as to implement synchronization. When message passing is used for communication and synchronization, processes send and receive messages instead of reading and writing shared variables. Communication is accomplished because a process, upon receiving a message, obtains values from some sender process. Synchronization is accomplished because a message can be received only after it has been sent, which constrains the order in which these two events can occur.
A message is sent by executing

send *expression_list*
    to *destination_designator*.

The message contains the values of the expressions in *expression_list* at the time **send** is executed. The *destination_designator* gives the programmer control over where the message goes, and hence over which statements can receive it. A message is received by executing

receive *variable_list*
    from *source_designator*

where *variable_list* is a list of variables. The *source_designator* gives the programmer control over where the message came from, and hence over which statements could have sent it. Receipt of a message causes, first, assignment of the values in the message to the variables in *variable__list* and, second, subsequent destruction of the message.[19]

Designing message-passing primitives involves making choices about the form and semantics of these general commands. Two main issues must be addressed: How are source and destination designators specified? How is communication synchronized? Common alternative solutions for these issues are described in the next two sections. Then higher level message-passing constructs, semantic issues, and languages based on message passing are discussed.

Specifying channels of communication

Taken together, the destination and source designators define a *communications channel*. Various schemes have been proposed for naming channels. The simplest channel-naming scheme is for process names to serve as source and destination designators. We refer to this as *direct naming*. Thus

send *card* **to** *executer*

sends a message that can be received only by the *executer* process. Similarly,

receive *line* **from** *executer*

permits receipt only of a message sent by this executer process.

```
program OPSYS;
    process reader;
      var card : cardimage;
      loop
        read card from cardreader;
        send card to executer
        end
      end;
    process executer;
      var card : cardimage;  line : lineimage;
      loop
        receive card from reader;
        process card and generate line;
        send line to printer
        end
      end;
    process printer;
      var line : lineimage;
      loop
        receive line from executer;
        print line on lineprinter
        end
      end
    end.
```

Figure 2.8 Batch operating system with message passing

[19] A broadcast can be modeled by the concurrent execution of a collection of **sends**, each sending the message to a different destination. A nondestructive **receive** can be modeled by a **receive**, immediately followed by a **send**.

Direct naming is easy to implement and to use. It makes it possible for a process to control the times at which it receives messages from each other process. Our simple batch operating system might be programmed using direct naming as shown in Figure 2.8.

The batch operating system also illustrates an important paradigm for process interaction—a pipeline. A *pipeline* is a collection of concurrent processes in which the output of each process is used as the input to another. Information flows analogously to the way liquid flows in a pipeline. Here, information flows from the *reader* process to the *executer* process and then from the *executer* process to the *printer* process. Direct naming is particularly well suited for programming pipelines.

Another important paradigm for process interaction is the *client/server relationship*. Some *server* processes render a service to some *client* processes. A client can request that a service be performed by sending a message to one of these servers. A server repeatedly receives a request for service from a client, performs that service, and (if necessary) returns a completion message to that client.

The interaction between an I/O driver process and processes that use it – for example, the lineprinter driver and the *printer* process in our operating system example – illustrates this paradigm. The lineprinter driver is a server; it repeatedly receives requests to print a line on the printer, starts that I/O operation, and then awaits the interrupt signifying completion of the I/O operation. Depending on the application, it might also send a completion message to the client after the line has been printed.

Unfortunately, direct naming is not always well suited for client/server interaction. Ideally, the **receive** in a server should allow receipt of a message from any client. If there is only one client, then direct naming will work well; difficulties arise if there is more than one client because, at the very least, a **receive** would be required for each. Similarly, if there is more than one server (and all servers are identical), then the **send** in a client should produce a message that can be received by *any* server. Again, this cannot be accomplished easily with direct naming. Therefore, a more sophisticated scheme for defining communications channels is required.

One such scheme is based on the use of *global names*, sometimes called *mailboxes*. A mailbox can appear as the destination designator in any process' **send** statements and as the source designator in any process' **receive** statements. Thus messages sent to a given mailbox can be received by any process that executes a **receive** naming that mailbox.

This scheme is particularly well suited for programming client/server interactions. Clients send their service requests to a single mailbox; servers receive service requests from that mailbox. Unfortunately, implementing mailboxes can be quite costly without a specialized communications network (Gelernter and Bernstein, 1982). When a message is sent, it must be relayed to all sites where a **receive** could be performed on the destination mailbox; then, after a message has been received, all these sites must be notified that the message is no longer available for receipt.

The special case of mailboxes, in which a mailbox name can appear as the source designator in **receive** statements in one process only, does not suffer these implementation difficulties. Such mailboxes are often called *ports* (Balzer, 1971). Ports are simple to implement, since all **receives** that designate a port occur in the same process. Moreover, ports allow a straight-forward solution to the multiple-clients/single-server problem. (The multiple-clients/multiple-server problem, however, is not easily solved with ports.)

To summarize, when direct naming is used, communication is one to one since each communicating process names the other. When port naming is used, communication can be many to one since each port has one receiver but may have many senders. The most general scheme is global naming, which can be many to many. Direct naming and port naming are special cases of global naming; they limit the kinds of interactions that can be programmed directly, but are more efficient to implement.

Source and destination designations can be fixed at compile time, called *static channel naming*, or they can be computed at run time, called *dynamic channel naming*. Although widely used, static naming presents two problems. First, it precludes a program from communicating along channels not known at compile time, and thus limits the program's ability to exist in a changing environment. For example, this would preclude implementing the I/O redirection or pipelines provided by UNIX (Ritchie and Thompson, 1974).[20] The second problem is this: if a program might *ever* need access to a channel, it must permanently have the access. In many applications, such as file systems, it is more desirable to allocate communications channels to resources (such as files) dynamically.

To support dynamic channel naming, an underlying, static channel-naming scheme could be augmented by variables that contain source or destination designators. These variables can be viewed as containing *capabilities* for the communications channel (Baskett *et al.*, 1977; Solomon and Finkel, 1979; Andrews, 1982).

Synchronization

Another important property of message-passing statements concerns whether their execution could cause a delay. A statement is *nonblocking* if its execution never delays its invoker; otherwise the statement is said to be *blocking*. In some message-passing schemes, messages are buffered between the time they are sent and received. Then, if the buffer is full when a **send** is executed, there are two options: the **send** might delay until there is a space in the buffer for the message, or the **send** might return a code to the invoker, indicating that, because the buffer was full, the message could not be sent. Similarly, execution of a **receive**, when no message that satisfies the source designator is available for receipt, might either cause a delay or terminate with a code, signifying that no message was available.

If the system has an effectively unbounded buffer capacity, then a process is never delayed when executing a **send**. This is variously called *asynchronous message passing* and *send no-wait*. Asynchronous message passing allows a sender to get arbitrarily far ahead of a receiver. Consequently, when a message is received, it contains information about the sender's state that is

---

[20] Although in UNIX most commands read from and write to the user's terminal, one can specify that a command read its input from a file or write its output to a file. Also, one can specify that commands be connected in a pipeline. These options are provided by a dynamic channel-naming scheme that is transparent to the implementation of each command.

not necessarily still its current state. At the other extreme, with no buffering, execution of a **send** is always delayed until a corresponding[21] **receive** is executed; then the message is transferred and both proceed. This is called *synchronous message passing*. When synchronous message passing is used, a message exchange represents a synchronization point in the execution of both the sender and receiver. Therefore, the message received will always correspond to the sender's current state. Moreover, when the **send** terminates, the sender can make assertions about the state of the receiver. Between these two extremes is *buffered message passing*, in which the buffer has finite bounds. Buffered message passing allows the sender to get ahead of the receiver, but not arbitrarily far ahead.

The blocking form of the **receive** statement is the most common, because a receiving process often has nothing else to do while awaiting receipt of a message. However, most languages and operating systems also provide a nonblocking **receive** or a means to test whether execution of a **receive** would block. This enables a process to receive all available messages and then select one to process (effectively, to schedule them).

Sometimes, further control over which messages can be received is provided. The statement

receive *variable__list*
from *source__designator* **when** *B*

permits receipt of only those messages that make *B* true. This allows a process to 'peek' at the contents of a delivered message before receiving it. Although this facility is not necessary – a process can always receive and store copies of messages until appropriate to act on them, as shown in the shortest-next-allocator example at the end of this section – the conditional receive makes possible concise solutions to many synchronization problems. Two languages that provide such a facility, PLITS and SR are described later.

A blocking **receive** implicitly implements synchronization between sender and receiver because the receiver is delayed until after the message is sent. To implement such synchronization with nonblocking **receive**, busy-waiting is required. However, blocking message-passing statements can achieve the same semantic effects as nonblocking ones by using what we shall call *selective communications*, which is based on Dijkstra's guarded commands (Dijkstra, 1975).

In a selective-communications statement, a *guarded command* has the form

guard → statement

The guard consists of a Boolean expression, optionally followed by a message-passing statement. The guard *succeeds* if the Boolean expression is true and executing the message-passing statement would not cause a delay; the guard *fails* if the Boolean expression is false; the guard (temporarily) neither succeeds nor fails if the Boolean expression is true but the message-passing statement cannot yet be executed without causing delay. The alternative statement

[21] Correspondence is determined by the source and destination designators.

```
if G1 → S1
[] G2 → S2
   . . .
[] Gn → Sn
fi
```

is executed as follows. If at least one guard succeeds, one of them, *Gi*, is selected nondeterministically; the message-passing statement in *Gi* is executed (if present); then *Si*, the statement following the guard, is executed. If all guards fail, the command aborts. If all guards neither succeed nor fail, execution is delayed until some guard succeeds. (Obviously, deadlock could result.) Execution of the iterative statement is the same as for the alternative statement, except selection and execution of a guarded command is repeated until all guards fail, at which time the iterative statement terminates rather than aborts.

To illustrate the use of selective communications, we implement a *buffer* process, which stores data produced by a *producer* process and allows these data to be retrieved by a *consumer* process:[22]

```
process buffer;
    var slots : array [0..N−1] of T;
        head, tail : 0..N−1;
        size : 0..N;
    head := 0;  tail := 0;  size := 0;
    do size<N;  receive slots[tail] from producer →
            size := size + 1;
            tail := (tail + 1) mod N
    [] size>0;  send slots[head] to consumer →
            size := size − 1;
            head := (head + 1) mod N
    od
end
```

The producer and consumer are as follows:

```
process producer;
    var stuff : T;
    loop
        generate stuff;
        send stuff to buffer
    end
end;

process consumer;
    var stuff : T;
    loop
        receive stuff from buffer;
        use stuff
    end
end
```

[22] Even if message passing is asynchronous, such a buffer may still be required if there are multiple producers or consumers.

If **send** statements cannot appear in guards, selective communication is straightforward to implement. A delayed process determines which Boolean expressions in guards are true, and then awaits arrival of a message that allows execution of the **receive** in one of these guards. (If the guard did not contain a **receive**, the process would not be delayed.) If both **send** and **receive** statements can appear in guards,[23] implementation is much more costly because a process needs to negotiate with other processes to determine if they can communicate, and these processes could also be in the middle of such a negotiation. For example, three processes could be executing selective-communications statements in which any pair could communicate; the problem is to decide which pair communicates and which one remains delayed. Development of protocols that solve this problem in an efficient and deadlock-free way remains an active research area (Schwartz, 1978; Silberschatz, 1979; Bernstein, 1980; Van de Snepscheut, 1981; Schneider, 1982; Reif and Spirakis, 1982).

Unfortunately, if **send** statements are not permitted to appear in guards, programming with blocking **send** and blocking **receive** becomes somewhat more complex. In the example above, the *buffer* process above would be changed to first wait for a message from the *consumer* requesting data (a **receive** would appear in the second guard instead of the **send**) and then to send the data. The difference in the protocol used by this new *buffer* process when interacting with the *consumer* and that used when interacting with the *producer* process is misleading; a producer/consumer relationship is inherently symmetric, and the program should mirror this fact.

Some process relationships are inherently asymmetric. In client/server interactions, the server often takes different actions in response to different kinds of client requests. For example, a shortest-job-next allocator (see *Definition*, p. 47) that receives 'allocation' requests on a *request_port* and 'release' requests on a *release_port* can be programmed using message passing as follows:

```
process shortest_next_allocator;

    var free : Boolean;
        time : integer;
        client_id : process_id;
        declarations of a priority queue and other local variables;

    free := true;
    do true; receive (time, client_id) from request_port →
        if free →
            free := false;
            send allocation to client_id
        [] not free →
            save client_id on priority queue ordered by time
        fi
    [] not free; receive release from release_port →
        if not priority queue empty →
            remove client_id with smallest time from queue;
            send allocation to client_id
        [] priority queue empty →
            free := true
        fi
    od
end
```

[23] Also note that allowing only **send** statements in guards is not very useful.

A client makes a request by executing

send (*time, my_id*) **to** *request_port*;
receive *allocation*
        from *shortest_next_allocator*

and indicates that it has finished using the resource by executing

send *release* **to** *release_port*

Higher level message-passing constructs

Remote procedure call
The primitives of the previous section are sufficient to program any type of
process interaction using message passing. To program client/server interactions, however, both the client and server execute two message-passing
statements: the client a **send** followed by a **receive**, and the server a **receive**
followed by a **send**. Because this type of interaction is very common, higher
level statements that directly support it have been proposed. These are
termed *remote procedure call* statements because of the interface that they
present: a client 'calls' a procedure that is executed on a potentially remote
machine by a server.

When remote procedure calls are used, a client interacts with a server by
means of a **call** statement. This statement has a form similar to that used for
a procedure call in a sequential language:

call *service*(*value_args*; *result_args*)

The *service* is really the name of a channel. If direct naming is used, *service*
designates the server process; if port or mailbox naming is used, *service*
might designate the kind of service requested. Remote **call** is executed as
follows: the value arguments are sent to the appropriate server, and the
calling process delays until both the service has been performed and the
results have been returned and assigned to the result arguments. Thus such a
call could be translated into a **send**, immediately followed by a **receive**. Note
that the client cannot forget to wait for the results of a requested service.

There are two basic approaches to specifying the server side of a remote
procedure call. In the first, the remote procedure is a declaration, like a
procedure in a sequential language.[24]

remote procedure *service*
    (**in** *value_parameters*;
    out *result_parameters*)
    body
    end

However, such a procedure declaration is implemented as a process. This
process, the server, awaits receipt of a message containing value arguments
from some calling process, assigns them to the value parameters, executes its
body, and then returns a *reply message* containing the values of the result
parameters. Note that even if there are no value or result parameters, the

---

[24] This is another reason this kind of interaction is termed 'remote procedure call.'

synchronization resulting from the implicit **send** and **receive** occurs. A remote procedure declaration can be implemented as a single process that repeatedly loops (Andrews, 1982), in which case **calls** to the same remote procedure would execute sequentially. Alternatively, a new process can be created for each execution of **call** (Brinch Hansen, 1978; Cook, 1980; Liskov and Scheifler, 1982); these could execute concurrently, meaning that the different instances of the server might need to synchronize if they share variables.

In the second approach to specifying the server side, the remote procedure is a statement, which can be placed anywhere any other statement can be placed. Such a statement has the general form

accept *service*(**in** *value__parameters*;
    out *result__parameters*) → *body*

Execution of this statement delays the server until a message resulting from a **call** to the *service* has arrived. Then the body is executed, using the values of the value parameters and any other variables accessible in the scope of the statement. Upon termination, a reply message, containing the values of the result parameters, is sent to the calling process. The server then continues execution.[25]

When **accept** or similar statements are used to specify the server side, remote procedure call is called a *rendezvous* (Department of Defense, 1981) because the client and server 'meet' for the duration of the execution of the body of the **accept** statement and then go their separate ways. One advantage of the rendezvous approach is that client **calls** may be serviced at times of the server's choosing; **accept** statements, for example, can be interleaved or nested. A second advantage is that the server can achieve different effects for **calls** to the same service by using more than one **accept** statement, each with a different body. (For example, the first **accept** of a service might perform initialization.) The final, and most important, advantage is that the server can provide more than one kind of service. In particular, **accept** is often combined with selective communications to enable a server to wait for and select one of several requests to service (U. S. Department of Defense, 1981; Andrews, 1981). This is illustrated in the following implementation of the bounded buffer:

process *buffer*;

```
    var slots : array [0..N−1] of T;
        head, tail : 0..N−1;
        size : 0..N;

    head := 0;   tail := 0;   size := 0;

    do size<N;   accept deposit(in value : T) →
        slots[tail] := value;
        size := size + 1;
        tail := (tail + 1) mod N
```

---

[25] Different semantics result depending on whether the reply message is sent by a synchronous or by an asynchronous **send**. A synchronous **send** delays the server until the results have been received by the caller. Therefore, when the server continues, it can assert that the reply message has been received and that the result parameters have been assigned to the result arguments. Use of asynchronous **send** does not allow this, but does not delay the server, either.

```
[] size>0; accept fetch(out value : T) →
    value := slots[head];
    size := size − 1;
    head := (head + 1) mod N
od

end.
```

The *buffer* process implements two operations: *deposit* and *fetch*. The first is invoked by a producer by executing

call *deposit* (*stuff*)

The second is invoked by a consumer by executing

call *fetch*(*stuff*)

Note that *deposit* and *fetch* are handled by the *buffer* process in a symmetric manner, even though **send** statements do not appear in guards, because remote procedure calls always involve two messages, one in each direction. Note also that *buffer* can be used by multiple producers and multiple consumers.

Although remote procedure call is a useful, high-level mechanism for client/server interactions, not all such interactions can be directly programmed by using it. For example, the *shortest_next_allocator* of the previous section still requires two client/server exchanges to service allocation requests because the allocator must look at the parameters of a request in order to decide if the request should be delayed. Thus the client must use one operation to transmit the request arguments and another to wait for an allocation. If there are a small number of different scheduling priorities, this can be overcome by associating a different server operation with each priority level. Ada (U. S. Department of Defense, 1981) supports this nicely by means of arrays of operations. In general, however, a mechanism is required to enable a server to accept a **call** that minimizes some function of the parameters of the called operation. SR (Andrews, 1981) includes such a mechanism (see Section under SR later in this Chapter).

Atomic transactions
An often-cited advantage of multiple-processor systems is that they can be made resilient to failures. Designing programs that exhibit this fault tolerance is not a simple matter. While a discussion of how to design fault-tolerant programs is beyond the scope of this survey, we comment briefly on how fault-tolerance issues have affected the design of higher level message-passing statements.[26]

Remote procedure call provides a clean way to program client/server interactions. Ideally, we would like a remote **call**, like a procedure call in a sequential programming notation, to have *exactly once* semantics: each remote **call** should terminate only after the named remote procedure has been executed exactly once by the server (Nelson, 1981; Spector, 1982). Unfortunately a failure may mean that a client is forever delayed awaiting the response to a remote **call**. This might occur if

---

[26] For a general discussion, the interested reader is referred to Kohler 1981.

(i) the message signifying the remote procedure invocation is lost by the network, or
(ii) the reply message is lost, or
(iii) the server crashes during execution of the remote procedure (but before the reply message is sent).

This difficulty can be overcome by attaching a time-out interval to the remote **call**; if no response is received by the client before the time-out interval expires, the client presumes that the server has failed and takes some action.

Deciding what action to take after a detected failure can be difficult. In Case (i) above, the correct action would be to retransmit the message. In Case (ii), however, retransmittal would cause a second execution of the remote procedure body. This is undesirable unless the procedure is *idempotent*, meaning that the repeated execution has the same effect as a single execution. Finally, the correct action in Case (iii) would depend on exactly how much of the remote procedure body was executed, what parts of the computation were lost, what parts must be undone, etc. In some cases, this could be handled by saving state information, called *checkpoints*, and programming special recovery actions. A more general solution would be to view execution of a remote procedure in terms of atomic transactions.

An *atomic transaction* (Lomet, 1977; Reed, 1979; Lampson, 1981) is an all-or-nothing computation – either it installs a complete collection of changes to some variables or it installs no changes, even if interrupted by a failure. Moreover, atomic transactions are assumed to be indivisible in the sense that partial execution of an atomic transaction is not visible to any concurrently executing atomic transaction. The first attribute is called *failure atomicity*, and the second *synchronization atomicity*.

Given atomic transactions, it is possible to construct a remote procedure call mechanism with *at most once* semantics – receipt of a reply message means that the remote procedure was executed exactly once, and failure to receive a reply message means the remote procedure invocation had no (permanent) effect (Liskov and Scheifler, 1982; Spector, 1982). This is done by making execution of a remote procedure an atomic transaction that is allowed to 'commit' only after the reply has been received by the client. In some circumstances, even more complex mechanisms are useful. For example, when nested remote **calls** occur, failure while executing a higher level call should cause the effects of lower level (i.e., nested) calls to be undone, even if those calls have already completed (Liskov and Scheifler, 1982).

The main consideration in the design of these mechanisms is that it may not be possible for a process to see system data in an inconsistent state following partial execution of a remote procedure. The use of atomic transactions is one way to do this, but it is quite expensive (Lampson and Sturgis, 1979; Liskov, 1981). Other techniques to ensure the invisibility of inconsistent states have been proposed (Lynch, 1981; Schlichting and Schneider, 1981) and this remains an active area of research.

An axiomatic view of message passing

When message passing is used for communication and synchronization, processes usually do not share variables. Nonetheless interference can still arise. In order to prove that a collection of processes achieves a common goal, it is usually necessary to make assertions in one process about the state of others. Processes learn about each other's state by exchanging messages. In particular, receipt of a message not only causes the transfer of values from sender to receiver but also facilitates the 'transfer' of a predicate. This allows the receiver to make assertions about the state of the sender, such as about how far the sender has progressed in its computation. Clearly, subsequent execution by the sender might invalidate such an assertion. Thus it is possible for the sender to interfere with an assertion in the receiver.

It turns out that two distinct kinds of interference must be considered when message passing is used (Schlichting and Schneider, 1982a). The first is similar to that occurring when shared variables are used: assertions made in one process about the state of another must not be invalidated by concurrent execution. The second form of interference arises only when asynchronous or buffered message passing is used. If a sender 'transfers' a predicate with a message, the 'transferred' predicate must be true when the message is received: receipt of a message reveals information about the state of the sender at the time that the message was sent, which is not necessarily the sender's current state.

The second type of interference is not possible when synchronous message passing is used, because, after sending a message, the sender does not progress until the message has been received. This is a good reason to prefer the use of synchronous **send** over asynchronous **send** (and to prefer synchronous **send** for the reply message in a remote procedure body). One often hears the argument that asynchronous **send** does not restrict parallelism as much as synchronous **send** and so it is preferable. However, the amount of parallelism that can be exhibited by a program is determined by program structure and not by choice of communications primitives. For example, addition of an intervening buffer process allows the sender to be executed concurrently with the receiving process. Choosing a communications primitive merely establishes whether the programmer will have to do the additional work (of defining more processes) to allow a high degree of parallel activity or will have to do additional work (of using the primitives in a highly disciplined way) to control the amount of parallelism. Nevertheless, a variety of 'safe' uses of asynchronous message passing have been identified: the 'transfer' of monotonic predicates and the use of 'acknowledged' protocols, for example. These schemes are studied in Schlichting and Schneider (1982b), where they are shown to follow directly from simple techniques to avoid the second kind of interference.

Formal proof techniques for various types of message-passing primitives have been developed. Axioms for buffered, asynchronous message passing were first proposed in connection with Gypsy (Good et al., 1979). Several people have developed proof systems for synchronous message-passing statements – in particular the input and output commands in CSP (Apt et al., 1980; Cousot and Cousot, 1980; Levin and Gries, 1981; Misra and Chandy, 1981; Soundararajan, 1981; Lamport and Schneider, 1982; Schlichting and Schneider, 1982a). Also, several people have developed proof rules for asynchronous message passing (Misra et al., 1982; Schlichting and Schneider, 1982b), and proof rules for remote procedures and rendezvous (Barringer and Mearns, 1982; Gerth, 1982; Gerth *et al.*, 1982; Schlichting and Schneider, 1982a).

Programming notations based on message passing

A large number of concurrent programming languages have been proposed that use message passing for communication and synchronization. This should not be too surprising; because the two major message-passing design issues – channel naming and synchronization – are orthogonal, the various alternatives for each can be combined in many ways. In the following, we summarize the important characteristics of four languages: CSP, PLITS, Ada and SR. Each is well documented in the literature and was innovative in some regard. Also, each reflects a different combination of the two design alternatives. Some other languages that have been influential – Gypsy, Distributed Processes, StarMod and Argus – are then briefly discussed.

Communicating sequential processes

Communicating Sequential Processes (CSP) (Hoare, 1978) is a programming notation based on synchronous message passing and selective communications. The concepts embodied in CSP have greatly influenced subsequent work in concurrent programming language design and the design of distributed programs.

In CSP, processes are denoted by a variant of the **cobegin** statement. Processes may share read-only variables, but use input/output commands for synchronization and communication. Direct (and static) channel naming is used and message passing is synchronous.

An *output command* in CSP has the form

destination!expression

where *destination* is a process name and *expression* is a simple or structured value. An *input command* has the form

source?target

where *source* is a process name and *target* is a simple or structured variable local to the process containing the input command.
The commands

Pr!expression

in process *Ps* and

Ps?target

in process *Pr match* if *target* and *expression* have the same type. Two processes communicate if they execute a matching pair of input/output commands. The result of communication is that the expression's value is assigned to the target variable; both processes then proceed independently and concurrently.

A restricted form of selective communications statement is supported by CSP. Input commands can appear in guards of alternative and iterative statements, but output commands may not. This allows an efficient implementation, but makes certain kinds of process interaction awkward to express, as was discussed under *Synchronization*, p. 62.

By combining communication commands with alternative and iterative statements, CSP provides a powerful mechanism for programming process interaction. Its strength is that it is based on a simple idea – input/output commands – that is carefully integrated with a few other mechanisms. CSP is not a complete concurrent programming language, nor was it intended to be. For example, static direct naming is often awkward to use. Fortunately, this deficiency is easily overcome by using ports; how to do so was discussed briefly by Hoare (Hoare, 1978) and is described in detail by Kieburtz and Silberschatz (1979). Recently, two languages based on CSP have also been described (Jazayeri *et al.*, 1980; Roper and Barter, 1981).

PLITS

PLITS, an acronym for 'Programming Language In The Sky,' was developed at the University of Rochester (Feldman, 1979). The design of PLITS is based on the premise that it is inherently difficult to combine a high degree of parallelism with data sharing and therefore message passing is the appropriate means for process interaction in a distributed system. Part of an ongoing research project in programming language design and distributed computation, PLITS is being used to program applications that are executed on Rochester's Intelligent Gateway (RIG) computer network (Ball *et al.*, 1976).

A PLITS program consists of a number of modules; *active modules* are processes. Message passing is the sole means for intermodule interaction. So as not to restrict parallelism, message passing is asynchronous. A module sends a message containing the values of some expressions to a module *modname* by executing

send *expressions* **to** *modname* [**about** *key*]

The '**about** *key*' phrase is optional. If included, it attaches an identifying *transaction key* to the message. This key can then be used to identify the message uniquely, or the same key can be attached to several different messages to allow messages to be grouped.

A module receives messages by executing

receive *variables* [**from** *modname*]
  [**about** *key*]

If the last two phrases are omitted, execution of **receive** delays the executing module until the arrival of any message. If the phrase '**from** *modname*' is included, execution is delayed until a message from the named module arrives. Finally, if the phrase '**about** *key*' is included, the module is delayed until a message with the indicated transaction key has arrived.

By combining the options in **send** and **receive** in different ways, a programmer can exert a variety of controls over communication. When both the sending and receiving modules name each other, communication is direct. The effect of port naming is realized by having a receiving module not name the source module. Finally, the use of transaction keys allows the receiver to select a particular kind of message; this provides a facility almost as powerful as attaching '**when** *B*' to a **receive** statement.

In PLITS, execution of **receive** can cause blocking. PLITS also provides primitives to test whether messages with certain field values or transaction keys are available for receipt; this enables a process to avoid blocking when there is no message available.

PLITS programs interface to the operating systems of the processors that make up RIG. Each host system provides device access, a file system, and job control. A communications kernel on each machine provides the required support for inter-processor communication.

Ada[27]

Ada (U. S. Department of Defense, 1981) is a language intended for programming embedded real-time, process-control systems. Because of this, Ada includes facilities for multiprocessing and device control. With respect to concurrent programming, Ada's main innovation is the rendezvous form of remote procedure call.

Processes in Ada are called *tasks*. A task is activated when the block containing its declaration is entered. Tasks may be nested and may interact by using shared variables declared in enclosing blocks. (No special mechanisms for synchronizing access to shared variables are provided.)

The primary mechanism for process interaction is the remote procedure call. Remote procedures in Ada are called *entries*; they are ports into a server process specified by means of an **accept** statement, which is similar in syntax and semantics to the **accept** statement described on p. 67. Entries are invoked by execution of a remote **call**. Selective communications are supported using the **select** statement, which is like an alternative statement.

Both **call** and **accept** statements are blocking. Since Ada programs might have to meet real-time response constraints, the language includes mechanisms to prevent or control the length of time that a process is delayed when it becomes blocked. Blocking on **call** can be avoided by using the *conditional entry call*, which performs a **call** only if a rendezvous is possible immediately. Blocking on **accept** can be avoided by using a mechanism that enables a server to determine the number of waiting **calls**. Blocking on **select** can be avoided by means of the **else** guard, which is true if none of the other guards are. Finally, a task can suspend execution for a time interval by means of the **delay** statement. This statement can be used within a guard of **select** to ensure that a process is eventually awakened.

In order to allow the programmer to control I/O devices, Ada allows entries to be bound to interrupt vector locations. Interrupts become **calls** to those entries and can therefore be serviced by a task that receives the interrupt by means of an **accept** statement.

Since its inception, Ada has generated controversy (Hoare, 1981), much of which is not related to concurrency. However, few applications using the concurrent programming features have been programmed, and at the time of this writing no compiler for full Ada has been validated. Implementation of some of the concurrent programming aspects of Ada is likely to be hard. A paper by Welsh and Lister (1981) compares the concurrency aspects of Ada to CSP and Distributed Processes (Brinch Hansen, 1978); Wegner and Smolka (1983) compare Ada, CSP and monitors.

SR

SR (Synchronizing Resources) (Andrews, 1981, 1982), like Ada, uses the

[27] Ada is a trademark of the U.S. Department of Defense.

rendezvous form of remote procedure call and port naming. However, there are notable differences between the languages, as described below. A compiler for SR has been implemented on PDP-11 processors and the language is being used in the construction of a UNIX-like network operating system.

An SR program consists of one or more *resources*.[28] The resource construct supports both control of process interaction and data abstraction. (In contrast, Ada has two distinct constructs for this – the task and the package.) Resources contain one or more processes. Processes interact by using *operations*, which are similar to Ada entries. Also, processes in the same resource may interact by means of shared variables.

Unlike Ada, operations may be invoked by either **send**, which is non-blocking, or **call**, which is blocking. (The server that implements an operation can require a particular form of invocation, if necessary.) Thus both asynchronous message passing and remote **call** are supported. Operations may be named either statically in the program text or dynamically by means of capability variables, which are variables having fields whose values are the names of operations. A process can therefore have a changing set of communication channels.

In SR, operations are specified by the **in** statement, which also supports selective communications. Each guard in an **in** statement has the form

op__name(*parameters*) [**and** *B*] [**by** *A*]

where *B* is an optional Boolean expression and *A* is an optional arithmetic expression. The phrase '**and** *B*' allows selection of the operation to be dependent on the value of *b*, which may contain references to parameters. The phrase '**by** *A*' controls which invocation of *op__name* is selected if more than one invocation is pending that satisfies *B*. This can be used to express scheduling constraints succinctly. For example, it permits a compact solution to the shortest-job-next allocation problem discussed earlier. Although somewhat expensive to implement because it requires reevaluation of *A* whenever a selection is made, this facility turns out to be less costly to use than explicitly programmed scheduling queues, if the expected number of pending invocations is small (which is usually the case).

Operations may also be declared to be *procedures*. In SR, a procedure is shorthand for a process that repeatedly executes an **in** statement. Thus such operations are executed sequentially.

To support device control, SR provides a variant of the resource called a *real resource*. A real resource is similar to a Modula device module: it can contain device-driver processes and it allows variables to be bound to device-register addresses. Operations in real resources can be bound to interrupt vector locations. A hardware interrupt is treated as a **send** to such an operation; interrupts are processed by means of **in** statements.

Some other language notations based on message passing
Gypsy (Good *et al.*, 1979), one of the first high-level languages based on message passing, uses mailbox naming and buffered message passing. A major focus of Gypsy was the development of a programming language well

---

[28] SR's resources are not to be confused with resources in conditional critical regions.

suited for constructing verifiable systems. It has been used to implement special-purpose systems for single- and multiprocessor architectures.

Distributed Processes (DP) (Brinch Hansen, 1978) was the first language to be based on remote procedure calls. It can be viewed as a language that implements monitors by means of active processes rather than collections of passive procedures. In DP, remote procedures are specified as externally callable procedures declared along with a host process and shared variables. When a remote procedure is called, a server process is created to execute the body of the procedure. The server processes created for different calls and the host process execute with mutual exclusion. The servers and host synchronize by means of a variant of conditional critical regions. An extension of DP that employs the rendezvous form of remote procedure call and thus has a more efficient implementation is described by Mao and Yeh (1980).

StarMod (Cook, 1980) synthesizes aspects of Modula and Distributed Processes: it borrows modularization ideas from Modula and communication ideas from Distributed Processes. A module contains one or more processes and, optionally, variables shared by those processes. Synchronization within a module is provided by semaphores. Processes in different modules interact by means of remote procedure call; StarMod provides both remote procedures and rendezvous for implementing the server side. In StarMod, as in SR, both **send** and **call** can be used to initiate communication, the choice being dictated by whether the invoked operation returns values.

Argus (Liskov and Scheifler, 1982) also borrows ideas from Distributed Processes – remote procedures implemented by dynamically created processes, which synchronize using critial regions – but goes much further. It has extensive support for programming atomic transactions. The language also includes exception handling and recovery mechanisms, which are invoked if failures occur during execution of atomic transactions. Argus is higher level than the other languages surveyed here in the sense that it attaches more semantics to remote **call**. A prototype implementation of Argus is nearing completion.

5.   Models of concurrent programming languages

Most of this survey has been devoted to mechanisms for process interaction and programming languages that use them. Despite the resulting large variety of languages, each can be viewed as belonging to one of three classes: procedure oriented, message oriented, or operation oriented. Languages in the same class provide the same basic kinds of mechanisms for process interaction and have similar attributes.

In *procedure-oriented* languages, process interaction is based on shared variables. (Because monitor-based languages are the most widely known languages in this class, this is often called the *monitor model*.) These languages contain both active objects (processes) and shared, passive objects (modules, monitors, etc.). Passive objects are represented by shared variables, usually with some procedures that implement the operations on the objects. Processes access the objects they require directly and thus interact by accessing shared objects. Because passive objects are shared, they are subject to concurrent access. Therefore, procedure-oriented languages provide means for ensuring mutual exclusion. Concurrent PASCAL, Modula, Mesa and Edison are examples of such languages.

Message- and operation-oriented languages are both based on message passing, but reflect different views of process interaction. *Message-oriented* languages provide **send** and **receive** as the primary means for process interaction. In contrast to procedure-oriented languages, there are no shared, passive objects, and so processes cannot directly access all objects. Instead, each object is managed by a single process, its *caretaker*, which performs the operation and then (possibly) responds with a completion message. Thus, objects are never subject to concurrent access. CSP, Gypsy, and PLITS are examples of message-oriented languages.

Operation-oriented languages provide remote procedure call as the primary means for process interaction. These languages combine aspects of the other two classes. As in a message-oriented language, each object has a caretaker process associated with it; as in a procedure-oriented language, operations are performed on an object by calling a procedure. The difference is that the caller of an operation and the caretaker that implements it synchronize while the operation is executed. Both then proceed asynchronously. Distributed Processes, StarMod, Ada, and SR are examples of operation-oriented languages.

Languages in each of these classes are roughly equivalent in expressive power. Each can be used to implement various types of cooperation between concurrently executing processes, including client/server interactions and pipelines. Operation-oriented languages are well suited for programming client/server systems, and message-oriented languages are well suited for programming pipelined computations.

Languages in each class can be used to write concurrent programs for uniprocessors, multiprocessors, and distributed systems. Not all three classes are equally suited for all three architectures, however. Procedure-oriented languages are the most efficient to implement on contemporary single processors. Since it is expensive to simulate shared memory if none is present, implementing procedure-oriented languages on a distributed system can be costly. Nevertheless, procedure-oriented languages can be used to program a distributed system – an individual program is written for each processor and the communications network is viewed as a shared object. Message-oriented languages can be implemented with or without shared memory. In the latter case, the existence of a communications network is made completely transparent, which frees the programmer from concerns about how the network is accessed and where processes are located. This is an advantage of message-oriented languages over procedure-oriented languages when programming a distributed system. Operation-oriented languages enjoy the advantages of both procedure-oriented and message-oriented languages. When shared memory is available, an operation-oriented language can, in many cases, be implemented like a procedure-oriented language (Habermann and Nassi, 1980); otherwise it can be implemented using message passing. Recent research has shown that both message- and operation-oriented languages can be implemented quite efficiently on distributed systems if special software/firmware is used in the implementation of the language's mechanisms (Nelson, 1981; Spector, 1982).

In a recent paper, Lauer and Needham argued that procedure-oriented and message-oriented languages are equal in terms of expressive power, logical equivalence, and performance (Lauer and Needham, 1979). (They did not consider operation-oriented languages, which have only recently come into existence.) Their thesis was examined in depth by Reid (1980), who reached many conclusions that we share. At an abstract level, the three types of languages are interchangeable. One *can* transform any program written using the mechanisms found in languages of one class into a program using the mechanisms of another class without affecting performance. However, the classes emphasize different styles of programming – the same program written in languages of different classes is often best structured in entirely different ways. Also, each class provides a type of flexibility not present in the others. Program fragments that are easy to describe using the mechanisms of one can be awkward to describe using the mechanisms of another. One might argue (as do Lauer and Needham) that such use of these mechanisms is a bad idea. We, however, favor programming in the style appropriate to the language.

6.   Conclusion

This paper has discussed two aspects of concurrent programming: the key concepts – specification of processes and control of their interaction – and important language notations. Early work on operating systems led to the discovery of two types of synchronization: mutual exclusion and condition synchronization. This stimulated development of synchronization primitives, a number of which are described in the paper. The historical and conceptual relationships among these primitives are illustrated in Figure 2.9.

The difficulty of designing concurrent programs that use busy-waiting and their inefficiency led to the definition of semaphores. Semaphores were then extended in two ways: (1) constructs were defined that enforced their structured use, resulting in critical regions, monitors, and path expressions; (2) 'data' were added to the synchronization associated with semaphores, resulting in message-passing primitives. Finally, the procedural interface of monitors was combined with message passing, resulting in remote procedure call.

Since the first concurrent programming languages were defined only a decade ago, practical experience has increased our understanding of how to engineer such programs, and the development of formal techniques has greatly increased our understanding of the basic concepts. Although there are a variety of different programming languages, there are only three essentially different kinds: procedure oriented, message oriented, and operation oriented. This, too, is illustrated in Figure 2.9.

At present, many of the basic problems that arise when constructing conncurrent programs have been identified, solutions to these problems are by and large understood, and substantial progress has been made toward the design of notations to express those solutions. Much remains to be done, however. The utility of various languages – really, combinations of constructs – remains to be investigated. This requires using the languages to develop systems and then analysing how they helped or hindered the development. In addition, the interaction of fault tolerance and concurrent programming is not well understood. Little is known about the design of distributed (decentralized) concurrent programs. Last, devising formal techniques to aid the programmer in constructing correct programs remains an important open problem.

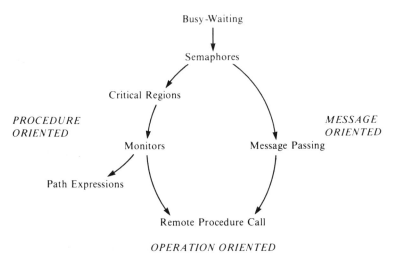

Figure 2.9 Synchronization techniques and language classes

Acknowledgments

Numerous people have been kind enough to provide very helpful comments on earlier drafts of this survey: David Gries, Phil Kaslo, Lynn Kivell, Gary Levin, Ron Olsson, Rich Schlichting, and David Wright. Three referees, and also Eike Best and Michael Scott, provided valuable comments on the penultimate draft. Tony Wasserman has also provided helpful advice; it has been a joy to have him as the editor for this paper. Rachel Rutherford critiqued the ultimate draft and made numerous useful, joyfully picturesque comments.

This work was supported in part by NSF Grants MCS 80-01668 and MCS 82-02869 at Arizona and MCS 81-03605 at Cornell.

Addendum*

Since the publication of this article in 1983, there have been several attempts to write validated Ada compilers. An example of such an attempt is the University of York Release 3 **SUN/UNIX** Ada compiler[†].[1] This release supports the *full* ANSI **ada** language and was successfully validated on a

* This note was added by the Editor regarding the material in the section on **Ada**
[†] **UNIX** is a trademark of AT & T Bell Laboratories
[1] Firth, J. R., Forsyth, C. H. and Wand, I. C., (1988). *York Ada Compiler Release 3 (SUN/UNIX) User Guide*, University of York, Department of Computer Science YCS 97, UK

SUN 3/50 using a 3/280 file server under **UNIX(SUNOS** 3.2) operating system on 26 November 1987 under version 1.9 of the test suite.

The compiler runs on any model of the SUN 3 range of machines. For this release the target is the host. The compiler is suitable for use with the **SUNOS** 3.2 operating system only.

The York Ada Workbench compiler project has been supported by grants and contracts from the Science and Engineering Research Council and the Alvey Directorate of Great Britain since 1979.

References

Akkoyunlu, E. A., Bernstein, A. J., Schneider, F. B., and Silberschatz, A. "Conditions for the equivalence of synchronous and asynchronous systems." *IEEE Trans. Softw. Eng.* **SE-4**, 6 (Nov. 1978), 507–516

Andler, S. "Predicate path expressions." In *Proc. 6th ACM Symp. Principles of Programming Languages* (San Antonio, Tex., Jan. 1979). ACM, New York, 1979, pp. 226–236

Andrews, G. R. "The design of a message switching system: An application and evaluation of Modula." *IEEE Trans. Softw. Eng.* **SE-5**, 2 (March 1979), 138–147

Andrews, G. R. "Synchronizing resources." *ACM Trans. Prog. Lang. Syst.* **3**, **4** (Oct 1981), 405–430.

Andrews, G. R. "The distributed programming language SR—Mechanisms, design, and implementation." *Softw. Pract. Exper.* **12**, 8 (Aug. 1982), 719–754

Andrews, G. R., and McGraw, J. R. "Language features for process interaction." In *Proc. ACM Conf. Language Design for Reliable Software, SIGPLAN Not.* **12**, 3 (March 1977), 114–127

Apt, K. R., Francez, N., and de Roever, W. P. "A proof system for communicating sequential processes." *ACM Trans. Prog. Lang. Syst.* **2**, 3 (July 1980), 359–385

Ashcroft, E. A. "Proving assertions about parallel programs." *J. Comput. Syst.* **10** (Jan. 1975), 110–135

Ball, E., Feldman, J., Low, J., Rashid, R., and Rovner, P. "RIG, Rochester's intelligent gateway: System overview." *IEEE Trans. Softw. Eng.* **SE-2**, 4 (Dec. 1976), 321–328

Balzer, R. M. "PORTS—A method for dynamic interprogram communication and job control." In *Proc. AFIPS Spring Jt. Computer Conf.* (Atlantic City, N. J., May 18–20, 1971), vol. 38. AFIPS Press, Arlington, Va., 1971, pp. 485–489

Barringer, H., and Mearns, I. "Axioms and proof rules for Ada tasks." *IEE Proc.* **129**, Pt. E, 2 (March 1982), 38–48

Baskett, F., Howard, J. H., and Montague, J. T. "Task communication in DEMOS." In *Proc. 6th Symp. Operating Systems Principles* (West Lafayette, Indiana, Nov. 16–18, 1977). ACM, New York, 1977, pp. 23–31

Ben-Ari, M. *Principles of Concurrent Programming.* Prentice-Hall, Englewood Cliffs, N. J., 1982

Bernstein, A. J. "Output guards and nondeterminism in communicating sequential processes." *ACM Trans. Prog. Lang. Syst.* **2**, 2 (Apr. 1980), 234–238

Bernstein, A. J., and Ensor, J. R. "A modification of Modula." *Softw. Pract. Exper.* **11** (1981), 237–255

Bernstein, A. J., and Schneider, F. B. "On language restrictions to ensure deterministic behavior in concurrent systems." In J. Moneta (Ed.), *Proc. 3rd Jerusalem Conf. Information Technology JCIT3.* North-Holland Publ., Amsterdam, 1978, pp. 537–541

Bernstein, P. A. and Goodman, N. "Concurrency control in distributed database systems." *ACM Comput. Surv.* **13**, 2 (June 1981), 185–221

Best, E. "Relational semantics of concurrent programs (with some applications)." In *Proc IFIP WG2.2 Conf.* North-Holland Publ., Amsterdam, 1982

Bloom, T. "Evaluating synchronization mechanisms." In *Proc. 7th Symp. Operating Systems Principles* (Pacific Grove, Calif., Dec. 10–12, 1979). ACM, New York, 1979, pp. 24–32

Brinch Hansen, P. "Structured multiprogramming." *Commun. ACM* **15**, 7 (July 1972), 574–578

Brinch Hansen, P. *Operating System Principles.* Prentice-Hall, Englewood Cliffs, N. J., 1973. (a)

Brinch Hansen, P. "Concurrent programming concepts." *ACM Comput. Surv.* **5**, 4 (Dec. 1973), 223–245. (b)

Brinch Hansen, P. "The programming language Concurrent Pascal." *IEEE Trans. Softw. Eng.* **SE-1**, 2 (June 1975), 199–206

Brinch Hansen, P. "The Solo operating system: Job interface." *Softw. Pract. Exper.* **6**, (1976), 151–164. (a)

Brinch Hansen, P. "The Solo operating system: Processes, monitors, and classes." *Softw. Pract. Exper.* **6**, (1976), 165–200. (b)

Brinch Hansen, P. *The Architecture of Concurrent Programs.* Prentice-Hall, Englewood Cliffs, N. J., 1977

Brinch Hansen, P. "Distributed processes: A concurrent programming concept." *Commun. ACM* **21**, 11 (Nov. 1978), 934–941

Brinch Hansen, P. "Edison: A multiprocessor language." *Softw. Pract. Exper.* **11**, 4 (Apr. 1981), 325–361

Campbell, R. H. "Path expressions: A technique for specifying process synchronization." Ph.D. dissertation, Computing Laboratory, University of Newcastle upon Tyne, Aug. 1976

Campbell, R. H., and Habermann, A. N. "The specification of process synchronization by path expressions." *Lecture Notes in Computer Science*, vol. 16. Springer-Verlag, New York, 1974, pp. 89–102

Campbell, R. H., and Kolstad, R. B. "Path expressions in Pascal". In *Proc. 4th Int. Conf. on Software Eng.* (Munich, Sept. 17–19, 1979). IEEE, New York, 1979, pp. 212–219

Conway, M. E. "Design of a separable transition-diagram compiler." *Commun. ACM* **6**, 7 (July 1963), 396–408. (a)

Conway, M. E. "A multiprocessor system design." In *Proc. AFIPS Fall Jt. Computer Conf.* (Las Vegas, Nev., Nov., 1963), vol. 24. Spartan Books, Baltimore, Maryland, pp. 139–146. (b)

Cook, R. P. "*MOD—A language for distributed programming." *IEEE Trans. Softw. Eng.* **SE-6**, 6 (Nov. 1980), 563–571

Courtois, P. J., Heymans, F., and Parnas, D. L. "Concurrent control with 'readers' and 'writers'." *Commun. ACM* **14**, 10 (Oct. 1971), 667–668

Cousot, P., and Cousot, R. "Semantic analysis of communicating sequential processes." In *Proc. 7th Int. Colloquium Automata, Languages and Programming (ICALP80), Lecture Notes in Computer Science*, vol. 85. Springer-Verlag, New York, 1980, pp. 119–133

Dennis, J. B., and Van Horn, E. C. "Programming semantics for multiprogrammed computations." *Commun. ACM* **9**, 3 (March 1966), 143–155

Dijkstra, E. W. "The structure of the 'THE' multiprogramming system." *Commun. ACM* **11**, 5 (May 1968), 341–346. (a)

Dijkstra, E. W. "Cooperating sequential processes." In F. Genuys (Ed.), *Programming Languages.* Academic Press, New York, 1968. (b)

Dijkstra, E. W. "Guarded commands, nondeterminacy, and formal derivation of programs." *Commun. ACM* **18**, 8 (Aug. 1975), 453–457

Dijkstra, E. W. *A Discipline of Programming.* Prentice-Hall, Englewood Cliffs, N. J., 1976

Dijkstra, E. W. "An assertional proof of a program by G. L. Peterson." EWD 779 (Feb. 1979), Nuenen, The Netherlands. (a)

Dijkstra, E. W. Personal communication, Oct. 1981. (b)

Feldman, J. A., "High-level programming for distributed computing." *Commun. ACM* **22**, 6 (June 1979), 353–368

Flon, L., and Habermann, A. N. "Towards the construction of verifiable software systems." In *Proc. ACM Conf. Data, SIGPLAN Not.* **8**, 2 (March 1976), 141–148

Floyd, R. W. "Assigning meanings to programs." In *Proc. Am. Math. Soc. Symp. Applied Mathematics*, vol. 19, pp. 19–31, 1967

Gelernter, D., and Bernstein, A. J. "Distributed communication via global buffer." In *Proc. Symp. Principles of Distributed Computing* (Ottawa, Canada, Aug. 18–20, 1982). ACM, New York, 1982, pp. 10–18

Gerth, R. "A sound and complete Hoare axiomatization of the Ada-rendevous." In *Proc. 9th Int. Colloquium Automata, Languages and Programming (ICALP82), Lecture Notes in Computer Science*, vol. 140. Springer-Verlag, New York, 1982, pp. 252–264

Gerth, R., de Roever, W. P., and Roncken, M. "Procedures and concurrency: A study in proof." In *5th Int. Symp. Programming, Lecture Notes in Computer Science*, vol. 137. Springer-Verlag, New York, 1982, pp. 132–163

Good, D. I., Cohen, R. M., and Keeton-Williams, J. "Principles of proving concurrent programs in Gypsy." In *Proc. 6th ACM Symp. Principles of Programming Languages* (San Antonio, Texas, Jan. 29–31, 1979). ACM, New York, 1979, pp. 42–52

Habermann, A. N. "Path expressions." Dep. of Computer Science, Carnegie-Mellon Univ., Pittsburgh, Pennsylvania, June, 1975

Habermann, A. N., and Nassi, I. R. "Efficient implementation of Ada tasks." Tech. Rep. CMU-CS-80-103, Carnegie-Mellon Univ., Jan. 1980

Haddon, Ь. K. "Nested monitor calls." *Oper. Syst. Rev.* **11**, 4 (Oct. 1977), 18–23

Hanson, D. R., and Griswold, R. E. "The SL5 procedure mechanisms." *Commun. ACM* **21**, 5 (May 1978), 392–400

Hoare, C. A. R. "An axiomatic basis for computer programming." *Commun. ACM* **12**, 10 (Oct. 1969), 576–580, 583

Hoare, C. A. R. "Towards a theory of parallel programming." In C. A. R. Hoare and R. H. Perrott (Eds.), *Operating Systems Techniques.* Academic Press, New York, 1972, pp. 61–71

Hoare, C. A. R. "Monitors: An operating system structuring concept." *Commun. ACM* **17**, 10 (Oct. 1974), 549–557

Hoare, C. A. R. "Communicating sequential processes." *Commun. ACM* **21**, 8 (Aug. 1978), 666–667

Hoare, C. A. R. "The emperor's old clothes." *Commun. ACM* **24**, 2 (Feb. 1981), 75–83

Holden, J., and Wand, I. C. "An assessment of Modula." *Softw. Pract. Exper.* **10** (1980), 593–621

Holt, R. C., Graham, G. S., Lazowska, E. D., and Scott, M. A. *Structured Concurrent Programming with Operating Systems Applications.* Addison-Wesley, Reading, Mass., 1978

Howard, J. H. "Proving monitors." *Commun. ACM* **19**, 5 (May 1976), 273–279. (a)

Howard, J. H. "Signaling in monitors." In *Proc. 2nd Int. Conf. Software Engineering* (San Francisco, Oct. 13–15, 1976). IEEE, New York, 1976, pp. 47–52. (b)

Jazayeri, M., et al. "CSP/80: A language for communicating processes." In *Proc. Fall IEEE COMPCON80* (Sept. 1980). IEEE, New York, 1980, pp. 736–740

Jones, A. K., and Schwarz, P. "Experience using multiprocessor systems—A status report." *ACM Comput. Surv.* **12**, 2 (June 1980), 121–165

Kaubisch, W. H., Perrott, R. H., and Hoare, C. A. R. "Quasiparallel programming." *Softw. Pract. Exper.* **6** (1976), 341–356

Keedy, J. L. "On structuring operating systems with monitors." *Aust. Comput. J.* **10**, 1 (Feb. 1978), 23–27. Reprinted in *Oper. Syst. Rev.* **13**, 1 (Jan. 1979), 5–9

Keller, R. M. "Formal verification of parallel programs." *Commun ACM* **19**, 7 (July 1976), 371–384

Kessels, J. L. W. "An alternative to event queues for synchronization in monitors." *Commun. ACM* **20**, 7 (July 1977), 500–503

Kieburtz, R. B., and Silberschatz, A. "Comments on 'communicating sequential processes.'" *ACM Trans. Program. Lang. Syst.* **1**, 2 (Oct. 1979), 218–225

Kohler, W. H. "A survey of techniques for synchronization and recovery in decentralized computer systems." *ACM Comput. Surv.* **13**, 2 (June 1981), 149–183

Lamport, L. "Proving the correctness of multiprocess programs." *IEEE Trans. Softw. Eng.* **SE-3**, 2 (March 1977), 125–143

Lamport, L. "The 'Hoare logic' of concurrent programs." *Acta Inform.* **14**, 21–37. (a)

Lamport, L. "The mutual exclusion problem." Op.56, SRI International, Menlo Park, Calif., Oct. 1980. (b)

Lamport, L., and Schneider, F. B. "The 'Hoare logic' of CSP, and all that." Tech. Rep. TR 82-490, Dep. Computer Sci., Cornell Univ., May, 1982

Lampson, B. W. "Atomic transactions." In *Distributed Systems—Architecture and Implementation, Lecture Notes in Computer Science*, vol. 105. Springer-Verlag, New York, 1981

Lampson, B. W., and Redell, D. D. "Experience with processes and monitors in Mesa." *Commun. ACM* **23**, 2 (Feb. 1980), 105–117

Lampson, B. W., and Sturgis, H. E. "Crash recovery in a distributed data storage system." Xerox Palo Alto Research Center, Apr. 1979

Lauer, H. C. and Needham, R. M. "On the duality of operating system structures." In *Proc. 2nd Int. Symp. Operating Systems* (IRIA, Paris, Oct. 1978); reprinted in *Oper Syst. Rev.* **13**, 2 (Apr. 1979), 3–19

Lauer, P. E., and Campbell, R. H. "Formal semantics of a class of high level primitives for coordinating concurrent processes." *Acta Inform.* **5** (1975), 297–332

Lauer, P. E., and Shields, M. W. "Abstract specification of resource accessing disciplines: Adequacy, starvation, priority and interrupts." *SIGPLAN Not.* **13**, 12 (Dec. 1978), 41–59

Lehmann, D., Pnueli, A., and Stavi, J. "Impartiality, justice and fairness: The ethics of concurrent termination." *Automata, Languages and Programming, Lecture Notes in Computer Science*, vol. 115. Springer-Verlag, New York, 1981, pp. 264–277

Levin, G. M., and Gries, D. "A proof technique for communicating sequential processes." *Acta Inform.* **15** (1981), 281–302

Liskov, B. L. "On linguistic support for distributed programs." In *Proc. IEEE Symp. Reliability in Distributed Software and Database Systems* (Pittsburgh, July 21–22, 1981). IEEE, New York, 1981, pp. 53–60

Liskov, B. L., and Scheifler, R. "Guardians and actions: Linguistic support for robust, distributed programs." In *Proc. 9th ACM Symp. Principles of Programming Languages* (Albuquerque, New Mexico, Jan. 25–27, 1982). ACM, New York, 1982, pp. 7–19

Lister A. "The problem of nested monitor calls." *Oper. Syst. Rev.* **11**, 3 (July 1977), 5–7

Loehr, K.-P. "Beyond Concurrent Pascal." In *Proc. 6th ACM Symp. Operating Systems Principles* (West Lafayette, Ind., Nov. 16–18, 1977). ACM, New York, 1977, pp. 173–180

Lomet, D. B. "Process structuring, synchronization, and recovery using atomic transactions." In *Proc. ACM Conf. Language Design for Reliable Software, SIGPLAN Not.* **12**, 3 (March 1977), 128–137

Lynch, N. A. "Multilevel atomicity—A new correctness criterion for distributed databases." Tech. Rep. GIT-ICS-81/05, School of Information and Computer Sciences, Georgia Tech., May 1981

Mao, T. W., and Yeh, R. T. "Communication port: A language concept for concurrent programming." *IEEE Trans Softw. Eng.* **SE-6**, 2 (March 1980), 194–204

Misra, J., and Chandy, K. "Proofs of networks of processes." *IEEE Trans. Softw. Eng.* **SE-7**, 4 (July 1981), 417–426

Misra, J., Chandy, K. M., and Smith, T. "Proving safety and liveness of communicating processes with examples." In *Proc. Symp. Principles of Distributed Computing* (Ottawa, Canada, Aug. 18–20, 1982). ACM, New York, 1982, pp. 201–208

Mitchell, J. G., Maybury, W., and Sweet, R. "Mesa language manual, version 5.0." Rep. CSL-79-3, Xerox Palo Alto Research Center, Apr. 1979

Nelson, B. J. "Remote procedure call." Ph.D. thesis. Rep. CMU-CS-81-119, Dep. of Computer Science, Carnegie-Mellon Univ., May 1981

Nygaard, K., and Dahl, O. J. "The development of the SIMULA languages." *Preprints ACM SIGPLAN History of Programming Languages Conference, SIGPLAN Not.* **13**, 8 (Aug. 1978), 245–272

Owicki, S. S., and Gries, D. "An axiomatic proof technique for parallel programs." *Acta Inform.* **6** (1976), 319–340 (a)

Owicki, S. S., and Gries, D. "Verifying properties of parallel programs: an axiomatic approach." *Commun. ACM* **19**, 5 (May 1976), 279–285 (b)

Parnas, D. L. "On the criteria to be used in decomposing systems into modules." *Commun. ACM* **15**, 12 (Dec. 1972), 1053–1058

Parnas, D. L. "The non-problem of nested monitor calls." *Oper. Syst. Rev.* **12**, 1 (Jan. 1978), 12–14

Peterson, G. L. "Myths about the mutual exclusion problem." *Inform. Process. Lett.* **12**, 3 (June 1981), 115–116

Reed, D. P. "Implementing atomic actions on decentralized data." *ACM Trans. Comput. Syst.* **1**, 1 (Feb. 1983), 3–23

Reid, L. G., "Control and communication in programmed systems." Ph.D. thesis, Rep. CMU-CS-80-142, Dep. of Computer Science, Carnegie-Mellon Univ., Sept, 1980

Reif, J. H., and Spirakis, P. G. "Unbounded speed variability in distributed communications systems." In *Proc. 9th ACM Conf. Principles of Programming Languages* (Albuquerque, New Mexico, Jan. 25–27, 1982). ACM, New York, 1982, pp. 46–56

Ritchie, D. M., and Thompson, K. "The UNIX timesharing system." *Commun. ACM* **17**, 7 (July 1974), 365–375

Roper, T. J., and Barter, C. J. "A communicating sequential process language and implementation." *Softw. Pract. Exper.* **11** (1981), 1215–1234

Schlichting, R. D., and Schneider, F. B. "An approach to designing fault-tolerant computing systems." Tech. Rep. TR 81-479, Dep. of Computer Sci., Cornell Univ., Nov. 1981

Schlichting, R. D., and Schneider, F. B. "Using message passing for distributed programming: Proof rules and disciplines." Tech. Rep. TR 82-491, Dep. of Computer Science, Cornell Univ., May 1982 (a)

Schlichting, R. D., and Schneider, F. B. "Understanding and using asynchronous message passing primitives." In *Proc. Symp. Principles of Distributed Computing* (Ottawa, Canada, Aug. 18–20, 1982). ACM, New York, 1982, pp. 141–147 (b)

Schneider, F. B. "Synchronization in distributed programs." *ACM Trans. Program. Lang. Syst.* **4**, 2 (Apr. 1982), 125–148

Schneider, F. B., and Bernstein, A. J. "Scheduling in Concurrent Pascal." *Oper. Syst. Rev.* **12**, 2 (Apr. 1978), 15–20

Schwartz, J. S. "Distributed synchronization of communicating sequential processes." Tech. Rep., Dep. of Artificial Intelligence, Univ. of Edinburgh, July 1978

Shaw, A. C. *The Logical Design of Operating Systems.* Prentice-Hall, Englewood Cliffs, N. J., 1974

Shaw, A. C. "Software specification languages based on regular expressions." In W. E. Riddle and R. E. Fairley (Eds.), *Software Development Tools.* Springer-Verlag, New York, 1980, pp. 148–175

Shields, M. W. "Adequate path expressions." In *Proc. Int. Symp. Semantics of Concurrent Computation, Lecture Notes in Computer Science,* vol. 70. Springer-Verlag, New York, pp. 249–265

Silberschatz, A. "On the input/output mechanism in Concurrent Pascal." In *Proc. COMPSAC '77—IEEE Computer Society Computer Software and Applications Conference* (Chicago, Ill., Nov. 1977). IEEE, New York, 1977, pp. 514–518

Silberschatz, A. "Communication and synchronization in distributed programs." *IEEE Trans. Softw. Eng.* **SE-5**, 6 (Nov. 1979), 542–546

Silberschatz, A., Kieburtz, R. B., and Bernstein, A. J. "Extending Concurrent Pascal to allow dynamic resource management." *IEEE Trans. Softw. Eng.* **SE-3**, 3 (May 1977), 210–217

Solomon, M. H., and Finkel, R. A. "The Roscoe distributed operating system." In *Proc. 7th Symp. Operating System Principles* (Pacific Grove, Calif., Dec. 10–12, 1979). ACM, New York, 1979, pp. 108–114

Soundararajan, N. "Axiomatic semantics of communicating sequential processes." Tech. Rep., Dep. of Computer and Information Science, Ohio State Univ., 1981

Spector, A. Z. "Performing remote operations efficiently on a local computer network." *Commun. ACM* **25**, 4 (Apr. 1982), 246–260

U.S. Department of Defense. *Programming Language Ada: Reference Manual,* vol. 106, *Lecture Notes in Computer Science.* Springer-Verlag, New York, 1981

Van de Snepscheut, J. L. A. "Synchronous communication between synchronization components." *Inform. Process. Lett.* **13**, 3 (Dec. 1981), 127–130

van Wijngaarden, A., Mailloux, B. J., Peck, J. L., Koster, C. H. A., Sintzoff, M., Lindsey, C. H., Meertens, L. G. L. T., and Fisker, R. G. "Revised report on the algorithm language ALGOL68." *Acta Inform.* **5**, 1–3 (1975), 1–236

Wegner, P., and Smolka, S. A. "Processes, tasks and monitors: A comparative study of concurrent programming primitives." *IEEE Trans. Softw. Eng.*, **9** (4), 446–462

Welsh, J., and Bustard, D. W. "Pascal-Plus—Another language for modular multiprogramming." *Softw. Pract. Exper.* **9** (1979), 947–957

Welsh, J., and Lister, A. "A comparative study of task communication in Ada." *Softw. Pract. Exper.* **11** (1981), 257–290

Wettstein, H. "The problem of nested monitor cells revisited." *Oper. Syst. Rev.* **12**, 1 (Jan. 1978), 19–23

Wirth, N. "Modula: A language for modular multiprogramming." *Softw. Pract. Exper.* **7** (1977), 3–35 (a)

Wirth, N. "The use of Modula." *Softw. Pract. Exper.* **7** (1977), 37–65 (b)

Wirth, N. "Design and implementation of Modula." *Softw. Pract. Exper.* **7** (1977), 67–84 (c)

Wirth, N. "Toward a discipline of real-time programming." *Commun. ACM* **20**, 8 (Aug. 1977), 577–583 (d)

Wirth, N. *Programming in Modula-2.* Springer-Verlag, New York, 1982

Wulf, W. A., Russell, D. B., and Habermann, A. N. BLISS: A language for systems programming. *Commun. ACM* **14**, 12 (Dec. 1971), 780–790

Chapter 3

Load balancing algorithms in loosely-coupled distributed systems: a survey

A. J. Harget and I. D. Johnson

With the advent of distributed computer systems with a largely transparent user interface, new questions have arisen regarding the management of such an environment by an operating system. One fertile area of research is that of load balancing, which attempts to improve system performance by redistributing the workload submitted to the system by the users. Early work in this field concentrated on static placement of computational objects to improve performance, given prior knowledge to process behaviour. Static load balancing seeks an optimal (or near-optimal) solution to processor allocation. More recently this has evolved into studying adaptive load balancing with process migration, thus allowing the system to adapt to varying loads. Adaptive load balancing is considered a superior approach for all but the most simple environments. This chapter gives an account of work conducted in the areas of both static and adaptive load balancing, thus providing a survey of this important aspect of distributed operating system design.

Introduction

With the traditional Von Neumann architecture reaching the physical limits of its capabilities, the trend in computer systems has been towards distributing processing power over a number of processors executing in parallel and connected via a communications medium. This can be viewed as a natural extension to the multiprogramming mechanism used to share a single CPU between a number of user processes. Through careful management by an operating system these processes appear to have exclusive access to the CPU, but are in fact being given periods of processor time, interleaved with their peers; thus when more than one processor is available much of this pseudo-parallel execution becomes truly parallel.

However, the advances in distributed processor technology need to be followed by similar developments in the design and implementation of operating systems capable of managing this new environment. The art of operating system design for uniprocessor architectures has made significant steps forward since the 'monolithic monitor' concept, in which large operating systems were developed which lacked any systematic use of abstraction in their design. New problems arise, however, for distributed systems. We are interested in such systems where processors are autonomous, each having its own local memory and resources. Such systems are more complex than the uniprocessor case because of the difficulty of retaining mutually exclusive access to system data structures, synchronization of operation and general consistency.

One of the most important questions which must be resolved to gain the maximum benefits of a distributed system, is that of allocating user processes to physical processors, since these are now a multiple rather than a shared resource. Initial work in this field concentrated on placing individual modules which constitute a user program on different processors in a static manner, taking into consideration the data flow between modules. Attempts were made to minimize interprocessor communications costs of such a system, with the consequent result that the thread of control of a program would move from one processor to another. This static allocation method, however, does not take account of the load imposed on processors in the system, and does not adapt to changes in the nature of user process arrival rates. Given this observation, researchers have striven to develop systems where the assignment of processes to processors is performed in a manner which balances the overall system load in order to avoid certain processors being overloaded whilst others remain idle.

Load balancing is an intuitively worthwhile goal, but necessititates some means of maintaining a global view of system activity, and a negotiation mechanism for redistributing processes to nodes on a network where they will most benefit in terms of execution time. A simple approach would be to have a central allocation processor which was periodically sent load information from all the other processors, and which would make process placement decisions based on its last-known state of the system. This approach, however, presents a single point of failure and could create a bottleneck. An alternative method is to distribute the responsibility for load measurement amongst all processors and to allow them to cooperate in making process-to-processor allocation. Again this approach is intuitively worthwhile, but adds complexity to the system in dealing with possibly out-of-date state information.

Since it has been shown (Zhou, 1986b) that the CPU is the resource which is most contended for in a computer system, an efficient mechanism must be found for performing processor allocation in a distributed system. Below we present previously studied approaches to this problem, in two main categories:

- static load balancing
- adaptive load balancing

Static load balancing

Typically in a computer network, interprocessor communications costs are significant relative to intraprocessor costs and will have a substantial effect on system performance. In order to reduce these overheads, an allocation strategy must be designed to calculate an assignment of processes to processors which minimizes execution and communications costs.

Early solutions to this problem assume a program to consist of a number of modules, which may be run separately on any processor in the network, and which exchange data by some communications mechanism. The cost of executing a particular module on a particular processor is assumed to be known a priori, as is the volume of data which will flow between modules. The problem then becomes one of assigning modules to processors in an optimal manner within the given cost constraints. Since such approaches do not consider the current state of the system when making their placement decisions, they are referred to as static load balancing algorithms and can be grouped into three major categories: graph theoretic, 0–1 integer programming and heuristic. Although these approaches have many aspects in common, this categorization illustrates the different conceptual views taken of the problem.

The graph theoretic approach

In the graph theoretic approach (Stone, 1977; Stone and Bokhari, 1978; Rao and Stone, 1979; Bokhari, 1981) to static load balancing, a program's modules are represented by nodes in a directed graph. Edges in the graph are used to show intermodule linkages and weights on these edges give the cost of sending the appropriate volume of data from one module to another. Intraprocessor communications costs are normally assumed to be zero if the program's modules reside on separate processors.

Stone (1977) recognized the similarity between this model of program structure and work carried out for commodity flow networks. Such networks consist of a number of source nodes which are capable of producing an infinite quantity of some commodity, which is directed to a number of sink nodes, capable of absorbing this infinite quantity. Edges from source to sink, via intermediate nodes, represent a commodity flow through the network and weights on these edges give the maximum capacity of an edge. The sum of the net flows out of the source nodes, and hence into the sink nodes, is termed the *value* of the commodity flow. A *feasible flow* through the network has the following properties:

1. the sum of flows into a node is equal to the sum of the flows out of that node
2. flows into sinks and out of sources are non-negative
3. flows do not exceed capacities

If a flow is found which is maximum among all feasible flows, then it is known as the maximum flow. A *cutset* determines the set of edges which, when removed from the network, totally disconnect source and sink nodes, and the weight of a cutset is defined as the sum of the capacities of edges in the cutset.

Figure 3.1 shows an example of such a network, due to Stone (1977), where circles labelled with letters represent modules of a program, and edges between these modules are labelled with numeric weights to show the amount of data passing from one module to another; processors are represented by the two nodes S1 and S2. In this example two-processor system, edges are added from each 'module' node to each 'processor' node, such that the weight of an edge from a 'module' node to (say) S_1 gives the execution cost of that module on processor P_2 and vice versa; if a module cannot be executed on a processor then the weight on the appropriate edge is set to infinity. Execution costs of a module will vary from processor to processor dependent on facilities available, for example specialized floating point hardware will tend to decrease execution costs. The minimum cutset for the network in Figure 3.1 is shown as a broad line. Stone shows that a cutset in this graph represents a particular module assignment (S_1 and S_2 in separate partitions), and that the weight of a cutset is therefore equal to the cost of the corresponding module assignment. Hence an optimal assignment can be found by calculating the minimum weight cutset in the graph, using an algorithm developed by Ford and Fulkerson (1962). If one of these two processors has limited memory, then the problem becomes much more complex, but it has been shown that techniques exist for complete solution of certain problems under memory constraints and a reduction in complexity for others (Rao and Stone, 1979).

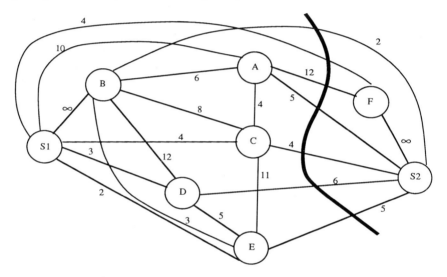

Figure 3.1 Graph Theoretic Module Assignment and minimum cutset for two processors

This network partitioning method can find an optimal assignment reasonably efficiently for two processors, and can theoretically be extended to an n-processor network, where n cutsets need to be found; this can be done by exhaustive enumeration, but its computational complexity makes it thoroughly undesirable. Stone suggests that the n-processor problem could be considered as a number of two-processor assignments, but significant difficulties exist in this solution, since nodes may be placed outside a minimum cost partition by successive two-processor solutions.

Although the max-flow, min-cut algorithm presented in Figure 3.1 is not easily extendable to n-processor systems for general programs, it has been shown (Bokhari, 1981) that an efficient implementation is possible if the program has a tree-structured call graph (known as an invocation tree) for its modules. Again assuming that all execution and communications costs are known, an assignment graph can be constructed from the invocation tree, where each node represents assignment of a module to a processor shown by a pair of numbers (i.e. (i,j) means that module i is resident on processor j). An edge between nodes (i,p) and (j,q) has a weight equal to the cost of assigning module j to processor q, given that module i has been assigned to processor p. An algorithm which then finds the least costly path through the assignment graph, constructs an assignment tree which gives the optimal module-to-processor allocation; such an algorithm has been shown by Bokhari (1981) to execute in time $0(mn^2)$ where m modules are assigned to n processors.

Chou and Abraham (1982) also use a graph model of module assignment, with nodes in the graph representing modules, but edges are used to indicate precedence relations. They introduce probabilistic branch points where the flow of the program may follow any one of two or more branches under a probability constraint; at fork points, execution will continue along each of the possible branches. A semi-Markov process with rewards is used to model dynamic execution of the program and this is augmented by 'policies' which indicate module-to-processor assignments. By iteratively examining the possible state transitions under each policy it is possible to find an optimal assignment for n-processor systems. Concurrent module execution is also built into the model. The disadvantage of this method is that it relies heavily on the accuracy of available data regarding program behaviour and the authors recognise that load balancing which adapts its placement decisions dynamically with the current system state is desirable, but would be too costly using their policy iteration algorithm.

The 0–1 integer programming approach

Due to the limitations of the graph-theoretic approach, other researchers (Chou and Abraham, 1982) have adopted an integer programming method for processor allocation. Again in this model, it is necessary to identify the execution and interprocess communications of modules, hence the following quantities are used:

C_{ij}:   coupling factor =   the number of data units transferred from module i to module j.

d_{kl}:   interprocessor distance =   the cost of transferring one data unit from processor k to processor l.

q_{ik}:   execution cost =   the cost of processing module i on processor k.

If i and j are resident on processors k and l respectively, then their total communications cost can be expressed as $C_{ij} * d_{kl}$. In addition to these quantities the assignment variable is defined as:

$$X_{ik} = \begin{cases} 1, \text{ module } i \text{ is assigned to processor } k \\ 0, \text{ otherwise} \end{cases}$$

Using the above notation, the total cost of processing a number of user modules is given as:

$$\sum_i \sum_k (q_{ik} X_{ik} + \sum_l \sum_j (c_{ij} * d_{kl}) X_{ik} X_{jl})$$

The major advantage of a programming solution to static load balancing is that constraints can be easily incorporated into the model, which is difficult, if not impossible, using graph theoretic techniques. For example, to ensure that processor k has sufficient memory available to process modules assigned to it the following constraint can be applied.

$$\sum_i M_i X_{ik} \leqslant S_k$$

where $M_i =$ memory requirements of module i
$\quad\quad S_k =$ memory capacity of processor k.

Constraints such as real-time requirements and processor speeds can also be expressed in a similar manner. Module allocation can then be performed by minimizing the above cost equation subject to the constraints imposed, by non-linear programming techniques, or further constraints can be added to linearize the problem. It has been shown (Chu et al., 1980), however, that on a CDC 6000 series mainframe, a problem involving 15 processors and 25 modules will take a *few minutes* to solve, and should hence be performed off-line in realistic environments.

An alternative approach is to use a branch and branch method (Ma et al., 1982) to construct and search in a depth-wise manner, a tree of possible assignments. Hence for allocating m modules, a tree of m level is constructed where a branch at each level represents assignment of that module to a particular processor. As this tree is being expanded, the constraints imposed on a solution are applied via branching nodes, thus eliminating the necessity to further expand certain branches, since they do not satisfy the constraints. A path from the root of such a tree to a lowest level node represents a complete assignment for all modules, and the optimal assignment is the lowest cost path. It is known that an optimal solution to searching a tree is an NP-complete problem, but Ma et al. (1982) show that the elimination of certain branches using constraints reduces the complexity considerably.

The major disadvantage of integer programming techniques using constraints, is that they are heavily parameterized and require substantial effort on the part of a system designer in specifying which constraints should apply in order to achieve a realizable load balancing solution.

The heuristic approach

Since finding optimal solutions to the module assignment problem is so computationally expensive, a number of heuristic approaches have been proposed to find a suboptimal solution (Gylys and Edwards, 1976; Efe, 1982; Lo, 1984). The essence of these algorithms is to identify clusters of modules which pass a large volume of data between them and to place them on the same processor.

One such algorithm (Gylys and Edwards, 1976) finds the module pair with most intermodule communication and examines whether the constraints imposed on their execution allows them to be co-resident on one processor. This continues until all possible pairings are found, but has the problem that it does not guarantee that the resultant number of clusters found will not be greater than the number of available processors.

A variation on this approach again due to Gylys and Edwards (1976) is to define a 'distance function' between modules, which is a measure of communications between two modules i and j, relative to communications between i and all other modules and j and all other modules. Using this function a 'centroid' of a possible candidate cluster can be found, and an iterative algorithm is then used to join modules having the lowest valued distance function from the centroid into the centroid's cluster. The centroid is then appropriately adjusted to take account of this addition. The iterations are stopped when an upper limit is reached or when no module clusters change.

This concept has been extended by Efe (1982). In his algorithm, clusters are formed as above, whilst recognizing that certain 'attached' modules must be executed on a single processor or a subset of the available processors, and hence these modules can form the 'centre' of a cluster. When clustering is completed, a queue length constraint can be imposed on each processor, and modules are then moved from processors whose load lies above the expected average plus some tolerance threshold onto a similarly underloaded processor, whilst still maintaining the restrictions of interprocessor communications cost. Efe shows that an optimal assignment with respect to execution cost and communications cost may not necessarily result in the most efficient assignment when queue lengths are considered.

This additional constraint is also investigated by Lo (1984), who identifies an extra cost to be considered, resulting from the contention for shared resources, such as CPU cycles in a multiprogramming environment, which she terms the interference cost defined as:

$$I_q(i,j) = \quad I_q^p(i,j) + I_q^c(i,j)$$

where

$I_q(i,j) =$ total interference cost of executing modules i and j on processor q

$I_q^p(i,j) =$ processor interference cost of i and j on processor q

$I_q^c(i,j) =$ communications interference cost due to contention for the communications mechanism by i and j running on q.

Lo also states that an increase in parallelism (i.e. running i and j on separate processors) reduces interference costs and hence assignments should have a weighting which consists of execution, communications, and interference costs. This is achieved by limiting the number of clusters which can be assigned to a single processor.

It has recently been suggested (Chu and Lan, 1987) in a study of static load balancing algorithms for real-time systems, that since queuing delays at a processor are non-linear with increasing load, then the major limiting factor on system performance is a single bottleneck processor which becomes overloaded; hence improvement can only be achieved by minimizing the chances of a bottleneck being created. A heuristic method of ensuring this, is to create module clusters in a manner similar to Lo (1984), and then to solve the equation:

$$\min_{x} \left\{ \max_{1 \leqslant r \leqslant s} [EXEC(r; x) + IPC(r; x)] \right\}$$

where $EXEC(r; x)$ is the total execution costs of modules assigned to processor r, and IPC $(r; x)$, the total communications costs of this assignment.

Simulation runs conducted using this method performed significantly better than previous results obtained from simply minimizing execution and communications costs.

Adaptive load balancing

The limitation of static load balancing is that this method assigns processes to processors in a once-and-for-all manner and solutions require a priori knowledge of program behaviour; most approaches ignore the effects of interference in a system comprising multiprogrammed nodes. Livny and Melman (1982) have shown that in a distributed system the probability that at least one process is waiting for service at one node, whilst at least one processor is idle can be calculated as:

$$P_{wi} = \sum_{i=1}^{N} {}^{N}C_i Q_i H_{N-i} = (1 - P_o^N)(1 - P_o^N) - (1 - P_o)^N)$$

where

$Q_i = P_o^i$ is the probability that i processors are idle
H_i is the probability that i processors are not idle and one process waits for service
P_o is the probability that a processor is idle
N is the number of processors

They propose that if P_{wi} can be reduced by transferring processes from one processor to another, then the expected turnaround time for processes in the system will also be reduced. It is to be noted that for systems exceeding 10 nodes, and with loads ranging from moderately light to moderately heavy, P_{wi} is high, unless process transfer is performed.

This important result, and the conclusions which can be drawn from it, suggests that if the current state of the system can be observed, then by maintaining a balanced load, performance improvement can be achieved. We choose to refer to algorithms which dynamically react to system state in this manner, as adaptive load balancing algorithms. Many researchers have suggested that such algorithms are the most effective way of managing processor allocation (Carey et al., 1985; Tantawi and Towsley, 1985; Leland, 1986).

Although the adaptive approach is intuitively worthwhile, a number of new questions are raised. A load balancing algorithm must ensure that it has a reasonably up-to-date view of the system state. This could be achieved by using a centrally-located allocation processor (Zhou, 1986a), but this gives a single point of failure, and so a fully-distributed solution is favoured. However, care must be taken that cooperation between different processors does not overload the communications mechanism used, as load information is exchanged. In addition, since an adaptive load balancing algorithm transfers processes from lightly-loaded to heavily-loaded processors, it must guard against instability (Kratzer and Hammerstrom, 1980), caused by many processors all sending processes to the same lightly-loaded node, making it heavily-loaded. In this case processes will spend most of their time migrating around the network, fruitlessly looking for a suitable execution location; this phenomenon has been termed *processor thrashing*, and is analogous to thrashing in virtual memory management schemes.

We identify the following components of an adaptive load balancing algorithm, and review some approaches taken to providing efficient implementations of these components, and the relevant issues involved:

— processor load measurement
— information exchange
— transfer policy
— cooperation and location policy

Processor load measurement

In order to begin making sensible placement decisions for processes in a multi-computer environment, it is necessary to have available from the operating system a measure of the current load on each processor. Due to the loosely-coupled nature of the systems we are considering in this study, this measure will be calculated independently by each processor, and then communicated through the network to its peers. Since the value representing a processor's load will be frequently calculated during normal operation, it must be efficiently evaluated and be a reasonable indicator of what service a process will receive running on that processor. Also the value should adapt swiftly to changes in load state, but not so much that out-of-date information will be held at other locations in the network (Alonso, 1986). If possible, the method of load measurement used in a policy should be generalizable so that it can be used in a variety of operating system environments.

One simple solution to this question is to use a specialized load estimation program (Ni *et al.*, 1985), which constantly runs, determining the time intervals between periods where it successfully acquires use of the CPU. If the interval is great, then processor load is high, and conversely, if it is small, then this indicates low processor load. Although this approach is very easily implementable, it suffers from the problem that it relies heavily on the local process scheduling discipline used, and may therefore not provide a sufficiently accurate estimate of load; additionally it introduces a further process onto each processor, which goes against the principle of trying to improve system performance.

A measure used by the Maitre d' (Bershad, 1985) load balancing program is the UNIX five-minute average which gives the length of the run queue exponentially smoothed over a five-minute period. This value gives a gross indication of processor activity but does not respond quickly to load changes. A quantity which does so, is the number of processes ready to run on the CPU at a given instant (instantaneous processor load), but this will fluctuate very rapidly, because many processes may be waiting for I/O operations to complete, thus giving the false impression of a lightly-loaded processor. This problem can be further exacerbated when process migration is introduced to offload processes from a heavily-loaded processor, since these will not yet be included in the recipient processor's ready queue. The problem is thus one of maintaining *stability*. We adopt the definition of a stable system due to Kratzer and Hammerstrom (1980), as being one where the costs of adaptive load balancing do not outweigh its benefits over a system using no load balancing. Such a situation would be caused by a large number of fruitless migrations, resulting from use of out-of-date or inaccurate state information. In order to use a measure with a reduced fluctuation, it has been suggested (Krueger and Finkel, 1984) that the instantaneous load value should be averaged over a period at least as long as the time necessary to migrate an average process. Extra stability is then introduced by using a *virtual* load value, being the sum of the *actual* load on a particular processor augmented by the number of processes currently in transit to that processor.

The local load measurement used by Barak and Shiloh (1985a) is a further enhancement of the instantaneous load value. A time period t is divided into a number, μ, of atomic time units or quanta of length q. If W_i is taken to be the number of ready processes on a processor in the time interval (q_{i-1}, q_i), $i = 1, 2, \ldots, \mu$, and if ω of the μ quanta were unavailable due to operating system overhead, then the load over time t (denoted by V_t) can be given as:

$$V_t = \frac{\sum\limits_{i=1}^{\mu} W_i}{\mu - \omega}$$

Bryant and Finkel (1981) have proposed that if the remaining service time of processes can be estimated (i.e. the time which they still require to complete execution), this value can be used to calculate the expected response time for a process arriving at a processor, and that this is an indication of processor load. They investigated the use of probability distributions in the evaluation of remaining service time, of a process at time t (denoted by $R_E(t)$) but found that a simple and quickly calculated value is to assume that $R_E(t) = t$ (in other words a process is expected to require the same service time as it has already received). If $J(P)$ is used to denote the set of jobs resident on processor P, and we take a job $K \notin J(P)$ then the expected response time of K on processor P (denoted by $RSP_E(K,J(P))$) is calculated using the following algorithm:

```
R: = R_E(t_k)
for all j in J(P) do
begin
            if R_E(t_j) < R_E(t_k)
            then R: = R + R_E(t_j)
            else R: = R + R_E(t_k)
end;
RSP_E(K,J(P)): = R;
```

Hence this method of calculation can be used to provide an estimate of a processor's load by evaluating $RSP_E(K',J(P))$, where K' is a job whose remaining service time is equal to the average overall service time of processes in the network.

The queue of ready processes is not the only queue which gives an indication of the activity on a processor. Ferrari (1985) has studied the possibility of using a linear combination of all main resource queues as a measure of load, where coefficients in this equation are given by the total time a process spends in a particular queue. Employing a queuing model of each processor, and using mean-value analysis, he seeks to define the response time of a given UNIX command as a single-valued function of the current load, in terms of resource queue lengths. In other words, given the expected resource usage of a command 'C' on an otherwise empty processor it is possible to calculate how 'C' will perform when a known mix of commands is concurrently executing with it. Unfortunately, Ferrari's 'load index' (the name he gives to this measure of processor load) assumes a steady-state system, and the queuing theoretic analysis used only holds for certain queuing disciplines for resources. This may well not apply in a practical system (Zhou, 1986b), since process arrival and departure are dynamic in nature. In addition, since the calculation of the load exerted by a command is dependent on its known resource usage, changes in command code will necessitate changing the coefficient values in the load index equation. In fact Cabrera (1986) has suggested that load balancing algorithms based on command names will be detrimental to user process performance.

State information exchange policy

In order for an adaptive load balancing policy to make placement decisions for processes arriving for service at a particular node, there must be a mechanism by which information regarding processor load (whose measurement was discussed in the previous section) is passed throughout the network. Since the network architecture is loosely-coupled, this information will vary in its degree of accuracy of the true system state since it will be out-of-date, but accuracy must be sufficient to avoid instability (as defined previously). However, frequent load exchange will result in added overhead and will, in the extreme, lead to performance degrading to a level worse than that achievable without load balancing.

The limited approach
It has been suggested (Eager et al., 1986) that load information exchange can be very limited whilst still achieving the goal of maintaining a global view of overall system load. In their study of the merits of very simple load balancing policies, Eager et al. (1986) propose that load information from other processors in the network should only be requested when an individual processor believes itself to be overloaded based purely on local data. In their threshold and shortest algorithms a number of random processors are probed, in an attempt to find a processor to which processes can be offloaded. They showed via simulation that performance improvements are possible even with this limited exchange policy. In a recent study which we conducted (Harget and Johnson, 1988; Johnson, 1988), we found that this is indeed the case for a simple environment of independent, short-lived processes; however, our study revealed that in a more complex environment of process groups co-operating via message-passing to achieve a common goal, extra complexity in a load balancing algorithm can bring significant performance improvement.

The pairing approach

A 'pairing' approach has been put forward by Bryant and Finkel (1981). In their algorithm, each processor cyclically sends load information to each of its neighbours in an attempt to 'pair' with a processor whose load differs greatly from its own; the load information sent consists of a list of all local jobs, together with jobs which are currently migrating to the sender of the load message. Under this scheme, the number of such message exchanges and pairings is reduced by introducing a relaxation period when the loads of all neighbours have been queried, in order to avoid excess overhead in this policy.

Load vector approach

Some researchers have chosen to maintain a load vector in each processor, which gives the most-recently received load value for a limited subset of the other processors in the network (Hac and Johnson, 1986). Load balancing decisions can then be made on the basis of the relative difference between a processor's own load, and the loads of those held in the load vector.

In the adaptive load balancing algorithm (Barak and Shiloh, 1985a) developed for the MOS distributed operating system (Barak and Litman, 1985b) at the Hebrew University of Jerusalem, such an information exchange policy has been studied in detail. A load vector L is used, of size v, where the first component contains a processor's own local load value, and the other $v-1$ components contain load values for a subset of the other processors. Updating the load vector is performed periodically; every unit of time t (which is a parameter of the algorithm) each processor executes the following operations:

1. Update own local load value
2. Choose a random processor i
3. Send the first half of the load vector to processor i.

When a processor receives a portion of another processor's load vector, it merges this with its own load vector using the mappings:

$$L[i] \rightarrow L[2i], \ 1 < i < v/2 - 1$$
$$L_R[i] \rightarrow L[2i + 1], \ 0 < i < v/2 - 1$$

where L_R is the received portion.

It can be seen from this description that the subset of processors whose load values will be known, changes as the above merging is carried out and a load vector may contain duplicate entries for a particular processor. It is essential to choose an appropriate value for v, large enough to ensure that sufficient information is available to each processor, but small enough to avoid unnecessary overheads. In order to investigate choice of both v (the load vector size) and t (the update interval), it was shown that using the strategy described above, at least $\log_2 v$ load vectors need to be received in order to guarantee that a processor's vector is totally updated in time interval T. In a system with a large number of processors the probability that processor X will be selected at the next update period by k processors is approximately equal to $1/(ek!)$. Using these results, Barak and Shiloh tabulated a number of possible values of v, together with the probabilities that a processor's load vector will be updated in a particular time interval.

This allows the designer to tune the load exchange mechanism to the characteristics of the system.

An alternative load vector approach is taken in the distributed drafting algorithm (Ni et al., 1985). The load of each processor is considered to be in one of three states: light, normal or heavy. A processor holds its most recent view of the load state of its neighbours in a load vector, which is updated when a state transition occurs; possible transitions are light-to-normal, normal-to-light, normal-to-high or high-to-normal (L–N, N–L, N–H, H–N). It would be possible for a processor to broadcast its new state every time a transition occurred, but this would greatly increase network traffic and the algorithm is intended to be network topology-independent, hence it should not rely on an efficient broadcast mechanism being available. A strategy has been developed to minimize the traffic caused by state transitions, whilst still maintaining a reasonably up-to-date account of the state of all neighbouring processors. In order to avoid many messages being sent when a processor frequently changes between H-load and N-load or between L-load and N-load, an 'L-load' message is only broadcast to its neighbours as the N–L transition is made, if the previous processor state was H-load. If a similar approach were taken to N–H transitions, Ni et al. (1985) show that this could have a detrimental effect on the performance of their algorithm. They choose to broadcast N–H transitions and only notify neighbours of an H–N transition when process migration between two processors is being negotiated, thus further reducing message traffic. They also note it would be easy to relax these restrictions if the underlying communications network allowed efficient broadcasting.

Broadcast approach
Certain adaptive load balancing policies adopt broadcasting for their load exchange component. In the Maitre d' systems (Bershad, 1985), daemon processes (i.e. processes whose sole purpose is to listen for and react to events in the system) play a prominent role. One such process executes on each processor and periodically examines the UNIX five-minute load average and decides whether this will permit user processes to be imported from other processors; a processor will then broadcast this availability, and the appropriate daemon process maintains a list of processors currently willing to accept work. Since load balancing is fairly 'coarse-grained' and only applies to certain long-running processes which have been modified to run under Maitre d', this method is adequate and does not exert a lot of extra load on the communications subsystem.

Livny and Melman (1982) have made a detailed study of algorithms using a broadcast approach. In the simplest of these algorithms, when the load state of a processor changes (in other words on the birth or death of a process), its load value is broadcast throughout the network, thus each processor has an accurate view of all other processors' loads delayed only by the speed of the communications network. They found that this accuracy of information improves performance for small numbers of processors, but as the size of the network increases, then the additional communications overhead results in performance degradation. To overcome this overhead, a modified version of the information policy was introduced which purely broadcasts a message when the processor becomes idle, thus announcing willingness to accept migrating processes. It should be noted that this form of policy is only applicable to networks with a broadcast communications medium.

Global system load approach

The information exchange policies presented thus far have dealt with the exchange of the load values of particular processors. It has been suggested (Krueger and Finkel, 1984) that rather than exchanging specific local load values, processors should strive to calculate the load on the whole system and to adjust their own load relative to this global value. This approach has the desirable feature of being able to detect overall heavy and light loads on the system, in which case attempting to move processes from one processor to another may be of little benefit.

The 'above average' algorithm (Krueger and Finkel, 1984) developed at the University of Wisconsin uses a policy which exchanges each processor's view of the global average system load. Whenever a processor's local load is significantly different from this average, and it is unable to find another processor whose load is in the complementary state it modifies its value for the global average, and broadcasts this fact to all other processors; for example if a processor is overloaded and is unable to find an underloaded processor, then the global average value should be increased. The amount by which processor loads are permitted to differ from the average before load balancing is attempted, needs to be set at a level which is not so small that processors spend most of their time migrating processes in order to maintain their load close to the average, and not so large that many possible fruitful migrations are neglected.

The Gradient Model algorithm (Lin and Keller, 1987) views global load in terms of a collection of distances of each processor from a lightly-loaded processor. If the distance between two processors i and j is denoted by d_{ij} then in an N-processor network, the diameter of the network is defined as:

$$D(N) = \max \{d_{i,j}, \ i \text{ and } j \in N\}$$

A processor i has a gate value g_i which is set to zero if the processor is lightly-loaded or W_{max} otherwise where $W_{max} = D(N) + 1$. The proximity (W_i) of a processor is calculated as its minimum distance from a lightly-loaded processor hence:

$$W_i = \min \{d_{i,k}, \text{ over } k, \text{ where } g_k = 0\}$$
$$\text{if } \exists \ k \,|\, g_k = 0$$
$$W_i = W_{max}, \text{ if for all } k, \ g_k = W_{max}$$

Since a processor's distance from itself is zero, the proximity of a lightly-loaded processor is zero. Global load can then be represented by a *gradient surface* which is the set of all proximities $GS = (W_1, W_2, W_3, \dots W_N)$. Such a measure of global load is useful, since it not only gives a network-wide indication of light-loading, but also gives a route to a lightly-loaded processor with minimum cost, from anywhere in the network.

Since proximities cannot be calculated with absolute certainty due to communications delay in the network, it is necessary to define an approximation to a proximity, which is termed the *propagated pressure*. This approximation is based on the fact that the information received from a processor's direct neighbour is likely to be more accurate than information obtained from further away in the network. Hence the propagated pressure of processor i (P_i) is calculated as:

$$P_i = \min \{g_i, 1 + \min \{P_j \text{ over all } j, \text{ where } d_{i,j} = 1\}\}$$

So the propagated pressure of a lightly-loaded processor will be zero (as expected), and that of a moderate or heavily-loaded processor will be one greater than the smallest propagated pressure of its direct neighbours. The collection of all propagated pressures is termed the *propagated surface* and approximates the gradient surface. This method quickly reacts to the absence of lightly-loaded processors in the network, and thus prevents fruitless migrations when the entire network is under moderate or heavy load. An example gradient surface for a 9-processor network, is shown in Figure 3.2, where a lightly-loaded processor (P3) is shaded, and the values associated with each processor give its proximity (W_i).

Transfer policy

The transfer policy component of an adaptive load balancing algorithm deals primarily with the questions of deciding under what conditions is migration of a process from one processor to another to be considered, and which processes are eligible for migration.

A very simple, but effective, method for determining when process movement may occur is to use a static threshold value (Eager *et al.*, 1986), which, when exceeded indicates that a processor's load is too heavy and work may need to be offloaded to another node in the network. This threshold should be chosen by experimentation to find a load value where performance degrades sharply without load balancing. If the threshold is too high then processors will remain heavily loaded for too long, but if it is too low many pointless migration attempts will occur. Lin and Keller (1987) use two thresholds in order to categorize a processor's load as light, moderate or heavy, and consider migration only when the heavy threshold is exceeded.

The transfer policy in Figure 3.2 strives to identify overloading to trigger process migration, but some researchers (Ni, 1982) have taken the opposite view that an underloaded processor should seek to accept processes from its peers in order to balance the load over the network. One extreme version of this policy is to only consider migration to a processor when it becomes idle. In the distributed drafting algorithm (Ni *et al.*, 1985) possible process migration is triggered when a processor makes the state transition from normal to light-load, whereupon it indicates its willingness to offload processes from processors whose current state is shown as heavy in its most-recently received entry in the load vector.

Some transfer policies approach this question by using the difference of a processor's load from that of its peers as the major criterion for process migration. In Stankovic's algorithms (Stankovic, 1984) this difference is calculated explicitly and if it exceeds some bias then migration is a viable proposition. The above average algorithm (Krueger and Finkel, 1984) also bases its transfer policy on difference in load, but achieves this implicitly by maintaining a global average load value, and considering migration when local load differs from the average by a tunable acceptance threshold.

Another method used which implicitly considers load difference is to examine periodically the response time which local processes would receive if migrated to another processor, based on the current estimate of the remote processor's load. If the response time would be significantly better, taking into account the overhead of migration, then movement of that process is desirable (Barak and Shiloh, 1985).

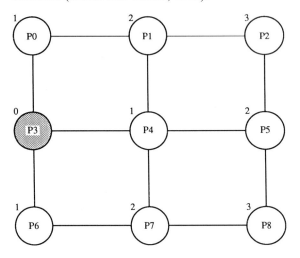

Figure 3.2 Gradient surface for the gradient model algorithm in a 9-processor network

Once it has been established that a process, or a number of processes, need to be executed remotely, part of the transfer policy is to decide which processes should be moved. A simple and easily implementable method is to consider only newly-arriving processes for migration; this is only really applicable where a threshold is being used in the transfer policy, so that an arriving process causing the threshold to be exceeded is the one chosen for migration. Migrated processes can be treated exactly the same as newly-created ones, but Eager *et al* (1986) have shown that this introduces instability into the system, and under heavy loads, processes may be constantly passed around, trying to find a suitable destination processor; this problem can be alleviated by limiting the number of times that a process is permitted to migrate (Ni *et al.*, 1985 chose to limit migration to once only).

If the main criterion used in the transfer policy is migrating a process to a processor where its response time will be improved, then the process to be sent is taken as the one which will benefit most from remote execution, assuming that a method is available for estimating a process's remaining service time. In order to be of maximum use, the transfer policy should only migrate processes which have been executing for some minimum amount of CPU time on a particular processor (Barak and Shiloh, 1985); this will help maintain stability and prevent a process from migrating too often.

Kreuger and Finkel (1984) have established a number of essential considerations when choosing a process to migrate:

1. Migration of a blocked process may not prove useful, since this may not effect local processor load.

2. Extra overhead will be incurred by migrating the currently scheduled process.
3. The process with the best current response ratio can better afford the cost of migration.
4. Smaller processes put less load on the communications network.
5. The process with the highest remaining service time will benefit most in the long-term from migration.
6. Processes which communicate frequently with the intended destination processor will reduce communications load if they migrate.
7. Migrating the most locally demanding process will be of greatest benefit to local load reduction.

All of these factors are of varying importance on the effectiveness of a transfer policy, and a load balancing algorithm should incorporate those features which best fit the system environment. Using a preemptive transfer policy (in other words one which migrates executing processes) has considerable advantages in that it adapts more quickly to changes in processor load; however, some load balancing algorithms (Ni, 1982; Bershad, 1985) do not use preemption, either because the operating systems for which they have been designed do not support such a facility, or because the costs of such migration are believed to be too high. These costs are significantly reduced if the distributed operating system has been developed with process migration in mind (Powell and Miller, 1983).

Cooperation and location policy

Once mechanisms for measuring local processor load, exchanging load values and deciding when process migration should occur have been established, a load balancing algorithm must define a method by which processors cooperate to find a suitable location for a migrating process. Many categorizations of cooperation and location policies are possible, but we choose to group them into sender-initiated (where an overloaded processor attempts to find an underloaded processor) and receiver-initiated (where the reverse applies) since we feel that this captures the most fundamental differences in approaching the load balancing problem (Eager *et al.*, 1985).

Sender-initiated approaches
Initiating load-balancing from an overloaded processor is by far the most studied method of cooperation policy. Eager *et al* (1986) examined the question of what level of complexity was appropriate for a load balancing algorithm, by evaluating the performance of three very simple policies which make their migration decisions based purely on local load information. Their goal was not to identify a suitable algorithm in absolute terms, but to analyse the relative merits of varying degrees of complexity; the transfer policy used in all three algorithms is a simple static threshold policy. The simplest of their algorithms chooses a destination processor at random for a process migrating from a heavily-loaded processor, and the number of times that a process is permitted to migrate is limited to once only. Since this policy has no regard for whether the destination processor itself is equally loaded or more heavily-loaded than the source processor, an enhancement

was proposed for a second algorithm known as *threshold*. Under this policy a random destination processor is chosen as before, and this processor is then sent a probe message to determine whether migration of a process would cause that processor's load to exceed the static threshold. If so, then another processor is chosen and probed, until either an appropriate destination is found, or the number of probe messages sent is greater than a statically set limit; if this limit is exceeded then the process is executed locally. The probe limit was introduced in order to prevent unbounded probing when the global system load is high. In the third algorithm investigated known as *shortest*, an attempt was made not only to determine whether a potential destination processor would have a load above the threshold, but also to establish the 'best' destination; this was achieved by polling a fixed number of processors, requesting their current queue lengths and selecting the processor with the shortest queue.

In order to evaluate the performance of these algorithms under simulation a queuing model was used, and to establish boundary conditions a k-processor network was modelled as k independent $M/M/1$ queues and an $M/M/k$ queue, to represent the no load balancing and optimal load balancing cases respectively. Results indicated that all three algorithms provided substantial improvement over no load balancing, and further that threshold and shortest provided extra improvement beyond a system load of above 0.5 (where system load of 1.0 is used to denote saturation); also the difference in performance between threshold and shortest was found to be negligible, with shortest performing slightly better. This led the authors to conclude that simple policies are adequate for adaptive load balancing, and that gains to be obtained from additional complexity are questionable.

The Maitre d' load balancing system (Bershad, 1985) uses daemon processes running on each processor to implement its cooperation and location policy. It works on a client/server basis where a local daemon known as maitrd runs on the client processor and negotiates remote process execution with a garçon daemon running on the server processor; in a typical configuration all nodes in the network can be both clients and servers depending on their relative loads. Communication between maitrd, garçon and application processes modified to run under Maitr d' is achieved using the socket mechanism of UNIX 4.2 BSD. When the user requests execution of an application, the local maitrd process receives a message at a known socket address. If the UNIX five-minute load average for the local processor is lower than a static threshold, then the application will run locally; if the load average exceeds the threshold, a message is sent to a remote garçon process, which has announced its processor's availability for importing work, again using sockets. The policy used to choose a remote processor is simply the one to which a remote request was least recently sent. When the garçon process accepts the request, it forks another copy of itself to act as a controller for the remote application process and a socket connection is set up back to the originating processor. In this manner both original maitrd and garçon processes can continue listening on their control sockets for further requests. Although this method showed significant performance improvements on the University of California VAX machines, it suffers from a need for application processes to be explicitly modified to use load balancing, and will only work for processes which use their standard I/O channels in a 'well-behaved' manner; there is also considerable difficulty in dealing with faulty processes which are part of a pipeline.

Stankovic (1984) has proposed three algorithms which are based on the relative difference between processor loads. The information exchange policy used in all three, is to periodically broadcast local load values. In the first of these algorithms, the least-loaded processor is chosen as a potential destination for migrating processes if the difference between that processor's load and the local load exceeds a tuneable bias value.

A similar method is used in Stankovic's second algorithm, but in this scheme a processor compares its load with each other processor in turn; for all differences greater than a value bias1, one process will be migrated there; if the difference exceeds bias2 then two processes are moved. In order to prevent instability, a static limit is imposed on the total number of processes that can migrate in a single pass through the load vector.

The third algorithm developed uses exactly the same policy as the first, except that when migration occurs to a particular processor this fact is recorded and no subsequent migrations will be performed to that processor for a time window of ∂t even if it is found to be underloaded. Results were obtained through simulation, and considerable analysis was carried out on the effect of changing the tuneable biasses and time window length. The major conclusion of this analysis was that parameter choice is a difficult and crucial question for the algorithms studied, and the second algorithm gave greater performance improvement than the others, only if appropriately tuned. This leads to the suggestion that an algorithm should, as much as possible, adapt to its environment by using variable parameters which do not need to be statically assigned.

The distributed scheduling algorithm designed at the University of Wisconsin (Bryant and Finkel, 1981), also used the load difference between processors to achieve load balancing. When a processor finds that it has more than two processes currently resident it enters what is termed the 'pairing state', where it attempts to locate one of its neighbours to which it can offload processes. In the pairing state, queries are sent cyclically to all neighbours, and a neighbour will respond by accepting pairing if it is sufficiently underloaded (i.e. it has less than two processes executing on it). Once a pair has been established both processors reject any further queries from their neighbours, and process migration is performed using expected service time improvement as explained in the previous section on transfer policies. The pair is then broken by common consent. An enhancement to this approach was investigated, whereby queries made during pairing would not be rejected if the querier's load differed significantly from that of the queried processor, but would be postponed until after the pairing state was left, in order to avoid missing possible fruitful migrations. A simulation of 25 processors connected in a square mesh topology showed that this method results in an evenly loaded network, and that even when a lightly-loaded processor is surrounded by heavily-loaded neighbours it does not get 'swamped' by migrating processes.

A later algorithm (Krueger and Finkel, 1984) from the same group of researchers at the University of Wisconsin uses a global-agreed average load value (as previously described) to negotiate process migration between processors. When a processor becomes overloaded, it broadcasts this fact and waits for an underloaded processor to respond with a message accepting migration of a process to it. The underloaded processor increases its local load value by the number of migrant processes which it believes it is going to receive in order to prevent subsequent overloading, but reduces its load when a timeout period expires indicating that another processor was chosen for migration. If the overloaded processor is unable to find a suitable location for offloading work, then it assumes that the global average value is too low and broadcasts an increased value. The advantage of this approach is that it adapts better to load fluctuations than the cooperation and location policies which migrate processes based on a static threshold for under- and overloading. It has the desirable feature of diminishing load balancing effort when the system is in a generally stable state, and increasing this effort when anomalies in load distribution occur. Simulation of a 40-processor network showed that this method drastically improved both mean processor load and average process response ratio. We have reported elsewhere (Johnson, 1988; Harget and Johnson, 1988) results which we obtained using a similar approach. In our study we experimented with using this algorithm in a receiver-initiated manner, and also one which switched between sender and receiver-initiated mode, depending on the current system load. The motivation behind the latter variant is that sender-initiated policies perform better at low load, and receiver-initiated policies better at high load; hence we used a 'load breakpoint' at which our algorithm would change from one mode to the other. In order to avoid the case where the algorithm frequently switches between modes, we added a 'tolerance range' around the breakpoint. Using this scheme, if the algorithm is operating in sender-initiated mode (i.e. at low load), and the average__load__value > load__breakpoint + tolerance__range, then the algorithm changes over to receiver-initiated mode. A change back to sender-initiated mode will then be made when average__load__value < load__breakpoint − tolerance__ range. This algorithm was found to give better performance than the global average algorithm over a range of load values.

The Gradient Model load balancing algorithm (Lin and Keller, 1987) uses the concept of a pressure surface approximation of the current network load distribution to make its process migration decisions. When a processor has calculated its own local load an action is taken depending on whether this is light, moderate or heavy. If local load is light then the processor's propagated pressure is set to zero and propagated pressures from neighbours are ignored; if load is moderate, the propagated pressure is set to one greater than the smallest propagated pressure of all direct neighbours, but no migration is attempted. Migration occurs only at heavy load: if the propagated pressure of all neighbours indicates that no lightly-loaded processors exist, then the network is saturated and migration will serve no purpose; if however, this is not the case, then a process is migrated to the neighbour whose propagated pressure is minimal. It should be noted that using this method, processes are not necessarily migrated *directly* to a lightly-loaded processor, but by definition are guaranteed to migrate *towards* them following the route implied by each processors's propagated pressure. The algorithm hence strives to achieve global load balancing by a series of local migration decisions; if the intended destination of a migrant process becomes overloaded whilst it is in transit, the algorithm will react to this and divert the process elsewhere. The use of the bounding value W_{max} (as described in the previous section on transfer policies) prevents unnecessary migrations and also serves as an indicator that a processor has failed.

In the MOS distributed load balancing algorithm (Barak and Litman, 1985), a quite complex combination of elements is taken into consideration when choosing a destination processor for local processes, which are caused to contemplate migration in a round-robin manner by a special system process. First, an estimation is made of the response time that a process can expect if it executes on each of the processors whose load is currently held in the periodically-exchanged load vector. This estimate includes communications costs with other processors, where the process's resources may reside and also a weighting to take into account the overheads of transferring the process based on its size. The processor chosen is the one which apparently offers the best expected response time. Tests using this algorithm were conducted using a network of four PDP-11 computers connected by a 10Mbit/second communications ring. A number of I/O-bound and CPU-bound processes were used and observed speed-up in processing was tabulated for various initial process placements. These results showed significant improvement over the no load-balancing case, but it is not clear what effect a larger network, with a greater variety of process behaviour would have.

Receiver-initiated approaches
Receiver-initiated location policies work with underloaded or idle processors requesting processes from more heavily-loaded parts of the network. They have been less well-studied than sender-initiated policies, but Eager *et al.* (1985) showed that they can perform well, especially at high overall system load. Similarly to their work on sender-initiated policies they investigated the level of complexity necessary to achieve efficient load balancing; as in their other study they based their policies on a simple threshold transfer policy. In an algorithm which they term 'receiver', when the load on a processor falls below the static threshold (T), it polls random processors to find one where transfer of a process from that processor would not cause its load to be below T; again unsuccessful probes are constrained by a static probe limit. In an attempt to remove the overhead of migrating an executing process, a modification to the above approach, known as the *reservation* policy was investigated. When a processor's load falls below the threshold T it polls its peers exactly as in the 'receiver' policy, but instead of accepting a process currently running on a particular processor, a reservation is made to migrate the next newly-arriving process, provided that no other reservations are already pending; a static probe limit is used as above. Simulation results using a queuing model indicated that despite the reservation policies avoidance of costly preemptive migration it did not perform as well as the receiver policy; it was also noted that the receiver policy performed better than an equivalent sender-initiated algorithm at loads greater than 0.7.

The distributed drafting algorithm (Ni *et al.*, 1985) is also an example of a location policy where lightly-loaded processors seek work from their heavily-loaded neighbours. Since the algorithm is intended to be network topology-independent, the processors which are candidates for migration are defined with regard to communications costs. When a processor enters the light-load state, a 'draft request' message is sent to all heavily-loaded candidate processors which then respond with a 'draft age' message; the draft age is calculated by considering the characteristics ('ages') of all processes which are suitable for migration and will have a value of zero if the processor's load is no longer heavy. When the original drafting processor has received all such draft ages, it selects the processor which sent the highest draft age value and sends it a 'draft standard' message based on the draft ages received. Finally, the receiver of the draft standard will then migrate any of its processes to the drafting processor whose ages exceed the standard; if there are no such processes it replies with a 'too late' message. The major drawback of this approach is that it contains a large collection of parameters which must be carefully tuned to suit the network topology (e.g. draft ages, draft standard, time-out periods). A five-processor simulation showed that this method can perform well, with correct parameter choice.

In a study of load balancing algorithms in broadcast networks, Livny and Melman (1982) proposed two receiver-initiated policies. Under the first of these a node broadcasts a status message when it becomes idle and receivers of this message carry out the following actions:

Assuming n_i denotes the number of processes executing on a processor i:
1. If $n_i > 1$ continue to step 2, else terminate algorithm.
2. Wait D/n_i time units, where D is a parameter depending on the speed of the communications subsystem; by making this value dependent on processor load, more heavily-loaded processors will respond more quickly.
3. Broadcast a reservation message if no other processor has already done so (if this is the case terminate algorithm).
4. Wait for reply.
5. If reply is positive and $n_i > 1$, migrate a process to the idle processor.

It was thought that this broadcast method might overload the communications medium, so a second algorithm was proposed which replaced broadcasting by polling when idle. In this algorithm the following steps are taken when a processor's queue length reaches zero:

1. Select a random set of R processors $(a_i, \ldots, a_R)$ and set a counter $j = 1$.
2. Send a message to processor a_j and wait for a reply.
3. The reply from a_j will either be a migrating process or an indication that it has no processes.
4. If the processor is still idle and $j < R$, increment j and go to step 2 else stop polling.

A large number of queuing model simulations with varying numbers of processors were performed, and it was found that both algorithms resulted in similar improvements in process turnaround time and similar overall communications costs.

Conclusion

In this paper, we have surveyed two main approaches to processor allocation in a loosely-coupled distributed computer system. The static load balancing algorithms presented use a priori knowledge of process behaviour and are extremely computationally expensive; indeed some approaches are infeasible as the number of nodes in the network increases above two or three. In order to modify the operation of a system depending on its current state, adaptive load balancing algorithms are employed, and we have presented a number of different strategies taken by researchers in this field.

We believe that as such processors as the INMOS Transputer are increasingly widely used as parallel computation servers, further work will be necessary into the efficient mapping of parallel algorithms onto these architectures, using load balancing and flow control techniques.

References

Alonso, R. (1986) The design of load balancing strategies for distributed systems. *Proceedings of a Workshop on Future Directions in Computer Architecture and Software*, Charleston, South Carolina, USA, May, pp. 202–207

Barak, A. and Shiloh, A. (1985) A distributed load-balancing policy for a multicomputer. *Software Practice and Experience*, **15**(9), 901–913

Barak, A. and Litman, A. (1985) MOS: A multicomputer distributed operating system. *Software Practice and Experience*, **15**(8), 725–737

Bershad, B. (1985) *Load balancing with Maitre d'*, Report ♯UCB/CSD86/276, December. Computer Science Division (EECS), University of California, Berkeley, California, USA

Bokhari, S. H. (1981) A shortest tree algorithm for optimal assignments across space and time in a distributed processor system. *IEEE Transactions on Software Engineering*, **7**(6), 583–589

Bryant, R. M. and Finkel, R. A. (1981) A stable distributed scheduling algorithm. *Proceedings of the 2nd International Conference on Distributed Computing Systems*, April, Paris, pp. 314–323

of the 2nd International Conference on Distributed Computing Systems, April, Paris, 314–323

Cabrera, L-F. (1986) The influence of workload on load balancing strategies. *Proceedings of the 1986 Summer USENIX Conference*, June, Atlanta, GA, USA, pp. 446–458

Carey, M. J., Livny, M. and Lu, H. (1985) Dynamic task allocation in a distributed database system. *Proceedings of the 5th International Conference on Distributed Computing Systems*, May, Denver, USA, pp. 282–291

Chou, T. C. K. and Abraham, J. A. (1982) Load balancing in distributed systems. *IEEE Transactions on Software Engineering*, **8**(4), 401–412

Chu, W. W., Holloway, L. J., Lan, L. M-T. and Efe, K. (1980) Task allocation in distributed data processing, *IEEE Computer*, **13**(11), 57–69

Chu, W. W. and Lan, L. M-T. (1987) Task allocation and precedence relations for distributed real-time systems, *IEEE Transactions on Computers*, **36**(6), 667–679

Eager, D. L., Lazowska, E. D. and Zahorjan, J. (1985) A comparison of receiver-initiated and sender-initiated adaptive load sharing. *Proceedings of the 1985 ACM SIGMETRICS Conference on Measurement and Modelling of Computer Systems*, August, Austin, Texas, USA, pp. 1–3

Eager, D. L., Lazowska, E. D., Zahorjan, J. (1986) Adaptive load sharing in homogeneous distributed systems. *IEEE Transactions on Software Engineering*, **12**(5), 662–675

Efe, K. (1982) Heuristic models of task assignment scheduling in distributed systems. *IEEE Computer*, **15**(6), 50–56

Ferrari, D. (1985) A study of load indices for load balancing schemes. Report ♯UCB/CSD86/262, October. Computer Science Division (EECS), University of California, Berkeley, California, USA

Ford, L. R. and Fulkerson, D. R. (1962) *Flows in Networks*, Princeton University Press, Princeton, New Jersey

Gylys, V. B. and Edwards, J. A. (1976) Optimal partitioning of workload for distributed systems. *Digest of Papers, COMPCON Fall 76*, September, pp. 353–357

Hac, A. and Johnson, T. J. (1986) A study of dynamic load balancing in a distributed system. *Proceedings of the ACM SIGCOMM Symposium on Communications, Architectures and Protocols*, August, Stowe, Vermont, USA, pp. 348–356

Harget, A. J. and Johnson, I. D. (1988) A study of load balancing algorithms in distributed systems. *Proceedings of the IASTED Conference on Applied Informatics*, February, Grindelwald, Switzerland, pp. 11–14

Johnson, I. D. (1988) A study of adaptive load balancing algorithms for distributed systems. PhD Thesis, Aston University, Birmingham, UK, January

Kratzer, A. and Hammerstrom, D. (1980) A study of load levelling. *Proceedings of the IEEE Fall COMPCON*, pp. 647–654

Krueger, P. and Finkel, R. (1984) An adaptive load balancing algorithm for a multicomputer. Computer sciences technical Report ♯539, University of Wisconsin-Madison, USA, April

Leland, W. E. and Ott, T. J. (1986) Load-balancing heuristics and process behaviour. *Proceedings of the ACM SIGMETRICS Conference*, May, pp. 54–69

Lin, F. C. H. and Keller, R. M. (1987) The gradient model load balancing method. *IEEE Transactions on Software Engineering*, **13**(1), 32–38

Livny, M. and Melman, M. (1982) Load balancing in homogeneous broadcast distributed systems. *Proceedings of the ACM Computer Network Performance Symposium*, April, 47–55

Lo, V. M. (1984) Heuristic algorithms for task assignment in distributed systems. *Proceedings of the 4th International Conference on Distributed Computing Systems*, pp. 30–39

Ma, P-Y.R., Lee, E. Y. S. and Tsuchiya, M. (1982) A task allocation model for distributed computing systems. *IEEE Transactions on Computers*, **31**(1), 41–47

Ni, L. M. (1982) A distributed load balancing algorithm for point-to-point local computer networks. *Proceedings of COMPCON Computer Networks*, September, pp. 116–123

Ni, L. M., Xu, C-W., Gendreau, T. B. (1985) A distributed drafting algorithm for load balancing. *IEEE Transactions on Software Engineering*, **11**(10), 1153–1161

Powell, M. L. and Miller, B. P. (1983) Process migration in DEMOS/MP. *Proceedings of the 9th ACM Symposium on Operating Systems Principles*, December, pp. 110–119

Rao, G. J. and Stone, H. S. (1979) Assignment of tasks in a distributed processor system with limited memory. *IEEE Transactions on Computers*, **28**(4), 291–298

Stankovic, J. A. (1984) Simulations of three adaptive, decentralized controlled, job scheduling algorithms. *Computer Networks*, **8**(3), 199–217

Stone, H. S. (1977) Multiprocessor scheduling with the aid of network flow algorithms. *IEEE Transactions on Software Engineering*, **3**(1), 85–93

Stone, H. S. and Bokhari, S. H. (1978) Control of distributed processes, *IEEE Computer*, **11**(7), 97–106

Tantawi, A. N., Towsley, D. (1985) Optimal static load balancing in distributed computer systems. *Journal of the ACM*, **32**(2), 445–465

Zhou, S. (1986a) A trace-driven simulation study of dynamic load balancing. Report ♯UCB/CSD/87/305, Computer Science Division (EECS), University of California, Berkeley, California, USA, September

Zhou, S. (1986b) An experimental assessment of resource queue lengths as load indices. Report ♯UCB/CSD/86/298, Computer Science Division (EECS), University of California, Berkeley, California, USA, June

Part 2

Special topics

Chapter 4

Debugging distributed real-time applications: a case study in ada

D. S. Snowden and A. J. Wellings

The increasing use of the **ada** language for the programming of distributed systems has served to highlight the lack of debugging support for such systems in general. In this paper we discuss the considerations involved in the design of a debugger for distributed **ada** programs, and we describe a *trace-replay* debugging system which is based on the recording of *inter-task events* during program execution. This system facilitates a wide range of debugging approaches; for any given program, the user can select the particular approach which provides the maximum of debugging assistance without significantly disturbing the behaviour of the program. We include in this paper a brief survey of related work in the area of multiprocess debugging.

Introduction

In the field of *embedded* computer systems, program distribution not only introduces the potential for improved performance, but also promises improved reliability through the use of redundant components. The **ada** programming language is increasingly being used to program such systems; perhaps more so than was originally envisaged by its designers. Unfortunately, it is not obvious how to go about designing distributed **ada** software; consequently a wide variety of approaches has been adopted (Burns, *et al.*, 1987a). There is also a critical lack of support for the debugging of distributed **ada** programs, reflecting the poor level of debugging support for distributed systems in general.

In this paper we describe the methodology which we have adopted for the design of distributed **ada** programs, and we discuss the considerations involved in the design of a debugger for such programs. We concentrate particularly upon the latter area, the background to the underlying methodology of which can be found in a previous paper by Harrison (Harrison, 1985). Whilst we consider the design and debugging of distributed **ada** programs in particular, the same basic principles apply to distributed programs written in other imperative languages.

Using ada in a distributed environment

One of the main issues in designing a distributed system is that of partitioning: deciding which code is to reside on which machine, and how the pieces of code are to interact. Two basic approaches may be identified (Burns *et al.*, 1987a, Burns *et al.*, 1987b):

   (i) distribute fragments of a single program across machines, and use normal intra-program communication mechanisms for interaction;
   (ii) write a separate program for each machine and devise a means of inter-program interaction.

For a detailed review of both (i) and (ii) see, Burns, *et al.*, 1987a. For a case study of (ii) see Keeffe *et al.*, 1985.

The chosen approach

The basic characteristic of our approach to distribution is that the application software is viewed as a single **ada** program distributed across the target system. The main advantage of this approach, over (ii) above, is that all interfaces between the distributed program fragments can be type-checked by the compiler. Within this approach two general strategies can be identified: *post-partitioning* and *pre-partitioning*. As the name implies, post-partitioning is based on partitioning the program after it has been written. The program is designed without regard to a target architecture; the programmer produces an appropriate solution to the problem in hand, and has the full language at his or her disposal.

The pre-partitioning strategy is to select a particular **ada** construct as the sole unit of partitioning to be used throughout the design and programming process. The programmer is obliged to accept any constraints that the choice of construct entails. The notion underlying this strategy is that of the *virtual node* (Hutcheon and Wellings, 1989a), which is an abstraction of a physical node in a distributed system. A virtual node consists of one or more tasks (which may share memory) communicating with other virtual nodes via message passing over a communications subsystem. More than one virtual node can be mapped onto a single physical node. The notion of the virtual node is found in most languages which have been designed with the specific intent of supporting distributed programming; for example, the 'guardian' of **argus** (Liskov and Scheifler, 1983), and the 'task module' of **conic** (Sloman, *et al.*, 1984).

We have chosen to adopt the pre-partitioning approach to programming distributed systems because we believe that:

   • potential distribution should be clearly visible to the programmer since it may affect the interfaces to be provided;
   • post-partitioning is difficult to implement for a language as sophisticated as **ada**, and we do not have the necessary resources; and
   • adopting virtual nodes allows a distributed system to be built from nodes written in different languages.

It is our view that the package is the most important feature of the **ada** programming language, and that **ada** programs should be constructed, wherever possible, by linking together existing library packages. This approach has the significant advantages that programs are easier to construct and that software modules can be shared between programs. For this reason we have chosen the package as the basis of the **ada** virtual node; hence, distributed programs can be constructed by linking virtual nodes together. However, by adopting this approach we are accepting that there may be some limitations imposed on dynamic reconfiguration.

We have also decided that communication between virtual nodes should be via remote procedure call (RPC), for the following reasons:

- the procedure call is common to many different languages as a mechanism for transferring control,
- RPC's allow the possibility of easy communication between virtual nodes written in different languages, and
- techniques for reliable remote procedure call implementation are now fairly well understood (Birrell and Nelson, 1984) by comparison with those for implementing reliable remote **ada** rendezvous (Burns *et al.*, 1987a).

A full discussion and formal definition of our approach can be found in previous papers (Hutcheon *et al.*, 1989; Hutcheon and Wellings, 1989b)

Debugging distributed ada programs

Whilst many of the issues associated with the use of **ada** in a distributed environment (for example, the construction of highly reliable distributed systems, and the implementation of a distributed rendezvous) have been well documented elsewhere (Wellings 1987), one issue which has not been so widely addressed is that of distributed debugging. In this section we outline the types of error which can arise in distributed **ada** programs, and explain the derivation of the basic mechanism of a debugger for such programs.

The debugging of **ada** programs which consist of multiple tasks has certain similarities to the debugging of single task programs, but there are also important differences. The similarities arise because in a multi-task system it is still possible, to a certain extent, to consider the individual tasks in isolation, and to apply conventional debugging techniques in order to discover various sorts of algorithmic error within those tasks. The differences arise because multi-task programs, whether they are run on a single processor or on multiple processors, are affected by a class of errors which are not applicable to single-task programs; these errors concern the ways in which tasks interact with one another.

Tasks interact in a limited number of well-defined ways, which generally concern the communication between pairs of tasks: in our model of distributed **ada** this involves rendezvous and shared variable communication between tasks residing in the same virtual node, and RPC communication between tasks residing in different virtual nodes. Other interactions concern such things as task creation, activation, and termination. These interactions will henceforth be referred to collectively as *Inter-Task Events* (ITEs). A summary of all the different types of ITE which apply to **ada** can be found in the appendix to this paper.

Whilst in theory it should be possible to detect errors of task interaction simply by observing the ITEs which occur, in practice the observation of ITEs in real time is not really practicable; ITEs can occur at quite high rates, and an observer would not be able to keep up with them. One solution to this problem is to monitor the execution of a collection of tasks in real time, and to record in a *trace* the details of the ITEs which occur. The trace can subsequently be examined at leisure.

Whilst examining the contents of an ITE trace is sufficient for determining the existence of an erroneous sequence of ITEs, it is not sufficient for determining the underlying algorithmic errors in the individual tasks which may have given rise to the erroneous ITE sequence. In order to do that, it is necessary to be able to tie the entries in the ITE trace back to the execution of the tasks themselves. This can be achieved by using the trace to drive a *replay* of some or all of the tasks in the original program. During such a replay the user can examine the behaviour of individual tasks at the statement level using the facilities of a conventional symbolic debugger; for example, examining the values of variables, setting breakpoints, and single-stepping execution.

We now proceed to discuss a number of issues relating to the design of a *trace-replay* debugging system for distributed **ada** programs, and to suggest a number of ways in which the facilities provided by such a system may be applied. In our discussion we concentrate upon a hardware configuration which consists of a collection of networked target machines with a link to a host machine. We also concentrate on the debugging of tasks in the target machine context; debugging in the virtual node context is broadly similar.

Primary requirements of the trace-replay mechanism

In this section we consider some of the basic requirements which apply to the design of the mechanism of a trace-replay debugging system.

Trace collection

When collecting a trace it is imperative that the action of recording the ITEs in the trace should disturb the behaviour of the monitored user program as little as possible. However, it is inevitable that some disturbance will result, and as a consequence of this there will always be some bugs which will disappear when trace collection is applied. We can only seek to minimize the likelihood of this by minimizing the disturbance caused by the collection of a trace.

One way in which to minimize the disturbance caused by the collection of a trace is to arrange for the ITEs relating to particular tasks to be recorded on the target machines where those tasks are executed. The alternative, to send details of every ITE back to the host, would have a greater effect on the behaviour of the user program, not least because of the extra load which it would place on the communications subsystem. If the traces are to be stored on the target machines then we must make the assumption that there is sufficient space available on the target machines for that purpose. However, the space on the target machines is obviously finite, and the trace collection mechanism must take this into account.

Snapshots

If it is wished to be able to replay the user program in such a way that a conventional, sequential symbolic debugger can be applied to individual tasks within the program, then it is necessary to precede the collection of the trace with a snapshot of the states of each of the tasks. If space on the target machines permits then the snapshots might also be stored there, otherwise they must be uplined to the host at some appropriate time. Wherever snapshots are stored, the action of recording them is likely to have some effect on the behaviour of the user program irrespective of whether the program is suspended whilst the snapshots are taken or not.

As the user program may be distributed over a number of target machines it is necessary to provide a mechanism for synchronizing the snapshots on each of the target machines so that together they represent a consistent starting state for the replay of the tasks of the user program.

Integrating snapshots and trace collection

The simplest implementation of a snapshot-and-trace mechanism involves taking a snapshot of the initial state of the tasks within the user program, and then recording ITEs in a trace for as long as is required. However, this could involve collecting a trace of arbitrary length, which is clearly infeasible given the limited amount of space likely to be available on the target machines. Given that the snapshot-and-trace mechanism is constrained by the space available on the target machines, it is essential to allow a reasonable degree of flexibility over when the snapshots are taken and the collection of the trace commences.

Replay

As far as the replay of a user program is concerned, the main consideration, apart from the way in which the trace is to be used to drive the replay, is the need to provide extra functionality on the target machines to support the facilities of the symbolic debugger; for example, the examination of variables, the setting of breakpoints, and the control of execution.

Monitoring considerations

In this section we consider various issues relating to the collection of traces and snapshots during the monitoring of a user program.

What to trace

We have already stated that a trace is used to record details of the ITEs which occur during the monitoring of the tasks within a program. Not surprisingly, each type of ITE corresponds closely to a particular routine within the **ada** run-time kernel, and so the most obvious way to record the occurrence of ITEs is to add code to the appropriate kernel routines to copy the details of each ITE into the trace. The details, or *attributes*, to be recorded include the type of the ITE, the identity of the task which gave rise to it, and the logical time (Lamport, 1978) at which it occurred.

It is not always necessary to record all of the ITEs which arise from the execution of a program, so it may be useful to facilitate the conditional recording of ITEs. The sort of conditions which might be applied can be based upon the attributes of the ITEs. The advantage of being selective about which ITEs are recorded is that fewer ITEs have to be recorded overall, hence reducing the space required to store them. The disadvantages are that the evaluation of the conditions increases the effect on the behaviour of the user program, and that the resulting trace cannot be used to drive a replay (see pages 118–119 on event level replay and full replay).

Trace collection

There are two possible approaches to collecting a trace; they differ in the ways in which they manage the *trace buffer* (the buffer which holds the ITE details which constitute the trace). These approaches are:

- one-off trace collection: recording ITEs only until the trace buffer becomes full.
- cyclic trace collection: recording ITEs in a circular trace buffer, or else reinitializing the trace buffer every time it becomes full. This method continues until the recording is terminated in some other way (see below).

The commencement of the collection of traces can be triggered in three ways:

- by the start of execution of the monitored program.
- by the user issuing an explicit command; as this is done on-the-fly its usefulness may be limited.
- by the occurrence of an ITE whose attributes satisfy some specified condition. Just how complex such conditions might be is a matter for debate; in general the more complex the condition is the longer it will take to evaluate, and the more likely it is that its evaluation will affect the behaviour of the user program. This applies particularly to conditions which relate to a sequence of ITEs, especially when the sequence involves ITEs arising from tasks which reside on different target machines.

The termination of the collection of traces can be triggered in three ways:

- by the trace buffer becoming full (this only applies to the one-off method of trace collection).
- by the user issuing an explicit command.
- by the occurrence of an ITE whose attributes satisfy some specified condition. The types of condition permitted here are the same as those which can be used to trigger the commencement of trace collection.

The synchronization of the commencement and termination of trace collection on each of the target machines requires the ability to request that all target machines start/stop trace collection instantaneously. In the absence of suitable hardware support such synchronization has to be achieved by the propagation of special 'software signals'. Inevitably this method will allow the target machines, and hence the tasks running on them, to get slightly out of step with one another. As a result, the behaviour of the user program may be affected. Unfortunately this is unavoidable.

What to snapshot

When considering the amount of information to be recorded in a snapshot, there are several possibilities. The simplest (brute force) approach is to snapshot the entire executable image of the parts of the user program residing on each of the target machines; this includes both code and data. If it can be assumed that the code on each of the target machines will not be damaged during monitoring because of bugs in the user program, then it is only really necessary to snapshot the *data* areas on each target machine; this will obviously reduce the size of the snapshots.

It is also possible to reduce the size of a snapshot by recording only the details pertaining to specific tasks within the program. This approach is complicated by the presence of shared variables which do not lie in the data areas belonging to any particular task, but which still need to be recorded. For this reason it may be more appropriate to snapshot individual virtual nodes rather than individual tasks.

Under some circumstances it can be sufficient to snapshot only a very limited amount of information pertaining to individual tasks; for example, their run-states, and the queues associated with each of their entries. This minimal information can be used in conjunction with the event level replay mechanism (see section on event level replay).

When to snapshot

There are two possible approaches to the selection of when to take a snapshot; they correspond directly to the approaches to trace collection listed on page 116.

- precede the collection of a one-off trace by a snapshot.
- repeat a cycle of snapshot and trace, taking an initial snapshot, and then further snapshots each time the trace buffer becomes full.

As the snapshots are to be used as the starting point for the replay of the user program, it is essential that the taking of snapshots on the individual target machines is synchronized so that together the snapshots form a consistent representation of the state of the user program at a given instant. Since snapshots are taken immediately prior to the commencement of the collection of a trace, their synchronization is a consequence of the mechanism for the synchronization of trace collection.

Multiple snapshots and traces

A potential drawback of the snapshot-and-trace mechanism is that a target machine may be instructed to cease trace collection when it has only just taken a snapshot, and hence when there is little or no subsequent trace available for use in a replay. For this reason it can be useful to retain at least one previous generation of snapshot and trace which can be called upon if required. This obviously increases the storage requirements for holding the snapshots and the traces.

Trace-based tools

In this section we describe a number of tools, of increasing levels of complexity, which can be applied to the snapshots and traces collected during monitoring.

Trace browser

One of the simplest approaches to using a trace as a basis for debugging is to browse through the ITEs contained within the trace. A trace browsing tool allows a user to look through the chronologically-ordered entries in an ITE trace, and provides them with the facilities to search for ITEs which satisfy certain conditions. These conditions can involve such things as the type of the ITE, the task or tasks involved, and the (logical) time at which the ITE occurred.

As the ITE traces are held in the trace buffers on the individual target machines at the end of the trace collection, some method of accessing these traces for browsing is required. This is most easily achieved by uplining the traces to the host machine and merging them to form a single, *combined trace* in which all the ITEs from different target machines are ordered by logical time. The trace browser can then be run entirely on the host machine.

Note that whilst snapshots are not required for trace browsing, there is no reason why the trace browser cannot be applied in situations where a snapshot has been collected as well as the trace.

Event level replay

A slight refinement on the simple trace browsing approach is to use the ITEs contained in the combined trace to drive a replay of the behaviour of the tasks within a program at the ITE level. Such a facility, running on the host machine, allows the user to step through the ITEs (either singly, or until an ITE with specified attributes is encountered) and observe such things as the run-states of the tasks, the states of their entry queues, and the values of the parameters of the individual entry calls. Note that the information which drives the event level replay is derived solely from the combined trace; no execution of the code of the user tasks is involved, and so no details of the internal states of the user tasks themselves are available. Note also that if no snapshots were collected along with the trace, the initial run-states of the tasks and the initial states of their entry queues will be unknown.

Event level replay will obviously benefit from the provision of a graphical interface to display some representation of the individual tasks, their run-states, and the states of their entry queues.

Full replay

Whilst the trace browser and the event level replay system facilitate varying degrees of examination of the behaviour of tasks at the ITE level, they do not address the problem of examining the code of the user tasks to determine the underlying algorithmic errors. This can be achieved by driving a full replay of the user program from the combined ITE trace. The facilities provided by full replay are similar to those provided by event level replay, but they are extended by the provision of a symbolic debugger which can be applied to the individual tasks within the program.

The most straightforward way to implement full replay is to run the code of the individual tasks on the target machines where they ran during trace collection, and to control the replay from the host machine. To prepare the system for replay it is first necessary to reset the target machines to a consistent state; this can be achieved by reloading the appropriate snapshot details into each machine. Replay is then driven by the contents of the combined trace in such a way that the order in which the ITEs occur during the replay is constrained to be the same as the order in which they occurred during monitoring. In order to achieve this it is necessary to alter the behaviour of the run-time kernel routines associated with particular ITEs so that, for example, a task which would receive an entry call direct from some other task during live running will actually have the details of the appropriate call provided from the combined trace by the host machine. The behaviour of the kernel routines also needs to be modified when replaying to prevent the collection of further traces and snapshots.

Note that, in order for it to be possible to replay a task, all of that task's ITEs must be recorded in the original trace. If only a subset of a task's ITEs is recorded then it is not possible to relate ITEs arising during replay to ITEs from the trace, and hence the detection of trace invalidation becomes impossible (see section on mechanism of replay).

Granularity of replay
It might be considered desirable to depict a number of tasks which ran on different target machines during monitoring as executing truly in parallel during replay, whether the execution be continuous or single-stepped. However, to guarantee accurate parallel replay at the level of the individual statement would require that each target machine enter a timestamped record of the execution of every statement into its trace. This would represent a very large overhead in terms of both the time and space required to record this information. It is clearly not practicable to collect such a detailed trace, and hence it is not possible to depict the parallel execution of tasks at the statement level.

Given that only ITEs are recorded in the trace, the granularity of the replay (at least in terms of the apparent relative execution of different tasks) is necessarily at the ITE level. Since any attempt to display parallel execution of tasks at the statement level would be meaningless, careful consideration has to be given to the way in which parallel execution is to be presented to the user. The best approach is probably to use a two-level presentation. The first level provides an overview of system execution in pictorial form, displaying the tasks which are being replayed, and illustrating their run-states and the rendezvous between them. The second level provides one window per task, and in those windows the full details of the individual ITEs are displayed in textual form as they are replayed.

Whilst the execution of a number of tasks may be observed at the ITE level at the same time, it is only meaningful to allow the execution of a single task to be observed at the statement level at any given time. The particular task selected to be observed at the statement level at any given time will be referred to as the *current task*, and is the one to which the facilities of the symbolic debugger may be applied. The selection of the current task may be explicit, or it may result from the occurrence of either a statement level breakpoint or a specified ITE within a task.

Mechanism of replay

When carrying out a full replay, the execution of the tasks is commenced from the states which they were in when the previous snapshot was taken. The replay of the tasks is then driven by the contents of the combined trace in the following way. Initially, the first ITE is taken from the combined trace, and the task which gave rise to that ITE during trace collection is then run until the next ITE occurs in it. A check is made to ensure that the newly arisen ITE corresponds to the one taken from the combined trace, and then the next ITE is taken from the trace, the corresponding task is run, and so on. It should be noted that although the tasks are replayed on the target machines, no actual parallel execution is involved.

If a statement level breakpoint or specified ITE occurs during the replay of a particular task, then the whole replay is halted. That particular task becomes the current task (if it was not already so), and the facilities of the symbolic debugger can be applied to it.

The implementation of statement-level single-stepping by the debugger is made more difficult because of the presence of statements which give rise to ITEs. It has already been stated that the normal execution mechanism for replay always selects the next ITE from the trace and runs the corresponding task. Whilst the user is single-stepping through the statements of a task it is possible to single-step the execution of a statement which gives rise to a particular ITE such that there were other ITEs in other tasks which should have arisen before that one. Although this might not always be significant, in some cases it can change the behaviour of the replayed program in important ways. For example, consider the case of single-stepping through a conditional entry call. It may be that the conditional entry call fails because the called task is apparently not waiting at an accept statement associated with the particular entry. However, it may also be that one of the ITEs which should have arisen previously would have signalled the readiness of the called task to accept the entry call, hence implying that the conditional entry call should have succeeded.

There are three possible ways to approach the problem of single-stepping statements which give rise to ITEs:

- to forbid the single-stepping of such statements, at least in those cases where preceding ITEs should have arisen. The consequent need to return to the ITE level in order to arrange for the preceding ITEs to be cleared would almost certainly be an impediment to the debugging process.
- to detect the single-stepping of such statements, and temporarily suspend the single-stepping whilst other tasks are allowed to catch up. Given this approach, it might well prove to be desirable to ignore breakpoints in the other tasks while they are catching up, otherwise the

single-stepping could become very complicated from the user's point of view. The disadvantage of this is that potentially important breakpoints would be ignored.

- to allow the user to single step such statements, but to warn them beforehand that single-stepping a particular statement would cause the trace to be invalidated (see below).

Another issue which needs to be considered concerns what changes, if any, the user should be allowed to make to the tasks and ITEs during replay. It is not immediately obvious whether the user should be allowed to change the values in a task's variables using the symbolic debugger. It is equally uncertain whether the user should be allowed to manipulate the ITEs by, for example, changing the values of particular attributes. In either case there would be a danger that the change which was made would affect the way in which the tasks interacted, thus invalidating the remainder of the ITE trace. Since the user would be investigating a trace which contained an erroneous sequence of ITEs, any change which they made to remedy the underlying algorithmic cause of the erroneous sequence would *ipso facto* invalidate the rest of the ITE trace. However, disallowing such changes would preclude the commonly employed debugging technique of altering a value and then allowing execution to proceed in order to check that the change which was made led to the correct behaviour of the program. The only alternative available to the user would be to edit the source, re-compile, re-load, and rerun the program, monitoring its execution again if it still failed to work properly. This would obviously not be a very satisfactory method.

If the user is to be allowed to make alterations to task states and ITEs then it is necessary to allow execution of a program to continue after the trace has been invalidated. As such execution can obviously not be driven from the trace, the only alternative is to allow 'live' execution of the program to be resumed. This execution could itself be monitored for subsequent replay.

The point at which the invalidation of the trace becomes apparent will depend upon the type of alteration which has caused the invalidation. If the alteration was to an ITE then the trace automatically becomes invalidated straight away, but if the alteration was to a task's state then it is not necessarily the case that the trace will be invalidated at all. In the latter case the invalidation of the trace will only become apparent when a subsequent ITE which arises from the replayed system is found not to match the corresponding ITE from the trace.

The resumption of live running of the tasks following the invalidation of the trace is a simple matter of sending an appropriate start-up message to each of the target machines. However, since the individual tasks are only synchronized at the ITE level (and not at the statement level) during replay, this (taken together with the inevitably non-synchronous start-up of the target machines) may limit the usefulness of the subsequent live running.

Interrupts

An area of the trace-replay mechanism which requires careful consideration is the way in which interrupts are to be handled. It is quite straightforward to record ITEs representing an interrupt and the corresponding 'accept' by an interrupt handler, but that alone is not sufficient. It is also necessary to record ITEs representing the accesses to device registers made from within an interrupt handler; particularly so when values are being *read* from the registers.

In order that accesses to device registers may be recorded, they must be easily identifiable. This can be achieved by adopting the approach recommended by Hibbard *et al.* (Hibbard 1981): that device registers are accessed only through the SEND__CONTROL and RECEIVE__CONTROL procedures of the package LOW__LEVEL__I/O and not by associating device registers with variables using address clauses. It can be arranged that the SEND__CONTROL and RECEIVE__CONTROL procedures make calls to appropriate routines in the run-time kernel which record ITEs containing the values read from or written to specific device registers.

Having considered the way in which interrupts are handled during monitoring, we now turn our attention to the way they are handled during replay. When replaying a program, further interrupts are disabled; all the interrupt-related ITEs are generated from the trace. Reads from device registers actually pick up the appropriate values from the corresponding ITEs in the trace, whilst writes to device registers have no effect at all.

Whilst it is the case that, during replay, interrupt ITEs will occur in the same order relative to other ITEs as they did during monitoring, they will be unlikely to occur at the same point relative to the execution of the individual statements of the tasks within the program. On first consideration, this may appear to limit considerably the usefulness of the trace-replay approach for the debugging of interrupt-related errors. However, such errors generally concern accesses to variables which are shared between interrupt handlers and other tasks; since accesses to such shared variables can be recorded (see next section), synchronization at the ITE level is actually sufficient in most cases.

Shared variables
Another area of the trace-replay mechanism which requires careful consideration is the way in which shared variables are to be dealt with. The main difficulty here is in trying to identify those variables in an **ada** program which are intended to be shared; this is quite difficult unless a given variable also happens to be specified as the argument of a 'shared' pragma. In order that shared variable access ITEs can be recorded, it is necessary to arrange for shared variable accesses to be carried out by calls to a routine in the run-time kernel.

We contend that the shared variable is not intended to be the primary means of inter-task communication in **ada**, and that where shared variables really are required they should be encapsulated within separate tasks in order to guarantee exclusive access to them. If such an approach can be assumed then the explicit recording of shared variable access ITEs becomes unnecessary. However, if 'free-standing' shared variables are used then we must accept that it may be difficult to record accesses to them.

Debugging approaches

The facilities which have been described so far can be used to implement a number of different approaches to the debugging of distributed **ada** programs. It is our intention to give a range of debugging methods which provide varying amounts of information, whilst disturbing the behaviour of the monitored program to different degrees. In general, the more information which a particular method provides, the greater will be the disturbance to the monitored program. The user can try to find a happy medium in any particular case between trying to maximize the amount of useful debugging information which is made available, and disturbing the behaviour of their program to such an extent that the sought bug disappears. It is realized that this strategy relies on the assumption that the particular bug under investigation can be made to manifest itself reasonably frequently. Some of the possible debugging methods are outlined below:

- single trace collection without snapshot: when the program is halted, for whatever reason, the trace which has been collected may be browsed or used to drive an event level replay. Whether the trace is collected on a one-off basis or cyclically, this method has the least effect on the behaviour of the monitored program.
- repeated trace collection without snapshots: when a buffer full of ITEs has been collected, the program is halted so that the trace may be browsed or used to drive an event level replay. The program may then be restarted to collect another trace which can then be browsed or replayed, and so on. The need to halt the monitored program to allow browsing or event level replay to take place means that this method is more likely to affect the behaviour of the program.
- single snapshot and trace: the collection of a single snapshot followed by a trace has a fairly minimal effect on program behaviour because the program is only halted once so that the snapshot may be taken. The resulting snapshot and trace may be used for trace browsing, event level replay, or full replay.
- single cyclic snapshot and trace (taking a new snapshot every time the ITE trace buffer becomes full): as the program has to be halted whenever a snapshot is to be taken, the effect of this method on the behaviour of the program increases with the number of cycles of snapshot and trace which take place. When the program is finally halted, for whatever reason, the most recent snapshot and trace may be used for trace browsing, event level replay, or full replay.
- repeated snapshot and trace: this involves collecting a snapshot followed by a trace, halting the program whilst the trace is used to drive a full replay, restarting the program to collect another snapshot and trace, and so on. The more often this cycle is repeated, the greater will be its effect on the behaviour of the program. Of course, the traces may also be used for browsing or for event level replay.

Related work

This section outlines other work, related to our own, which has been reported in the literature. The related work has considered various aspects of the monitor-based debugging of distributed multiprocess systems. We divide the related work into two categories, which are considered below: that which has used monitoring of system behaviour to collect a trace for subsequent use; and that which has used monitoring to investigate the behaviour of live systems. Most of this work has concentrated on the message-passing model of inter-process communication, and much of it has not restricted itself to the consideration of any one particular programming language.

Monitoring for trace collection

The work within this category can be subdivided into that which has specifically considered the types of event which should be recorded in a trace; that which has used a trace to produce a static display of program behaviour; that which has investigated the use of traces to drive system replays; that which has investigated the use of traces as a basis for answering queries regarding system execution; and that which has investigated the use of traces as a form of input to a knowledge-based fault localization system. These subcategories are considered below.

Types of event
This work has given consideration to the types of event which need to be recorded in order to provide the required information for subsequent use.

Fairley (1978) appreciated that the collection of large amounts of information in a trace is expensive in terms of both time and space, and that the more information that is collected the harder it is for a user to find the information they require. Hence, he aimed to restrict the size of a trace by being fairly selective in the recording of events. He recommends sixteen types of event which should be recorded; these mainly involve the entry into and exit from various programming language constructs, but also concern assignment operations and the values of parameters.

Stankovic (1980) lists various classes of information which would be required in order to debug certain types of errors which can occur in distributed programs. These classes include such things as process creation and termination, the uses of a particular data item, and the communications between processes. He details five actions, including snapshots and tracing, which could be used to record the required information.

Lantz (1982) identifies nine types of information which need to be derived from the data collected by the monitor on **RIG** (Rochester's Intelligent Gateway), a system of multiple processors connected by an Ethernet. These types of information include the state of a process at a given time, the states of system queues, the scheduling sequence, and the messages which are exchanged between processes. Lantz determined that all of this information could be derived from just four, parametrized, types of event recorded by the monitor; these concern the receipt of messages, the scheduling of processes, swapping, and page replacement.

Display
Gordon (1985) describes the **tap** system which generates timing graphs depicting interprocess communications. The user can examine these graphs to discover any communication events which have occurred in an unacceptable order. **tap** generates the timing graphs from a *communication history* collected during program execution; this records details of the processes and

links involved in each communication, and an initial portion of the messages themselves.

Replay

This work has sought to provide a facility for replaying the execution of a program based upon the contents of a trace collected during its original execution. During the replay the user is able to examine the program without disturbing its behaviour.

Some of the earliest work in this area was carried out by Balzer (1969). He developed a system called **exdams** (Extendable Debugging and Monitoring System) which, during program execution, records details of assignments of values to variables and transfers of control in an *execution history*. This can then be used to drive a limited replay of the user program; stepping forwards (or backwards) to the next (previous) assignment of a value to a given variable, at which point it is possible to request to see both the value of any variable and the way in which that value was derived. Balzer's system was strictly limited to working with single process systems, but the idea was extended to multiprocess systems by Hadjioannou (1976). He suggested that the execution history needed to be augmented by including processor identification tags on events, and by recording events representing the initiation, termination, and synchronization of processes.

Curtis and Wittie (1982) describe a system, called **bugnet**, which allows multiple processes, or subsets of such processes, to be monitored and subsequently replayed. Whilst the monitoring of processes evidently involves the taking of snapshots, no mention is made of the way in which the snapshots on different processors are synchronized. The replay mechanism provides some debugging facilities, such as altering the values of variables, but it is not clear whether breakpoints and single-stepping are also facilitated. It is interesting to note that this system is capable of working with multiprocess systems based on rendezvous and remote invocation as well as those based on message passing.

LeBlanc and Mellor-Crummey (1987) consider a trace-replay approach, called Instant Replay, for tightly-coupled distributed systems (they say that the same approach could also be applied to loosely-coupled systems). Whilst this approach is based upon recording the relative order of significant events during execution, it does not require the data associated with all such events to be recorded too. Instead, a version number is maintained for each shared object, and the version number is recorded in place of the object itself. This can achieve a significant saving in the amount of space required to store the trace information. During replay, the values of the shared objects are regenerated by the processes themselves, and the recorded version numbers are used to ensure that accesses to the shared objects by the different processes occur in the correct sequence. LeBlanc and Mellor-Crummey point out that any form of process interaction, such as message passing, can be catered for using this approach since they can all be modelled as operations on shared objects. They also list several other types of event which need to be recorded, concerning such things as the outcomes of nondeterministic selects, and the clock values returned by system calls. Using this approach, it is generally not possible to trace and replay partial systems, but single stepping at the statement level within individual processes is possible. The main drawback of this approach is that it cannot handle real-time programs, largely because of the difficulties of dealing with interrupts.

Query answering
This work has sought to provide a facility for answering queries about the execution of a program, based on a trace of events collected during its execution. The systems which are described provide no mechanisms for relating unexpected behaviour back to algorithmic errors in the individual processes.

Cohen and Carpenter (1977) describe a system which records, in a *Label Trajectory*, details of the assignments of values to variables, the execution of operators (including transfers of control), and the passing of program labels. They provide an *inquiry language* in which the user can phrase questions concerning such things as the maximum value assigned to a given variable, the number of additions which took place between passing a given pair of labels, and the number of times a given expression evaluated to one particular value when another particular expression evaluated to some other value. This system is, however, only designed to work with single process programs.

Snodgrass (1982) allows considerable flexibility in selecting exactly what is to be monitored and what is not. The collected information is viewed as constituting a relational database which can subsequently be queried about the occurrence of arbitrarily complex sequences of events.

Knowledge-based fault localization
Gupta and Seviora (1984) describe the Message Trace Analyzer, a knowledge-based system which examines a message trace collected from a multi-process system, identifies illegal message sequences, and attempts to localize the underlying fault to a particular process. It is apparently left to the user to determine the exact algorithmic problem in that process. The Analyzer incorporates domain knowledge about a large class multiprocess, real-time systems, and system specific knowledge about the processes and messages of the particular system under investigation.

Monitoring for live investigation

The work within this category can be subdivided into that which has addressed the automatic checking of the behaviour of monitored systems, and that which has addressed the interactive debugging of such systems. These subcategories are considered below.

Automatic checking
This work has addressed the recognition of sequences of events as a means of comparing the behaviour of a program against some specified expected behaviour. The comparison of observed and expected behaviours takes place in real time, and the action upon discovering a discrepancy between the two can be to invoke a symbolic debugger.

Baiardi *et al.* (1983, 1986) work with the CSP-based language 'MuTeam'. The expected behaviour of a program is specified in terms of the expected behaviour of its individual constituent processes. The specification of the expected behaviour of an individual process is contained in a *behaviour specification* which consists of an ordering on sequences of primitive events occurring in that process, and sets of assertions to be checked when a given sequence has been recognized. If these assertions fail, then the user is given the option of aborting the program, changing the values of variables, or resuming execution from another instruction. An interesting mechanism introduced by this work is the DELAY clause which can be used to suspend specific processes when necessary in order that the timing behaviour of the program as a whole is not affected by the imposition of the checking mechanism.

Bates and Wileden, (Bates and Wileden, 1982 and 1983; Bates *et al.*, 1983) specify the expected behaviour of a program using the *event definition language* which allows sequences of primitive events to be considered as higher level events which can themselves be combined to form further events. This enables various levels of abstraction of program behaviour to be built up as required. It is also possible to apply *filtering* in order to restrict the recognition of particular events to specific circumstances.

Bruegge and Hibbard (1983), specify the expected behaviour of Pascal programs using *path rules*, a development of the path expressions which were originally devised to express the synchronization of concurrent processes. Their work considers program behaviour at a comparatively high level of abstraction; their specifications are in terms of statements within the program rather than events representing such things as inter-process communication. No mention is made of the extent to which the imposition of the mechanism affects the timing behaviour of a program.

Interactive debugging

This work has sought to use monitoring as the basis for interacting with the live execution of programs.

Smith, 1981, monitors systems of loosely-coupled processes by recording details of the various stages involved in the movement of messages between processes. This system does not encounter problems arising from the arbitrary suspension of processes whilst the user intervenes, simply because it works with only a single target machine (i.e. it does not support distributed programs). The system allows limited inspection of the variables within a process, but provides no other debugging facilities at the statement level. It is interesting to note that the user is allowed to create and alter messages. The system apparently facilitates a limited trace and replay; the replay is restricted to the event level, and does not involve the execution of the processes within the program.

Garcia-Molina, Germano and Kohler, 1984, suggest that multiprocess debugging should proceed in two stages: the first stage is to monitor the multiprocess system in an effort to discover which processes are giving rise to the observed error, and the second stage is to construct an artificial environment in which those processes can be run again in order that conventional debugging techniques may be applied. The second stage relies upon the use of software signals to achieve synchronous suspension and resumption of processes running on different processors.

Schiffenbauer, 1981, describes a system which is primarily intended to provide the user with the means of experimenting with the behaviour of their program under various conditions; hence it places great emphasis on allowing the user to manipulate events. In particular, the user is given the opportunity to manipulate every message sent by every process. The manipulation of a message can take the form of allowing it to proceed, delaying it, discarding it, or altering its contents. The system runs on a network of Altos in which one machine is dedicated to controlling the messages moving around the rest of the system, and to providing interaction with the user. The system relies upon an ability to suspend processes when necessary to compensate for delays caused by the intervention of the monitoring system. One command which the user can issue to this system requests that a symbolic debugger process be started up on one of the other machines, but the actual extent to which the symbolic debugger is integrated with the overall mechanism of message control is unclear.

Gait, 1985, describes the **CBUG** debugger which can be applied to programs written in a concurrent implementation of the **C** language. Apart from providing the usual symbolic debugging facilities, **CBUG** can monitor interprocess activities and provides single stepping at the granularity of interprocess communication (via shared memory) or synchronization points. Gait intends to provide a version of **CBUG** which will run in a multiprocessor environment where the communications will be based on message passing.

Helmbold and Luckham, 1985, apply live monitoring to multi-task **ada** programs to detect *deadness* errors and *task sequencing* errors. Upon detection of such an error, various debugging information is printed relating to the tasking state of the program as a whole. Their approach also permits stepping through arbitrary numbers of events, printing snapshots of task states upon halting. It is not clear whether this work has been applied to truly distributed programs.

Fainter and Lindquist, 1986, utilize a three tier approach to debugging **ada** programs with a system called **adaTAD**. The first tier of the approach involves the conventional investigation of logical errors within individual tasks considered in isolation. The second tier involves the, monitor-based, investigation of interactions between tasks through rendezvous and synchronized access to shared data. This tier employs a pictorial display of the interaction statuses of the tasks in a system, depicting task run-states, entry calls and rendezvous. The third tier of the approach concerns the investigation of application-specific errors of task interaction; these include subtle timing problems. The facilities of this tier are mainly an extension of those of the second tier; the extra facilities include the collection of frequency counts relating to statement execution, entry calls, and accepts. Fainter and Lindquist acknowledge that this system, since it works with live tasks, will alter the behaviour of the program under investigation to some extent.

Summary

In this paper we have presented a methodology for the design of distributed **ada** programs, and we have discussed the design of a debugger which can be applied to such programs. The debugging mechanism is based upon the collection of snapshots and traces during the execution of a user program, and the subsequent use of such information in a number of ways, ranging from the simple browsing of a trace to the full reply of the user program on the target machines. Given such a range of approaches, the user is able to select, for debugging a given program, the particular approach which provides the maximum amount of debugging assistance possible without significantly disturbing the behaviour of the program.

Whilst we have concentrated on the design and debugging of distributed programs written in **ada**, the approaches which we have presented are generally applicable to distributed programs written in other imperative languages; the main area of language dependence being the types of ITE (or, more generally, Inter-*Process* Event) which are appropriate.

Table 4.1

Ada Inter-Task Events	
ITE	Description
TASK_CREATED	the task has been created by elaboration or by an allocator
START_ACTIVATION	the task has started its activation
ACTIVATION_COMPLETE	the task has finished its activation
TASK_COMPLETED	the task has completed
TASK_TERMINATED	the task has terminated
ACTIVATE_TASKS	the task is activating dependent tasks
ACTIVATE_TASKS_COMPLETE	the activation of the dependent tasks has finished
WAIT_FOR_DEP_TASKS	the task is waiting for its dependent tasks to terminate
DEP_TASK_TERMINATED	a dependent task has terminated
WAIT_FOR_DEP_TASKS_COMPLETE	all dependent tasks have terminated
DELAY_STATEMENT	the task has executed a delay statement
DELAY_TIMEOUT	the delay on which a task is waiting has expired
ENTRY_CALL_STATEMENT	the task has encountered an entry call statement
CONDITIONAL_ENTRY_CALL	the task has encountered a conditional entry call
TIMED_ENTRY_CALL	the task has encountered a timed entry call
COMMENCE_ENTRY_CALL	the (calling) task has commenced a rendezvous
ENTRY_CALL_COMPLETE	the (calling) task has finished a rendezvous
ACCEPT_STATEMENT	the task has encountered an accept statement
SELECTIVE_WAIT	the task has encountered a selective wait statement
ACCEPT_ENTRY_CALL	the (accepting) task has commenced a rendezvous
ACCEPT_ENTRY_CALL_COMPLETE	the (accepting) task has finished a rendezvous
ENTRY_COUNT	the number of calls queued on a task's entry has been requested
ABORT_STATEMENT	the task has aborted other tasks
TASK_ABORTED	the task has been aborted
EXCEPTION	an exception has been raised in the task
INTERRUPT	an interrupt has been raised
READ_DEVICE_REGISTER	the task has read from a device register
WRITE_DEVICE_REGISTER	the task has written to a device register
COMMENCE_SV_ACCESS	the task has commenced a shared variable access
SV_ACCESS_COMPLETE	the shared variable access has finished
CALL_RP	the task has called a remote procedure
RP_READY	the remote procedure is ready to execute
RP_COMPLETE	the execution of the remote procedure has finished
RETURN_FROM_RP	the remote procedure call has returned
START_TASK	the task has been scheduled
SUSPEND_TASK	the task has been suspended

Appendix: ada inter-task events

Table 4.1 summarizes the types of ITE which we have identified as being of
relevance when considering **ada** programs. We assume that the reader has a
detailed knowledge of **ada** task states and the transitions between them
(Burns *et al.*, 1987a). A full specification of these types of ITE, along with a
formal specification, written in **Z** (Sufrin *et al.*, 1985), of a prototype trace-
replay debugging system can be found in a previous document by Snowden
(1987).

References

Baiardi, F., De Francesco, N., Matteoli, E., Stefanini, S. and Vaglini, G. (1983) Development of
a debugger for a concurrent language. *SIGPLAN Notices* **18**(8), 98–106
Baiardi, F., De Francesco, N. and Vaglini, G. (1986) Development of a debugger for a
concurrent language. *IEEE Transactions on Software Engineering*, **12**(4), 547–553
Balzer, R. M. (1969) EXDAMS – extendable debugging and monitoring system. In *Proceedings AFIPS*, pp. 567–580
Bates, P. C. and Wileden, J. C. (1982) EDL: a basis for distributed system debugging tools. In
Proceedings Fifteenth Hawaii International Conference on System Sciences, 86–93.
Bates, P. C. and Wileden, J. C. (1983) An approach to high-level debugging of distributed
systems. *SIGPLAN Notices* **18**(8), 107–111
Bates, P. C., Wileden, J. C. and Lesser, V. R. ((1983) A debugging tool for distributed systems.
Proceedings Second Annual Phoenix Conference on Computers and Communications.
pp. 311–315
Birrell, A. D. and Nelson, B. J. (1984) Implementing remote procedure calls, *ACM Transactions on Computer Systems* **2**(1), 39–59
Bruegge, B. and Hibbard, P. (1983) Generalized path expressions: a high level debugging
mechanism. *SIGPLAN Notices* **18**(8), 34–44
Burns, A., Lister, A. M. and Wellings, A. J. (1987a) *A Review of ADA Tasking*, Lecture Notes in
Computer Science, Volume 262, Springer-Verlag, Berlin
Burns, A., Lister, A. M. and Wellings, A. J. (1987b) Ada Tasking Implementation Issues. *Ada User* **8**(2), 30–39
Cohen, J. and Carpenter, N. (1977) A language for inquiring about the run-time behaviour of
programs. *Software Practice and Experience* **7**(4), 445–460
Curtis, R. and Wittie, L. (1982) BugNet: a debugging system for parallel programming
environments. *Proceedings IEEE Third International Conference on Distributed Computing Systems*, October, pp. 394–399
Fainter, R. G. and Lindquist, T. E. (1986) Debugging Tasks with AdaTAD. *Proceedings of
First International Conference on Ada Programming Language Applications for the NASA
Space Station*, June, Houston
Fairley, R. E. (1978) Static analysis and dynamic testing of computer software. *IEEE Computer* **11**(4), 14–23
Gait, J. (1985) A debugger for concurrent programs. *Software Practice and Experience* **15**(6), 539–554
Garcia-Molina, H., Germano, F. Jr. and Kohler, W. H. (1984) Debugging a distributed
computing system. *IEEE Transactions on Software Engineering*, **10**(2), 210–219
Gordon, A. J. (1985) Ordering errors in distributed programs. Technical Report #611,
Computer Sciences Department, University of Wisconsin, Madison, USA, August
Gupta, N. K. and Seviora, R. E. (1984) Knowledge based message trace analyzer. *Proceedings
Real-Time Systems Symposium*, Austin, Texas
Hadjioannou, M. (1976) Debugging of parallel programs. In *Proceedings of Ninth Hawaii
International Conference on System Sciences*, January, pp. 20–22

Harrison, M. D. (1985) Monitoring a target network to support subsequent host simulation. *Journal of Microcomputer Applications*, **8**, 75–85

Helmbold, D. and Luckham, D. (1985) Debugging Ada tasking programs. *IEEE Software* **2**(2), 47–57

Hibbard, P., Hisgen, A., Rosemberg, J. and Sheiman, M. (1981) Programming in Ada: examples. In *Studies in Ada Style*, Springer-Verlag, Berlin

Hitchcock, P. (ed.) (1989) *ASPECT: An Integrated Project Support Environment*, MIT Press, Cambridge, Massachusetts

Hutcheon, A. D. and Wellings, A. J. (1989a) The virtual node approach to designing distributed Ada programs. *Ada User* **10**(1)

Hutcheon, A. D. and Wellings, A. J. (1989b) Distributed embedded computer systems in Ada – an approach and experience. In *Hardware and Software for Real Time Process Control, Proceedings of the IFIP WG 5.4/IFAC/EWICS Working Conference*, (eds J. Zalewski and W. Ehrenberger), North Holland, pp. 55–64

Hutcheon, A. D., Snowden, D. S. and Wellings, A. J. (1989) Programming and debugging distributed target systems. In *ASPECT: An Integrated Project Support Environment*, (ed. P. Hitchcock), MIT Press, Cambridge, Massachusetts

Keeffe, D., Tomlinson, G. M., Wand, I. C. and Wellings, A. J. (1985) *PULSE: An Ada-based Distributed Operating System*, APIC Studies in Data Processing Series, Academic Press, London

Lamport, L. (1978) Time, clocks, and the ordering of events in a distributed system. *Communications of the ACM*, **21**(7), 558–565

Lantz, K. A. (1982) Rochester's intelligent gateway. *IEEE Computer* **15**(10), 54–68

LeBlanc, T. J. and Mellor-Crummey, J. M. (1987) Debugging parallel programs with instant replay. *IEEE Transactions on Computers* **36**(4), 471–482

Liskov, B. and Scheifler, R. (1983) Guardians and actions: linguistic support for robust, distributed programs. *ACM Transactions on Programming Languages and Systems* **5**(3), 381–404

Schiffenbauer, R. D. (1981) Interactive debugging in a distributed computational environment. Technical Report MIT/LCS/TR-264, Laboratory for Computer Science, Massachusetts Institute of Technology, Cambridge, Massachusetts, September

Sloman, M., Magee, J. and Kramer, J. (1984) Building flexible distributed systems in Conic. In *Distributed Computing Systems Programme*, (ed. D. A. Duce), Peter Peregrinus, Stevenage

Smith, E. T. (1981) Debugging techniques for communicating, loosely-coupled processes. Report No. TR 100, Department of Computer Science, University of Rochester, New York, USA, December

Snodgrass, R. (1982) Monitoring distributed systems: a relational approach. Report CMU-CS-82-154, Department of Computer Science, Carnegie-Mellon University, Pittsburgh, USA

Snowden, D. S. (1987) Specification of a trace-replay system for Ada programs. Aspect Document wb/pub/dds/dss1, Department of Computer Science, University of York, York, UK, January

Stankovic, J. A. (1980) Debugging commands for a distributed processing system. *Proceedings of The IEEE Fall COMPCON*, pp. 701–705

Sufrin, B., Morgan, C., Sorensen, I. and Hayes, I. (1985) *Notes for a Z Handbook Part 1 – Mathematical Language*, Oxford University Computing Laboratory, Programming Research Group, Oxford, UK, July

Wellings, A. J. (1987) Issues in distributed processing – session summary. Proceedings of the International Workshop on Real-Time Ada Issues, October, *ACM Ada Letters* **7**(6), 57–60

Chapter 5

Reliable systems in occam

H. S. M. Zedan

In this chapter we propose a scheme to support error recovery in the programming language **occam**. The scheme is based on structuring the concurrent **occam** program into a set of communication-closed layers ('layer' for short) which are then run sequentially. (Note that for every concurrent **occam** program there exists an 'equivalent' quasi-sequential one).

Each layer is in fact a 'basic' atomic action. To achieve consistency, each layer is made recoverable. A recovery scheme is proposed and incorporated into the layered structure of the system.

Introduction

Distributed computer systems have increasingly become a versatile and an important area of research. This interest has been motivated not only by the many challenging problems in the field but also due to the ever-falling cost of microprocessors which allow building these systems more economically.

Furthermore, these systems offer the potential to develop decentralized operating systems which support highly concurrent and 'reliable computation' which is needed in many applications such as large scale distributed real-time control systems. This gives rise to the need for the development of provably 'consistent' and correct concurrency control and failure recovery mechanisms. Concurrency control mechanisms must ensure the consistency and correctness of concurrent execution of a system.

By 'system consistency' we mean that systems must function reliably despite any software or hardware failures. Hence failure 'recovery' mechanisms must be able to maintain the consistency and correctness of concurrency control in the face of system failures.

An appropriate environment for the design of a fault-tolerant system must be provided. We believe that issues related to the development of such systems must be properly addressed by the semantics of the (concurrent) language: The semantics should be such that the events and constructs relative to fault treatment are naturally included in the general cooperation of events and constructs.

Many existing programming languages have considered error recovery in some form. **ada, CLU** (Liskov and Snyder, 1979) **mesa,** and **ECSP** (Baiardi

* Earlier version of parts of this paper was published in *Microprocessing and Microprogramming* **23** (1988).

et al., 1984) have considered forward error recovery in the form of exception handling. **argus** (Liskov and Scheifler, 1983) and **ECSP** have proposed backward error recovery facilities.

The provision of both backward and forward error recovery within the same concurrent programming language remains a problem. Recently an attempt was made (Jalot and Campbell, 1986), to resolve this problem within the semantics of **CSP**.

In this chapter we propose a scheme to support error recovery in the programming language **occam** (**occam** programming manual, 1984). The scheme is based on structuring the concurrent **occam** program into a set of *communication-closed* layers ('layers' for short) which are then run sequentially. (Note that for each concurrent **occam** program *there exists one*). Each layer is in fact a 'simple' atomic action. Using this technique it is possible to achieve consistency by making each layer recoverable. Furthermore, it allows flexibility in adopting the various recovery schemes.

A recovery scheme to support both forward and backward error recovery in a unified manner is proposed. The scheme is then incorporated within the layered structure of the system.

The chapter is organized as follows. In the first section we provide a brief introduction to the computational model of **occam** and then give an outline to the layer model which is based on Zedan (1985). The utilization of the layer structure to achieve atomicity in **occam's** system is also described. We then present a failure model in **occam** and give our principles of error recovery which are incorporated in the system's overall structure. Linguistic support for both forward and backward error recovery in a given layer is outlined in the final section.

Actions in occam

The increasing demand for reliable systems has resulted in the development of techniques and mechanisms for the design of 'fault-tolerance' software systems.

In any software system, errors may occur at any level. Some errors are machine dependent and should be masked from the application level. Others are purely application dependent and should be dealt with at the application level. In this study we concentrate on application level errors.

It has been realized that fault-tolerance facilities for concurrent systems are complicated by the possibility of communicating erroneous information and the need to coordinate processes which are engaged in the recovery. Hence, additional structure for communication and synchronization is needed.

Generally, in system recovery, it is required that the error be detected, identified and then dealt with by any appropriate error recovery technique. Because of the delay between the erroneous behaviour of the system (caused by the fault) and the detection of the error, the damage may very well spread through the system. Therefore it is essential to assess the extent of the damage due to the fault. The assessment of the damage depends on the way that the system is structured. The concept of atomic action plays an important role in providing a useful system structure for error recovery techniques.

In the present work we view atomic actions as basic atomic actions (Jalot and Campbell, 1986). A basic atomic action is an action where indivisibility is the only requirement of atomicity. It is also a planned action in the sense that its boundary is statically defined. In this section we show how basic atomic action can be achieved in **occam**. To begin with, however, a brief overview of the **occam**'s model of computation is in order.

The occam model

The programming language **occam** is a strongly typed and highly structured concurrent language. **occam** was principally designed for the microprocessor known as the **transputer**.* The language follows the ideas presented in Hoare's CSP very closely (Hoare, 1985). It is particularly suited for a loosely coupled environment and an efficient implementation of it on a multiprocessor computer is also possible. Fundamental to its design was the idea that the language should have close ties with formal methods of designing and verifying programs.

occam is based on two basic concepts: **PROC**esses amd **CHAN**nels. The process is the main building block and communication between processes (or the outside world) is via channels (Figure 5.1).

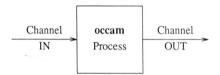

Figure **5.1** An **occam** process

An **occam** process starts, executes and then terminates. The process structure is semi-static (i.e. processes are defined at any level of the program text and are created implicitly when the corresponding level is entered.) The number of extant processes is determined at compile-time.

The 'core' of **occam** mainly consists of four primitive processes: The assignment process, $:=$, the output process, !, the input process, ?, and the null process, **SKIP**. Other processes can be constructed from these primitive processes as follows: Let S_1 and S_2 be two primitive processes:

(1) Sequential processes:

> **SEQ**
> S_1
> S_2

(The execution of S_1 followed by the execution of S_2. The whole process terminates upon the termination of S_2.)

(2) Concurrent processes:

> **PAR**
> S_1
> S_2

---

* **occam** and **transputer** are both trade marks of Inmos PLC.

(The execution of processes S_1 and S_2 is performed concurrently. The whole process terminates only when both processes terminate.)

(3)   Choices processes:

(3.1) Deterministic:

IF

    g_1

       P_1

    g_2

       P_2

    .

    .

    .

    g_n

       P_n

(The guarded process, g_i, is a Boolean expression while P_i is any other process. P_i is executed only if its guard is passable and then the whole process terminates. If none of the guards were passable the whole process does not terminate.)

(3.2) Non-deterministic:

ALT

    g_1

       P_1

    g_2

       P_2

    .

    .

    .

    g_n

       P_n

(The guarded process is either an input process and/or Boolean expression or Boolean expression and the null process. If more than one guard is passable then the choice between their corresponding processes is undefined.)

Other processes such as loops are also available in the language. **occam** supports nesting of parallel commands. Thus an **occam** program has a hierarchical parallel structure which aids the implementation of the required degree of modularity and parallelism. For more detail we refer the reader to the **occam** programming manual, 1984.

The layer model

A distributed **occam** application is viewed as a set of sequential processes which are communicating together in order to provide a service. Let p_1, $p_2, \ldots, p_N$ be N communicating processes such that p_i is of the form:

  p_i ::

        SEQ

         S_1^i

         S_2^i

         .

         .

         S_k^i

S_j^i is any program segment. The application program P will take the form:

P ::

    PAR

        p_1

        p_2 (1)

        .

        .

        .

        p_N

The components (threads) of P (i.e p_1, p_2), communicate via a set of predeclared channels. The decomposition (1) above is called 'distributed decomposition'. Let us further consider the following parallel programs:

L_j ::

    PAR

        $S_j'^1$

        $S_j'^2$

        .

        .

        .

        $S_j'^N$

Note that $S_j'^i$ is either the null process **SKIP**, or S_j^i.

Let us define a 'communication-closed' layer to be a layer which does not contain an I/O command whose matching (corresponding) I/O command belongs to a different layer. A communication-closed layer may be represented as a 'cut' in the time-diagram of the application. Horizontal lines represent the time axis of the processes (involved in the application) and arrows represent communication from a sender to a receiver process. A cut divides the time-diagram into two halves (or layers). A communication-closed layer is such that no arrow starts on the right-hand side of the cut and ends on the left-hand side of it (Figure 5.2).

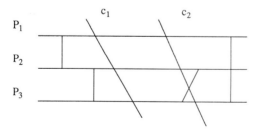

Figure 5.2 An application of three processes. c_1 forms a communication-closed layer. c_2 does not form a communication-closed layer

Furthermore, consider the new layered (quasi-) sequential application P' which corresponds to the distributed application P in (1):

P'::

$$\textbf{SEQ } i = [\,1 \textbf{ FOR } k \,] \tag{2}$$
$$L_i$$

The program in Figure 5.2 is said to be a 'sequential decomposition'. However, the question that needs to be addressed now is: under what condition(s) are the distributed decomposition (program (1)) and the sequential decomposition (program (2)) semantically equivalent?

To address this question, let us make some more definitions: The sequential decomposition (2) is said to be safe if and only if all its layers are communication closed. (Intuitively, a sequential and distributed decomposition is semantically equivalent if and only if the sequential decomposition is safe.) We should note here that if the distributed decomposition P is a real-time application, then the relation 'semantic equivalency' does not guarantee a 'safe' sequential decomposition. Stronger conditions to guarantee safe decomposition of these types of applications, have been established (Zedan, 1988).

Using the **SKIP** process in **occam**, we can easily construct a safe decomposition as illustrated in the following example.

Example (1)
Consider the distributed program Q:

Q ::

    PAR
      Q_1
      Q_2 (3)
      Q_3

where

  Q_1 ::

    SEQ
      { Q_1 : Non I/O segment }

      .
      .

      $C_1 ! M_1$
      .
      .

      { Q_1 : Non I/O segment }
      .
      .

      $C_3 ? Z$

  Q_2 ::

    SEQ
      $C_1 ? X$
      .

      .
      {Q_2 : Non I/O segment}
      .

      .
      $C_2 ! M_2$

Q_3 ::

SEQ

.

.

{Q_3 : Non I/O segment}

.

.

C_2 ? Y

.

.

.

{Q_3 : Non I/O segment}

.

.

C_3 ! M_3

and C_1, C_2, and C_3 are three pre-declared **occam** channels. The following layers are easily constructed:

L_1 ::

PAR
{Q_1 : Non I/O segment}
SKIP
{Q_3 : Non I/O segment}

L_2 ::

PAR
C_1 ! M_1
C_1 ? X
SKIP

L_3 ::

PAR
{Q_1 : Non I/O segment}
{Q_2 : Non I/O segment}
SKIP

L_4 ::

PAR
SKIP
C_2 ! M_2
C_2 ? Y

L_5 ::

PAR
SKIP
SKIP
{Q_3 : Non I/O segment}

L_6 ::

    PAR
      $C_3 ? Z$
      SKIP
      $C_3 ! M_3$

It can be easily verified that each of the above six layers is a communication-closed layer. Thus the distributed program Q can be decomposed into the following

Q ::

    SEQ
      L_1
      L_2
      L_3 (4)
      L_4
      L_5
      L_6

which is clearly a safe decomposition.

The sequential decomposition in the above example is just one of the many possible decompositions that could be constructed. In fact a distributed decomposition of an application program can be looked upon as a sequential decomposition that is composed of a single layer (such decomposition will be referred to as the 'trivial' decomposition). The number of layers in a decomposition is not unique and depends on the designers of the application program. The 'width' of all layers is nevertheless, the same and must be equal to the number of threads in the original distributed decomposition (e.g. N in (1)).

Layers as atomic actions

It has been recognized that 'atomic actions' are an important programming concept. They were first introduced as a means of characterizing programs by their input/output relations, but interest in the concept has increased due to the fact that it can be used to generalize the concept of error recovery in concurrent languages.

Intuitively, an atomic action is a segment of the program that enjoys a simple 'primitive' status with regard to its environment, though it may have a complicated internal processing structure. In shared database systems, atomic actions have been used quite extensively and they are usually called 'transactions'.

Properties of atomic actions have been frequently characterized by the 'serializability' property: An action is atomic if it can be considered, as far as its environment is concerned, to be indivisible and instantaneous. Adopting this view of atomic action allows recoverability in a simple manner.

The layer model presented in the previous section offers a general framework for structuring, building and designing fault-tolerant systems. In fact, with the definition of a communication-closed layer, the structure provides a means to decompose any given distributed system into a set of 'basic' atomic actions. Moreover, as a result of the decomposition, the new sequential system may be looked upon as a 'planned' system which is designed explicitly as a set of 'planned atomic actions'. A planned system is sometimes referred to as an 'atomic system'. (We note here that the layer structure does not allow for what is known as 'spontaneous' atomic actions that arise from the dynamic sequences of events occurring in the system (application).) Because the communication-closedness property of a layer delimits any error propagation caused by interprocess communication, it also supports the idea of error confinement.

Furthermore, layers in a sequential decomposition can be nested to any required degree providing the communication-closedness property is preserved to ensure safety decomposition. The following example shows how such nesting may be achieved:

Example (2)
Let us consider the following layer L (which may be regarded as a part of a given sequential decomposition):

    L::

                    PAR
                    SEQ
                      A
                      α
                      β
                      γ
                    SEQ
                      $\bar{\alpha}$
                      $\bar{\beta}$
                      $\bar{\gamma}$

Where a, β, γ are any I/O processes and $\bar{a}$, $\bar{\beta}$, $\bar{\gamma}$ are their matching I/O processes respectively. A being any non-communicating process(es). Figure 5.3 illustrates the reconstruction of L as nested layers L_1, L_2 and L_3:

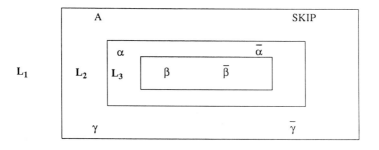

Figure 5.3 Nested layers

L_1::

    PAR
      SEQ
        A
        L_2^1
        γ
      SEQ
        SKIP
        L_2^2
        $\overline{\gamma}$

L_2::

    PAR
      SEQ
        α
        L_3^1
      SEQ
        $\overline{\alpha}$
        L_3^2

L_3::

    PAR
      β
      $\overline{\beta}$

where L_j^i is the ith thread of the jth layer.

Error recovery in the layer structure

In the last section we have shown how an application program written in **occam** can be structured into a set of basic atomic actions which may be nested. We shall now show how such atomic action can be made recoverable.

Failure model in occam

We take the view that an error (or a fault) in the system corresponds to an inconsistent behaviour of a set of processes. It is therefore the responsibility of the language run-time system to support mechanisms that transform any error to an inconsistent behaviour.

An inconsistent behaviour takes, for example, the form of the termination of a process unexpectedly or an erroneous communication attempt. Let us now take the **occam** model of computation and add a failure model upon which an error recovery system may be designed and be incorporated into the layer framework.

(a) Communication
Taking **occams**'s protocol of communication, we may categorize the termination conditions of an I/O process as follows:

(TC1) Successful termination: The I/O process has successfully matched its corresponding process.

(TC2) Failure: The I/O process fails if one of the following conditions occurs

   (a) Its corresponding process has terminated.

   (b) The processor (node) on which its partner process lives has crashed (or the link (channel) between the two processors does not exist).

Note that both (TC1) and (TC2) take into account the two ways of selecting an I/O process for execution; namely deterministic and non-deterministic.

(b) Concurrency
The distributed termination convention which is adopted in **occam** implies that a layer terminates 'successfully' only if all its threads terminate. Unlike ECSP, for example, a thread in a layer terminates (implicitly) upon a 'successful' execution of its body. For a non-communicating layer (i.e. one which does not contain any I/O process) the following termination conditions may be identified:

(TC3) Successful termination: all threads have successfully terminated

(TC4) Failure termination: at least one thread has not terminated. This may be because the thread's processor has crashed, or because abnormal results have occurred. In such situations the whole layer should 'terminate with a failure'.

Principles of error recovery in the layer structure

To begin with, it should be realized that, if successful, provisions for fault-tolerance within a layer are invisible to the rest of the layers. This leads to the encapsulation of such measures in modular components (known here as 'sub-layers').

Second, as pointed out by Campbell and Randell (1983), the specification of a layer is constituted by the relationship between the states at the beginning and termination of the layer.

Let us now assume that an error E has occurred at the layer L_i. A recovery procedure may be informally described as follows. For each layer there is what we call a 'layer__handler'. (A layer__handler acts as a local handler for the given layer.) An attempt will be made to correct E through software which is available to the local handler H_i. If this attempt is successful, then the computation is resumed at layer L_{i+1}, otherwise the computation is backed up to a previously saved consistent state. However, if a failure occurs after the resumption then the whole application must be aborted (see Figure 5.4 and 5.5).

Furthermore, in the case of nested layers, the following philosophy for error recovery is adopted. Any internal layer should have its own private ('local') handler which deals with any exception raised by any of its threads.

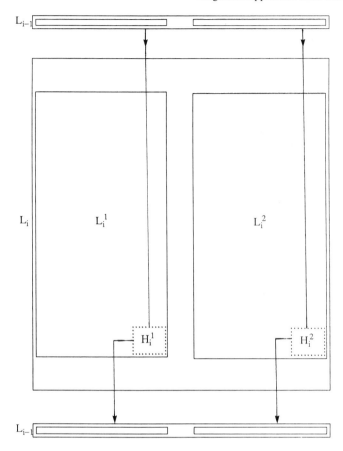

Figure 5.4 Normal activity

If the exception cannot be handled internally, then it should be raised in its containing layer (this will be known as 'layer-failure') and by *all* its threads. However, if different exceptions are raised by more than one thread in a layer and at least one cannot be handled locally a layer-failure should be raised.

Linguistic support for error recovery in occam

It has been a common practice, in writing fault-tolerant software, to classify erroneous situations into 'anticipated' and 'unanticipated' situations. Programming languages provide the user with facilities to cope with anticipated abnormalities e.g. the 'ON FAIL' clause in **ECSP** and 'ON units' in PL1). These techniques are best known as 'forward error recovery' techniques.

'Backward error recovery' is usually adopted for unanticipated situations, so facilities must be provided to enable programmers to employ this technique (e.g. 'OUT' and 'IN' in **ECSP** and volatile and stable parameters in **argus**).

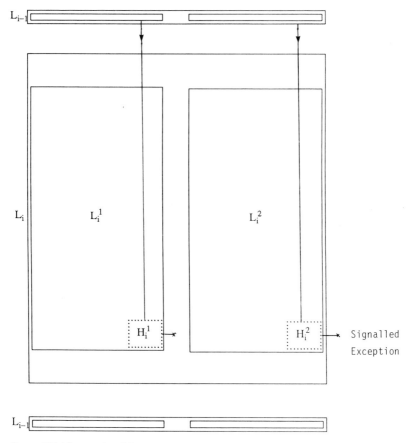

Figure 5.5 Abnormal activity

In order to design and write fault-tolerant **occam** system, each of its layers must be made recoverable. This is achieved by adding linguistic support to the language so that forward and backward error recovery schemes may be adopted.

Forward error recovery

Forward error recovery aims to remove or isolate a specific fault. The fault must be correctly identified and the erroneous state of the system is corrected before proceeding with further processing. In this recovery scheme, a precise and detailed knowledge of the erroneous state is needed (these errors are often called 'anticipated' errors). It has become a common practice to use 'exception handling' mechanisms in dealing with these types of errors. In what follows we propose some language features which provide such a mechanism.

As was mentioned earlier, for a given layer L_i there is a 'local' handler (namely the layer__handler H_i) which is viewed as a sub-layer to L_i and handles all exceptions raised in its layer. For each error, E, there will be an exceptional value, VE, which qualifies E. The VE's are all declared, as a part of the layer declarations (see later), as **EXCEPTION**. If an exception is raised by any process in the given layer then all other processes are notified of the exception and execute its VE. On the other hand, if no exception is raised then the given layer is successfully terminated.

The structure of the layer_handler, **ALT*** takes a form similar to the process **ALT**. Unlike **ALT**, **ALT*** is deterministic:

ALT*
   V.E
      {Action Process}

The Action Process is an **occam** process including the new primitive process **SIGNAL**. **SIGNAL** is a process which indicates the abnormal termination of a layer_handler, and hence a layer, with an exception. The following example illustrates this structure.

Example (3)
A familiar and simple example to illustrate the use of the proposed features is the iterative calculation of factorial. The program is designed as three (communication-closed) layers: 'Inputter' (transmits an integer from one thread to another), 'Calculate' (to calculate the required factorial) and 'Outputter' (to output the results). Each layer has two threads.

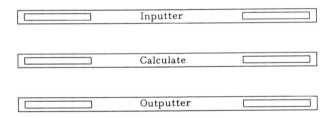

We shall only consider the first layer (Inputter): let us assume that the two threads are connected via a channel 'Input'. Further, we assume that three errors can be anticipated: OverFlow (when the integer value n is greater than say N_{max}), Negative (if $n < 0$) and Fail (due to (TC2) in our failure model above).

```
LAYER Inputter ( Params. list ):
--
-- Declarations
--
EXCEPTION OverFlow, Negative, Fail:
-- Other declarations
--
PAR
   SEQ
      Input ! n
```

```
IF
  n > Nmax
    OverFlow
  n < 0
    Negative
ALT*
  Negative ∨ OverFlow
    Input ! n
  Fail
    SIGNAL
SEQ
  Input ? n
  ALT*
    Negative ∨ OverFlow
      Input ? n
    Fail
      SIGNAL
```

Upon raising an exception, the control goes, with the exception value, to the layer__handler, ALT*, and executes the appropriate Action Process. We choose the retransmission of the value of n for both exceptions Negative and OverFlow. As for the exception Fail, the Action Process is the new **occam** primitive process **SIGNAL**. It is the responsibility of the layer's run-time system and its recovery system to deal with the **SIGNAL** process by aborting the layer. The forward error recovery for the layer terminates after the completion of the Action Process. If, however, the communication of Input was correctly performed and the value of n was such that $0 \leqslant n < N_{max}$ then we say that the layer has been successfully terminated and the control goes to the layer Calculate.

Backward error recovery

Backward error recovery involves backing up the process involved to a previous state which is expected to be error free and then attempting to continue further processing.

Backward error recovery may be incorporated within the layer structure of the application program. Our technique closely follows those adopted in **ECSP**, (Baiardi *et al.*, 1984), and **argus**, (Liskov and Scheifler, 1983).

In our structure, the (static) upper boundary of a layer serves as a natural 'recovery line' for backward error recovery. Thus in case of an error, a mechanism must be established to undo the whole layer with the activation of an alternative method for that particular layer. In order to achieve this mechanism the state of the layer must be saved after it commits. (Note that the saved state acts as a recovery point for the layer.)

The saved state is accomplished by parametrizing the layer itself. The parameters in the layer play a similar role to the formal parameter list in a procedure environment.

```
LAYER name ( {;parameter} )
  body
```

The parameter values in the **LAYER**'s heading are transmitted to their corresponding variables in the appropriate threads of the body. The role of parameter transmission is illustrated in the following example.

Example (4)
Let us consider layer L_6 in Example (1). To employ backward error recovery, the layer takes the form

    LAYER SIX $(Z; ; M_3)$

    --
    -- Declarations
    --

        PAR
            C_3 ? Z -- thread 1
            SKIP -- thread 2
            C_3 ! M_3 -- thread 3

The value of Z is assigned to the variable in thread 1, while the value of M_3 is assigned to the variable in thread 3. Note that the above form is equivalent to

    LAYER SIX $(M_3;Z;)$

    --
    -- Declarations
    --
    PAR
        C_3 ! M_3
        C_3 ? Z
        SKIP

The above assignment of the values is only performed if and when the **PAR** construct has successfully terminated otherwise a retry to the layer is performed from a consistent state. The procedure, therefore, ensures that an update on a layer's state is completed only if the state transition is consistent, otherwise the state is not affected. Furthermore, as the **PAR** construct fails if at least one of its threads fails, the assignment procedure is performed after a consensus decision of all threads. An algorithm such as the one described in Hazari and Zedan (1987), may be used.

Conclusion

The work described in this chapter is aimed at high-level tools for the design of reliable application programs. The relatively new programming language **occam** was chosen for this task.

    A control structure, **LAYER**, was suggested with which an application program was viewed as a set of 'quasi-sequential' communication-closed layers. As the layer is communication-closed, it is considered as a basic atomic action, where indivisibility does not constitute recoverability. This, in fact, gives us great flexibility in employing the various recovery schemes. A failure model in **occam** was studied and a forward error recovery scheme was added by introducing what we called a layer__handler. Parametrization of the layer was introduced to guarantee that an update on a layer state is completed only if the state transition is consistent, otherwise the state is not affected and a new update may be tried. Hence a backward error recovery scheme may be applied.

We are currently implementing the concept of layers and we are also investigating an extended version of the **occam** formal model which includes **LAYERS**.

References

Baiardi, F., Ricci, L., Tomasi, A. and Vanneschi, M. (1984) Structuring Process For a Cooperative Approach to Fault-tolerant Distributed Software. *Proceedings of the Fourth IEEE Symposium on reliability in distributed software and database systems*, pp. 218–230

Campbell, R. H. and Randell, B. (1983) Error recovery in asynchronous systems. Report UIUCDCS-R-83-1148, Department of Computer Science, University of Illinois at Urbana-Champaign USA

Hazari, C. and Zedan, H. (1987) A distributed algorithm for distributed termination. *Information Processing Letters*, **24**, 293–297

Hoare, C. A. R. (1985) *Communicating Sequential Processes*, Prentice-Hall International, Hemel Hempstead

Horning, J., Lauer, H. C., Melliar-Smith, P. M. and Randell, B. (1974) A program structure for error detection and recovery. In *Lecture Notes in Computer Science*, **16**, Springer Verlag, Berlin

Jalot, P. and Campbell, R. H. (1986) Atomic action for fault-tolerance using CSP, *IEEE Transactions in Software Engineering*, **12**, 59–68

Liskov, B. and Snyder, A. (1979) Exception handling in CLU. *IEEE Transactions in Software Engineering* **5**, 546–558

Liskov, B. and Scheifler, R. (1983) Guardians and actions: linguistic support for robust, distributed programs. *ACM TOPLAS*, **5**(3), 381–404

occam programming manual (1984) Prentice-Hall, Englewood Cliffs, New Jersey

Randell, B., Lee, P. A. and Treleaven, P. C. (1978) Reliability issues in computing system design. *ACM Computer Surveys*, **10**(2), 123–165

Shrivastava, S. K. and Banatre, J. P. (1978) Reliable resource allocation between unreliable processes. *IEEE Transactions on Software Engineering* **4**(3)

Zedan, H. (1985) Safe Decomposition of Distributed Programs. *ACM SIGPLAN Notices* **20**(8)

Zedan, H. (1988) On the analysis of **occam** real-time distributed computations, *Microprocessing and Microprogramming*, **24**, 491–500

Chapter 6

The architecture of real-time distributed databases for computer network monitoring

C. H. C. Leung and J. Z. Lu

The architecture of a real-time distributed database system used for computer network management is described. The computer network management system is an integrated system which includes monitoring, administration and control of both local area and wide area communications networks. The monitoring data are collected in real-time by various probes distributed over the network which are used for network control and management. A distributed database system provides a natural solution here because the entire communications network has a number of sites, each having its own collection of data, and effective monitoring requires their integration to form a global picture of the entire network status. The architecture of the resultant distributed database system is an integration of dynamic databases with partitioned data replication, and static databases with sophisticated query processing facilities. In order to meet the performance requirements of real-time databases, a special transaction protocol based on the ISO reference model is adopted. This protocol is able to significantly reduce the time for incorporating distributed updates, and offers substantial improvements in processing speed. The present distributed database architecture, in addition, is able to provide a high degree of resilience and reliability. This is achieved by the use of a novel crash recovery mechanism which is superior to conventional ones; it makes use of network status monitoring information to detect in advance any network failures before the instigation of database transactions.

Introduction

Real-time Distributed Database System (RDDBS) is increasingly essential for a wide variety of applications, such as network monitoring, military command and control, industrial process control, telecommunication and factory automation (Andriopoulos *et al.*, 1985; Moore, 1985). The features and characteristics of real-time distributed database systems are significantly different from most commercial database systems; Among the most critical requirements of RDDBS is system performance in terms of query process- ing, inter-site communication, and transaction concurrency. The techniques and structure used in commercial database systems are not capable of dealing with the problems relating to real-time requirements. As a result, the architecture of real-time distributed database systems needs to be significantly different from conventional ones; the approaches available for achieving the high performance in real-time systems include increasing the data processing speed, the communication speed, the transaction commitment rate, and processing concurrency.

In this paper, a computer network monitoring system is employed to highlight the features and demonstrate a possible architecture of RDDBS. As an application of the RDDBS, the computer network monitoring system collects various network information in real-time from various sensors, called probe servers, in a distributed fashion. It has the characteristics of real-time from data manipulation, non-stop processing of sequential tasks of processes with high query and update rates, high inter-site communication performance, pre-defined query facilities, and good failure resilience. The real-time constraints coupled with the above characteristics are used to determine the design criteria and the architecture of the system. Some of the features of our system consists of: non-blocking pre-commit concurrency control mechanism; low level failure detection based recovery mechanism; high data replication; heterogeneity; and failure detection for system reliability.

The next section describes the requirement of the present RDDBS and the network monitoring environment. The corresponding distributed database model, the schema mapping, together with an example are given in the third section. The concurrency control and revovery mechanisms, and their relationships to the ISO reference model are presented in the final section.

The distributed database architecture in the network monitoring environment

The network monitoring model

Computer network management system consists of three main components: network monitoring, network control and network administration. The central part of the system is network monitoring which has the principal function of collecting network information in real-time from various probes; these probes poke the network components at different layers of OSI model and relay the information back to the data collecting processes (Ma, 1984). The data collection facility, often called probe server, is sensor based and operates in real-time. As network control action is based on the monitoring information, the monitoring data are added and manipulated in real-time at high speed.

The network being monitored consists of six sites, each of which has a satellite terminal and ring-satellite bridge, and communication with each other is via the Orbital Test Satellite. One of the monitoring sites is located at University College London whose local network consists of three Cambridge Rings. The present network monitoring system monitors both Wide Area Network and Local Area Network, and the monitoring activities include network status monitoring, configuration monitoring, performance monitoring and event and fault monitoring. These different types of collected data will need to be managed in real-time and supported with a high degree of reliability, availability and performance; thus a real-time distributed database system provides a natural solution here (Ma, 1984).

The real-time database requirement

The requirements of the present system are significantly different from most commercial database systems (Hughes, 1980; Kopetz, 1981; Andriopoulos *et al.*, 1985; Moore, 1985) and has the following characteristics.

1 Speed

The response time of a real-time distributed database system is critical. In the network monitoring environment, the data collected by various probes will need to be accessed and updated frequently. Particularly during 'system blast' intervals, all types of data, such as error report, events report, status changing report, traffic report will flood into the database at an enormous rate. Any hold up in the functioning of the database manipulating processes will result in loss of data and possible malfunction in the subsequent network control and administration action. The approaches adopted in achieving the required speed comprise fast data manipulating tools, efficient communication protocols, processing parallelism and optimal data distribution.

2 Data type

The network monitoring system includes various activities such as status monitoring, configuration monitoring, performance monitoring, and event and fault monitoring. These collected data are naturally classified into two categories; dynamic data which is rapidly changing and reflects the current world-wide picture of the computer network, and static data which is relatively inactive and has a low update frequency. The dynamic data are those collected, updated, and accessed in real-time; they consist of current network topologies, throughput data, status data, events data, error data and so on. The amount of dynamic data is relatively small, however, but their storage requirement is highly variable, because of the possibility of data explosion during network blast. The queries of the dynamic data are pre-defined and generated by the processes in real-time. The static data consist of network planned topology, name tables, and user directories, queries on them are generally more sophisticated.

3 Reliability and availabilty

Like a military command and control system, a network monitoring and control system has very stringent reliability requirements. It should be resilient to network failures; in particular, the failure of a part of the system must not affect the rest of the system. To achieve this, a system with a high degree of data replication is necessary. Moreover, a high degree of data replication will improve the data availability and increase the access speed.

The distributed database model

The architecture of the distributed database

Figure 6.1 shows the architecture of the present system which consists of two parts, the distributed database (DDB), and the network monitoring subsystem. The network monitoring system acts like a real-time user of the distributed database, retrieving and updating the data at high speed. The distributed database on the other hand provides the network monitoring system with high performance data manipulating facilities.

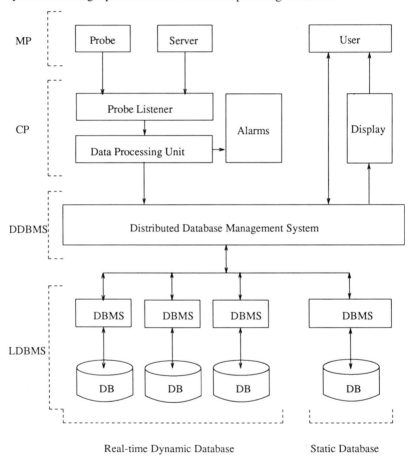

Figure 6.1 The distributed database model

At the highest level of the model are the probe servers called Monitoring Processes (MP) which poke various network components, discover the abnormal situations of the network, and send reports back to probe listeners. The function of probe server is similar to sensor processing in industrial process control.

At the next lower level is the Collection Processes (CP) which consists of probe listener and Data Processing Unit (DPU). The probe listener collects the monitoring data from the reports sent by probe server and passes it to the Data Processing Unit. The DPU then generates a query to the DDB to check whether network component status has changed. If so then an update is issued to the DDB to change this status, and at the same time a trigger is generated to raise alarms and network control actions. The kind of queries and updates generated by the DPU are predefined. The DPU accesses and changes the dynamic data distributed in the Real-time Dynamic Databases which support fast response to the access. Other accesses to the DDB come from users for network administration. The user can ask a fairly sophisticated query to the Static Database for administrative information and receive a graphic display of network status. The overlapping between the dynamic database and the static database is defined in the schema mapping dictionary.

At the third level is the Distributed Management System (DDBMS) which is the core of the entire system. It contains a data dictionary describing the three-layered schema structure. The three layers are the global schema, fragmentation schema, and allocation schema and they govern data partition and distribution (Ceri and Pelagatti, 1984). The data dictionary is used at each site to direct the decomposition and recomposition of the query and update to distributed local sites, so that the distribution of data is transparent to the users. A universal query interface is used to integrate all the local databases. It consists of both pre-defined queries from the DPU and sophisticated queries from the network administrator. Being a subset of the universal query language, the pre-defined queries mainly contain the primary read and write operations, while the universal query language is an INGRES-like relational query language.

At the lowest level are the local distributed databases containing Real-time Dynamic Database and Static Database. Each local database receives the decomposed query or update from the DDBMS and performs data manipulation on the local database and returns the appropriate response to the DDBMS.

Schema mapping

The data dictionary at each site is used to define the three layered schema mapping (ANSI, 1978; Ceri *et al.*, 1984). The global schema, i.e. the virtual database, is the global view of the physical databases distributed over the network.

The global schema is defined by a set of relations

$$\mathbf{R} = \{\, r_i : 1 \leqslant i \leqslant m \},$$

where m is the number of the global relations. The fragmentation schema is defined by set

$$\mathbf{F} = \{F_i : 1 \leqslant i \leqslant m\} = \{f_{ij} : 1 \leqslant i \leqslant m, 1 \leqslant j \leqslant n_i\}.$$

Here we have

$$F_i = \{f_{ij} : 1 \leqslant j \leqslant n_i\},$$

where $\{f_{ij} : 1 \leqslant j \leqslant n_i\}$ are the fragments partitioned from relation R_i, and n_i is the number of fragments of relation R_i. The allocation schema is defined by set

$$S = \{s_k : 1 \leqslant k \leqslant N\},$$

where N is the number of physical sites.

The mapping from global schema to fragmentation schema is that each relation R_i is partitioned into several fragments

$$\{f_{ij} : 1 \leqslant j \leqslant n_i\},$$

so we have

$$R_i = \bigcap_{j=1}^{n_i} f_{ij}.$$

The fragment f_{ij} is further mapped to several physical allocations which are defined in set S_{ij} by a function

$$S_{ij} = M(f_{ij}) = a_1 s_1 + a_2 s_2 + \ldots + a_N s_N,$$

where $a_k = 1$ if fragment f_{ij} is allocated to site s_k, otherwise $a_k = 0$.

An example of the schema mapping is shown in Figure 6.2. There, the global schema contains three relations R_1, R_2, and R_3. The three logical fragments partitioned from relation R_1 are fragments f_{11}, f_{12}, and f_{13}. Each of these three fragments is distributed among sites s_1, s_2, and s_3. The mapping from fragments $\{f_{1j} : 1 \leqslant j \leqslant 3\}$ to physical sites, for instance, is that f_{11} is allocated to sites s_1, s_2, and s_3; f_{12} to s_2 and s_3; and f_{13} to s_1 and s_2. The rest of the mapping is indicated in the same way.

From the user's viewpoint, only the global schema **R** can be seen, the other parts are transparent to them. The query and update issued by a user or a processor are decomposed according to the schema mapping from R_i to F_i and then further to the physical sites $S_{ij} = M(f_{ij})$. The essential operations of the database are read and write. The read operation $Read\ (f_{ij})$ reads f_{ij} from any site defined in S_{ij}, while for a write operation, $Write\ (f_{ij})$ has to be propagated to all the sites defined in S_{ij}. So the write operation generates several concurrent transactions to different sites. The degree of concurrency has a strong bearing on the performance of the system. The concurrency control and recovery mechanisms are discussed later.

An example

Figure 6.3 shows an example of the global relation of the distributed network monitoring databases. There exist seven entity sets with ten relations among them.

The probe servers defined in the set 'PROBER' probe various network components defined in set 'COMPONENT', which are further defined by the 'NAME' set. The 'COMPONENT' set has the current status given by set 'STATUS'. Each change of status is recorded in the 'HISTORY' set for network fault diagnosis. The reason for change of status and other important network information are specified in the set 'NETINFO', and the important network event information is relayed to the set 'NURSE' which will also raise the appropriate alarms to alert the network administrators.

The universal query language is an INGRES-like language which can be

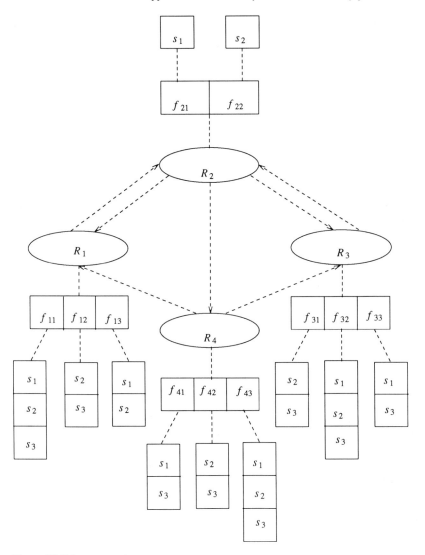

Figure 6.2 Schema mapping

used by both network administrators and processes (Stonebraker, 1976). Various sophisticated queries can be made from the relations defined in the global schema.

Real-time approach to concurrency control and recovery protocols

Protocol structure in the ISO model

The protocol structure for our distributed databases is based on the

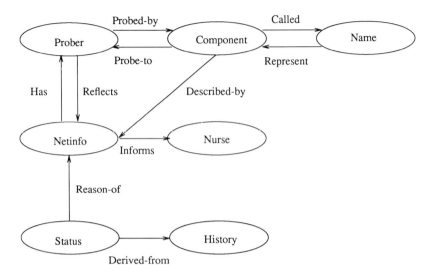

Figure 6.3 The global schema of distributed network monitoring database

transaction oriented high level, protocol, supported by the top three layers of the ISO reference model (ISO, 1982), namely, the application layer, presentation layer, and the session layer. It has the following characteristics:

1. Common presentation for both query language and data format.
2. Reliable procedure for the exchange of information between sites.
3. Concurrency control for distributed transactions.
4. Failure detection facility for cooperative sites.

In most existing DDBs, database functions are incorporated at the application layer (Stonebraker, 1979; Bernstein, 1981), the performance of such protocol is not satisfactory because of the high level time-out, and excessive communication delay. In a real-time system this is unacceptable, and a hierarchical rather than horizontal (i.e. one level flat structure) protocol structure appears to be more appropriate. Moreover, this protocol should be able to achieve low communication delay, maximum concurrency, and maximum reliability.

The functions of DDB protocol described above are decomposed into several subfunctions which are scattered into layer five to seven which is shown in Figure 6.4.

At the application layer, the global transaction management controls the initiation and termination of an integrated transaction which consists of several decomposed subtransactions. For example, a write operation to data copy can result in several sub-write operations to the same data copy distributed in different local databases. The user authentication and view definition, i.e. the global schema, are also managed at this level.

At the presentation layer, the form of the local information including both query language and data format is translated into a common presentation form, and then decomposed into several logical fragments using the data dictionary. Each logical fragment is a unit of the logical transaction which will be sent to a given destination.

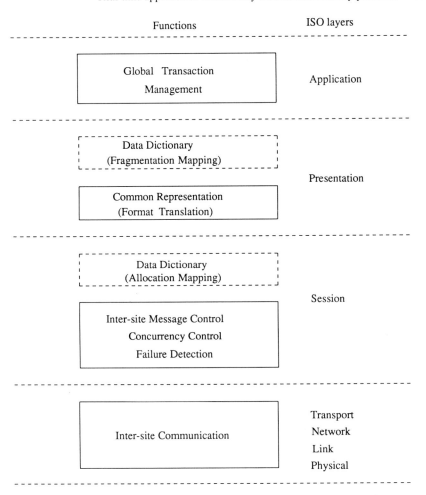

Figure 6.4 1S0 model vs database protocol architecture

At the session layer, the logical transactions are mapped to the physical location using an allocation mapping data dictionary, which will give rise to several atomic transactions. The control of these atomic transactions is held at the session control layer. The atomic transactions are first assembled with the destination addresses; then the session protocol controls the initiation and termination of the atomic transactions. The concurrency control mechanism is also encapsulated in this layer in order to control these parallel atomic transactions to gain maximum concurrency. The concurrency control mechanism is described in the next section.

The failure detection facility is usually established at the application layer in most DDB systems (Chang, 1984), which is triggered off by a high level time-out, so that it is quite time consuming. In order to enhance the performance of the system, the failure detection facility is encapsulated in the session layer. It detects the site status of the cooperative systems at a low cost and with enhanced performance (Ma, 1984).

The lowest four layers are mainly used for inter-site communications. The protocols used at the transport layer are network independent. At the network layer, various protocols for different networks such as X.75 Internet Virtual Call in CCITT Adopted Standards and Internet Datagram Protocol in DARPA/DoD Internet model are adopted as the basis of the transport protocol (Davies *et al.*, 1979).

Concurrency control

In order to achieve high performance in a real-time system, maximum concurrency could be obtained through the concurrency control protocol (Stonebraker, 1979; Bernstein, 1981). The design of the concurrency control mechanism is to meet the following criteria. First, during the execution of the concurrent distributed transactions copies of affected data should not be blocked. Second, the phases of protocol should be reduced to a minimum in order to obtain high speed commitment. Third, because the monitoring data reflect the real world in real-time, only the most recent data are useful. As a result, it is not necessary to restore the previous data after failure. In order to gain maximum speed, a small degree of inconsistency is allowed for a short period of time. Our concurrency control protocol, which is based on these design criteria, has two phases:

Phase I
Coordinator:
- Issue an atomic transaction.
- Write in log.
- Check site status from failure detection facility.
  If the participant site is unavailable then mark the transaction and write in log.
- Send the transactions to participants.

Participants:
- Wait for a transaction.
- Receive a transaction.
  If not available, then mark it for later execution.
- Write in log.
- Execute the transaction if available.
- Send 'READY' to coordinator.

Phase II
Coordinator:
- Wait for answer messages.
  If any 'READY' message is received, then send 'COMMIT' to participants write 'Complete' in log.
  If no 'READY' message is received at time-out, send 'ABORT' to all participants write 'Abort' in log.
- As a background process, the coordinator checks all the answers from the participants when time-out.
  If any participant has not commited, then mark it for later recovery phase and write it in log.

Participants:
- Wait for command message.
- Write 'ABORT' or 'COMMIT' in log.

In the first phase, the coordinator issues the concurrent transactions to all the participants. It first checks the participant's status from the failure detection facility to see whether the cooperative participants are available. If a participant is not available, a mark is written in the recovery log, and the transaction to the corresponding participant will be saved at the coordinator's site for later recovery. The coordinator then sends the transactions to all the participants available at the time. The participants, on the other hand, wait to be called. Once they receive the transaction, they write it in the log, and then execute the transaction and send 'READY' and the result to the coordinator.

At the second phase, the coordinator waits for the answer messages from the participants. If any of them answers 'READY', the coordinator sends 'COMMIT' to all the participants, and then writes 'Complete' in the log. If at time-out, no 'READY' answer is received from participants, the coordinator then sends 'ABORT' to all the participants. Regardless of the transaction commitment, a background process is collecting all the 'READY' answers from participants until time-out. The uncommitted transactions will be marked and written in the log for later recovery purposes. On the participants' side, the command message of either 'COMMIT' or 'ABORT' is expected from the coordinator, and it will also be written in the log.

Summary and conclusions

The architecture of a real-time distributed database used for computer network monitoring is presented, which makes use of a number of features to achieve real-time performance. First, different types of information are given different treatment so that the dynamic time-critical data can be processed at high speed, while the less critical static data are provided with sophisticated query facility. Second, the communication protocol is designed with a hierarchical structure to reduce unnecessary communication delay to minimize the possibility of transaction blocking. Third, the concurrency control procedure is designed to attain maximum parallelism while reducing the processing overhead; it adopts a non-blocking pre-commit mechanism. Fourth, failure detection at high level is avoided and a low level detection tool is used to reduce the detection time. Fifth, the system is designed to be resilient with a high degree of data replication.

The present architecture appears to be sufficiently general, and is suitable not only for computer network monitoring but also for a wide variety of real-time distributed database applications such as command and control, telecommunication, industrial processes control, and factory automation. Accordingly, it can be usefully adopted in most practical real-time distributed systems which support an appreciable amount of database functions.

References

ANSI/X3/SPARC/Study Group (1978) *Database Management Systems, Framework Report on Database Management Systems*, AFIP Press

Andriopoulos, X. and Sloman, M. (1985). A Database model for distributed real-time systems, Research Report Doc 85/8, Imperial College, London

Bernstein, P. A. (1981) A sophisticate's introduction to distributed database concurrency control. *Proceedings of the International Conference on Very Large Data Bases*, **8**, 62–76

Ceri, S. and Pelagatti, G. (1984) *Distributed Data Base*, McGraw-Hill, New York

Chang, J. M. (1984) Simplifying distributed database systems design by using a broadcast network. *SIGMOD 84*, **14**(2), 22–233

Davies, D. W. *et al.*, (1979) *Computer Networks and their Protocols*, John Wiley, Chichester

Hughes, G. R. and Ward, S. D. (1980) Engineer oriented power station control in the UK central electricity generating board. In *Real-time Data Handling and Process Control*, (ed. H. Meyer)

ISO/DIS/7498 (1982) *Information Processing Systems—Open Systems Interconnection—Basic Reference Model*, International Standards Organisation, Geneva, Switzerland

Kopetz, H. (1981) High level programming of distributed process control systems. In *Real-time Data Handling and Process Control—II* (ed. E. G. Kingham)

Ma, Z. (1984a) Universe configuration monitoring. Internal Note 1525, Department of Computer Science, University College, London, UK

Ma, Z. (1984b) Universe status monitoring. Internal Note 1526, Department of Computer Science, University College, London, UK

Moore, R. B. (1985) Distributed data management in a real-time environment. *Proceedings of the Fourth British National Conference on Databases*, **4**, 157–176

Stonebraker, M. (1976) The design and implementation of INGRES. *ACM Transactions on Database System*, **1**(3), 189–222

Stonebraker, M. (1979) Concurrency control and consistency of multiple copies of data of distributed INGRES. *IEEE Transactions on Software Engineering*, **5**, 188–194

Chapter 7

A distributed model of computation for combinatory code

Andy Cheese

Up until now the widespread use of functional languages has been hindered by the lack of any sort of efficient implementation. The main reason for this has been the need to support an environment, a mapping of variables in scope to their current values. By using combinatory logic it is possible to translate a functional program into a form in which all bound variables have been removed. The transformed program will be a string of constants which selectively ship to each expression that part of the environment it references. As a result of this the hardware needed to produce a physical realization of the model should be very much simpler than that of normal Von Neumann computing engines. In order to exploit the implicit parallelism present in a functional program a computational model based upon a parallel packet-based graph reduction scheme is proposed which allows code to be treated in exactly the same manner as data. In particular the code graph can be regarded as a lazily constructed data structure.

Introduction

A feature of all lambda-calculus based languages is the presence of bound variables. In a conventional implementation of a functional language the current value of all these variables is stored in a structure called an environment. At each step of the computation the bindings of the relevant variables have to be looked-up. It is this operation which is partly responsible for the popular complaint that functional language systems are slow. But, using combinatory logic (Curry and Feys, 1958), it is possible to transform a functional language program into a form which is free of variables. During this process a number of extra constants called combinators are added. However, each combinator has a fixed specific rewrite rule associated with it, thus the elevation process becomes very simple due to the now small number of primitive executable operations.

Maintaining storage for and searching an environment to find the value of a free variable are major sources of inefficiency in a conventional system. Usually there are two methods of structuring this environment. One is deep binding which consists of maintaining an association list of variable-value pairs. This means function calling and return is quite fast but variable look-up is very inefficient. The other alternative is shallow binding where the environment is stored as a table of variables and their corresponding bindings. This means variable look-up does not require much overhead but function call and return requires the switching of these table entries which can prove to be expensive. Because combinators are higher order functions having no free variables in their function bodies, the need for any environment can be dispensed with. Furthermore because combinators neither cause nor rely on side effects, several can be reduced in parallel (Turner, 1979a).

Combinators

A combinator is simply a lambda expression which contains no unbound variables. The transformation of a source functional language program into one consisting solely of combinators is a process of abstraction. It is known as abstraction since bound variables are abstracted out of the source-level expression yielding another expression. If this new expression is now applied to a variable the original source-level expression is obtained.

It is possible to define the abstraction process by the following set of equations:

$$[x] (E_1\ E_2) = S\ ([x]\ E_1)\ ([x]\ E_2)$$
$$[x]\ x\qquad = I$$
$$[x]\ y\qquad = Ky$$

where E_1 and E_2 are expressions, y is a variable other than x, and S, K and I are three combinators each having a strictly limited power of beta conversion. '$[x]\ E$' denotes the result of abstracting the variable x from the expression E.

The first equation tells us that to abstract a variable from an application we introduce a new constant, the S combinator, which is to be applied to the results of abstracting x from the two sub-expressions. The second equation states that to abstract a variable from an expression consisting solely of that variable we replace it by the identity combinator, I. The final equation deals with the case when the variable in the expression x needs to be abstracted from is different.

The defining equations for these newly introduced combinators are given below:

$$S\,x\,y\,z = (x\ z)\ (y\ z)$$
$$K\,x\,y\quad = x$$
$$I\,x\quad\ = x$$

The abstraction algorithm, if used as illustrated, will produce considerable amounts of combinatory code compared to the size of the original applicative expression. An improved version can be obtained by taking into account the special cases where the variable currently being abstracted does not appear in one or more subexpressions. This desirable property can be realized by introducing two new combinators, B and C, which are simply degenerate versions of S. These are defined by the following two equations.

$$B\,f\,g\,x = f(g\ x)$$
$$C\,f\,g\,x = f\,x\,g$$

Four optimizations can now be defined by:

$$S(K E_1) (K E_2) = K (E_1 E_2)$$
$$S (K E_1) I = E_1$$
$$S (K E_1) E_2 = B E_1 E_2$$
$$S E_1 (K E_2) = C E_1 E_2$$

where E_1 and E_2 are arbitrary expressions and the above rewrite rules are applied in the order presented. The correctness of the algorithm can be inferred by observing that for each of these rules, the term on the right-hand side is extensionally equal to the original term on the left-hand side. That is if each side of the equation is applied to the same argument, the resulting expressions will be equal. The computational model given below will be based solely upon the definitions of these combinators and built-in functions, such as the arithmetic functions, to improve efficiency, although everything could be implemented in terms of SKI combinators.

An abstract model of computation

SKI combinators by their nature are fully lazy. That is they only evaluate their subexpressions when they require their corresponding canonical values. There is also the need to support the definition and manipulation of infinite data structures. Both of these properties mean that the model of computation must in essence be demand-driven. The evaluation strategy will therefore be normal order but will exploit low-level parallelism because of the strictness of the various built-in operations. A mechanism that allows us to achieve this is packet-based graph reduction. The natural mode of execution of this model is call-by-need hence realizes our desired behaviour that the evaluation of an expression will only ever be performed once. Recursion is also easily handled by this computational model. The computational mechanism is essentially code copying so recursive definitions can be evaluated by taking a separate copy of the function body for each invocation of it, (Watson, 1985).

Each node of the graph corresponding to an applicative expression is represented as a packet structure. The first and second fields of a packet represent the left and right subbranches of that node. At any moment in time, a packet can be in any one of four possible states. These are respectively rewritable, suspended, evaluated or dormant. The abstract computational model describes the manner in which packets move between these states.

The fields of a packet can be of type value or type reference. A packet is rewritable if its first field is a function value and has fields of type value for all the functions arguments that are strict. This information is a priori provided for all of the built-in functions. If such a packet has a field of type reference instead of type value in a strict argument field then that packet moves into the suspended state. It activates the reference sets of packets, representing the subgraphs, and the packet will wake up when the fields are all of type value. Packets in the dormant state are waiting to be activated and hence become rewritable. An evaluated packet contains the result of the corresponding rewrite of the original active packet. It is tagged with the address of a suspended packet to which it must return its result.

A computation begins by demanding the value of the root packet of the program graph. The dormant root packet then changes state to rewritable. In general the first field of an active rewritable packet is of type difference and points to a dormant packet. The dormant packet is then inspected in order to determine the type of its first field. If it is a pointer the original rewritable packet will change state to suspended and the dormant packet will be made rewritable. If the first field of the dormant packet is a basic operation then a copy of it is taken. The corresponding argument fields of the rewritable packet are inserted into their respective fields in the packet. If this copy has the correct number of argument fields present, as required by the basic operation, then the return address of the rewritable packet is inserted into the copy and the dormant packet moves into the rewritable state. If there is a mismatch between the required number of argument fields and the actual number that are present, a packet in the evaluated state is created. The address in the packet store of the dormant packet is placed in the first field of the evaluated packet. The return address of the evaluated packet is made equal to the return address of the original-rewritable packet.

A rewritable packet whose first field is a basic operation value and also has the correct number of non-null strict argument fields which are not pointer values can be executed. If there are pointers present in any of the active packet's strict argument fields, the state of the rewritable packet changes to that of being suspended. Also stored in the suspended packet is a count of the number of pending argument values; this is so the suspended packet will only change state to rewritable if it is able to do some work. The original pointer value fields are then nullified. Although this is not actually necessary it does make the debugging of the combinator machine code more tractable. For every designated strict argument field that is of pointer value a new rewritable packet is created. For each new packet a copy of the appropriate pointer value field of the suspended packet is inserted into its first field. The return address of each new rewritable packet is made equal to the address in the packet store of the suspended packet. The number of the field in the suspended packet where the result of the rewritable packet should return will be the number of the field in the original rewritable packet that possessed its corresponding pointer value field.

The result of the execution of a rewritable packet will be stored in a newly created evaluated packet. An evaluated packet copies its first field into the field of the appropriate suspended packet as specified by its return address. The suspended packet to which this value is returned then has its pending argument value count decremented. If the count is now zero the state of this packet changes to rewritable.

A consequence of using graph reduction is the property that shared calculations are only performed once. The fact that the S, K and I combinators are fully lazy determines that calculations are only performed when needed. To preserve this property in our model a new type of suspended packet called a ghost is introduced. If the first field of a rewritable packet is a pointer value, the referenced dormant packet is inspected. If this dormant packet has a basic operation present in its first field then the computation will proceed as described above. If the dormant packet's first field is a pointer value then the rewritable packet suspends and its pending values count field is incremented. A ghost packet is then created. Its return address field has a return address equal to that of the place in the packet store where the suspended packet is now located with the appropriate field number to return its value to set, in this case the first. The dormant packet then becomes rewritable. Its return address is equal to the packet store address of the ghost packet. If the reference packet is a ghost, the rewritable packet moves into the suspended state. A null field in the ghost packet is altered to a return address value field, the inserted return address being equal to the packet store address of the suspended packet, the return address value field having a returning-value-field number equal to the number of the strict argument field in the previously rewritable packet.

If the return address of an evaluated packet references a ghost packet, then the ghost is overwritten with a copy of the evaluated packet. The return address field of this copy being set to null, this allows the result of the computation to be shared. A copy of the evaluated packet is made for each of the ghost packets non-null fields, these will be of type return address value. The return address fields of these copies will be equal to their respective return address value fields in the ghost. If the evaluated packet just contains a reference then the ghost will be overwritten with a packet which contains an indirection combinator as its first field and the reference now in its second field. This packet will then act as an indirection node thus preserving the simplicity of the model.

The structural composition of a packet is depicted below:

| PT | SC | GCF | Field 1 | Field 2 | Field 3 | Field 4 | RAddr |

The bar '|' characters denote field separators. The PT field is used to hold the type of the packet. Because of the simplicity of the model there is only a need to support two types of packet, these being a ghost, GH, and a non-ghost, NGH. SC is the suspended pending values count field. This is an integer which will range from 0 to the number of possible argument fields. GCF is a garbage collection field. This allows a choice of reference counting as well as parallel mark-scan methods to be used. RAddr is the return address field of the packet. This is made up of two components, an address and a field number of the packet it will return its evaluated result to. The other fields are used to house arguments in non-ghosts and return addresses in ghosts. These fields belong to one of five possible types. A pointer type field is a packet address ranging from 1 to the size of the current addressable packet store. The Nilptr type field is a representation of the nil pointer used as a basis for constructed types. A field containing Null denotes an unused nullified field. A return address type field has exactly the same structure as the reserved RAddr field. The other possible field type is Value which can be any one of six possible subtypes. A function subtype consists of a basic operation and an argument descriptor indicating which fields are used and their strictness properties. The other, self-explanatory, field subtypes are, Integer value, Real value, Character value, and Boolean value.

As an illustration of this model the initial and final packet configurations for an application of the S combinator are depicted below:

! | NGH | 0 | 0 | (a) | x | Null | Null | RetAddr |

@a | NGH | 0 | 1 | (b) | g | Null | Null | NullRA |

@b | NGH | 0 | 1 | S | f | Null | Null | NullRA |

‖
‖
V

! | NGH | 0 | 0 | (c) | (d) | Null | Null | RetAddr |

@c | NGH | 0 | 1 | f | x | Null | Null | NullRA |

@d | NGH | 0 | 1 | g | x | Null | Null | NullRA |

The '!' symbol denotes that the packet in question is active, that is, it is currently being manipulated by a processing element. The '@a' notation indicates that the following packet is stored at address a in the packet pool store. 'RetAddr' is the return address, address and field number, for the parent packet which is blocked waiting for the value of this computation. In this case it happens to be the application of the S combinator defining equation which rewrites $S\,f\,g\,x$ to $(f\,x)\,(g\,x)$. 'NullRA' is the null return address symbol, indicating the return address field has not been set to a specific value.

By way of illustration of a packet rewrite, the initial and final packet configurations for applications of the K and I combinator equations are given below:

! | NGH | 0 | 0 | (a) | y | Null | Null | RetAddr |

@a | NGH | 0 | 1 | K | x | Null | Null | NullRA |

‖
‖
V

! | NGH | 0 | 0 | x | Null | Null | Null | RetAddr |

! | NGH | 0 | 0 | I | x | Null | Null | RetAddr |

‖
‖
V

! | NGH | 0 | 0 | x | Null | Null | Null | RetAddr |

In order to allow more general selector and constructor functions than simply those dealing with lists, special pairing and unpairing combinators are not used. The constructors and selectors are themselves used. Active selector function packets, such as those for head and tail, simply inspect the packet their second pointer value field references. If the first field of this referenced packet is of the required constructor form, the appropriate fields out of the constructor packet are selected as the value to be returned by the selector. If it is not a constructor form, the selector packet is suspended pending the coalescing of the reference packet into a constructor packet. An active packet which consists of a constructor function in its first field, changes state to dormant and returns to a self-reference packet to the selector function packet that originally demanded its value.

As an example of the packet representation of a data structure, the collection of packets for the list (cons 1 (cons 2 (cons 3 nil))) is depicted below. All selector accesses to lists mean a traversal through their heads, the second field of the packet. Hence to modify a particular element one just applies the head selector function until the wanted element is found. The traversed cons cell packets are copied on the way. The required packet is updated, leaving the remainder of the list unaltered. The cloning of packets is reduced to the copying of those con cells that are before the required element in the list. This ensures that all references to the original list remain unaltered:

@a | NGH | 0 | 0 | CONS | 1 | (b) | Null | Null | NullRA |

@b | NGH | 0 | 1 | CONS | 2 | (c) | Null | Null | NullRA |

@c | NGH | 0 | 1 | CONS | 3 | Nilptr | Null | Null | NullRA |

A value packet which is made up of a single reference, such as the result of the coalescing of a constructor packet, requires special consideration. The initial and final collections of packets for the event of returning an evaluated reference packet to a ghost packet are shown below.

@a | GH | 0 | 2 | b.1 | Null | Null | Null | c.1 |

VA | NGH | 0 | 1 | (d) | Null | Null | Null | a.1 |

$$\begin{array}{c} \| \\ \| \\ V \end{array}$$

VA | NGH | 0 | 1 | (d) | Null | Null | Null | c.1 |

VA | NGH | 0 | 1 | (d) | Null | Null | Null | b.1 |

@a | NGH | 0 | 0 | IND | (d) | Null | Null | NullRA |

The 'VA' notation means that the following packet form is in the evaluated state. The format of the syntax for a return address field is illustrated best by an example. 'a.1' for instance is a return address where 'a' is the destination address in the packet pool where this evaluated packet

must return its value and '1' is the field number in the destination packet
which is to be overwritten with the value. 'IND' is the indirection combinator which when activated simply returns a value packet consisting solely of
its second field, as shown below. This is to avoid long chains of references
building up. It also means that selector functions can be implemented very
simply. If it were not for the indirection packets they would have to chase
down these long chains at runtime:

! | NGH | 0 | 0 | IND | x | Null | Null | RetAddr |

$$\begin{array}{c} \| \\ \| \\ V \end{array}$$

VA | NGH | 0 | 0 | x | Null | Null | Null | RetAddr |

@a | NGH | 0 | 0 | IND | x | Null | Null | NullRA |

Output can be treated as a side-effect free operation by treating it as a stream
concatenation. However, because of the need to output the head of the list
before its tail some form of artificial sequencing of output values is
necessary. One solution to this problem is to compute the head and wait
until this value is output before attempting to output the tail of the stream.
This is easily achieved by coding the output routine as a set of rewriting
rules, using conditionals, in which the output operation simply returns a
Boolean value on completion thus preserving the declarative semantics of
the language.

Improving the model of computation

The free variable abstraction algorithm can be improved even further by
introducing a new long range combinator S' and two other combinators B'
and C'. Where B' and C' take into account the cases where the variable
being abstracted does not occur in one or more subexpressions (Turner,
1979b). In fact they play the same part as B and C do for the S combinator.
The defining equations for these three further combinators are given below.
'k' is a term consisting entirely of combinators:

$$S' \, k \, x \, y \, z = k \, (x \, z) \, (y \, z)$$
$$B' \, k \, x \, y \, z = k \, x \, (y \, z)$$
$$C' \, k \, x \, y \, z = k \, (x \, z) \, y$$

As noted previously for the case of the ordinary combinator set S, K and I
there are a set of optimisations which can be applied to the abstracted
combinatory code. These are given below.

$$S \, (B \, k \, E1) \, E2 = S' \, k \, E1 \, E2$$
$$B \, (k \, E1) \, E2 = B' \, k \, E1 \, E2$$
$$C \, (B \, k \, E1) \, E2 = C'k \, E1 \, E2$$

From an implementation point of view there is only one difference between
the long range combinator set and their ordinary counterparts. This is in the

number of arguments they require before they constitute a fully populated application. The number of fields per packet needs to be increased from four to five to accommodate this. The physical overhead incurred being the number of bits per packet will have to be increased by the number of bits used to represent a field along with the added strictness indicator. The garbage collection field will have to be able to cope with the possibility of there being an extra reference than in the *SKI* case to a packet. The advantages now are that the number of actual code packets needed for the program and the number of steps needed to execute the program will both be reduced.

A further improvement can be obtained by instead of returning references to partially evaluated packets as results, the complete whole evaluated packet is returned. This should be regarded as an optimization of the general computation mechanism. The number of times pointers will have to be dereferenced to inspect packets during the evaluation of a program will be greatly reduced. The numbers of stored packets and active packets will also be less since ghost packets are now overwritten with the complete evaluated packet instead of a reference to it. This will reduce the communication between the packet pool and the processing elements and also the amount of activity of the memory representing the packet pool.

The lexical ordering of variables in unabstracted expressions can drastically alter the amount of combinatory code generated. As an example of this consider the two expressions and their corresponding *SKI* combinator code forms given below:

$$f\,x\,y\,z = +\,x(+\,y\,z)$$
$$f = C'S\,(S'C(B\ K(K(B' +)))I) +$$

and

$$f\,x\,y\,z = +(+\,x\,y)z$$
$$f = C(S'C'(K(S' +))\,(C'S\,(S'\ S\ (S'\ C\ (B\ K\ (K\ (B' +)))\ I)\ K))\ I)$$

For the first equation the number of code packets generated is ten, whereas for the second it is seventeen. Even for this very simple case there is enough evidence to suggest that some amount of program transformation should be attempted before the abstraction in order to decrease the size of the code produced. One very simple case where transformation can be applied is in the case of the set of basic built-in arithmetic operations. These are all associative and strict upon both arguments. The lexical ordering of these arguments can be interchanged quite safely without disturbing the semantics of the original program.

The model of computation as a means to a distributed computing environment

By performing a static analysis of the program at compile-time it is possible to determine approximately which functions require evaluated arguments in order to become candidates for evaluation themselves. This compilation technique is known as strictness analysis. A function which needs the value of an argument, that is if the argument is undefined the value of the function is undefined, is said to be strict upon that argument. Among the functions that are strict upon all of their arguments are the basic operations $+$, $-$, $*$, $/$, $>$ and $<$. The conditional operator 'ITE', if-then-else, is strict upon its first argument and lazy upon its second and third. In layman's terms this means if one of the arms of the conditional were evaluated and found to diverge it does not hold that the value of the conditional expression will necessarily be undefined. The list selector operations head and tail are non-strict on their arguments; this is because they should only evaluate that part of a list they require, to return a result.

In the computational model if an argument of an operation is designated as strict and the corresponding packet field is a pointer value then the active packet will suspend and wait for the argument to become evaluated before proceeding. This information could be collected during the compilation phase and the definitions of strictness of the combinators altered appropriately. Using this information it is possible to evaluate those arguments that are strict without violating the natural lazy semantics of the program.

Accessing elements that are near the end of a list can be extremely inefficient, due to a large amount of copying of packets which will have to be done as the chain of tail pointers is traversed. This problem would be solved if a more general random access structure were incorporated into the functional environment. One possible solution is a tree, the size of the node being restricted to the number of fields in a packet. The more fields there are per packet then the more amenable to random access the structure becomes. As packets grow larger though, the storage and communication overheads grow in proportion to the size of the packet. Since the majority of basic operations use only two or three of their arguments, fields will be unused for most of the time representing a waste of store, communications bandwidth, and time when copying packets.

Conclusions

A parallel packet based incremental code-copying computational model has been devised based on the $SKI(BC)$ set of combinators and a small set of primitive operations. A pascal simulator and a simple functional language compiler for the model has been written and has performed correctly on all programs that have been currently tested.

The model has given promising results for the small number of programs tested so far. The double recursive sum of the first 100 numbers has an average parallelism of 51, the double recursive factorial of 50 an average parallelism of 29, and the inherently sequential generate and filter primes program computing the first 25 prime numbers has an average of 2. Although these results are very promising when compared to a conventional implementation of a functional language they must be balanced out against the low level nature of the SKI combinators.

A number of current novel implementations such as **GRIP** (Peyton Jones, 1987), (a supercombinator approach), and **ALICE** (Darlington and Reeve, 1981), (a source code level approach), have been shown to outperform an SKI model considerably. It is very hard to quantify the simplicity of the hardware required to implement a particular computational model. Undoubtedly due to the simplicity and their implementation of the small number of fixed combinators as basic hardware functions it would be a much simpler engine than any current Von Neumann computer. However, experience with the hardware implementations of **GRIP**, **ALICE** and **FLAG-SHIP** has shown these to be not much more complex with respect to the amount of information represented in a packet. In particular though one should note the minimal number of packet types in the *SKI* model, the simulator only needs to distinguish between ordinary packets, of type 'NGH' and ghosts, of type 'GH'.

Acknowledgments

I would like to thank Ian Watson of the Manchester architecture group of the Flagship Project for supervising me whilst I successfully completed this project for my MSc. I also wish to express my thanks to the Science and Engineering Research Council for funding this research project.

References

Curry H. B. and Feys R. (1958) *Combinatory Logic* Volume 1, North-Holland Publishing Company, Amsterdam

Darlington J. and Reeve M. J. (1981) ALICE – A multi-processor reduction machine for the parallel evaluation of applicative languages. *Proceedings of 1981 ACM Conference on Functional Programming Languages and Computer Architecture*

Peyton Jones S. L. (1987) GRIP – A high-performance architecture for parallel graph reduction. Internal Note No. 2079, Department of Computer Science, University College, London, UK, presented at the 3rd International Conference on Functional Languages and Computer Architecture, Portland, USA, September

Turner, D. A. (1979a) A new implementation technique for applicative languages, *Software Practice and Experience*, **9** 31–49

Turner D. A. (1979b) Another algorithm for bracket abstraction. *Journal of Symbolic Logic*, **44**(2)

Watson I. (1985) A parallel SKI(BC) combinators model, Document PMP/MU/IW/00005, Department of Computer Science, University of Manchester, UK, March

Chapter 8

isaac: a high-level distributed language

Jerud J. Mead

Introduction

A major advantage of sequential high-level languages such as **pascal** and **fortran** is the 'easy-to-use' standard interface to complex system-level features such as terminal and file I/O. More recent languages such as **modula**-2 (Wirth, 1985) and **ada** (US Dept. of Defense, 1983) add the ability to describe the high-level logical structure of a program in terms of modules or packages. However, for those who would write distributed programs there are also the complexities of process communication with which to deal. Certainly many high-level languages have been defined and implemented for the description of distributed programs. These languages, though high-level in the sense of **pascal**, require sophistication when it comes to process communication. Existing distributed languages also provide little support for managing the communication structure of a distributed program.

isaac is a high-level language for writing distributed programs with communication structure as its central design point. The language is being implemented on a network of **SUN** workstations and is meant to be used by students and faculty to experiment with distributed programming. This points up a second design point: ease of use by those with minimal distributed systems sophistication. We do assume that the user understands the notion of process as a program in execution.

An example

The following example is introduced to provide a focus for the discussion of **isaac** language features. It is a simplified version of a class project in an operating systems course. The project is carried out on a network of **apollo** workstations and is designed to confront the students with standard operating system and distributed system problems. (This class project has been the source of much of the motivation for the design of **isaac**.)

For the example consider a simple single user calculator implemented in software using two communicating processes.* One process acts as a command interpreter or user interface, the other as the calculator. The

---

* The actual class project involves the design and implementation of a multiuser stack-based calculator which accepts either single entries (numbers or operations) or infix expressions.

command interpreter repeatedly accepts and verifies a single operation or operand. The user interface passes each entry to the calculator and waits for two values to be returned by the calculator: the value at the top of the computation stack and a code specifying the status of the just executed entry.

The PI model

Because communication structure is to be central to the **isaac** language, it is necessary to have a model of distributed programs which emphasizes this point. This section introduces such a model. The *process/interface* (*PI*) *model* is a hierarchical representation of the communication structure for systems of communicating processes (Mead, 1986). The PI model is based on the two abstractions *process* and *interface*, interface representing the object used by two processes for communication and process, of course, representing the unit of system activity. The *hierarchical process composition* (*HPC*) model (Leblanc and Friedberg, 1985) is similar but is oriented toward the design of operating systems.

Interface

An interface represents the composite of all communication mechanisms used by two communicating processes and is defined to be a set of typed, one-way communication components. Here *typed* refers to the set of data values which can be transmitted on a component and *one-way* refers to the fact that each component is dedicated for transmission of data from one process to another.

The calculator example has been specified as consisting of two communicating processes, so we should be able to define a PI-model interface between them. When the user interface sends a value to the calculator it either specifies an operation or an operand. One way to ensure that the calculator can distinguish between operations and operands is to provide separate interface components. In the other direction, the calculator must be able to return a status code and the current top of stack value. This can also be handled by having two components, one for transmitting the status and the other for the top of stack value. The interface can be summarized as the following collection of four components.

operand	user interface	→ calculator
operation	user interface	→ calculator
status	user interface	← calculator
top of stack	user interface	← calculator

The arrows indicate which process can transmit data to which component. Though the types of data for each component have not been specified they can be easily determined from a more detailed description of the project.

It is important to notice that in this example the interface is not an active agent, it is simply the mechanism for conducting data. The interface acts as an opaque boundary between the communicating processes. The only information one process has of the state of its communication partner is that which is transmitted via the interface components.

Process

Process is defined recursively in the PI model. At the lowest level it corresponds to the usual notion of process, i.e., the unit of asynchronous sequential activity or the execution of a sequential program. A higher-level process in the PI model is an abstraction of this familiar idea and can be thought of as the execution of a distributed program; it comprises two or more lower-level communicating processes and their associated interfaces.

We say that two processes communicate if there is one and only one interface associated with them and the interface components are split into two disjoint sets, where each set can be written by one process and read by the other (one of the sets can be empty). The *environment* of a process is defined to be the set of interfaces to which it has access.

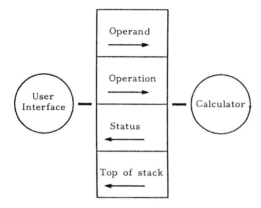

Figure 8.1

A simple diagram depicts the structure we have discussed for the calculator example (see Figure 8.1). The user interface process can send data via the operand or operation components. While the calculator process may perceive the user interface process as a sequential process, it can be modelled, and implemented, as a set of processes. To illustrate this point consider Figure 8.2. The diagram shows the user interface process of our example decomposed into a set of two processes and one additional interface. Such a decomposition yields a tree structure of processes (ignoring communication). As is customary, we will say that the user interface process is the *parent* of the get input process, with the term *child* being used in the obvious way.

A child process can communicate with a process outside its parent only if the parent communicates with that process; the communication can only be carried on via a subset of the interface which the parent uses. For example, the get input process (Figure 8.2) has access to the *operation* and *operand* components of the interface but not the *status* or *top of stack* components. For the get input process, the two components form an interface used to communicate with the calculator process. The calculator process, of course, is not even aware that there is a get input process; it sees only sequential activity through the interface.

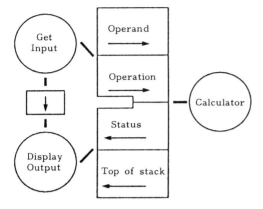

Figure 8.2

System

One implication of the previous section is that at the highest level of abstraction a system (including its 'users') is closed; it can be modelled as a single process with no interfaces. This process can then be seen as a combination of child processes and interfaces; each child process can in turn become a parent by decomposition. This gives us a methodology for describing the parallel activity which goes on in many systems.

isaac language features

An **isaac** program consists of two (required) sections, as illustrated in Figure 8.3. The **structure** section contains a formal description of the program's process/communication structure based on the PI model. The second section is a list of process descriptions, the code to be executed by each of the (lowest level) processes comprising the program.

```
<program> ::=
    <structure>
    <process description list>

<structure> ::=
    process <name> [using <interface list>];
        [structure
            <interface declarations>;
            <structure>
            {<structure>}
        end <name>;]

<process description list> ::=
    <process description>
    {<process description>}
```

Figure 8.3

A process description is based on **pascal** (Jensen and Wirth, 1976) with extensions to permit system-independent process communication. In the next two sections we will look in detail at the syntax and semantics of the two basic parts of an **isaac** program. Rather than presenting formal syntax for all constructs, selected examples drawn from an implementation of the RPN calculator will be presented. The complete implementation (up to procedures) is presented in Appendix A.

Communication structure

To specify communication structure based on the PI model we must be able to specify the structure of each interface as well as the association of processes and interfaces. The segment of **isaac** code in Figure 8.4 formalizes the RPN calculator structure depicted in Figure 8.2. This code defines interfaces, processes and the environment for each process.

```
process RPNCalculator;
   structure

   CommunicationType =
      interface
         Operation    --> OperationType;
         Operand      --> Integer;
         Status       <-- StatusType;
         TOSValue     <-- Integer
      end;

   Comm : CommunicationType;

   process Calculator using Comm(<--);

   process UserInterface using Comm(-->);
      structure

      PipeType=
         interface
            Line     --> LineType;
            TurnOff--> signal
         end;

      Pipe : PipeType;

      process GetInput
         using Comm (Operation, Operand),
               Pipe(-->);

      process PrintResults
         using Comm (Status, TOSValue),
               Pipe(<--);

      end UserInterface;

   end RPNCalculator;
```
Figure 8.4

One of the difficulties in formalizing the PI model is defining language constructs which will describe the relationship between a process and an interface component, i.e., whether the process can read or write the component. When writing an **isaac** program a 'direction' (the arrow notation) is associated with each interface component and process/interface pair (in the **using** clause). In Figure 8.4, for example, the definition line for process *Calculator* has the notation '*Comm*(←)', while in the interface definition of *Comm* the component *Status* has ' ← ' associated. Since the arrows are the same, we say that *Calculator matches* the component *Status*. On the other hand, *Calculator* does not match the component *Operand*, since their respective arrows point in opposite directions. The **isaac** convention specifies that a process can write to any component it matches and read from any component it does not match. Thus, *Calculator* can read from both *Operation* and *Operand* and write to *Status* and *TOSValue*.

The one exception to the above description involves a child process which communicates via one of its parent's interfaces. The process *GetInput* communicates with *Calculator* via the same interface used by *UserInterface*. This is specified in the *using* part of the process definition line by giving the interface name and listing those components to which *GetInput* is to have access. Notice that an arrow is unnecessary because the child process inherits the communication direction from its parent. A key point in the definition of the PI model is that the decomposition of a process cannot alter the environment of the process.

It should be noted that the high-level processes specified by the PI model are only structural, they are never associated with actual processes at run time. This means that only the lowest level processes (those with no **structure** block) are described in the process description list.

Process description

In standard **pascal** (Jensen and Wirth, 1976) the program heading line defines the program's environment (i.e., the internal file names which will be associated at run-time with external files). The operations **read** and **write** are provided for interacting with this environment. Generalizations of **read** and **write** are provided in **isaac** for specifying the interactions between a process and its environment. With the necessity of handling asynchronous communication in a distributed program, **isaac** also provides a mechanism patterned after Dijkstra's guarded command (Dijkstra, 1975), for asynchronous communication. The characteristics of these features will be discussed in terms of the following framework, proposed by Scott (Scott, 1985):

- processes
- communication paths and naming
- synchronization
- message receipt
- message screening
- side issues

Processes
isaac processes run under the control of the underlying operating system; there is no mechanism in **isaac** to interfere with this control. Thus, an **isaac**

program cannot create or terminate processes, set process priorities or cause a process to migrate from one processor to another. Processes in an **isaac** implementation have disjoint address spaces, so communication cannot take place by using shared variables. These restrictions are adopted to ensure that the **isaac** language is powerful, yet easy to use.

Communication paths and naming

In **isaac**, communication paths are defined by interfaces and their components. **isaac** restricts paths to be many (senders) to one (receiver). Since it is possible for processes to share an interface, the compiler must check that if two processes have the same orientation to a shared interface there can be no common readable component. For a process to communicate with another it must name the interface and components which they share; processes do not know the names of other processes in a program.

Synchronization

Data is sent to another process by writing to the appropriate components of the shared interface. This is done in **isaac** with the **write** statement. The following **isaac** statement is from the procedure *Respond* in the process *Calculator* (see Appendix A for the complete code):

write (Comm, Status : Stat, TOSValue : TOS)

This statement specifies that the process writes the values in the process variables *Stat* and *TOS* to the components *Status* and *TOSValue* of the interface *Comm*.* The major difference between this statement and a **pascal** **write** statement is that in **isaac** it is necessary to specify the interface and components which are being written.

The process executing a **write** statement must have output access to the components listed in the statement and the expression types must match those of the associated component. A **write** statement need not write data to every component of an interface and cannot write to more than one interface. Components provide buffered data transfer, so when a **write** statement is executed the process is not blocked unless the component has insufficient room for the data.

Message receipt

Message receipt in **isaac** is explicit and is implemented by the **read** statement. The syntax of the **read** statement is similar to that of the **write** statement described above. As with the **write** statement, the compiler will check that each interface component listed is an input component for the process and that the local variable has the same type as the corresponding interface component. A **read** statement need not read from every input component of the interface and cannot read from more than one interface. When executed the **read** statement blocks until all specified interface components have received data.

Message screening

Since it is possible for a process to have access to several interfaces it is

---

* A value being written to a component can be more generally specified by an expression.

necessary to have a mechanism for receiving data from whichever interface has data currently available. It is also convenient to have a non-blocking **read** capability. **isaac** uses a variant of Dijkstra's guarded command for this purpose (Dijkstra, 1975). In this case the guards are always **read** statements. The **select** statement has the following form:

```
select
    read (<arg list>) --> <statement>  |
        .
        .
        .
    read (<arg list>) --> <statement>
end
```

When the **select** statement is executed, if one or more of the **read** statements can execute immediately (i.e., without blocking) then one of the guards is chosen, the guard is executed and then the guard's <statement> is executed. Control then transfers to the next statement after the **end**. If no guard can proceed, the process blocks until one of the guards becomes ready.

An alternative form of the statement relieves this problem by introducing an else clause as the last guard; this guard is always ready to run but is only selected if no other guard is ready. This makes it possible for the programmer to implement a non-blocking read.

Side issues

All process communication in **isaac** is via interfaces; there is no mechanism for sharing memory space among processes. This does not mean that the implementation of **isaac** cannot make use of shared variables for efficiency reasons, just that the programmer has no ability to specify shared variables.

To give the **isaac** programmer some control over unreliable communication the **select** command has a parameterized variant which provides a timeout mechanism.

```
select ( <numeric expression> )
    read (<arg list>) --> <statement>  |
        .
        .
        .
    read (<arg list>) --> <statement>  |

    else --> <statement>
end
```

The process executing this instruction waits up to <numeric expression> time units for a **read** guard to be ready. If a guard becomes ready, the corresponding <statement> is executed as with the standard **select** command. If the time expires, the **else** <statement> is executed if it is present; if no **else** guard is present, execution continues with the statement following the end.

Implementation

The **isaac** language is designed to expose the communication structure of a distributed program while hiding from the programmer the complexities of process communication. This characteristic of **isaac** raises two important implementation questions. First, how are processes to be matched up with processors at run time? Second, how is process communication to be provided and managed? These issues are examined in the next two sections.

Run-time model

An executing distributed program can be decomposed into disjoint sets of processes, called *execution sets*, where the processes in each execution set run on the same processor. It is, of course, conceivable that distinct executions of a distributed program result in different execution sets. The **isaac** design, however, assumes that there is a standard decomposition of an **isaac** program into execution sets.

Each execution set is represented by a separate source file containing the complete PI description followed by the process descriptions for the processes in the execution set. The compiler then generates a run-unit for each execution set. The run unit for an execution set will contain an encoded description of the PI characteristics of the program, the translated version of each process and an initialization routine for starting the processes.

The expectation is that on a network of workstations each execution set would be run on a separate workstation, though this is not required. In fact when testing a system it might be more feasible to run all execution sets on the same workstation. The RPN calculator example could be set up as one execution unit (all processes run on one workstation) or as two units, with the process *Calculator* in one, and the processes *GetInput* and *PrintResults* in the other.

Isaac kernel

The setup just described presents a problem: which execution set should be started first? In fact, in what order should the execution sets be started? The assumption for **isaac** is that the order doesn't matter. Thus, when an execution set is executed there must be some mechanism for the new processes to establish communication with other processes.

The programmer's view of process communication in **isaac** is in terms of reading or writing a set of interface components. This abstract view must be translated in terms of the IPC facilities provided by the target system; the logical communication paths of the **isaac** program must be bound to actual communication paths provided by the underlying system.

One approach to these two problems is to have the compiler generate a run-time environment which manages the communication. This approach, however, will yield a compiler which is highly system dependent. To make **isaac** more easily ported a second approach has been chosen: implement the communication manager as a user-level distributed service, an **isaac** kernel, a virtual machine which handles communication requests from **isaac** programs. This kernel provides two basic services: registration and communication.

The **isaac** compiler generates calls to the procedures which provide the kernel services.

The purpose of the kernel's registration service is to make it possible for processes in one execution set to find the other processes in the **isaac** program. The initialization routine of a run unit calls the **register** service and passes it the program name, the PI description and the names of the processes in the execution set. If the program is already executing **register** updates the kernel data structures for the program to reflect the inclusion of the new processes (establishes the necessary communication paths). If the program is not yet in execution then **register** initializes the kernel data structures for this program and establishes communication paths necessary among the currently executing processes of the program. When a process terminates, it calls the **unregister** service which removes the process from the program data base.

The **isaac** kernel's communication service handles all communications between processes. The service is defined in terms of two procedures: **send** and **receive**. The **send** routine is passed the process name, interface, and component names and data lists; **receive** is defined similarly. These two routines are implemented using whatever IPC mechanism is available on the system.

Conclusions

If the distributed environment is to become commonplace, especially in engineering and scientific applications, it will be necessary to have distributed programming languages which hide from the user the details of process communication while allowing the user to specify the communication structure of the program. Though high level languages tend to be less efficient than special purpose ones, they are usually easier to use and give users a chance to enhance their understanding of the computer systems on which they work. This is especially true in the academic environment where students can do little distributed programming because the tools are too sophisticated. **isaac** is a language which has been designed to fill the need for a truly high-level distributed language based on an intuitive model of communicating processes.

References

Dijkstra, E. W. (1975) Guarded commands, non-determinancy and formal derivation of programs, *Communications of the ACM*, 453–457

Jensen, A. K. and Wirth, N. (1976) *Pascal User Manual and Report*, (2nd edn) Springer-Verlag, Berlin

LeBlanc, T. J. and Friedberg, S. A. (1985) Hierarchical process composition in distributed operating systems. In *Proceedings 5th International Conference on Distributed Computing Systems*, May, pp. 26–34

Mead, J. J. (1986) *Specifying the Structure of Concurrent Communicating Processes*, Computer Science Technical Report ♯86–1, Bucknell University, Lewisburg, USA, June

Scott, M. L. (1985) *Design and Implementation of a Distributed Systems Language*, Computer Sciences Technical Report ♯596, University of Wisconsin, Madison, USA, May

Wirth, N. (1985) *Programming in Modula-2*, Texts and Monographs in Computer Science, 3rd edn, (ed. D. Gries), Springer-Verlag, Berlin
United States Department of Defense (1983) *Reference Manual for the Ada Programming Language*, (ANSI/MIL-STD-1815A-1983), February

Appendix

```
process RPNCalculator;
  structure

    CommunicationType =
      interface
        Operation      --> OperationType;
        Operand        --> Integer;
        Status         <-- StatusType;
        TOSValue       <-- Integer
      end;
    Comm : CommunicationType;

    process Calculator using Comm(<--);

    process UserInterface using Comm(-->);
      structure

        PipeType =
          interface
            Line       --> LineType;
            TurnOff    --> signal
          end;
        Pipe : PipeType;

        process GetInput
          using Comm (Operation, Operand),
                Pipe(-->);
        process PrintResults
          using Comm (Status, TOSValue),
                Pipe(<--);
      end UserInterface
  end RPNCalculator;

process GetInput;
  var Op : OperationType;
      Val : integer;
      On : boolean;
  procedure GetInput (Op, Val, On);
  begin
    read  (Input, CommandLine);
    write (Pipe, Line : CommandLine);
    Translate (CommandLine, Op, Val, On)
    if not On then
        write (Pipe, TurnOff)
  end GetInput;
  procedure Send (Op, Val);
  begin
    if Op = Push then
        write (Comm, Value : Val)
    else
        write (Comm, Operation : Op)
    endif
  end Send;
```

```
begin { GetInput}
  Initialize;
  repeat
        GetInput (Op, Val, On)
        Send      (Op, Val)
  until not On
end GetInput;

process PrintResults;
  var TOS : integer;
      CommandLine : StringType;
      Done : boolean;
begin { PrintResults }
  Initialize;
  repeat
    select
      read (Comm, Status : Stat,
              TOSValue : TOS) -->
              DisplayResults (Stat, TOS) |
      read (Pipe, Line : CommandLine) --:
              DisplayLine (CommandLine) |
      read (Pipe, TurnOff) -->
              Done := true
    end
  until Done
end PrintResults;

process Calculator;
  var TOS : integer;
      Op : OperationType;
      Val : integer;
      Stat : StatusType;
  procedure Receive (Op, Val);
  begin
    select
      read (Comm, Operation : Op)  -->
              Val := 0 |
      read (Comm, Value : Val) -->
              Op := Push
    end
  end Receive;
  procedure Respond (Stat, TOS);
  begin
      write (Comm, Status   : Stat,
              TOSValue : TOS)
  end Respond;
begin { Calculator }
  Initialize;
  repeat
      Receive (Op, Val);
      Compute (Op, Val, Stat, TOS);
      Respond (Stat, TOS)
  until false
end Calculator;
```

Part 3

Annotated bibliography and key references

Over 1600 references on distributed/concurrent languages, systems and
related topics (theory and practice) covering the period from 1959 to
1989 are compiled. This.extensive and rather comprehensive set of
references is drawn from books, national and international journals,
Proceedings of Workshops, Conferences and meetings, and finally
internal reports and research papers in academic establishments and
industrial research centres. In addition, an annotated bibliography to the
'key' papers in the field is also given.

Concurrent programming: an annotated bibliography

H. S. M. Zedan

Introduction

For the past three decades research and development has been rather extensive in both the theory and practice of distributed computing systems. However, there are few 'key' contributions which are considered to be the milestones of the subject. In this chapter, an annotated bibliography of these contributions is given. The bibliography deals with the following topics: models for concurrent programming, formal treatments of concurrency and concurrent programming languages.

Models for concurrent programming

The ever-increasing decline in the cost of hardware has resulted in the rapid advance of network and distributed systems technologies. With the advent of these technologies, new questions have arisen regarding concurrency, synchronization, design methodology analysis of complexities and so on.

However, concurrency, for over three decades, has been the major concern of many researchers and models for concurrency have been developed. The important contributions concerning concurrency and synchronization models will be given in this section.

Dijkstra, E. W. (1968) Co-operating sequential processes. In *Programming Languages* (ed. F. Genuys), Academic Press, New York, pp. 43–112
In this influential paper, Professor Dijkstra has discussed in detail the way in which a number of 'independent' processes may cooperate. A parallel command, *parbegin...parend* was introduced to specify the execution of its constituent sequential processes. All the processes start simultaneously, and the parallel command ends only when they are all terminated. The paper also introduced the concept of semaphore as a synchronization primitive.

Hoare, C. A. R. (1974) Monitors: An operating system structuring concept. *Communications of the ACM*, **17**(10), pp. 549–557
In this paper, Hoare has developed the notion of 'monitor' as a synchronization mechanism and a programming language feature that aids in the designing of operating systems. A monitor has a collection of data structures and a set of procedures that operate on these structures. The data internal to the monitor are only seen by the monitor's procedures and invisible to the outside world. These data may be accessed by external processes through the specified visible procedures. The visible procedures are executed in a mutually exclusive fashion.

Peterson, J. L. (1977) Petri nets. *ACM Computing Surveys*, **9**(3), 223–252
Petri net was initially developed by C. A. Petri in his thesis 'Kommunikation mit Automaten' (1962) Schriften des Rheinisch-Westfalischen Institutes fur Instrumentalle Mathematik an der Universitat Bonn, Bonn, West Germany, "where he developed a new model of information flow in systems. The model was based on asynchronous and concurrent operation by the parts of the system and the realization that the relationship between the parts could be represented by graph or net." In this survey James Peterson has given an account of the basic concept and usage of Petri nets. Languages based on Petri net are also discussed. Other computation models that are related to Petri nets are also analysed.

Campbell, R. H. (1979) Path Expressions: a technique for a specifying process synchronization. PhD Thesis. Computing Laboratory, University of Newcastle-upon-Tyne, UK
Path expression is a synchronization mechanism which was first introduced in Campbell, R. H. and Habermann, A. N. (1974). The specification of process synchronization by Path Expressions, *Lecture Notes in Computer Science*, **16**, pp. 89–102. Similar to the monitor structure, the module that implements a resource has its own local data and procedures (that perform operations on these data). Path Expressions are added representing a set of synchronization constraints. These constraints define all legal sequences of operation executions for a resource. The bodies of the module procedure contain no synchronization code.

Hoare, C. A. R. (1978) **Communicating Sequential Processes,** *Communications of the ACM*, **21**(8), 666–677
This classical paper is the first version of Hoare's celebrated **CSP** which has been propounded in his book *Communicating Sequential Processes*, Prentice-Hall International Series in Computer Science. **CSP** was the first attempt to introduce input, output and concurrency as primitives in programming language design. Many have subsequently used it as notation to describe concurrency. **CSP** is basically composed of input (?), output (!), SKIP, and the assignment as simple commands. Compound commands such as sequence (;), parallel (∥), alternation ([...]) and repetition (*[..]) are also available. Both alteration and repetition are formed from sets of Djikstra's guarded command. Communication between two processes is synchronized at the matching i/o commands. Note that explicit naming of processes is required for communication.

Hansen, P. B. (1978) Distributed processes: a concurrent programming concept. *Communications of the ACM*, **21**(11), 934–940
Distributed Processes (or **DP**) is another interesting and also an influential programming concept for distributed systems. A **DP** concurrent program consists of a (fixed) number of sequential processes that run simultaneously. Each of these processes has its own variables, common procedures and an initial statement. Procedures may be called from remote processes. Execution of the process code and the procedures are interleaved (i.e. procedure code can only be executed if the process code – its initial statement – is waiting on condition). Nondeterminism is also available through guarded commands and guarded regions.

Milner, R. (1980) A calculus of communicating systems. *Lecture Notes on Computer Science*, Springer-Verlag, Berlin
In this book, Professor Robin Milner gives a detailed account of his well known model **CCS (Calculus of Communicating Systems)**. **CCS** is an attempt to provide an analogous paradigm for concurrent computation, conducted by communication among independent 'agents'. **CCS** have been used widely in theoretical research and have been provided with a variety of semantics (operational as well as denotational).

Andrews, G. R. (1981) Synchronizing resources. *ACM TOPLAS*, **3**(4), 405–430
Synchronizing Resources (or **SR**) provides a new approach to parallel programming. **SR** is based on the idea that a parallel system is composed of a set of resources that define operations and these resources may be connected or loosely related. A resource consists of one or more processes that implement operations together with the variables that they share. Operations in **SR** are a generalization of procedures and message passing. Synchronization and schedule of processes are by Boolean expressions and arithmetic expressions respectively.

Liskov, B. and Scheifler, R. (1983) *Guardians* and actions: linguistic support for robust, distributed programs. *ACM TOPLAS*, **5**(3), pp. 381–404
This is an important contribution in concurrent programming models. In particular, the way in which the structure of *Guardians* takes into account the concepts of invisibility and recoverability in distributed systems. A *Guardian* resides at a single physical node, although a node may support several *Guardians*. Typically, a *Guardian* encapsulates and controls access to one or more resources. Access to a resource is provided by a set of operations called 'handlers'. The internal structure of a *Guardian* consists of a collection of data objects and processes to manipulate those objects. The state of a *Guardian* consists of 'stable' and 'volatile' objects. In the event of a crash, the stable objects remain intact while the volatile objects get lost.

Agha, G. (1985) *Actors* a model of concurrent computation in distributed systems, PhD Thesis, University of Michigan, Ann Arbor, USA
The '*Actor*' abstraction has been developed to exploit message-passing as a basis for concurrent computation. An *Actor* is essentially a computational agent which carries out actions (such as sending communication to itself or others, creating new *Actors* or specifying the replacement behaviour) in response to accepting a communication. In order to send a communication, the sender must specify a mail address, called the 'target'. The mail system buffers the communication until it can be delivered to the target. (Note that the order in which the communication is delivered is nondeterministic.) *Actors* have their own (unique) mail address which may be communicated just like any other value. These mail addresses provide a means to dynamically reconfigure a system of *Actors*. All *Actors* in a system carry out their actions concurrently. Several concurrent programming languages have been developed which are based on the *Actor* model, for example see the paper by Agah, G. and Hewitt, C. (1985) 'Concurrent Programming using Actors: exploiting large-scale parallelism' In *Foundation of Software Technology and Theoretical Computer Science*, (ed. S. N. Maheshwari) *Lecture Notes in Computer Science*, **206**, Springer-Verlag, Berlin, pp. 19–41. In this paper they have described the concurrent programming language '**ACT3**'.

Formal treatments of concurrency

Methods on formal treatments of concurrency depend on the type of concurrency dealt with. Generally there are two types of concurrency. Concurrency based on shared variable technique, and concurrency based on message passing mechanism. In what follows, we list the major references for each type followed by a brief comment on the method proposed. For more detailed exposure on each of the methods we refer the reader to the excellent book by Howard Barringer:

Barringer, H. (ed.) (1985) A Survey of Verification Techniques for Parallel Programs, *Lecture Notes in Computer Science*, **191**, Springer-Verlag, Berlin

In this book Professor Barringer has surveyed nine different verification methods for concurrency. The survey includes, for each method, a list of major references to the work, worked examples and a summary of the proof system. Furthermore, the paper by Lamport and Schneider gives a good and general introduction to formal specification and verification of concurrent programs: Lamport, L. and Schneider, F. B., Formal foundation for specification and verification

The use of 'Temporal Logic' in the verification of concurrent systems is not dealt with in Barringer's book. However, Hailpern's thesis is devoted to the subject: Hailpern, B. T. (1982) Verifying concurrent processes using temporal logic, *Lecture Notes in Computer Science*, **129**, Springer-Verlag, Berlin. More recently, a short survey on program logic including, among others, temporal logic has been given in: Fisher, M. and Barringer, H. (1986) Program Logics – a short survey, Report UMCS-86-11-1, *Department of Computer Science*, Manchester University, UK

Shared variable concurrency

Owicki, S. and Gries, D. (1976) An axiomatic proof technique for parallel programs I. *Acta Informatica*, **6**, 319–340
> In their technique, verification of a parallel program P consists of three steps: (1) a sequential proof for each of the sequential processes, P_i, that form P, (2) These proofs must be shown to be 'interference-free' and finally (3) the pre- and post-condition for P is formed as a conjunction of the pre- and post-conditions of P_i.

Lamport, L. (1980) The 'Hoare Logic' of concurrent programs. *Acta Informatica*, **14**, 21–37
> In this paper, Leslie Lamport has introduced what is known as **Generalized Hoare Logic (GHL)** for concurrent programs. In **GHL**, correctness formulae are expressed in the form $\{P\}\ S\ \{Q\}$ to mean that if execution is begun anywhere within S with P true, then Q will be true upon the termination of S and further P will still remain true (i.e. P is invariantly true throughout the execution of S). Assertions in **GHL** involve the use of both program variables and control locations. Control predicates 'at', 'in' and 'after' are used to state whether control resides at, in or after the statement labelled by the control predicate's argument. The semantics for a single programming language is given.

Flon, L. and Suzuki, N. (1978) Consistent and complete proof rules for the total correctness of parallel programs. Xerox Report, CSL-78-6, November
> In their system, a parallel program is realized to have an equivalent non-deterministic program. Proof rules are given in the paper in the form of weakest precondition predicate transformer. Inference rules are derived to prove properties such as invariance, deadlock freedom, starvation freedom, and blocking freedom.

Message-based concurrency

Apt, K. R., Francez, N. and de Roever, W. P. (1980) A proof system for **Communicating Sequential Processes**. *ACM Transactions on Programming Languages and Systems*, **2**(3), 359–385
> This proof system is for **CSP** parallel programs to prove partial correctness and absence of deadlock. The processes are viewed initially as acting in isolation where proof outlines for each process are given. Such proofs cooperate if, when taken together, they validate the assertions of the i/o commands mentioned in the isolated proofs. Global invariant is introduced to determine which pair of input and output commands correspond.

Levin, G. M. and Gries, D. (1981) A proof technique for **Communicating Sequential Processes**. *Acta Informatica*, **15**, 281–300
This proof system was given for an extended form of **CSP** as it is suitable for distributed systems. The proof system is composed of three parts: sequential proofs, satisfaction proofs and non-interference proofs. The sequential proofs are considered in isolation and need assumptions about the effect of communication; these assumptions are however shown to be valid using the satisfaction proofs. Rules dealing with total correctness are given and also sufficient conditions for showing that a program is deadlock-free are given. The proof system is similar, in merit, to that given by Apt, Francez, and de Roever above.

Misra, J. and Chandy, K. M. (1981) Proofs of networks of processes. *IEEE Transactions on Software Engineering*, 7(4), 417–426
Using a **CSP**-like notation, Misra and Chandy provide a proof system for networks of processes. Processes in the network communicate via message passing and using named communication channels. A process P is specified by two assertions over its communication traces and the notation '$r|P|s$' is used to mean that 'if s is true initially in P and that r holds at all times prior to some message transmission of P, then s holds at all times prior to and following that communication'. Specification of a network may be internal or external and is composed of the network's component specifications.

Hoare, C. A. R. (1981) A calculus of total correctness for communicating processes. *Science of Computer Programming*, **1**, 49–72
The work presented in this paper extends the system which was developed in the Technical Monograph: Zhou, C. C. and Hoare, C. A. R. (1981). Partial correctness of communicating processes and protocols, *Technical Monograph PRG-20*, University of Oxford, UK, May. The system given in this monograph provides interference rules for proving that processes satisfy given specifications. The specification of a process is taken as a set of assertions over its communication histories. Unlike **CSP** the processes in the network cover a set of named channels. Total correctness is achieved by changing the assertions to include channel variables which relate readiness for some communication.

There are other approaches to formal reasoning such as the rigorous approach of Cliff Jones in Jones, C. B., (1983) Tentative steps towards a development method for interfering programs, *ACM TOPLAS*, **5**, 576–619. This work has started for sequential processes and has been documented in his book *Software Development: A Rigorous Approach*, (1980) Prentice-Hall International, Stevenage.

Concurrent programming languages

As parallel machines become more common, more powerful and 'affordable', concurrent languages are expected to follow the same trend. However, the development of (practical) concurrent programming languages has progressed rather slowly and closely followed the evolution in concurrency models. The difficulties are due to the implementation problems of communication and synchronization mechanisms.*

There have been several comparative surveys on concurrent languages: T.

* See R. Bornat, Imperative languages in distributed computing, in *Distributed Computing Systems Program* (ed. D. A. Duce), 1984, Peter Peregrinus, Stevenage.

Bloom in his report 'Synchronization mechanisms for modular programming languages' *MIT/LCS/TR-211*, (1979), MIT, Cambridge, Massachusetts, has analysed different synchronization mechanisms and presented a set of synchronization problems to test their expressive power. Stotts, in Stotts, Paul David, Jr. (1982) A comparative survey of concurrent programming languages, *SIGPLAN Notices*, **17**(10), has concentrated on design issues of concurrent languages and compared 13 different languages including **CSP**, **ada**, **DP**, and **modula**. Other comparative studies such as Wegner, P. and Smolka, S. A. (1983) Processes, tasks, and monitors: a comparative study of concurrent programming primitives, *IEEE Transactions on Software Engineering*, **9**, 446–462, concentrated on analysing concurrent programming primitives for process creation and synchronization in **ada** and **CSP**. A rather comprehensive and important survey is the one by Andrews and Schneider which is included in this book.

We do not intend to present yet another comparative study to concurrent programming languages nor do we wish to provide an annotated bibliography to all concurrent programming languages in the literature. In what follows, we shall consider some of these languages which have been studied and been considerably used in the literature. These are **Concurrent pascal**, **modula-2**, **pascal plus**, **path pascal**, **ada**, **conic** and **occam**.

Wirth, N. (1978) **modula-2**, *ETH, Institut for Informatik, Report 27*
  Modula-2 is a general purpose programming language primarily designed for system implementation. It was influenced by Pascal and Modula, and later revised and extended in: Wirth, N. (1984) Schemes for multiprogramming and their implementation in **modula-2**, *ETH, Institut for Informatik, Report 59*. The concept of processes and their synchronization with signals, which was adopted in **modula**, is replaced by a lower level notion of *Coroutines*. Hence, the language offers only some basic facilities which allow the specification of quasi concurrent processes and of genuine concurrency for peripheral devices. A process can be created by a predefine procedure (*Newprocess*). A *Module* may possibly contain a number of *import* lists (which specify all identifiers of objects that are declared outside but used within the *Module*) and *Export* lists (which specify all identifiers of objects that are declared within the *module* and used outside it).

Welsh, J. and Bustard, D. W. (1979) **pascal-plus** another language for modular multiprogramming. *Software Practice and Experience*, **9**, 947–957
  pascal plus is a superset of **pascal** which was evolved from a series of language experiments for operating systems and simulation modelling at the Queen's University, Belfast. The extension to **pascal** may be divided into two groups: *ENVELOP* construct (which defines data structure, operations that can be applied on the data structure, and control structure) and parallel programming facilities. The latter includes process structure and the monitor structure. Processes represent independent actions which can be executed in parallel. Processes communicate via the monitor. A monitor contains shared data which is protected by mutual exclusion. Conditions are used to identify queues of waiting processes. The language represents a natural progression in concurrent language evolution from **modula-2**. The use of the language in structuring operating systems and compilers can be found in: Welsh, J. and McKeag, R. M. (1980) *Structuring System Programming*, Prentice-Hall, Englewood Cliffs, New Jersey

Kolstad, R. B. and Campbell, R. H. (1980) **path pascal** user manual. *ACM SIGPLAN Notices*, **15**(9), 15–24
  path-pascal is an experimental language which was designed to study the effect of

using *Path Expressions* as a technique for specifying process synchronization. The P4 subset of **pascal** was augmented with an encapsulation mechanism, *Open Path Expressions* and a process mechanism. Access to encapsulated data is performed by operations synchronized by *Open Paths*. A process invoking such operations may execute the operation only if permitted by the *Open Path Expressions* associated with the shared data object. An instance of a process is dynamically created by invoking the process name in the same manner as a procedure invocation. The termination of the creating process does not depend on the created process(es). A brief discussion on the design aspects of the language may be found in: Campbell, R. H. and Kolstad, R. B. (1980) An Overview of **path pascal's** Design, *ACM SIGPLAN Notices*, **15**(9), pp. 13–14.

Department of Defense (1983) Reference Manual for the **ada** Programming Language, ANSI/MIL-STD-1815A-1983, Washington, D.C., USA

ada was developed by the US Department of Defense for real-time process control. The language is very complex, large and contains rich sets of data types and abstraction mechanisms. It has mechanisms for exception handling, a package structure for information hiding, decomposition and separate compilation. Mechanism for handling non-determinism is also available through the *select* statement. The unit of parallelism in **ada** is the *task*. A task is defined with similar syntax to other modules of **ada**, the procedure and package. Ordinary tasks depend on their declaring procedure or task, and are activated at the same time. The declaring task or procedure terminates only when all of its dependent tasks have terminated. Tasks can be created dynamically after the start of their declaring procedure or task by the use of access (pointer) types. Tasks communicate via either shared variable or message passing based mechanism (known as the *rendezvous*). Synchronization of access to shared variables is not guaranteed and must be programmed. A comprehensive review of the **ada** tasking model may be found in Burns, A., Lister, A. M. and Wellings, A. J. (1987) A Review of **ada** Tasking, *Lecture Notes in Computer Science*, **262**, Springer-Verlag, Berlin

Kramer, J., Magee, J., Sloman, M., Twidle, K. P. and Dulay, N. (1984) The **conic** programming language: version 2.4. Imperial College Research Report, DOC 84/19, London, UK

conic was designed to be used for the production of large, distributed embedded systems. The main design principle of **conic** is the ease of incorporating new 'functionality to the system in response to evolutionary changes and to allow reorganization of existing components in response to operational changes.' The language is based on **pascal**, which has been extended to support modularity and message-passing primitives. The process-structuring construct in **conic** is the MODULE-TASK, which is a self-contained sequential task. A MODULE TASK is written and compiled independently from any given configuration. There are two types of ports: *entryport* where message transaction can be received and *exitport* which denotes the interface at which message transaction can be initiated. **conic** also has a configuration language which is used to specify both the initial system and any subsequent changes to it. The book by Sloman, M. and Kramer, J. (1987) *Distributed Systems and Computer Networks*, Prentice-Hall International, Stevenage, presents, among other things, an overview of the **conic** system in some detail. However, the following papers give more detailed information about the **conic** language and system: Kramer, J., Sloman, M., Magee, J. and Lister, A. (1984) **conic**: an integrated approach to distributed computer control systems, *IEEE Proceedings, Part E*, **130**(1); Kramer, J. and Magee, J. (1984) Dynamic configuration for distributed systems, *IEEE Transactions on Software Engineering*, **11**(4); Sloman, M., Kramer, J. and Magee, J. (1985) The **conic** Toolkit for building distributed systems, *Proceedings of the 6th IFAC Workshop on distributed Computer Control Systems*, California, Pergamon, Press, Oxford.

Inmos PLC (1984) **occam** *Programming Manual*, Prentice-Hall International, Hemel Hempstead

The programming language **occam** is both elegant and simple. Its design principle follows directly the concepts of Hoare's **CSP**. The main building block in **occam** is the process which communicates with other processes (or the outside world) via a pre-declared set of channels. The communication is synchronous and a channel represents one-to-one link between processes. Parallelism in **occam** is explicitly expressed through the parallel command **par**. Non-determinism is also available in the language. **occam** is highly structured and uses identation instead of explicit bracketing. The language has been extended to what is known as **occam 2**: Inmos Limited (1988) *occam 2 Reference Manual*, Prentice-Hall International. **occam 2** differs from the prototype **occam 1** in that it introduces floating point representation of real numbers, functions and data types. The language has a configuration part which associates the component of an **occam** program with a set of physical nodes (or resources).

Key references in distributed computer systems 1959–1989

H. S. M. Zedan

Over 1600 references on distributed/concurrent languages, systems and related topics covering the period from 1959 to 1989 are compiled. This set of references has been drawn from books, national and international journals, Proceedings of Workshops, Conferences and meetings, and finally internal reports and research papers in academic establishments and industrial research centres. I would like to apologize in advance to any researcher whose work was accidentally not referred to in here. I have also deliberately avoided any classification to the references as I believe that an overlap of interests is inevitable under any given classification. Therefore the references are only classified by the year of their publications.

1959

Conway, R. W., Johnson, B. M. and Maxwell, W. L., A queue network simulator for the IBM 650 and Burroughs 220. *Communications of the ACM*, **2**(12)

Cook, J. M., Remarks on 'An efficient method for generating uniformly distributed points on the surface of an *n*-dimensional sphere'. *Communications of the ACM*, **2**(10)

Hicks, J. S. and Wheeling, R. F., An efficient method for generating uniformly distributed points on the surface of an *n*-dimensional sphere. *Communications of the ACM*, **2**(4)

1960

Harper, S. D., Automatic parallel processing. *Proceedings of the Computing and Data Processing Society of Canada, 2nd Conference*, June, pp. 321–331

Yarbrough, L. D., Some thoughts on parallel processing. *Communications of the ACM*, **3**(10)

1961

Caldwell, T., On finding minimum routes in a network with turn penalties. *Communications of the ACM*, **4**(2)

Lasser, D. J., Topological ordering of a list of randomly-numbered elements of a network. *Communications of the ACM*, **4**(4)

Neklora, M. R., Comment on a paper on parallel processing. *Communications of the ACM*, **4**(2)

1962

Kahn, A. B., Topological sorting of large networks. *Communications of the ACM*, **5**(11)

Petri, C. A., Kommunikation mit Automaten. Report, University of Bonn, Bonn, West Germany

1963

Cantrell, H. N., Incompressible flow network calculators. *Communications of the ACM*, **6**(6)
Estrin, G., Bussell, B., Turn, R., and Ribb, J., Parallel processing in a restructurable computer system. *IEEE Transactions on Electronics and Computers*, **12** 747–755
Gordon, R. M., Checking for loops in networks. *Communications of the ACM*, **6**(7)
Gregory, J. and McReynolds, R., The SOLOMON computer. *IEEE Transactions on Electronics and Computers*, **12** 774–781
Katz, J. H., Simulation of a traffic network. *Communications of the ACM*, **6**(8)

1964

Goldstine, H. H., Horwitz, L. P., Karp, R. M., and Miller, R. E., On the parallel execution of macroinstructions. IBM Research Report, RC-1262, August
Nievergelt, J., Parallel methods for integrating ordinary differential equations. *Communications of the ACM*, **7**(12)

1965

Anderson, J. P., Program structures for parallel processing. *Communications of the ACM*, **8**(12)
Anon. Proposed American Standard-parallel signalling speeds for data transmission. *Communications of the ACM*, **8**(3)
Dijkstra, E. W., Solution of a problem in concurrent program control. *Communications of the ACM*, **8**(9)
Larsen, R. P. and Mano, M. M., Modeling and simulation of digital networks. *Communications of the ACM*, **8**(5)
Loomis, R. G., Boundary networks. *Communications of the ACM*, **8**(1)
Opler, A., Procedure-oriented language statements to facilitate parallel processing. *Communications of the ACM*, **8**(5)
Senzig, D. N. and Smith, R. V., Computer organization for array processing. In *Fall Joint Computer Conference, AFIPS Conference Proceedings*, **27**, AFIPS Press, Montvale, New Jersey, pp. 117–128

1966

Anon., X3.3, ASA, Proposed American Standard – character structure and character parity sense for parallel-by-bit data communication in the ASCII. *Communications of the ACM*, **9**(9)
Bernestein, A. J., Analysis of programs for parallel processing. *IEEE Transactions on Electronics and Computers*, **15**, October, 757–763
Dennis, J. B. and Van Horn, E. C., Programming semantics for multiprogrammed computations. *Communications of the ACM*, **9**, March, 143–155
Gosden, J. A., Explicit parallel processing description and control in programs for multi- and uni-processor computers. *Fall Joint Computer Conference, AFIPS Conference Proceedings*, **29**, Washington DC, USA, Spartan Press, East Lansing, Michigan, pp. 651–660
Horwitz, L. P., Karp, R. M., Miller, R. E. and Winograd, S., Index register allocation. *Journal of the ACM*, **13**(1), 43–61
Hyman, H., Comments on a problem in concurrent program control. (Letter). *Communications of the ACM*, **9**(1)
Karp, R. M. and Miller, R. E., Properties of a model for parallel computations; determinancy, termination, queuing. *SIAM Journal on Computing*, **14**(6), 1390–1411
Knuth, D. E., Additional comments on a problem in concurrent program control, (Letter). *Communications of the ACM*, **9**(5)
Lehman, M., A survey of problems and preliminary results concerning parallel processing and parallel processors. *Proceedings of the IEEE*, **54**, December, 1889–1901

Miller, R. E. and Rutledge, J. D., Generating a data flow model of a program. *IBM Technical Disclosure Bulletin*, **8**, 1550–1553

Mrutha, J. C., Highly parallel information processing systems. *Advances in Computers*, **6**, 1–116

Parnas, D. L., On facilitating parallel and multiprocessing in ALGOL. (Letter). *Communications of the ACM*, **9**(4)

Petri, C. A., Communication with automata. Suppl. 1 to Technical Report, RAD C-TR-65-337, Vol 1, Griffiss Air Force Base, New York, USA

Karp, R. M., Miller, R. E. and Winograd, S., The organization of computations for uniform recurrence equations. IBM Research Report, RC-1667

Rohrbacher, D. L., Advanced computer organization study. Rome Air Development Corporation Technical Report, RADC-TR-66, 7(2 Vols)

Schwartz, J., Large parallel computer. *Journal of the ACM*, **13**(1), 25–32

Wirth, N., A note on 'Program structures for parallel processing', (Letter). *Communications of the ACM*, **9**(5)

1967

Anderson, D. W., Sparacio, F. J. and Tomasulo, R. M., Machine philosophy and instruction handling. *IBM Journal of Research and Development*, **11**, January, 8–24

Aschenbrenner, R. A., Flynn, M. J. and Robinson, G. A., Intrinsic multiprocessing. In *Spring Joint Computer Conference, AFIPS Conference Proceedings*, **30**, AFIPS Press, Montvale, New Jersey, pp. 81–86

Bruijn de, N. G., Additional comments on a problem in concurrent program control. *Communications of the ACM*, **10**(3)

Karp, R. M. and Miller, R. E., Parallel program schemata: a mathematical model for parallel computation. *Conference Record, IEEE 8th Annual Symposium on Switching and Automata Theory*, October, pp. 55–61

Klein, M. M., Scheduling project networks, *Communications of the ACM*, **10**(4)

Martin, D. F. and Estrin, G., Models of computations and systems – evaluation of vertex probabilities in graph models of computations. *Journal of the ACM*, **14**, April, 281–299

Patil, S. S., Coordination of asynchronous events. PhD Thesis, Project MAC Report, TR-72, MIT, Cambridge, Massachusetts, USA, September

Phillips, C. S. E., Networks for real-time programming. *BCS Computer Journal*, **10**(1), 46–52

Shedler, G. S., Parallel numerical methods for the solution of equations. *Communications of the ACM*, **10**(5)

Stone, H. S., One-pass compilation of arithmetic expressions for a parallel processor. *Communications of the ACM*, **10**(4)

1968

Barnes, G. T., *et al.*, The ILLIAC IV computer. *IEEE Transactions on Electronics and Computers*, **17**, August, 746–757

Dijkstra, E. W., Co-operating sequential processes. In *Programming Languages* (ed. F. Genuys) Academic Press, New York

Dill, J. C., Randall, D. L. and Richer, I., PLEXUS – an on-line system for modeling neural networks. *Communications of the ACM*, **11**(9)

Fisher, A. C., Liebman, J. S. and Nemhauser, G. L., Computer construction of project networks. *Communications of the ACM*, **11**(7)

Karp, R. M. and Miller, R. E., Parallel program schemata. IBM Research Report, RC-2053

Kotov, V. E. and Maringani, A. S., On transformation of sequential programs into asynchronous parallel programs. *Proceedings of the IFIPS Congress*, pp. J37–J45

Luconi, F. L., Output functional computational structures. *Conference Records of the IEEE 9th Annual Symposium on Switching and Automata Theory*, pp. 76–84

Noronha, L. G., Po, C. Y. and Womack, J. W., Hybrid computation of the dynamics of a distributed system. *BCS Computer Journal*, **11**(2), 196–205

Schurmann, A., GAN, a system for generating and analyzing activity networks. *Communications of the ACM*, **11**(10)

Slutz, D. R., The flowgraph schemata model of parallel computation, PhD Thesis, MIT, Cambridge, Massachusetts, USA

1969

Cocke, J. and Miller, R. E., Some analysis techniques for optimising computer programs. *Proceedings of 2nd Hawaii International Conference on Systems Sciences*, January, pp. 143–146

Davis, R. L., The ILLIAC IV processing element. *IEEE Transactions on Computers*, **18**, September, 800–816

Dennis, J. B., Programming generality, parallelism and computer architecture. *Information Processing Letters*, **68**, 484–492

Fateman, R. J., Optimal code for serial and parallel computation (short communication). *Communications of the ACM*, **12**(12)

Marin, M. A., Synthesis of TANT networks using a Boolean analyzer. *BCS Computer Journal*, **12**(3), 259–267

Nudds, D., Methods of computing event times in project networks. *BCS Computer Journal*, **12**(1) 38–40

Parnas, D. L., On simulating networks of parallel processes in which simultaneous events may occur. *Communications of the ACM*, **12**(9)

Ramamoorthy, C. V. and Gonzalez, J. M., A survey of techniques for recognizable parallel processable streams in computer programs. *Joint Computer Conference, AFIPS Conference Proceedings*, **35**, AFIPS Press, Montvale, New Jersey, pp. 1–15

Rodriguez, J. E., A graph model for parallel computation. MIT, ESL, and Project MAC Report ESL-R-398, MAC-TR-64, September

Rosenfeld, A., Picture processing by computer. *ACM Computing Surveys*, **1**(3), 147–176

Rosenfeld, J. L., A case study in programming for parallel-processors. *Communications of the ACM*, **12**(12)

Russell, E. C., Automatic program analysis. PhD Thesis, University of California, Los Angeles, USA

Sakai, T. and Nagao, M., Simulation of traffic flows in a network. *Communications of the ACM*, **12**(6)

Shapiro, R. M. and Saint, H., The representation of algorithms. Applied Data Research Inc., Rome Air Development Centre, Technical Report, TR-69-313, September

Shoshani, A. and Bernstein, A. J., Synchronization in a parallel-accessed data base. *Communications of the ACM*, **12**(11)

Ulrich, E. G., Exclusive simulation of activity in digital networks. *Communications of the ACM*, **12**(2)

1970

Adams, D. A., A model for parallel computations. In *Parallel Processor Systems, Technologies and Applications* (eds L. C. Hobbs, *et al.*), Spartan Press, Washington DC, pp. 311–333

Anon., X3, ANSI, proposed American National Standard – identification of states of the United States (including the district of Columbia) for information interchange. *Communications of the ACM*, **13**(8)

Baer, J. L., Bovet, D. P. and Estrin, G., Legality and other properties of graph models of computations, *Association for Computing Machinery Journal*, **17**, 543–552

Bredt, T. H. and McClusckey, E. J., Analysis and synthesis of control mechanisms for parallel processes. In *Parallel Processor Systems, Technologies and Applications* (eds L. C. Hobbs, *et al.*), Spartan Press, Washington DC, pp. 287–296

Bredt, T. H., A survey of models for parallel computing. Stanford University Electronics Laboratory, Technical Report 8, August

Dennis, J. B., Modular asynchronous control structures for high performance processor. In *Records of Project MAC Conference on Concurrent Systems and Parallel Computation*, ACM, New York, pp. 55–80

Flynn, M. J., Podvin, A. and Shimizu, K., A multiple instruction stream processor system. In *Parallel Processor Systems, Technologies and Applications* (eds L. C. Hobbs, *et al.*), Spartan Press, Washington DC, pp. 251–286

Fuchs, E. and Jackson, P. E., Estimates of distributions of random variables for certain computer communications traffic models, (short communication). *Communications of the ACM*, **13**(12)

Gonzales, M. J. and Ramamoorthy, C. V., Recognition and representation of parallel processable streams in computer programs. In *Parallel Processor Systems, Technologies and Applications* (eds L. C. Hobbs, *et al.*), Spartan Press, Washington DC, pp. 335–371

Graham, W. R., The impact of future developments in computer technology. Presented at the Joint Air Force and Lockheed Aircraft *Conference on Computer Oriented Analysis of Shell Structures* August

Graham, W. R., The parallel and the pipeline computers. *Datamation*, April, 68–71

Lamport, L., Comment on Bell's quadratic quotient method for hash code searching, (short communication). *Communications of the ACM*, **13**(9)

Patil, S. S., Closure properties of interconnections of determinate systems. In *Records of Project MAC Conference Concurrent Systems and Parallel Computation*, ACM, New York, pp. 10–116

Reigel, E. W., Parallelism exposure and exploitation. In *Parallel Processor Systems, Technologies and Applications*, (eds, L. C. Hobbs, *et al.*), Spartan Press, Washington DC, pp. 417–438

Rose, C. W., A system of representation for general purpose digital computer systems. PhD Thesis, Case Western Reserve University, Cleveland, Ohio, USA, September

Rutledge, J. D., Parallel processes, schemata and transformation. IBM Research Report, RC-2912, June

Rutledge, J. D., Program schemata as automata, Part I. *Conference Record, IEEE 11th Annual Symposium on Switching and Automata Theory*, pp. 7–24

Slutz, D. R., Flow graph schemata. In *Records of Project MAC Conference on Concurrent Systems and Parallel Computation*, ACM, New York

Stone, H. S., A pipeline push-down stack computer. In *Parallel Processor Systems, Technologies and Applications* (eds L. C. Hobbs, *et al.*) Spartan Press, Washington DC, pp. 235–249

Tjaden, G. S. and Flynn, M. J., Detection and parallel execution of independent instruction. *IEEE Transactions on Computers*, **19**, October, 889–895

Woods, W. A., Transition network grammars for natural language analysis. *Communications of the ACM*, **13**(10)

1971

Bradshaw, F. T., Structure and representation of digital computer systems, PhD. Thesis, Case Western Reserve University, Cleveland, Ohio, USA, January

Brinsfield, W. A. and Miller, R. E., On the composition of parallel program schemata. *Conference Record IEEE 12th Annual Symposium on Switching and Automata Theory*, October, pp. 20–23

Chen, T. C., Parallelism, pipelining and computer efficiency. *Computer Design*, January

Chen, T. C., Unconventional superspeed computer systems. In *Spring Joint Computer Conference, AFIPS Conference Proceedings*, **38**, AFIPS Press, Montvale, New Jersey, pp. 365–371

Coffman, E. G., A formal microprogram model of parallelism and register sharing. In *Symposium on Computers and Automata*, Polytechnic Institue of Brooklyn, New York, April, pp. 215–223

Commoner, F., Holt, A. W., Evan, S. and Pnueli, A., Marked directed graphs, *Journal of Computer and System Sciences*, **5**, October, 511–523

Courtois, P. J., Heymans, F. and Parnas, D. L. Concurrent control with 'Readers' and 'Writers'. *Communications of the ACM*, **14**(10)

Denning, P. J., Third generation computer systems. *ACM Computing Surveys*, **3**(4) 175–216

Dijkstra, E. W., Hierarchical ordering of sequential processes. *Acta Informatica*, **1**, 115–138

Etherton, M., Data structures for a network design system. *BCS Computer Journal*, **14**(4), 366–374

Gonzales, M. J. and Ramamoorthy, C. V., Program suitability for parallel processing, *IEEE Transactions on Computers*, **20**, June, 647–654

Hoare, C. A. R., Towards a theory of parallel programming. In *Operating Systems Techniques* (ed. R. H. Perrot), Academic Press, London, pp. 61–71

Hurwitz, H. Jr., On the probability distribution of the values of binary trees. *Communications of the ACM*, **14**(2)

Izbicki, H., On marked graphs. Report LR 25.6.023, IBM Laboratories, Vienna, Austria, September

Miranker, W. L., A survey of parallelism in numerical analysis. *SIAM Review*, **13**, October

Munro, I. and Paterson, M. Optimal algorithms for parallel polynomial evaluation. *Conference Records, IEEE 12th Annual Symposium on Switching and Automata Theory*, October, pp. 132–139

Nielson, N. R., The merit of regional computer networks. *Communications of the ACM*, **14**(5)

Noe, J. D., A Petri net model of the CDC 6400. Report 71-04-03, Computer Science Department, University of Washington, USA

Rose, C. W. and Bradshaw, F. T., The LOGOS representation system. Report, Case Western Reserve University, Cleveland, Ohio, USA, October

Shapiro, R. M. and Saint, H., The representation of algorithms as cyclic partial orderings. NASA Final Report, Contract NASW-2097, July

1972

Ahrens, J. H. and Dieter, U., Computer methods for sampling from the exponential and normal distributions. *Communications of the ACM*, **15**(10)

Hansen, B. P., A comparison of two synchronization concepts. *ACTA Informatica*, **1**, 190–199

Baker, H. G., Petri nets and languages. AT & T Bell Laboratories, internal memorandum, New York, USA, May

Beaven, P. A. and Lewin, D. W., An associative parallel processing system for non-numerical computation. *BCS Computer Journal*, **15**(4), 343–349

Bruno, J. L., Coffman, E. G. and Hosken, W. H., Consistency of synchronization nets using P and V operations. *Proceedings of the IEEE 13th Annual Symposium on Switching and Automata Theory*, October, pp. 71–77

Davis, E. W., Concurrent processing of conditional jump trees. In *IEEE Compcon 1972*, IEEE, New York, September, pp. 279–281

Dennis, J. B., Fosseen, J. B. and Linderman, J. P., Data flow schemas. *International Symposium on Theoretical Programming*, Novosibirsk, USSR, August

Dijkstra, E. W., Notes on structured programming. In *Structure Programming*, Academic Press, New York, pp. 1–82

Eisenberg, M. A. and McGuire, R., Further notes on Dijkstra's concurrent programming control problem, (short communication). *Communications of the ACM*, **15**(11)

Findler, N. V., Short note on a heuristic search strategy in long-term memory networks. *Information Processing Letters*, **1**(5), 191–196

Gilbert, P. and Chandler, W. J., Interference between communicating parallel processes. *Communications of the ACM*, **15**(6)

Hansel, A. and Schweb, G. M., On marked graphs III. Report LN 25.6.038, IBM Laboratories, Vienna, Austria, September

Hebermann, A. N., Synchronisation of communicating processes. *Communications of the ACM*, **15**(3), 171–176

Henhapl, W., Firing sequences of marked graphs. Report LN 25.6.023, IBM Laboratories, Vienna, Austria, February

Henhapl, W., Firing sequences of marked graphs II. Report LN 25.6.036, IBM Laboratories, Vienna, Austria, June

Hoare, C. A. R., Towards a theory of parallel programming. In *Operating Systems Techniques*, Academic Press, London

Izbicki, H., On marked graphs II. Report LN 25.6.029, IBM Laboratories, Vienna, Austria, January

Keller, R. M., On the decomposition of asynchronous systems. *IEEE 13th Annual Symposium on Switching and Automata Theory*, pp. 78–89

Keller, R. M., Vector replacement systems: a formalism for modelling asynchronous systems. EE Technical Report No. 117, Princeton University, December, (revised January 1974)

Kotov, V. E., Towards automatic construction of parallel programs. *International Symposium on Theoretical Programming*, Novosibirsk, USSR, August

Kuck, D. J., Muraoka, Y. and Chen, S. C., On the number of operations simultaneously executable in FORTRAN-like programs and their resulting speed-up. *IEEE Transactions on Computers*, **21**, December, 1293–1409

Ligrippo, L., Renamings in program schemas. *Conference Records of the IEEE 13th Annual Symposium on Switching and Automata Theory*, pp. 67–70

Miller, R. E. and Cocke, J., Configurable computers: a new class of general purpose machines. IBM Research Report, RC 3897

Miller, R. E., Some undecidability results for parallel program schemas, *SIAM Computing Journal*, **1**(1), 119–129

Narinyani, A. S., Looking for an approach to a theory of models for parallel computation. *International Symposium on Theoretical Programming*, Novosibirsk, USSR, August

Patil, S. S. and Dennis, J. B., The description and realisation of digital systems. Computation Structures Group Memo 71, Project MAC, MIT, Cambridge, Massachusetts, USA (also appears in the *IEEE Computer Society's 6th Annual International Conference* proceedings)

Patrick, M. L., A highly parallel algorithm for approximating all zeros of a polynomial with only real zeros. *Communications of the ACM*, **15**(11)

Riddle, W. E., The modelling and analysis of supervisory systems. PhD Thesis, Computer Science Department, Stanford University, California, USA, March

Rose, C. W., LOGOS and the software engineer. In *Fall Joint Computer Conference, AFIPS Conference Proceedings*, **41**, AFIPS Press, Montvale, New Jersey, pp. 311–323

Simmons, R. and Slocum, J., Generating English discourse from semantic networks. *Communications of the ACM*, **15**(10)

Vantilborgh, H. and van Lansweerde, A., On an extension of Dijkstra's semaphore primitives. *Information Processing Letters*, **1**, October, 181–186

Vranesic, Z. G. and Hamacher, V. C., Ternary logic in parallel multipliers. *BCS Computer Journal*, **15**(3), 254–258

Walden, D. C., A system for interprocess communication in a resource sharing computer network. *Communications of the ACM*, **15**(4)

Winograd, S., Parallel interactive methods. In *Complexity of Computer Computations* (eds R. E. Miller and J. W. Thatcher), Plenum Press, New York

1973

Agerwala, T. and Flynn, M., Comments on capabilities, limitations and 'correctness' of Petri nets. *Proceedings of the 1st Annual Symposium on Computer Architecture*, (eds G. J. Lipovski and S. A. Szygenda) December, pp. 81–86

Baer, J. L., A survey of some theoretical aspects of multiprocessing. *ACM Computing Surveys*, **5**(1), 31–80

Baker, H. G., Equivalence of Petri nets. Thesis, Department of Electrical Engineering, MIT, Cambridge, Massachusetts, USA, June

Baker, H. G., Rabin's proof of the undecidability of the reachability set inclusion problem of vector addition systems, AT & T Bell Laboratories, internal memorandum, New York, USA, July

Balpaire, G. and Wilmotte, J. P., Semantic aspects of concurrent processes. *Proceedings of ACM SIGPLAN-SIGOPS Interface Meeting on Programming Languages-Operating Systems*, **8**(9), 42–45

Buzen, J. P., Computational algorithms for closed queueing networks with exponential servers. *Communications of the ACM*, **16**(9)

Dosinski, P. R., A data flow programming language. IBM Technical Journal, Watson Research Centre Report RC-4264, March

Gelenbe, E., The distribution of a program in primary and fast buffer storage. *Communications of the ACM*, **16**(7)

Hack, M., A Petri net version of Rabin's undecidability proof for vector addition systems. AT & T Bell Laboratories, internal memorandum, New York, USA, December

Hansen, P. B., Concurrent programming concepts. *ACM Computing Surveys*, **5**(4), 223–245

Hansen, P. B., *Operating System Principles*, Prentice-Hall, Englewood Cliffs, New Jersey

Horning, J. J. and Randell, B., Process structuring. *ACM Computing Surveys*, **5**(1), 5–30

Keller, R. M., Parallel program schemata and maximal parallelism. *Journal of the ACM*, **20**(3), 514–537

Keller, R. M., Parallel program schemata and maximal parallelism. *Journal of the ACM*, **20**(4), 696–710

Kosaraju, S. R., Limitations of Dijksta's semaphore primitives and Petri nets. *Operating Systems Review*, **7**(4), 122–126

Lipton, R. J., On synchronization of primitive systems., PhD Thesis, Carnegie-Mellon University, Pittsburgh, Pennsylvania, USA

Meadows, N. G., Automatic frequency and Mikhailov locus plotting for systems with distributed lags: a new analogue computer technique. *BSC Computer Journal*, **16**(3), 266–268

Miller, R. E. and Brinsfield, W. A., Insertion of parallel program schemata. *Proceedings of the IEEE 7th Annual Princeton Conference on Information Sciences and Systems*, March

Miller, R. E., A comparison of some theoretical models of a parallel computation. *IEEE Transactions on Computers*, **22**(8), 710–717

Misunas, D., Petri nets and speed independent design. *Communications of the ACM*, **16**(8), 474–481

Nash, B. O., Reachability problems in vector addition systems. *The American Mathematical Monthly*, **80**(3), 292–295

Noe, J. D. and Nutt, G. J., Macro E-nets for representation of parallel systems. *IEEE Transactions on Computers*, **22**(8), 718–727

Randel, B., Process structuring. *ACM Computing Surveys*, **5**, March, 5–30

Rosenfeld, A. and Milgram, D. L., Parallel sequential array automata. *Information Processing Letters*, **2**(2), 43–46

Sethi, R., A note on implementing parallel assignment instructions. *Information Processing Letters*, **2**(4), 91–95

White, W. W., A status report on computing algorithms for mathematical programming. *ACM Computing Surveys*, **5**(3), 135–166

Yoeli, M., Petri nets and asynchronous control networks. Applied Analysis and Computer Science Research Report CS-73-07, University of Waterloo, Ontario, Canada, April

1974

Adam, T. L., Chandy, K. M. and Dickson, J. R., A comparison of list schedules for parallel processing systems. *Communications of the ACM*, **17**(12)

Anon., Parallel processing. Proceedings 1974. In *Lecture Notes in Computer Science*, **24**, Springer-Verlag, Berlin

Agerwala, T., A complete model for representing the coordination of asynchronous processes. Hopkins Computer Research Report ♯32, Computer Science program, The Johns Hopkins University, Baltimore, Maryland, USA, July

Agerwala, T., An analysis of controlling agents for asynchronous processes. Hopkins Computer Research Report ♯35, Computer Science program, Johns Hopkins University, Baltimore, Maryland, USA, August

Allery, G. D., Data communications and public networks. *IFIP Congress*, Stockholm, Sweden, pp. 117–122

Atkinson, M. P., PIXIN: a data language for network modelling, *IFIP Congress*, Stockholm, Sweden, pp. 296–300

Bahrs, A. A., Operation patterns (an extensible model of an extensible language). In *Lecture Notes in Computer Science*, **5**, Springer-Verlag, Berlin, pp. 217–246

Boudin, F., Madsule, F. and Mendelblaum, H. G., General purpose, programmable interface between computers and physical devices. *IFAC–IFIP Workshop on Real-Time Programming*, Budapest, Hungary, pp. 169–176

Campbell, A. H. and Habermann, A. N., The specification of process synchronization by path expressions. *Lecture Notes in Computer Science*, **16**, Springer-Verlag, Berlin, pp. 89–102

Chandra, A. K., The power of parallelism and nondeterminism in programming. *IFIP Congress*, Stockholm, Sweden, pp. 461–465

Chupin, J. C., Control concepts of a logical network machine for data banks. *IFIP Congress*, Stockholm, Sweden, pp. 291–295

Corradi, C. and Gambetta, G., A numerical method for estimating distributed lag models. *IFIP Congress*, Stockholm, Sweden, 638–641

Culik, K.II and Maibaum, T. S. E. Parallel rewriting systems on terms. In *Lecture Notes in Computer Science*, **14**, Springer-Verlag, Berlin, pp. 495–510

Davies, D. W., Packet switching, message switching and future data communication networks. *IFIP Congress*, Stockholm, Sweden, pp. 147–150

Dennis, J. B. and Misunas, D. P., A computer architecture for highly parallel signal processing. *Proceedings of the ACM Annual Conference*, November, pp. 402–409

Dezani-Ciancaglini, M. and Zacchi, M., Application of Church-Rosser properties to increase the parallelism and efficiency of algorithms. In *Lecture Notes in Computer Science*, **14**, Springer-Verlag, Berlin, pp. 170–184

Dijkstra, E. W., Self-stabilizing systems in spite of distributed control, (short communication). *Communications of the ACM*, **17**(11)

Duff, M. J. B., Watson, D. M. and Deutsch, E. S., A parallel computer for array processing, *IFIP Congress*, Stockholm, Sweden, pp. 94–97

Eswaran, K. P., Placement of records in a file and file allocation in a computer network. *IFIP Congress*, Stockholm, Sweden, pp. 304–307

Even, S., Parallelism in tape-sorting. *Communications of the ACM*, **17**(4)

Ghosh, S. P. and Astrahan, M. A., A Translator optimizer for obtaining answers to entity set queries from an arbitrary access path network. *IFIP Congress*, Stockholm, Sweden, pp. 436–439

Grauer, H., Computer graphics in process control and monitoring. *IFAC–IFIP Workshop on Real-Time Programming*, Budapest, Hungary, pp. 177–186

Groner, L. H. and Goel, A. L., Concurrency in hashed file access. *IFIP Congress*, Stockholm, Sweden, pp. 431–435

Hack, M., Correction to 'Analysis of production schemata by Petri nets'. *Computation Structures Note 17*, Project MAC, MIT, Cambridge, Massachusetts, USA, (June 1974)

Hack, M., Decision problems for Petri nets and vector addition systems. *Computation Structures Memo 95-1*, Project MAC, MIT, Cambridge, Massachusetts, USA, August

Hine, J. H. and Fitzwater, D. R. Modelling a drum in a queuing network. *IFIP Congress*, Stockholm, Sweden, pp. 226–229

Hoare, C. A. R., Monitors: an operating system structuring concept. *Communications of the ACM*, **17**(10), 549–557

Houston, I. N., The run-time characteristics of CAMAC computer systems. *IFAC–IFIP Workshop on Real-Time Programming*, Budapest, Hungary, pp. 135–142

Howard, V. J., A model to investigate inter-process communication in a distributed computer system. *IFAC–IFIP Workshop on Real-Time Programming*, Budapest, Hungary, pp. 187–194

Jackson, L. W. and Dasgupta, S., The identification of parallel micro-operations. *Information Processing Letters*, **2**(6), 180–184

Kahn, G., The semantics of a simple language for parallel programming. *IFIP Congress*, Stockholm, Sweden, pp. 471–475

Kleinrock, L., Resource allocation in computer systems and computer-communication networks. *IFIP Congress*, Stockholm, Sweden, pp. 11–18

Lagrippo, L., Renamings in parallel program schemas. PhD Thesis, University of Waterloo, Ontario, Canada, February

Lamport, L., A new solution to Dijkstra's concurrent programming problem. *Communications of the ACM*, **17**(8)

Lamport, L., On concurrent reading and writing. Report CA-7409-0511, Masachussets Computer Associates, Inc., September (revised from March 1976)

Lamport, L., The parallel execution of DO loops. *Communications of the ACM*, **17**(2)

Lautenbach, K. and Schmid, H. A., Use of Petri nets for proving correctness of concurrent process systems. *IFIP Congress*, Stockholm, Sweden, pp. 187–191

Lesser, V. R., The design of an emulator for a parallel machine language. *ACM SIGPLAN Notices*, **9**(8), 23–36

Lewis, A., The implementation of the CAMAC intermediate language in real-time computer systems. *IFAC–IFIP Workshop on Real-Time Programming*, Budapest, Hungary, pp. 143–150

Liskov, B., A note on CLU. Computation Structure Group, MIT, Cambridge, Massachusetts, USA

Maravac, N., A method for defining general networks for CAD, using interactive computer graphics. *BCS Computer Journal*, **17**(4), 332–336

Martel, C. C., Cunningham, I. M. and Gruschow, M. S., The BNR network: a Canadian experience with packet switching technology. *IFIP Congress*, Stockholm, Sweden, pp. 160–164

Meyer, S. C., An analysis of two models for parallel computations. PhD Thesis, Department of Electrical Engineering, Rice University, Houston, Texas, USA

Miller, R. E. and Cocke, J., Configurable computers: a new class of general purpose machines. *Lecture Notes in Computer Science*, **5**, Springer-Verlag, Berlin, pp. 285–298

Morgan, D. E., Banks, W., Colvin, W. and Sutton, D., A performance measurement system for computer networks. *IFIP Congress*, Stockholm, Sweden, pp. 29–33

Nielson, N. R., The implications of star computing networks. *IFIP Congress*, Stockholm, Sweden, pp. 908–912

Parent, M., Presentation of the control graph models. In *Lecture Notes in Computer Science*, **16**, Springer-Verlag, Berlin, pp. 279–292

Peterson, J. L. and Bredt, T. H., A comparison of models of parallel computation. *IFIP Congress*, Stockholm, Sweden, pp. 466–470

Peterson, J. L., Modelling of parallel systems. PhD Thesis, *Electrical Engineering Department*, Stanford University, January

Pfeiffer, K., Real-Time CAMAC interfacing in interpretive programming systems. *IFAC–IFIP Workshop on Real-Time Programming*, Budapest, Hungary, pp. 161–168

Pouzin, L., CIGALE, the packet switching machine of the CYCLADES computer network. *IFIP Congress*, Stockholm, Sweden, pp. 155–159

Price, W. L., Simulation studies of an isarithmically controlled store and forward data communication network. *IFIP Congress*, Stockholm, Sweden, pp. 151–154

Raymond, J. and du Masle, J., NJCI, a network job control language *IFIP Congress*, Stockholm, Sweden, pp. 301–303

Reiser, M. and Kobayashi, H., The effects of service time distributions on system performance. *IFIP Congress*, Stockholm, Sweden, pp. 230–234

Rice, J. R., Parallel algorithms for adaptive quadrature-convergence. *IFIP Congress*, Stockholm, Sweden, pp. 600–604

Riddle, W. E., The equivalence of Petri nets and message transmission models. SRM 97, University of Newcastle-upon-Tyne, UK, August

Salomaa, A., Parallelism in rewriting systems. In *Lecture Notes in Computer Science*, **14**, Springer-Verlag, Berlin, pp. 523–533

Schomberg, M. G., The use of CAMAC in multi-programming real-time systems. *IFAC–IFIP Workshop on Real-Time Programming*, Budapest, Hungary, pp. 151–160

Sharma, R. L., Shah, J. C., El-Bardai, M. T. and Sharma, K. K., C-system: multiprocessor network architecture. *IFIP Congress*, Stockholm, Sweden, pp. 19–23

Sonnenburg, C. R. A configurable parallel computing system. PhD dissertation, University of Michigan, Ann Arbor, USA, October

Tam, W. C. and Karplus, W. J. PDEL-ID: an extension of the PDEL for distributed parameter system identification. *ACM SIGPLAN Notices*, **9**(4), 82–90

Traub, J. F., Parallel alogorithms and parallel computational complexity. *IFIP Congress*, Stockholm, Sweden, pp. 685–690

Tsao, N., On the distributions of significant digits and roundoff errors. *Communications of the ACM*, **17**(5), 269

Wedburg, G. H. and Hauschild, L. W., The general electric network monitor system. *IFIP Congress*, Stockholm, Sweden, pp. 24–28

Van Leeuwen, J., A partial solution to the reachability problem for vector-addition systems. *Proceedings, 6th Annual ACM Symposium on Theory of Computing*, May, pp. 303–309

1975

Anderson, G. A. and Jensen, E. D. Computer interconnection structures: taxonomy, characteristics, and examples. *ACM Computing Surveys*, **7**(4), 197–213

Anon., Axiomatic proof techniques for parallel programs. PhD Thesis, Cornell University, Ithaca, New York, USA

Anon., Parallel processing, Proceedings 1974. In *Lecture Notes in Computer Science*, **24**, Springer-Verlag, Berlin

Barta, B. Z., PACOL: a parallel control language. *ACM SIGPLAN Notices*, **10**(3), 44–53

Chambers, J. A. and Poore, R. V., Computer networks in higher education: socio-economic-political factors. *Communications of the ACM*, **18**(4)

Chen, T. C., Overlap and pipeline processing. In *Introduction to Computer Architecture* (ed. H. S. Stone), SRA, Palo Alto, California, USA, pp. 375–431

Cremers, A. and Hibbard, T. N., An algebraic approach to concurrent programming control and related complexity problems. Report, USC Computer Science Program, USA, November

Crepsi-Reghizzi, S. and Mandriolli, D., A decidability theorem for a class of vector-addition systems. *Information Processing letters*, **3**(3), 78–80

Diehl, W. and Sanders, D., Real-time BASIC used in a distributed network. *IFAC–IFIP Workshop on Real-Time Programming*, Boston/Cambridge, Massachusetts, USA, pp. 159–164

Dijkstra, E. W., Guarded commands, nondeterminacy, and formal derivation of programs. *Communications of the ACM*, **18**(8), 453–457

Dniestrowski, A. and Equer, B., Implementation of a real-time pattern recognition system on a multiprocessor configuration. *IFAC–IFIP Workshop on Real-Time Programming*, Boston/Cambridge, Massachusetts, USA, pp. 171–178

Dumas, J. M. and Prunet, F., Searching for properties on a parallel process model. *IFAC–IFIP Workshop on Real-Time Programming*, Boston/Cambridge, Massachusetts, USA, pp. 97–104

Ellis, C. A., The validation of parallel co-operating processes. Report UC-CS-065-75 Computer Science Department, University of Colorado, Boulder, Colorado, USA, April

Gavril, F., Merging with parallel processors. *Communications of the ACM*, **18**(10)

Geller, D. P. and Weinberg, G. M. The principle of sufficient reason: a guide to language design for parallel processing. *ACM SIGPLAN Notices*, **10**(3), 34–38

Hack, M., Petri net languages. Computation Structures Group Memo 124, Project MAC, MIT, Cambridge, Massachusetts, USA, June

Halling, H., A distributed control system using the CAMAC serial highway and microprocessor modules. *IFAC–IFIP Workshop on Real-Time Programming*, Boston/Cambridge, Massachusetts, USA, pp. 13–24

Hansen, P. B., The programming language Concurrent Pascal, *IEEE Transactions on Software Engineering*, **1**(2), 199–207

Hansen, P. B., The purpose of Concurrent Pascal. *ACM SIGPLAN Notices*, **10**(6), 305–309

Hansen, P. B., Universal types in Concurrent Pascal, *Information Processing Letters*, **3**(6), 165–166

Irani, K. B. and Sonnenburg, C. R., Exploitation of implicit parallelism in arithmetic expressions for an asynchronous environment. Report, Department of Electronic and Computer Science Engineering, University of Michigan, Ann Arbor, USA

Keller, R. M. Look-ahead processors. *ACM Computing Surveys*, **7**(4), 177–195

Kimbleton, S. R. and Schneider, G. M., Computer communication networks: approaches, objectives, and performance considerations. *ACM Computing Surveys*, **7**(3), 129–173

Kirkman, H. C., Evolution of the daresbury computer network. *IFAC–IFIP Workshop on Real-Time Programming*, Boston/Cambridge, Massachusetts, USA, pp. 165–170

Kobayashi, H., Horner's rule for the evaluation of general closed queuing networks. *Communications of the ACM*, **18**(10)

Krohn, H., A parallel approach to code generation for FORTRAN-like compilers. *ACM SIGPLAN Notices*, **10**(3), 146–152

Lamport, L., On programming parallel computers. *ACM SIGPLAN Notices*, **10**(3), 25–33

Lamport, L., Multiple byte processing with full-word instructions. *Communications of the ACM*, **18**(8)

Laure, P. E. and Campbell, R. H., Formal semantics of high-level primitives for coordinating concurrent processes. *ACTA Informatica*, **5**, 247–332

Lipton, R. J., Miller, R. E. and Snyder, L., Introduction to linear asynchronous structures. *Proceedings of the Symposium on Petri Nets and Related Methods*, MIT, Cambridge, Massachusetts, USA

Lipton, R. J., Reduction: a method of proving properties of parallel programs. *Communications of the ACM*, **18**(12)

Lipton, R. J., Miller, R. E. and Snyder, L., Synchronization and computing capabilities of linear synchronous structures. *Proceedings of the 16th Annual Symposium on Foundations of Computer Science*, Berkeley, California, USA, pp. 19–28

Marcus, R. S., A translation computer interface for a network of heterogeneous interactive retrieval systems. *ACM SIGPLAN Notices*, **10**(1), 2–12

Miller, R. E., Eight lectures on parallelism. Presented at CIME International Mathematical Summer Centre on 'Theoretical Computer Science', June, pp. 5–63

Miller, R. E., Relationships among models of parallelism and synchronization *Proceedings of the Symposium on Petri Nets and Related Methods*, MIT, Cambridge, Massachusetts, USA, July

Morris, D. and Treleaven, P. C., A stream processing network. *ACM SIGPLAN Notices*, **10**(3), 107–112

Nelson, J. M. and Cohn, C. E., Parallel processing in FORTRAN with floating-point hardware. *Software Practice and Experience*, **5**(1), 65–68

Osterweil, J. P. and Nutt, G. J., Modelling process-resource activity. Report UC-CS-084-75 Computer Science Department, University of Colorado, Boulder, Colorado, USA

Pertridge, D., A dynamic database which automatically removes unwanted generalisation for the efficient analysis of language features that exhibit a disparate frequency distribution. *BCS Computer Journal*, **18**(1), 43–48

Presberg, D. L. and Johnson, N. W., The paralyzer: IVTRAN's parallelism analyzer and synthesizer., *ACM SIGPLAN Notices*, **10**(3), 9–16

Presser, L., Multiprogramming coordination. *ACM Computing Surveys*, **7**(1), 21–44

Reddi, S. S. and Feustel, E. A., A restructurable computer system. Report, Laboratory for Computer Science and Engineering, Rice University, Texas, USA, March

Roussopoulos, N. and Mylopoulos, J., Using semantic networks for data base management. In *Proceedings of the International Conference on Very Large Databases*, IEEE, Framingham, Massachusetts, September

Russell, R. D. and Sparrman, P., A technique for integrating remote minicomputers into a general computer's file system. *IFAC–IFIP Workshop on Real-Time Programming*, Boston/Cambridge, Massachusetts, USA, pp. 179–184

Sayward, F. G., A correctness criterion for CSP parallel programs. *ACM SIGPLAN Notices*, **10**(9), 30–38

Schneck, P. B., Movement of implicit parallel and vector expressions out of program loops. *ACM SIGPLAN Notices*, **10**(3), 103–106

Schoeffler, J. D., Haelsig, M. and Rose, C. W., Microprocessor-based communication and instrument control for distributed control systems. *IFAC–IFIP Workshop on Real-Time Programming*, Boston/Cambridge, Massachusetts, USA, pp. 153–158

Sekino, L. C., Multiple concurrent updates. In *Proceedings of the International Conference on Very Large Databases*, IEEE, Framingham, Massachusetts, USA, September

Shooman, M. L. and Bolsky, M. I., Types, distribution, and test and correction times for programming errors. *ACM SIGPLAN Notices*, **10**(6), 347–357

Shrivastava, S. K., A view of concurrent process synchronisation. *BCS Computer Journal*, **18**(4)

Sintzoff, M. and van Lamsweerde, A., Constructing correct and efficient concurrent programs. *ACM SIGPLAN Notices*, **10**(6), 319–326

Smedema, C. H., Real-time concepts and Concurrent Pascal. *IFAC–IFIP Workshop on Real-Time Programming*, Boston/Cambridge, Massachusetts, USA, pp. 31–38

Syre, J. C., From the single assignment software concept to a new class of multiprocessor architecture. Report, Department d'Informatique, CERT BP4025, 1055, Toulouse, France

Thurber, K. J. and Wald, L. D., Associative and parallel processors. *ACM Computing Surveys*, **7**(4), 215–255

Waite, W. M., Hints on distributing portable software. *Software Practice and Experience*, **5**(3), 295–308

1976

Anshel, M., Decision problems for HNN groups and vector addition systems. *Mathematics of Computation*, **30**(133), 154–156

Barak, A. B., On the parallel evaluation of division-free arithmetic expressions with fan-in of three, *Information Processing Letters*, **5**(1), 18–19

Campbell, R. H., Path expressions: a technique for a specifying process synchronization. PhD Thesis, Computing Laboratory, University of Newcastle-upon-Tyne, UK

Cardoza, E., Lipton, R. and Meyer, A. R., Exponential space complete problems for Petri nets and commutative semigroups: preliminary report. *Proceedings ACM Theory of Computing Symposium*, May, pp. 50–54

Chrobot, S., Layer – a language construction for concurrent structural program design. *Information Processing Letters*, **4**(5), 113–117

De Millo, R. A. and Vairavan, K., On the efficiency of on-line versus off-line scheduling strategies. Report TR-CS-76-8, University of Wisconsin-Milwaukee, USA

De Millo, R. A., Vairavan, K. and Sycara-Cyranski, E., A study of schedules as models of synchronous parallel computation, Report TR-CS-76-5, University of Wisconsin-Milwaukee, USA, March

Decour, K. and Duijvestein, A. J. W., Enclosures: an access control mechanism with applications in parallel programming and other areas of system programming. *Information Processing Letters*, **5**(5), 125–135

Dijkstra, E. W., In *A Discipline of Programming*, Prentice-Hall, Englewood Cliffs, New Jersey, USA

Dill, F. H., Alternative computer architectures using LSI. IBM Research Report, RC 5555, June

Fishman, G. S., Sampling from the gamma distribution on a computer. *Communications of the ACM*, **19**(7), 407

Fry, J. P. and Sibley, E. H., Evolution of database management systems. *ACM Computing Surveys*, **8**(1), 7–42

Gairola, B. K. and Rajaraman, V., A distributed index sequential access method. *Information Processing Letters*, **5**(1), 1–5

Hansen, P. B., The solo operating system: a Concurrent Pascal program. *Software Practice and Experience*, **6**(2), 141–150

Howard, J. H., Signalling in monitors. *Proceedings of the 2nd International Conference on Software Engineering*, San Francisco, USA, October

Keller, R. M., Formal verification of parallel programs. *Communications of the ACM*, **19**(7)

Kessels, J. L. W., Parallel programming concepts in a definitional language. *ACM SIGPLAN Notices*, **11**(10), 19–31

Lamport, L., Comments on 'A synchronization anomaly'. *Information Processing Letters*, **4**(4), 88–89

Lennon, W. J., Baatz, E. L., Collusi, S. and Kinnear, K. E., Jr., Using a distributed mini-computer network to automate a biochemical laboratory. *ACM SIGPLAN Notices*, **11**(4)

Lipton, R. J., The reachability problem requires exponential space. Research Report #62, Computer Science Department, Yale University, New Haven, Connecticut, USA, January

Madsen, N. K., Rodrigue, G. H. and Karush, J. I., Matrix multiplication by diagonols on a vector–parallel processor. *Information Processing Letters*, **5**(2), 41–45

Mahmoud, S. and Roirdon, J. S., Optimal allocation of resources in distributed information networks. *ACM Transactions on Database Systems*, **1**, 66–78

Maruyama, K. and Smith, S. E., Optimal reorganization of distributed space disk files. *Communications of the ACM*, **19**(11)

Merlin, P. M., A methodology for the design and implementation of communication protocols. *IEEE Transactions on Communications*, **24**(6), 614–621

Metcalfe, R. M. and Boggs, D. R., Ethernet: distributed packet switching for local computer networks. *Communications of the ACM*, **19**(7)

Michaels, A. S., Mittman, B. and Carlson, C. R., A comparison of the relational and CODASYL approaches to data-base management. *ACM Computing Surveys*, **8**(1), 125–151

Miller, R. E., Mathematical studies of parallel computation. *Proceedings 1st IBM Symposium on Mathematical Foundations of Computer Science*, IBM Amagi, Japan, October

Owicki, S. and Gries, D. An axiomatic proof technique for parallel programs I. *Acta Informatica*, **6**, 319–340

Owicki, S. and Gries, D., Verifying properties of parallel programs: an axiomatic approach. *Communications of the ACM*, **19**(5)

Rivest, R. L. and Pratt, V. R., The mutual exclusion problem for unreliable processes: preliminary report. *Proceedings of the 17th Annual Symposium on Foundations of Computer Science*, October, pp. 1–8

Schmid, H. A., On the efficient implementation of conditional critical regions and construction of monitors. *ACTA Informatica*, **6**, 227–249

Schneider, E. A., Synchronization of finite state shared resources. PhD Thesis, Computer Science Department, Carnegie-Mellon University, Pittsburgh, Pennsylvania, USA, March

Tsichritzis, D. C. and Lochovsky, F. H., Hierarchical data-base management: a survey. *ACM Computing Surveys*, **8**(1), 105–123

Zave, P., On the formal definition of processes. *Proceedings of International Conference on Parallel Processing*, Maryland, USA

1977

Andler, S., Synchronisation primitives and the verification of concurrent programs. Report, Department of Computer Science, Carnegie-Mellon University, Pittsburgh, Pennsylvania, USA, 25 May

Aspinall, D. and Daglass, E. L., Design methods for digital systems including parallelism. *IEE Journal Electronic Circuits and Electronic Engineering*, **1**(2), 49–56

Baer, J.-L. and Ellis, C. S., Model, design, and evaluation of a compiler for a parallel processing environment. *IEEE Transactions on Software Engineering*, **3**(6), 394–405

Balbo, G., Bruell, S. C. and Schwetman, H. D., Customer classes and closed network models – a solution technique, *IFIP Congress*, Toronto, Canada pp. 559–564

Baran, P., Some perspectives on networks – past, present and future. *IFIP Congress*, Toronto, Canada, pp. 459–464

Baudet, G. M., Brent, R. P. and Kung, H. T., Parallel, execution of a sequence of tasks on an asynchronous multiprocessor. Report, Department of Computer Science, Carnegie-Mellon University, Pittsburgh, Pennsylvania, USA, June

Benson, D. B. and Jeffords, R. D., Parallel decomposition, of LR(k) parsers. *Lecture Notes in Computer Science*, **52**, Springer-Verlag, Berlin, pp. 76–86

Bisiani, R., Paging behaviour of knowledge networks. Department of Computer Science, Carnegie-Mellon University, Pittsburgh, Pennsylvania, USA, 10 August

Buhr, R. J. A., Bowen, B. A. and Paquet, J. L., PL/M as a concurrent high level language. In *Proceedings of the International Symposium on Mini and Micro Computers*, IEEE, New York, USA, November, pp. 306–311

Cahit, I., Realization of graceful permutation by a shuffle-exchange network. *Information Processing Letters*, **6**(5), 171–173

Chandi, K. M., Howard, J. H. and Towsley, D. F., Product form and local balance in queuing networks, *Journal of the ACM*, **24**(2), 250–263

Dasgupta, S., Parallelism in loop-free microprograms. *IFIP Congress*, Toronto, Canada, pp. 745–750

Dawes, N. W., A simple network interacting program's executive (SNIPE). *Software Practice and Experience*, **7**(3), 341–346

De Millo, R. A., Vairavan, K. and Sycara-Cyranski, E., A study of schedules as models of synchronous parallel computation. *Journal of the ACM*, **24**(4), 544–565

Dennis, J. B., A language design for structured concurrency. In *Design and Implementation of Programming Languages*, (eds D. A. Fisher and J. H. Williams.), Springer-Verlag, Berlin, pp. 231–242

Dowsing, R. D., Structured programming constructs for concurrency in program optimisation. *ACM SIGPLAN Notices*, **12**(9), 31–35

Emery, J. C., Managerial and economic issues in distributed computing. *IFIP Congress*, Toronto, Canada, pp. 945–956

Feldman, J. A., Synchronising distant cooperating processes. Report TR26, Department of Computer Science, University of Rochester, October

Flon, L. and Suzuki, N., Nondeterminism and the correctness of parallel programs. Report, Department of Computer Science, Carnegie-Mellon University, Pittsburgh, Pennsylvania, USA, May

Ford, M. L., Business problems in planning of international data communications networks. *IFIP Congress*, Toronto, Canada, pp. 437–440

Forgy, C. L., A production system monitor for parallel computers. Department of Computer Science, Carnegie-Mellon University, Pittsburgh, Pennsylvania, USA, April

Goto, E., Ida, T. and Gunji, T., Parallel hashing algorithms. *Information Processing Letters*, **6**(1), 8–13

Gries, D. An exercise in proving parallel programs correct. *Communications of the ACM*, **20**(12)

Hansen, P. Experience with modular concurrent programming. *IEEE Transactions on Software Engineering*, **3**(2), 156–159

Hartmann, A. C., A concurrent pascal compiler for minicomputers. *Lecture Notes in Computer Science*, **50**, Springer-Verlag, Berlin

Herschberg, I. S. and Boekhorst, J. C. A., Concurrent file access under unpredictability. *Information Processing Letters*, **6**(6), 203–208

Hewitt, C. and Baker, H., Laws for communicating parallel processes. *IFIP Congress*, Toronto, Canada, 987–992

Hillman, A. L. and Schofield, D., EDIT – an interactive network service: design and implementation. *Software Practice and Experience*, **7**(5), 595–612

Holmes, G., Programming languages-real time becomes concurrent. *Computer Industry Annual Review*, Walker-Ellis, Tonbridge, Kent, UK, p. 18

Hutchinson, D. A., Riordan, J. S. and Mahmoud, S. A., A recursive algorithm for deadlock preemption in computer networks. *IFIP Congress*, Toronto, Canada, pp. 241–246

Hyafil, L. and Kung, H. T., The complexity of parallel evaluation of linear recurrences. *Journal of the ACM*, **24**(3), 513–521

Ida, T. and Goto, E., Performance of a parallel hash hardware with key deletion. *IFIP Congress*, Toronto, Canada, pp. 643–648

Johnson, D. B., Efficient algorithms for shortest paths in sparse networks. *Journal of the ACM*, **24**,(1), 1–13

Kahn, G. and Baker, H., Coroutines and networks of parallel processes. *IFIP Congress*, Toronto, Canada

Kleinrock, L., Performance of distributed multi-access computer communication systems. *IFIP Congress*, Toronto, Canada, pp. 547–552

Krzesinski, A., Gerber, A. S. and Teunissen, P., A multiclass network model of a multiprogramming timesharing computer system. *IFIP Congress*, Toronto, Canada, pp. 481–486

Kuck, D. J., A survey of parallel machine organization and programming. *ACM Computing Surveys*, **9**(1), 29–59

Kung, H. T. and Song, S. W., An efficient parallel garbage collection system and its correctness proof. Report, Department of Computer Science, Carnegie-Mellon University, Pittsburgh, Pennsylvania, USA, September

Lamport, L., Concurrent reading and writing. *Communications of the ACM*, **20**(11)

Lamport, L., Proving the correctness of multiprocess programs. *IEEE Transactions on Software Engineering*, **3**(2), 125–143

Le Lann, G., Distributed systems – towards a formal approach. *IFIP Congress*, Toronto, Canada, pp. 155–160

Lipsky, L. and Church, J. D., Applications of a queuing network model for a computer system. *ACM Computing Surveys*, **9**(3), 205–221

Maekawa, M., Interprocess communications in a highly diversified distributed system. *IFIP Congress*, Toronto, Canada, pp. 149–154

Mamrak, S. A., Dynamic response time prediction for computer networks. *Communications of the ACM*, **20**(7), 461

McGibbon, C. I. and Gibbs, H., DATAPAC – a phased approach to the introduction of public packet-switched network. *IFIP Congress*, Toronto, Canada, pp. 509–514

Miller, R. E. and Yap, C. K., Formal specification and analysis of loosely connected processes. IBM Research Report RC-6716, September

Miller, R. E., Theoretical studies of synchronous and parallel processing. *Proceedings of the 1977 Conference on Information Sciences and Systems*, Johns Hopkins University, Baltimore, Maryland, USA, March, pp. 333–339

Milne, G. and Milner, R., Concurrent processes and their syntax. Report CSR-2-77, Department of Computer Science, University of Edinburgh, UK, May

Mockapetris, P. V., Lyle, M. R. and Fisher, D. J., On the design of local network interfaces. *IFIP Congress*, Toronto, Canada, pp. 427–430

Morgan, H. L. and Levin, K. D., Optimal program and data locations in computer networks. *Communications of the ACM*, **20**(5), 315

Nishimura, T., Formalization of concurrent processes. *IFIP Congress*, Toronto, Canada, pp. 929–938

Nutt, G. J., A parallel processor operating system. *IEEE Transactions on Software Engineering*, **3**(6), 467–475

Paquet, J. L., Buhr, R. J. A. and Bowen, B. A., Concurrent high level language machines and kernel. *Proceedings of the International Symposium on Mini and Micro Computers*, IEEE, New York, USA, November, pp. 293–298

Peterson, J. L. and Fischer, M. J., Economical solutions for the critical section problem in a distributed system. *Proceedings of the 9th Annual ACM Symposium on Theory of Computing*, May, pp. 91–97

Peterson, J. L., Petri Nets. *ACM Computing Surveys*, **9**(3), 223–252

Pouzin, L., Packet networks – issues and choices. *IFIP Congress*, Toronto, Canada, pp. 515–522

Price, W. L., Adaptive routing in store-and-forward networks and the importance of load splitting. *IFIP Congress*, Toronto, Canada, pp. 309–314

Rackoff, C., The covering and boundedness problems of vector addition systems. *Theoretical Computer Science Journal*, **10**, 338–342

Roberts, L. G., Packet network design – the third generation. *IFIP Congress*, Toronto, Canada, pp. 541–546

Rudin, H., Analysis of flow control in switched data networks. *IFIP Congress*, Toronto, Canada, pp. 321–326

Sacerdote, G. S. and Tenney, R. L., The decidability of the reachability problem for vector addition systems. *Proceedings ACM Theory of Computing Symposium*, May

Sakai, T., Hayashi, T., Kitazawa, S., Tabata, K. and Kanade, T., Inhouse computer network kuipnet, *IFIP Congress*, Toronto, Canada, pp. 161–166

Sayward, F. G., Research issues in synchronization primitives for operating systems languages. *In Research Divisions in Software Technology*, (ed. P. Wagner), MIT Press, Cambridge, Massachusetts

Sevcik, K. C., Priority scheduling disciplines in queuing network models of computer systems. *IFIP Congress*, Toronto, Canada, pp. 565–570

Silberschatz, A., Extending Concurrent Pascal to allow dynamic resource managment. *IEEE Transactions on Software Engineering*, **3**(3), 210–217

Silberschatz, A., On the input/output mechanism in Concurrent Pascal. *The IEEE Computer Society's 1st International Conference on Computer Software and Applications*, Chicago, Illinois, USA, November

Steele, K. A., CPM network analysis with a storage tube terminal. *BCS Computer Journal*, **20**(4), 330–334

Stone, H. S., Multiprocessor scheduling with the aid of network flow algorithms, *IEEE Transactions on Software Engineering*, **3**(1), 85–93

Subramanian, K., A model for concurrent diagnosis in a microprogrammable system using a dynamic test scheme. *IFIP Congress*, Toronto, Canada, pp. 421–426

Szentes, R., Concurrent programming and the concurrent Pascal language. *Inf. Elektron (Hungary)*, **12**(6), 352–356

Tajibnapis, W. D., A correctness proof of a topology information maintenance protocol for a distributed computer network. *Communications of the ACM*, **20**(7)

Thompson, C. D. and Kung, H. T., Sorting on a mesh-connected parallel computer. *Communications of the ACM*, **20**(4)

Tomita, S., Shibayama, K., Oyanagi, S. and Hagiwara, H., Hardware organization of a low level parallel processor. *IFIP Congress*, Toronto, Canada, pp. 855–860

Turner, R. and Strecker, B., Use of the LRU stack depth distribution for simulation of paging behaviour. *Communications of the ACM*, **20**(11)

Van Sickle, L. and Chandy, K. M., Computational complexity of network design algorithms. *IFIP Congress*, Toronto, Canada, pp. 235–240

Wallach, Y., Scheduling algorithms for concurrent execution. *BCS Computer Journal*, **20**(2), 132–136

Warren, H. S. Jr., Functions realizable with word-parallel logical and two's complement addition instructions (short communication). *Communications of the ACM*, **20**(6)

Wood, D., Two variations on n-parallel finite state generators. *BCS Computer Journal*, **20**(1), 63–67

Zave, P. and Fitzwater, D. R., Specification of asynchronous interaction using primitive functions. Technical Report, Department of Computer Science, University of Maryland, College Park, Maryland, USA

Ziegler, K. Jr., Distributed data base where are you? (a tutorial). *IFIP Congress*, Toronto, Canada, pp. 113–116

Zuczek, R., The universal space for parallel computation. *Information Processing Letters*, **6**(2), 42–45

1978

Armstrong, J. L., Programming a parallel computer for robot vision. *BCS Computer Journal*, **21**(3), 215–218

Bard, Y., The VM/370 performance predictor. *ACM Computing Surveys*, **10**(3), 333–342

Barry, P. T., The regional computing organisational network. *BCS Computer Journal*, **21**(2), 184–187

Bernstein, P. A., Rothnie, J. B., Jr., Goodman, N. and Papadimitriou, C. A., The concurrency control mechanism of SDD-1: A system for distributed databases (the fully redundant case), *IEEE Transactions on Software Engineering*, **4**(3), 154–168

Bochmann, G. V., Compile time memory allocation for parallel processors. *IEEE Transactions on Software Engineering*, **4**(6), 517–520

Bonczek, R. H., Holsapple, C. W. and Whinston, A. B., Information transferral within a distributed data base via a generalised mapping language. *BCS Computer Journal*, **21**(2), 110–116

Bowen, B. A., Buhr, R. J. A. and Paquet, J. L., Kernel application techniques for multiple microprocessor systems. *Proceedings of the International Symposium on Mini and Micro Computers*, November, 1977, IEEE, New York, USA, pp. 299–302

Briggs, F. A., Performance of memory configurations for parallel-pipelined computers. In *5th Annual Symposium on Computer Architecture Conference Proceedings*, ACM, New York, p. 202

Buhr, R. J. A., Concurrent high level language model applied to multimicroprocessor system development. *2nd International sur les systems d'exploitation* (2nd International Conference on Operating Systems), Institute de Recherche d'informatique et d'Automatique, Le Chesnay, France, October

Burton, W., Comments on: sorting by distributive partitioning. *Information Processing Letters*, **7**(4), 205

Butler, J. T., Analysis and design of fanout-free networks of positive symmetric gates. *Journal of the ACM*, **25**(3), 481–498

Buzen, J. P., A queuing network model of MVS. *ACM Computing Surveys*, **10**(3), 319–331

Carlbom, I. and Paciorek, J., Planar geometric projections and viewing transformations. *ACM Computing Surveys*, **10**(4), 465–502

Cert, O., Parallelism, control and synchronisation expression in a single assignment language. *ACM SIGPLAN Notices*, **13**(1), 25–33

Chandy, K. M. and Sauer, C. H., Approximate methods for analyzing queuing network models of computer systems. *ACM Computing Surveys*, **10**(3), 281–317

Chin, Y. H., An analysis of 'distributed free space' in an operating and data management systems environment. *IEEE Transactions on Software Engineering*, **4**(5), 436–441

Cohen, H. and Kaufeld, J. C., Jr., The network operations center systems. *AT & T Bell Laboratories Technical Journal*, **57**(6 part 2), 2289–2304

Czaja, L., Implementation approach to parallel systems. *Information Processing Letters*, **7**(5), 244–249

Czaja, L., Parallel implementation of path expressions. *Information Processing Letters*, **7**(6), 291–295

Davenport, R. A., Distributed or centralised data base. *BCS Computer Journal*, **21**(1), 7–14

Davies, D. W., The protection of data by cryptography. In *Distributed Computing Systems* (ed. B. Shaw), Computing Laboratory, University of Newcastle-upon-Tyne, UK, September, pp. 1–14

Denning, P. J. and Buzen, J. P., The operational analysis of queuing network models. *ACM Computing Surveys*, **10**(3), 225–261

Devillers, R. E. and Lauer, P. E., A general mechanism for avoiding starvation with distributed control. *Information Processing Letters*, **7**(3), 156–158

Dijkstra, E. W., Aspects of reasoning effectively about distributed systems. In *Distributed Computing Systems* (ed. B. Shaw), Computing Laboratory, University of Newcastle-upon-Tyne, UK, September, pp. 15–29

Dijkstra, E. W., Lamport, L., Martin, A. J., Scholten, C. S. and Seffens, E. M. F., On-the-fly garbage collection: an exercise in cooperation. *Communications of the ACM*, **21**(11)

Dobosiewicz, W., Author's reply to Warren Burton's comments on distributive partitioning sorting. *Information Processing letters*, **7**(4), 206

Dobosiewicz, W., Sorting by distributive partitioning. *Information Processing Letters*, **7**(1), 1–6

Flon, L. and Suzuki, N., Consistent and complete proof rules for the total correctness of parallel programs. Xerox Report, CSL-78-6, November

Flon, L. and Suzuki, N., Non-determinism and the correctness of parallel programs. In *Proceedings of the IFIP Working Conference on the Formal Description of Programming Concepts* (ed. E. Neuhold), North-Holland, Amsterdam

Flynn, M. J., Computer organization and architecture. In *Operating Systems. An Advanced Course* (eds R. Hayer, R. M. Graham and G. Seegmuller), Springer-Verlag, Berlin, pp. 17–98

Gentleman, W. M., Some complexity results for matrix computations on parallel processors. *Journal of the ACM*, **25**(1), 112–115

Gjessing, S., Compile time preparations for run time scheduling in monitors. *BIT (Sweden)*, **18**(1), 72–83

Gries, D., Corrigendum: an exercise in proving parallel programs correct. *Communications of the ACM*, **21**(12), 1048

Hansen, P. B., Distributed processes: a concurrent programming concept. *Communications of the ACM*, **21**(11), 934–940

Hansen, P. B., A keynote address on concurrent programming. In *Proceedings of COMPSAC 78 Computer Software and Applications Conference*, Chicago, Illinois, USA, IEEE New York, November, pp. 1–6

Hirschberg, D. S., Fast parallel sorting algorithms. *Communications of the ACM*, **21**(8)

Hoare, C. A. R., Communicating sequential processes. *Communications of the ACM*, **21**(8), 666–677

Hollaar, L. A., Specialized merge processor networks for combining sorted lists. *ACM Transactions on Database Systems*, **3**(3), 272–284

Holthouse, M. A., Automated concurrent process analysis technique. *Proceedings of the Texas Conference on Operating Systems*, University of Houston, Texas, USA, pp. 4.19–4.24

Holt, R. C., Graham, G. S., Lazowska, E. D., and Scott, M. A., Announcing Concurrent SP/k. *ACM SIGPLAN Notices*, **13**(5)

Iglehart, D. L. and Shedler, G. S., Regenerative simulation of response times in networks of queues. *Journal of the ACM*, **25**(3), 449–460

Itoh, K., Tabata, K. and Ohano, Y., An evaluation system for concurrent processes by the traversing method. In *Proceedings of the 3rd USA–JAPAN Computer Conference*, San Francisco, AFIPS Press, Montvale, New Jersey, October, pp. 41–45

Kafura, D. G. and Shen, V. Y. and Logrippo, L., Renamings and economy of memory in program schemata. *Journal of the ACM*, **25**(1), 10–22

Kant, R. M. and Takayuki, K., Decentralized parallel algorithms for matrix computation. In *5th Annual Symposium on Computer Architecture Conference Proceedings*, ACM, New York, p. 96

Karayiannis, A. and Loizou, G., Cycle detection in critical path networks. *Information Processing Letters*, **7**(1), 15–19

Kumar, B. and Davidson, E. S., Performance evaluation of highly concurrent computers by deterministic simulation. *Communications of the ACM*, **21**(11), 904–913

Kung, H. T. and Lehman, P. L., A concurrent database manipulation problem: binary trees. In *Proceedings of the 4th International Conference on Very Large Databases*, IEEE, Berlin, West Germany, September

Lamport, L., Time, clocks, and the ordering of events in a distributed system. *Communications of the ACM*, **21**(7), 558–564

Landweber, L. H. and Robertson, E. L., Properties of conflict-free persistent Petri Nets, *Journal of the ACM*, **25**(3), 352–364

Lawler, E. L. and Labetoulle, J., On pre-emptive scheduling of unrelated parallel processors by linear programming. *Journal of the ACM*, **25**(4), 612–619

Lea, R. M., Text compression with an associative parallel processor. *BCS Computer Journal*, **21**(1), 45–56

Malhotra, V. M., Kumar, M. P. and Maheshwari, S. N., An $O(|V|\hat{~}3)$ algorithm for finding maximum flows in networks. *Information Processing Letters*, **7**(6), 277–278

Merlin, P. M., Modelling and validation of protocols. In *Distributed Computing Systems* (ed. B. Shaw), Computing Laboratory, University of Newcastle-upon-Tyne, UK, September, pp. 39–69

Miller, R. E. and Yap, C. K., On formulating simultaneity for studying parallelism and synchronization. *Proceedings of the 10th Annual ACM Symposium on Theory of Computing*, May, pp. 105–113

Mulvey, J. M., Pivot strategies for primal-simplex networks codes. *Journal of the ACM*, **25**(2), 266–270

Muntz, R. R., Queuing networks: a critique of the state of the art and directions for the future. *ACM Computing Surveys*, **10**(3), 353–359

Neal, D. and Wallentine, V., Experiences with the portability of Concurrent Pascal. *Software Practice and Experience*, **8**(3), 341–354

Needham, R. M. and Schroeder, M. D., Using encryption for authentication in large networks of computers. *Communications of the ACM*, **21**(12), 993–998

Needham, R. M., User-server distributed computing. In *Distributed Computing Systems* (ed. B. Shaw), Computing Laboratory, University of Newcastle-upon-Tyne, UK, September, pp. 71–78

Neuhold, E. J., The distribution of data and processes in computer networks. In *Distributed Computing Systems* (ed. B. Shaw), Computing Laboratory, University of Newcastle-upon-Tyne, UK, September, pp. 79–100

Nygaard, K., Concepts and tasks relating to system description. In *Distributed Computing Systems* (ed. B. Shaw), Computing Laboratory, University of Newcastle-upon-Tyne, UK, September, pp. 101–107

Oleinick, P. N. and Fuller, S. H., The implementation and evaluation of a parallel algorithm on C.mmp. Report, CMU-CS-78-125, Department of Computer Science, Carnegie-Mellon University, Pittsburgh, Pennsylvania, USA, 6 June

Oleinick, P. N. and Fuller, S. H., The implementation and evaluation of a parallel algorithm on C.mmp. Report, CMU-CS-78-151, Department of Computer Science, Carnegie-Mellon University, Pittsburgh, Pennsylvania, USA, November

Preparata, F. P. and Sarwate, D. V., An improved parallel processor bound in fast matrix inversion, *Information Processing Letters*, **7**(3), pp. 148–150

Price, R. J., Multiprocessing made easy. In *AFIPS Conference Proceedings*, **47**, National Computer Conference, AFIPS Press, Montvale, New Jersey, June, pp. 589–596

Price, W. L., Simulation studies of data communication networks operating in datagram mode. *BCS Computer Journal*, **21**(3), 219–223

Reghbati, H. K. and Hamacher, V. C., Hardware support for the concurrent programming in loosely coupled multiprocessors. In *5th Annual Symposium on Computer Architecture Conference Proceedings*, ACM, New York, p. 195

Ritchie, G. D., Augmented transition network grammars and semantic processing. Report CSR-20-78, Department of Computer Science, University of Edinburgh, January

Rose, C. A., A measurement procedure for queuing network models of computer systems. *ACM Computing Surveys*, **10**(3), 263–280

Rosenkrantz, D. J., Stearns, R. E. and Lewis, P. M., System level concurrency control for distributed database systems. *ACM Transactions on Database Systems*, **3**(2), 178–198

Sameh, A. H. and Kuck, D. J., On stable parallel linear systems solvers. *Journal of the ACM*, **25**(1), 81–91

Savitch, W., Parallel and nondeterministic time complexity classes. In *Lecture Notes in Computer Science*, **62**, Springer-Verlag, Berlin, pp. 411–424

Schlageter, G., Process synchronization in database systems. *ACM Transactions on Database Systems*, **3**(3), 248–271

Schneider, F. B. and Bernstein, A. J., Scheduling in Concurrent Pascal. *Operating System Reivew (USA)*, **12**(2), 15–20

Schnorr, C. P., Multiterminal network flow and connectivity in unsymmetrical networks. In *Lecture Notes in Computer Science*, **62**, Springer-Verlag, Berlin, pp. 425–439

Siegel, H. J. and Smith, S. D., Study of multistage SIMD interconnection networks. In *5th Annual Symposium on Computer Architecture Conference Proceedings*, ACM, New York, p. 223

Srodawa, R. J., Positive experiences with a multiprocessing system. *ACM Computing Surveys*, **10**(1), 73–82

Stone, H. S., Critical load factors in two-processor distributed systems. *IEEE Transactions on Software Engineering*, **4**(3), 254–258

Toffoli, T., Integration of the phase-difference relations in asynchronous, sequential networks. In *Lecture Notes in Computer Science*, **62**, Springer-Verlag, Berlin, pp. 457–463

Towsley, D., Chandy, K. M. and Browne, J. C. Models for parallel processing within programs: application to CPU:I/O and I/O:I/O overlap. *Communications of the ACM*, **21**(10), 821–830

Tsur, S., Analysis of queuing networks in which processes exhibit locality-transition behaviour. *Information Processing Letters*, **7**(1), 20–23

Vantilborgh, H., Exact aggregation in expotential queuing networks. *Journal of the ACM*, **25**(4), 620–629

Vigder, M. R. and Buhr, R. J. A., A firmware kernel to support a concurrent high level language. *Proceedings of Distributed Processing Conference*, Ottawa, Ontario, Canada, May, pp. 100–109

Wolf, J. J. and Liu, M. T., A distributed double-loop computer network (DDLCN). *Proceedings of the Texas Conference on Operating Systems*, University of Houston, Texas, USA

Wong, J. W., Queuing network modeling of computer communication networks. *ACM Computing Surveys*, **10**(3), 343–351

1979

Ancillotti, P., Lijtmaer, N. and Boari, M., Mechanisms for allocation and protection in languages for concurrent programming. *Riv. Inf. (Italy)*, **9**(4), 367–371

Anon., Semantics of concurrent computation. Proceedings 1979. *Lecture Notes in Computer Science*, **70**, Springer-Verlag, Berlin

Arora, R. K. and Rana, S. P. On module assignment in two-processor distributed systems. *Information Processing Letters*, **9**(3), 113–117

Babich, A. F., Proving total correctness of parallel programs. *IEEE Transactions on Software Engineering*, **5**(6), 558–574

Badler, N. I. and Smoliar, S. W., Digital representations of human movement. *ACM Computing Surveys*, **11**(1), 19–38

Barlow, R. H. and Evans, D. J. A parallel organisation of the bisection algorithm. *BCS Computer Journal*, **22**(3), 267–269

Bentley, J. L. and Kung, H. T., Two papers on a tree-structured parallel computer. Report, Department of Computer Science, Carnegie-Mellon University, Pittsburgh, Pennsylvania, USA, August

Bernard, D., Management issues in cooperative computing. *ACM Computing Surveys*, **11**(1), 3–17

Bernstein, P. A., Marco, A., Casanova, A. and Goodman, N., Comments on 'Process synchronization in database systems'. *ACM Transactions on Database Systems*, **4**(4), 545–546

Bernstein, P. A., Shipman, D. W. and Wong, W. S., Formal aspects of serializability in database concurrency control. *IEEE Transactions on Software Engineering*, **5**(3), 203–216

Best, E., A note on the proof of a concurrent program. *Information Processing Letters*, **9**(3), 103–104

Bochman, G. V., Architecture of distributed computer systems. In *Lecture Notes in Computer Science*, **77**, Springer-Verlag, Berlin

Bozyigit, M. and Paker, Y., A fixed routing problem in large and high connectivity networks. *BCS Computer Journal*, **22**(3), 246–250

Brent, R. P. and Kung, H. T., A regular layout for parallel adders. Report, Department of Computer Science, Carnegie-Mellon University, Pittsburgh, Pennsylvania, USA, June

Brock, J. D. and Montz, L. B., Translation and optimization of data flow programs, *Proceedings of the International Conference on Parallel Processing*, IEEE, New York, August, pp. 47–54

Bucci, G. and Streeter, D. N., A methodology for the design of distributed information systems. *Communications of the ACM*, **22**(4), 233–244

Chandy, K. M. and Misra, J. Distributed simulation: a case study in design and verification of distributed programs. *IEEE Transactions on Software Engineering*, **5**(5), 440–452

Chandy, K. M. and Misra, J., Deadlock and absence proofs for networks of communicating processes. *Information Processing Letters*, **9**(4), 185–189

Chattergy, R. and Pooch, U. W., A distributed function computer with dedicated processors. *BCS Computer Journal*, **22**(1), 37–40

Cockayne, E. J., Ruskey, F. and Thomason, A. G., An algorithm for the most economic link addition in a tree communications network. *Information Processing Letters*, **9**(4), 171–175

Coleman, D., Gallimore, R. M., Hughes, W. and Powell, M. S., An assessment of Concurrent Pascal. *Software Practice and Experience*, **9**(10), 827–838

Cornish, M., The IT data flow architectures: the power of concurrency for avionics. *Proceedings of the 3rd digital Avionics Systems Conference*, Fort Worth, Texas, November, pp. 19–25

Czaja, L., A specification of parallel problems. *Information Processing Letters*, **8**(4), 162–167

Dasgupta, S. The organization of microprogram stores. *ACM Computing Surveys*, **11**(1), 39–65

Deliyanni, A. and Kowalski, R. A., Logic and semantic networks. *Communications of the ACM*, **22**(3), 184–192

Denning, D. E., Secure personal computing in an insecure network. *Communications of the ACM*, **22**(8), 476–482

Eaglestone, B. M. and Partington, N. J., A campus network based on ICL2900 series protocol. *Software Practice and Experience*, **9**(11), 959–968

Farrell, E. P., Ghani, N. and Treleaven, P. C., A concurrent computer architecture and a ring based implementation. In *6th Annual Symposium on Computer Architecutre Conference Proceedings*, ACM, New York

Feldman, J. A., High level programming for distributed computing, *Communications of the ACM*, **22**(6), 353–367

Feng, T., Wu, C. and Agrawal, D. P., A microprocessor-controlled asynchronous circuit switching network. In *6th Annual Symposium on Computer Architecture Conference Proceedings*, ACM, New York

Fjellheim, R. A., A message distribution technique and its application to network control. *Software Practice and Experience*, **9**(6), 499–506

Francez, N., Hoare, C. A. R., Lehmann, D. J. and de Rover, W. P., Semantics of nondeterminism concurrency and communication. *Journal of Computer and System Sciences*, **19**(3), 290–308

Franklin, M. A., Kahn, S. A. and Stucki, M. J., Design issues in the development of a modular multiprocessor communications network. In *6th Annual Symposium on Computer Architecture Conference Proceedings*, ACM, New York

Galil, Z. and Megiddo, N., A fast selection algorithm and the problem of optimum distribution of effort. *Journal of the ACM*, **26**(1), 58–64

Gligor, V. D., Review and revocation of access privileges distributed through capabilities. *IEEE Transactions on Software Engineering*, **5**(6), 575–586

Gonnet, G. H. and Morgan, D. E., Analysis of closed queuing networks with periodic servers. *IEEE Transactions on Software Engineering*, **5**(6), 653–659

Graef, N., Kretschmar, H., Loehr, K.-P. and Morawetz, B., How to design and implement small time-sharing system using Concurrent Pascal. *Software Practice and Experience*, **9**(1), 17–24

Hevner, A. R. and Yao, S. B., Query processing in distributed database systems. *IEEE Transactions on Software Engineering*, **5**(3), 177–187

Hirschberg, D. S., Chandra, A. K. and Sarwate, D. V., Computing connected components on parallel computers. *Communications of the ACM*, **22**(8), 461–464

Huits, M. and Kumar, V., The practical significance of distributive partitioning sort. *Information Processing Letters*, **8**(4), 168–169

Jackowski, B. L., Kubiak, R. and Sokolowski, S., Complexity of sorting by distributive partitioning. *Information Processing Letters*, **9**(2), 100

Jelinek, J., An algebraic theory for parallel processor design. *BCS Computer Journal*, **22**(4), 363–375

Jensen, K., Kyng, M. and Lehrmann-Madsen, O., A Petri net definition of a system description language. In *Semantics of Concurrent Computations*, (ed. G. Kahn), Springer-Verlag, Berlin. pp. 348–368

Jerrum, M., Applications of algebraic completeness to problems of network reliability and monomer-dimer systems. Report CSR-45-79, Department of Computer Science, University of Edinburgh, September

Jones, S., A network display program. *BCS Computer Journal*, **22**(2), 98–104

Joseph, M., Towards more general implementation languages for operating systems. In *Operating Systems. Theory and Practice* (ed. D. Lanciaux), North-Holland, Amsterdam, pp. 321–331

Kieburtz, R. B., Comments on 'Communicating sequential processes'. *ACM Transactions on Programming Languages and Systems*, **1**(2), 218–225

Kim, W., Relational database systems. *ACM Computing Surveys*, **11**(3), 185–211

Kowalski, R. and Deliyanni, A., Logic and semantic networks. In *Artificial Intelligence/ Language Processing*, Department of Computing, Imperial College of Science and Technology, London, UK

Kruijer, H. S. M., Self-stabilization (in spite of distributed control) in tree-structured systems. *Information Processing Letters*, **8**(2), 91–95

Kung, H. T., The complexity of coordinating parallel asynchronous processes. Report, Department of Computer Science, Carnegie-Mellon University, Pittsburgh, Pennsylvania, USA, July

Kung, H. T., The structure of parallel algorithms. Report, Department of Computer Science, Carnegie-Mellon University, Pittsburgh, Pennsylvania, USA, August

Kung, H. T. and Lehman, P. L., Concurrent manipulation of binary search trees. Report, Department of Computer Science, Carnegie-Mellon University, Pittsburgh, Pennsylvania, USA, September

Kung, H. T. and Papadimitriou, C. H. An optimality theory of concurrency control for databases. Department of Computer Science, Carnegie-Mellon University, Pittsburgh, Pennsylvania, USA, September

Kung, H. T. and Robinson, J. T., On optimistic methods for concurrency control. Report, Department of Computer Science, Carnegie-Mellon University, Pittsburgh, Pennsylvania, USA, September

Kung, H. T. and Robinson, J. T., On optimistic methods for concurrency control. In *Proceedings of the IEEE International Conference on Very Large Databases*, Rio de Janeiro, Brazil, October

Lamport, L., A general construction for expression repetition. *ACM SIGPLAN Notices*, **14**(3)

Lamport, L., A new approach to proving the correctness of multiprocess programs. *Transactions on Programming Languages and Systems*, **1**(1), 84–97

Lamport, L., On the proof of correctness of a calendar program. *Communications of the ACM*, **22**(10), 557–559

Lemme, J. M. and Rice, J. R., Speedup in parallel algorithms for adaptive quadrature. *Journal of the ACM*, **26**(1), 65–71

Lesser, V. R. and Erman, L. D., An experiment in distributed interpretation. Report, Department of Computer Science, Carnegie-Mellon University, Pittsburgh, Pennsylvania, USA, May

Logrippo, L., Renamings, maximal parallelism, and space-time tradeoff in program schemata. *Journal of the ACM*, **26**(4), 819–833

Lotfi, Z. M. and Tosser, A. J., Minimising the NAND-NOR-XOR network of Modula 2 sum of Boolean products. *BCS Computer Journal*, **22**(3), 251–255

Manzo, M. D., Frisiani, A. L. and Olimpo, G., Loop optimisation for parallel processing, *BCS Computer Journal*, **22**(3), 234–239

Mao, T. W. and Yeh, R. T., Communication port-a language concept for concurrent programming. *Proceedings of the 1st International Conference on Distributed Computing Systems*, Huntsville, Alabama, USA, October, pp. 252–260

Marie, R. A., An approximate analytical method for general queuing networks. *IEEE Transactions on Software Engineering*, **5**(5), 530–538

McGraw, J. R. and Andrews, G. R., Access control in parallel programs. *IEEE Transactions on Software Engineering*, **5**(1), 1–9

Menasce, D. A. and Muntz, R. R., Locking and deadlock detection in distribution data bases. *IEEE Transactions on Software Engineering*, **5**(3), 195–202

Milne, G. and Milner, R., Concurrent processes and their syntax. *Journal of the ACM*, **26**(2), 302–321

Narayana, K. T., Prasad, V. R. and Joseph, M., Some aspects of concurrent programming in CCNPASCAL. *Software Practice and Experience*, **9**(9), 749–770

Nehmer, J., The implementation of concurrency for a PL/1-like language *Software Practice and Experience*, **9**(12), 1043–1058

Noetzel, A. S., A generalised queuing discipline for product form network solutions. *Journal of the ACM*, **26**(4), 779–793

Ortiz, J. J., Database concurrent processor. In *Proceedings of the 5th International Conference on Very Large Databases*, Rio de Janeiro, Brazil, IEEE, New York, October

Papadimitriou, C. H., The serializability of concurrent database updates. *Journal of the ACM*, **26**(4), 631–653

Popek, G. J. and Kline, C. S., Encryption and secure computer networks. *ACM Computing Surveys*, **11**(4), 331–356

Price, R. J., A language for distributed processing. In *Proceedings of AFIPS Conference, National Computer Conference*, AFIPS Press, Montvale, New Jersey, June, pp. 957–967

Ramming, F. J., The concurrent programming languaging CAP and the *n*-processor oriented CAP CAD-system. In *Microprocessors and their Applications* (eds J. Tiberghien, G. Carlstedt and J. Lewi), North-Holland, Amsterdam, pp. 249–258

Reeves, C. M., Free store distribution under random fit allocation: Part 1. *BCS Computer Journal*, **22**(4), 346–351

Reghbati, H. K., An efficient time-shared link processors for supporting communication in parallel systems with dynamic structure. In *6th Annual Symposium on Computer Architecture Conference Proceedings*, ACM, New York, p. 147

Ries, D. R. and Stonebraker, M. R., Locking granularity revisited. *ACM Transactions on Database Systems*, **4**(2), 210–227

Rouff, C. F., TEACH – a concurrent robot control language. *Proceedings of COMPSAC, the IEEE Computer Society's 3rd International Computer Software and Application Conference*, Chicago, Illinois, USA, November, pp. 442–445

Rychener, M. D., A semantic network of production rules in a system for describing computer structures. Report, Department of Computer Science, Carnegie-Mellon University, Pittsburgh, Pennsylvania, USA, June

Sauer, C. H. and Chandy, K. M., The impact of distributions and disciplines on multiple processor systems. *Communications of the ACM*, **22**(1), 23–25

Sauer, C. H. and MacNair, E. A., Queuing network software for systems modelling. *Software Practice and Experience*, **9**(5), 369–380

Savitch, W. J. and Stimson, M. J., Time bounded random access machines with parallel processing. *Journal of the ACM*, **26**(1), 103–118

Schmidt, J. W., Parallel processing of relations: a single assignment approach. In *Proceedings of the 5th International Conference on Very Large Data Bases*, Rio de Janeiro, Brazil, IEEE, New York, October, pp. 398–408

Schutz, H. A., On the design of a language for programming real-time concurrent processes. *IEEE Transactions on Software Engineering*, **5**(3), 248–255

Shields, M. W. and Lauer, P. E., A formal semantics for concurrent systems. In *Automata, Languages and Programming* (ed. H. A. Maurer), Springer-Verlag, Berlin, pp. 571–584

Shiloach, Y., Strong linear orderings of a directed network. *Information Processing Letters*, **8**(3), 146–148

Shrivastava, S. K., Concurrent Pascal with backward error recovery: language features and examples. *Software Practice and Experience*, **9**(12), 1001–1020

Shrivastava, S. K., Concurrent Pascal with backward error recovery: implementation. *Software Practice and Experience*, **9**(12), 1021–1034

Silberschatz, A., Communication and synchronization in distributed systems. *IEEE Transactions on Software Engineering*, **5**(6), 524–546

Silberschatz, A., On the safety of the IO Primitive in Concurrent Pascal. *BCS Computer Journal*, **22**(2), 142–145

Smith, S. D. and Siegel, H. J., An emulator network for SIMD machine interconnection networks. In *6th Annual Symposium on Computer Architecture Conference Proceedings*, ACM, New York,

Spirn, J. R., Queuing networks with random selection for service. *IEEE Transactions on Software Engineering*, **5**(3), 287–289

Spragins, J., Lewis, T. and Jafari, H., Some simplified performance modeling techniques with applications to a new ring-structured microcomputer network. In *6th Annual Symposium on Computer Architecture Conference Proceedings*, ACM, New York, p. 111

Stonebraker, M., Concurrency control and consistency of multiple copies of data in distributed INGRES. *IEEE Transactions on Software Engineering*, **5**(3), 188–194

Thomas, R. H., A majority consensus approach to concurrency control for multiple copy databases. *ACM Transactions on Database Systems*, **4**(2), 180–209

Tripathi, A. R. and Lipovski, G. J., Packet switching in banyan networks. In *6th Annual Symposium on Computer Architecture Conference Proceedings*, ACM, New York

Trivedi, K. S. and Wagner, R. A., A decision model for closed queuing networks. *IEEE Transactions on Software Engineering*, **5**(4), 328–332

Turner, J. C., The conditional distribution of waiting time given queue length in a computer system. *BCS Computer Journal*, **22**(1), 57–62

Zweben, S. H. and Halstead, M. H., The frequency distribution of operators in PL/1 programs. *IEEE Transactions on Software Engineering*, **5**(2), 91–95

1980

Abelson, H., Lower bounds on information transfer in distributed computations. *Journal of the ACM*, **27**(2), 384–392

Accetta, M., Robertson, G., Satyanarayanan, M. and Thompson, M., The design of a network-based central file system. Report, Department of Computer Science, Carnegie-Mellon University, Pittsburgh, Pennsylvania, USA, August

Adiba, M., Andrade, J. M., Fernandez, F. and Toan, N. G., An overview of the POLYPHEME distributed database management system. *IFIP Congress*, Tokyo/Melbourne, pp. 475–480

Ahuja, S. R. and Roberts, C. S., An associative/parallel processor for partial match retrieval using superimposed codes. In *7th Annual Symposium on Computer Architecture Conference Proceedings*, ACM, New York

Allison, D. C. S. and Noga, M. T., Selection by distributive partitioning. *Information Processing Letters*, **11**(1), 7–8

Altaber, J., Frammery, V., Gareyte, C. and van der Stok, P. D. V., An interpretive approach for interactive real-time control through a network. *IFAC–IFIP Workshop on Real-Time Programming*, Leibnitz, Austria, pp. 1–8

Anon., The 'Hoare Logic' of concurrent programs. *Acta Informatica*, **14**, 21–37

Apt, K. R., Francez, N. and de Roever, W. P., A proof system for communicating sequential processes. *ACM Transactions on Programming Languages and Systems*, **2**(3), 359–385

Arora, R. K. and Rana, S. P. Heuristic algorithms for process alignment in distributed computing systems. *Information Processing Letters*, **11**(4,5), 199–203

Badal, D. Z., The analysis of the effects of concurrency control on distributed data base system performance. In *Proceedings of the 6th International Conference on Very Large Databases*, Montreal, Canada, IEEE, New York, October

Barnden, J. A., A characterization of systems derived from terminating concurrent histories. *Information Processes Letters*, **10**(3), 148–152

Batcher, K. E., Architecture of a massively parallel processor. In *7th Annual Symposium on Computer Architecture Conference Proceedings*, ACM, New York

Bayer, R., Elhardt, K. Heller, H. and Reiser, A., Distributed concurrency control in database systems. In *Proceedings of the 6th International Conference on Very Large Databases*, Montreal, Canada, IEEE, New York, October

Bayer, R., Heller, H., and Reiser, A., Parallelism and recovery in database systems. *ACM Transactions on Database Systems*, **5**(2), 139–156

Bernstein, A. J., Output guards and nondeterminism in 'Communicating sequential processes. *ACM Transactions on Programming Languages and Systems*, **2**(2), 234–238

Bernstein, P. A. and Goodman, N., Timestamp-based algorithms for concurrent control in distributed database systems. In *Proceedings of the 6th International Conference on Very Large Databases*, Montreal, Canada, IEEE, New York, October

Bernstein, P. A., The correctness of concurrency control mechanisms in a system for distributed databases (SDD-1). *ACM Transactions on Database Systems*, **5**(1), 52–68

Bernstein, P. A., Shipman, D. W. and Rothnie, J. B., Concurrency control in a system for distributed databases (SDD-1). *ACM Transactions on Database Systems*, **5**(1), 18–51

Binns, S. E., Dallas, I. N. and Lee, M. N. A., UKC papers on the Cambridge Ring presented at Networkshops 4, 5 and 6. Computing Laboratory Report, 2, University of Kent at Canterbury, UK, October

Bowen, B. A. and Buhr, R. J. A. *Logical Design of Multiple-microprocessor Systems*, Prentice-Hall, Englewood Cliffs, New Jersey

Bozzetti, M., A general overview of the Olivetti network file system. *IFIP Congress*, Tokyo/Melbourne, pp. 551–556

Brassard, J. P. and Gecsei, J., Path building in cellular partitioning networks. In *7th Annual Symposium on Computer Architecture Conference Proceedings*, ACM, New York

Browning, S. A., The tree machine: a highly concurrent computing environment, Report 3760: 80, California Institute of technology, Pasadena, USA, January

Broy, M., Transformational semantics for concurrent programs. *Information Processing Letters*, **11**(2), 87–91

Cellary, W. and Mayer, D., A simple model of query scheduling in distributed data base systems. *Information Processing Letters*, **10**(3), 137–147

Chandy, K. M. and Misra, J., A simple model of distributed programs based on implementation-hiding and process autonomy. *ACM SIGPLAN Notices*, **15**(7–8), 26–35

Chandy, K. M. and Sauer, C. H., Computation algorithms for product form queuing networks. *Communications of the ACM*, **23**(10)

Chow, W. M., The cycle time distribution of exponential cyclic queues. *Journal of the ACM*, **27**(2), 281–286

Clarke, E. M., Synthesis of resource invariants for concurrent programs. *Transactions on Programming Languages and Systems*, **2**(3), 338–358

Coleman, D., Concurrent Pascal–an appraisal. In *On the Construction of Programs* (eds R. M. McKeag and A. M. Macnaghten), Cambridge University Press, Cambridge, pp. 213–227

Cook, R. P., *MOD – a language for distributed programming. *IEEE Transactions on Software Engineering*, **6**(6), 563–571

Cunningham, R. J. and Kramer, J., The design of stable distributed processing systems. Report 80/10, Department of Computing, Imperial College of Science and Technology, London, 11th November

Czaja, L., Parallel system schemas and their relation to automata. *Information Processing Letters*, **10**(3), 153–158

Czaja, L., Deadlock and fairness in parallel schemas: a set-theoretic characterization and decision problems. *Information Processing Letters*, **10**(4,5), 234–239

Dadam, P. and Schlageter, G., Recovery in distributed databases based on non-synchronized local checkpoints. *IFIP Congress*, Tokyo/Melbourne, 457–462

Dasgupta, S., Some aspects of high level microprogramming. *ACM Computing Surveys*, **12**(3), 295–323

de Cindio, F., de Michelis, G. and Simone, C., GCP: symmetry and control termination in communication between processes. *Atti del Congresso Annuale AICA 1980*, Bologna, Italy, October, pp. 495–505

Francesco, de N., Perego, G., Vaglini, G. and Vannischi, M., A framework for dataflow distributed processing. *Calcolo (Italy)*, **17**(4), 333–363

Dyer, C. R., A fast parallel algorithm for the closes pair problem. *Information Processing Letters*, **11**(1), 49–52

Ehrig, H. and Rosen, B. K., Parallelism and concurrency of graph manipulations. *Theoretical Computer Science*, **11**, 247–275.

Ellis, C. A. and Nutt, G. J., Office information systems and computer science. *ACM Computing Surveys*, **12**(1), 27–60

Emerson, E. A. and Clarke, E. M., Characterizing correctness properties of parallel programs using fixpoints. *Lecture Notes in Computer Science*, **85**, Springer-Verlag, Berlin, pp. 169–181.

Evans, D. J. and Williams, S. A., Analysis and detection of parallel processable code. *BCS Computer Journal*, **23**(1), 66–72

Fisher, M. L. and Hochbaum, D. S., Database location in computer networks. *Journal of the ACM*, **27**(4), 718–735

Foley, J. D., Optimum design of two-computer networks. *IFIP Congress*, Tokyo/Melbourne, pp. 587–592

Folkjaer, P. and Bjorner, D., A formal model of a generalized CSP-like language. *IFIP Congress*, Tokyo/Melbourne, pp. 95–100

Francez, N., Distributed termination. *Transactions on Programming Languages and Systems*, **2**(1), 42–55

Fredrickson, G. N. and Johnson, D. B., Generating and searching sets induced by networks. *Lecture Notes in Computer Science*, **85**, Springer-Verlag, Berlin, pp. 221–233

Furuya, T., A Concurrent Pascal on a multiprocessor system. *Bull. Electrotech. Lab*, (Japan) **44**(11–12), 694–706

Gaude, C., Langet, J., Palassin, S. and Kaiser, C., Distributed programming as a key to reliable and evolving software for real-time applications. *IFIP Congress*, Tokyo/Melbourne, pp. 315–320

Gligor, V. D. and Shattuck, S. H., On deadlock detection in distributed systems. *IEEE Transactions on Software Engineering*, **6**(5), 435–439

Haessig, K. and Jenny, C. J., Partitioning and allocating computational objects in distributed computing systems. *IFIP Congress*, Tokyo/Melbourne, pp. 593–598

Halstead, R. H. Jr. and Ward, S. A., The MUNET: a scalable decentralized architecture for parallel computation. In *7th Annual Symposium on Computer Architecture Conference Proceedings*, ACM, New York

Hamacher, V. C. and Shedler, G. S., Performance of a collision-free local bus network having asynchronous distributed control. In *7th Annual Symposium on Computer Architecture Conference Proceedings*, ACM, New York

Hammer, M. and Shipman, D., Reliability mechanisms for SDD-1: a system for distributed databases. *ACM Transactions on Database Systems*, **5**(4), 431–466

Hansen, P. B. and Fellows, J., The trio operating system. *Software Practice and Experience*, **10**(11), 943–948

Harland, D. M., High speed data acquisition: running a realtime process and a time-shared system (Unix) concurrently. *Software Practice and Experience* **10**(4), 273–282

Helms, R. W., A distributed flat file strategy for managing research data. *Proceedings of the ACM 1980 Annual Conference*, Nashville, Tennessee, USA, October 27–29, pp. 279–285

Hennessey, M. and Milner, R., On observing nondeterminism and concurrency. *Lecture Notes in Computer Science*, **85**, Springer-Verlag, Berlin, 299–309

Hikita, T. and Kawai, S., Parallel sieve methods for generating prime numbers. *IFIP Congress*, Tokyo/Melbourne, pp. 257–262

Hoey, D. and Leiserson, C. E., A layout for the shuffle-exchange network. Report, Department of Computer Science, Carnegie-Mellon University, Pittsburgh, Pennsylvania, USA, July

Hogger, C. J., Logic representation of a concurrent algorithm. Report, Department of Computing, Imperial College of Science and Technology, London, UK

Ibarra, O. H., Moran, S. and Rosier, L. E., A note on the parallel complexity of computing the rank of order in matrices. *Information Processing Letters*, **11**(4,5), 162

Inose, H., Aspects of data communications and computer networks. *IFIP Congress*, Tokyo/Melbourne, pp. 543–550

James, E. B. and Ireland, D., Microcomputers as protective interfaces in computing networks. *Software Practice and Experience*, **10**(12), 953–958

Jones, A. K. and Schwarz, P., Experiences using multiprocessor systems – a status report. *ACM Computing Surveys*, **12**(2), 121–165

Kaufman, L. C., Gopinath, B. and Wunderlich, E. F., Sparse matrix algorithms for a packet network control analysis. Computing Science Technical Report, **82**, May, AT & T Bell Laboratories, New York, USA

Kawai, H., A formal system for parallel programs in discrete time and space. *Information Processing Letters*, **11**(4,5), 204–210

Kent, S. A., A minicomputer based high level network control language. *BCS Computer Journal*, **23**(2), 124–131

Kotov, V. E., On basic parallel language. *IFIP Congress*, Tokyo/Melbourne, pp. 229–240

Kritzinger, P., Kryzesinski, A. E. and Teunissen, P., Incorporating system overhead in queuing network models. *IEEE Transactions on Software Engineering*, **6**(4), 381–389

Kuhl, J. G. and Reddy, S. M., Distributed fault-tolerance for large multiprocessor systems. In *7th Annual Symposium on Computer Architecture Conference Proceedings*, ACM, New York

Kung, H. T. and Lehman, P. L., Concurrent manipulation of binary search trees. *ACM Transactions on Database Systems*, **5**(3), 354–382

Labetoulle, J. and Pujolle, G., Isolation methods in a network of queues. *IEEE Transactions on Software Engineering*, **6**(4), 373–380

Ladner, P. E. and Fischer, M. J., Parallel prefix computation. *Journal of the ACM* **27**(4), 831–838

Landskov, D., Davidson, S., Shriver, B. and Mallet, P. W., Local microcode compaction techniques. *ACM Computing Surveys*, **12**(3), 261–294

Lev, G., Pippenger, N. and Valiant, L. G., A fast parallel algorithm for routing in permutation networks. Report CSR-63-80, Department of Computer Science, University of Edinburgh, September

Lipsky, L., A study of time sharing systems considered as queuing networks of exponential servers. *BCS Computer Journal*, **23**(4), 290–297

Lister, A., Magee, J., Sloman, M. and Kramer, J., Distributed process control systems. Report 80/12, Department of Computing, Imperial College of Science and Technology, London, May

Liu, Ming T., Mamrak, S. A. and Ramanathan, J., The distributed double-loop computer network (DDLCN). *Proceedings of the ACM 1980 Annual Conference*, Nashville, Tennessee, USA, October 27–29, pp. 164–178

Manning, E., Livesey, N. J. and Tokuda, H., Interprocess communication in distributed systems: one view. *IFIP Congress*, Tokyo/Melbourne, pp. 513–520

Mao, T. W. and Yeh, R. T., Communication port: a language concept for concurrent programming. *IEEE Transactions on Software Engineering*, **6**(2), 194–204

Marchuk, G. I. and Il'in, V. P., Parallel computations in grid methods for solving mathematical physics problems. *IFIP Congress*, Tokyo/Melbourne, pp. 671–676

Marti, J., Compilation techniques for a control-flow concurrent LISP system. *Conference Record of the 1980 LISP Conference*, Stanford, California, USA, August, pp. 203–207

Martin, A. J., A distributed implementation method for parallel programming. *IFIP Congress*, Tokyo/Melbourne, pp. 309–314

Maryanski, F. J., Backend database systems. *ACM Computing Surveys*, **12**(1), 3–25

Mattsson, S. E., Implementation of Concurrent Pascal on LSI-11. *Software Practice and Experience*, **10**(3), 205–218

Mayor, M. A., A language for network analysis and definintion. *ACM SIGPLAN Notices*, **15**(1), 130–138

McGraw, J. R., Data flow computing-software development. *IEEE Transactions on Computers*, **19**(12)

McMillen, R. J. and Siegel, H. J., MIMD machine communication using the augmented data manipulator network. In *7th Annual Symposium on Computer Architecture Conference Proceedings*, ACM, New York

Meek, B., Serial attitudes, parallel attitudes. *ACM SIGPLAN Notices*, **15**(6), 61–63

Mekly, L. J. and Yau, S. S., Software design representation using abstract process networks. *IEEE Transactions on Software Engineering*, **6**(5), 420–433

Menasce, D. A., Popek, G. J. and Muntz, R. R., A locking protocol for resource coordination in distributed databases. *ACM Transactions on Database Systems*, **5**(2), 103–138

Milner, R., A calculus of communicating systems. *Lecture Notes in Computer Science*, **92**, Springer-Verlag, Berlin

Mohan, C., Distributed data base management: some thoughts and analyses. *Proceedings of the ACM 1980 Annual Conference*, Nashville, Tennessee, USA, October 27–29, pp. 399–410

Munz, R., Transaction management in the distributed database system VDN. *IFIP Congress*, Tokyo/Melbourne, pp. 481–486

Murala, T., Synthesis of decision-free concurrent systems for prescribed resources. *IEEE Transactions on Software Engineering*, **6**(6), 525–530

Mylopoulos, J., Bernstein, P. A. and Wong, H. K. T., A language facility for designing database-intensive applications. *ACM Transactions on Database Systems*, **5**(2), 185–207

Nassimi, D. and Sahni, S., An optional routing algorithm for mesh-connected parallel computers. *Journal of the ACM*, **27**(1), 6–29

Nassimi, D. and Sahni, S., A self-routing benes network. In *7th Annual Symposium on Computer Architecture Conference Proceedings*, ACM, New York

Noodt, T. and Belsnes, D., A simple extension of Pascal for quasi-parallel processing. *ACM SIGPLAN Notices*, **15**(5), 56–65

Notkin, D. S., An experience with parallelism in Ada. *ACM SIGPLAN Notices*, **15**(11), 9–15

O'Neill, P. and O'Neill, A., Performance statistics of a time sharing network at a small univeristy. *Communications of the ACM*, **23**(1), 10–13

Ousterhout, J. K., Partitioning and cooperation in a distributed multiprocessor operating system: MEDUSA. Report, Department of Computer Science, Carnegie-Mellon University, April

Ousterhout, J. K., Scelza, D. A. and Redell, D. D., Medusa: An experiment in distributed operating system structure. *Communications of the ACM*, **23**(2), 92–104

Patterson, D., Management and editing of distributed modular documentation. In *Proceedings 1980 ACM Annual Conference*, ACM, New York, p. 143

Pease, M., Shostak, R. and Lamport, L., Reaching agreement in the presence of faults. *Journal of the ACM*, **27**(2), 228–234

Pereira, F. C. N. and Warren, D. H. D., Definite clause grammars for language analysis – a survey of the formalism and a comparison with augmented transition networks. *Artificial Intelligence*, **13**(3), 231–278

Preparata, F. P. and Vuillemin, J. E., Area-time optimal VLSI networks for multiplying matrices. *Information Processing Letters*, **11**(2), 77–80

Prini, G., Explicit parallelism in LISP-like languages. *Conference Record of the 1980 LISP Conference*, Stanford, California, USA, pp. 13–18

Ramamoorthy, C. V. and Ho, G. S., Performance evaluation of asynchronous concurrent systems using Petri nets. *IEEE Transactions on Software Engineering*, **6**(5), 440–449

Ramamritham, K., Specification and synthesis of synchronizers. *Proceedings of the International Conference on Parallel Processing*, Columbus, Ohio, August

Reeves, C. M., Free store distribution under random fit allocation: Part 2. *BCS Computer Journal*, **23**(4), 298–306

Reiser, M. and Lavenberg, S. S., Mean-value analysis of closed multichain queuing networks. *Journal of the ACM*, **27**(2), 313–322

Rothnie, J. B., Bernstein, P. A., Fox, S., Goodman, N., Hammer, M., Landers, T. A., Reeve, C., Shipman, D. W. and Wong, E., Introduction to a system for distributed databases (SDD-1). *ACM Transactions on Database Systems*, **5**(1), 1–17

Salton, G. and Bergmark, D., Parallel computations in information retrieval. Report TR-80-439, Department of Computer Science, Cornell University, Ithaca, New York, USA, September

Schneider, F. B., Broadcasts: a paradigm for distributed programs. Report TR 80-440, Department of Computer Science, Cornell University, Ithaca, New York, USA, October

Sharp, J. A., Data oriented program design. *ACM SIGPLAN Notices*, **15**(9), 44–57

Shave, M. J. R., Problems of integrity and distributed databases. *Software Practice and Experience*, **10**(2), 135–148

Shen, J. P. and Hayes, J. P., Fault tolerance of a class of connecting networks. In *7th Annual Symposium on Computer Architecture Conference Proceedings*, ACM, New York

Shibayama, K., Tomita, S., Hagiwara, H., Yamazaki, K. and Kitamura, T., Performance evaluation and improvement of a dynamically microprogrammable computer with low-level parallelism. *IFIP Congress*, Tokyo/Melbourne, pp. 181–186

Shoch, J. R. and Hupp, J. A., Measured performance of an ethernet local network. *Communications of the ACM*, **23**(12)

Spratt, E. B., Operational experiences with a Cambridge Ring local area network in a university environment. Computing Laboratory Report, 3, University of Kent at Canterbury, UK, October

Stonebraker, M., Retrospection on a database system. *ACM Transactions on Database Systems*, **5**(2), 225–240

Sumpter, A. G. and Quick, G. E., Concurrency specification in high level languages. *ACM SIGPLAN Notices*, **15**(12), 75–81

Takizawa, M. and Hamanaka, E., Query translation in distributed databases. *IFIP Congress*, Tokyo/Melbourne, pp. 451–456

Taylor, R. N. and Osterweil, L. J., Anomaly detection in concurrent software by static dataflow analysis. *IEEE Transactions on Software Engineering*, **6**(3), 265–277

Texier, A. G., New telecommunication services and network architecture: a tentative survey. *IFIP Congress*, Tokyo/Melbourne, pp. 537–542

Towley, D., Queuing network models with state-dependent routing. *Journal of the ACM*, **27**(2), 323–337

Valiant, L. G., Computing multivariate polynomials in parallel. *Information Processing Letters*, **11**(1), 44–45

Valiant, L. G., Experiments with a parallel communication scheme. Report CSR-73-80, Department of Computer Science, University of Edinburgh, September

Voss, K., Using predicate/transition nets to model and analyse distributed database systems. *IEEE Transactions on Software Engineering*, **6**(6), 539–544

Van der Nat, M., A fast sorting algorithm, a hybrid of distributive and merge sorting. *Information Processing Letters*, **10**(3), 163–167

Von Issendorff, H. and Grunewald, W. An adaptable network for functional distributed systems. In *7th Annual Symposium on Computer Architecture Conference Proceedings*, ACM, New York

Walke, B. and Rosenbaum, W., Deadline-oriented servicing waiting-time distribution. *IEEE Transactions on Software Engineering*, **6**(3), 304–312

Winkowski, J., Behaviours of concurrent systems. *Theoretical Computer Science*, **12**, 39–60

Wittie, L. D. and Van Tilborg, A. M., MICROS, a distributed operating system for MICRO-NET, a reconfigurable network computer. *IEEE Transactions on Computers*, **29**(12), 1133–1144

Yau, S. S. and Chen, F. C., An approach to concurrent control flow checking. *IEEE Transactions on Software Engineering*, **6**(2), 126–137

Yoeli, M. and Ginzburg, A., Control nets for parallel processing. *IFIP Congress*, Tokyo/Melbourne, pp. 71–76

1981

Andrews, G. R., Parallel programs: proofs, principles, and practice. *Communications of the ACM*, **24**(3), 140–145

Andrews, G. R., Synchronizing resources. *TOPLAS*, **3**(4), 405–430, ACM, New York, USA

Anon., Communication issues in the design and analysis of parallel algorithms. *IEEE Transactions on Software Engineering*, **7**(2), 174–188

Anon., Automatic construction of verification condition generators from Hoare Logics. In *Lecture Notes in Computer Science*, **115**, Springer-Verlag, Berlin, pp. 363–377

Anon., The total correctness of parallel programs. *SIAM Journal on Computing*, **10**(2), 227–246

Apt, K. R., Ten years of Hoare's Logic: A survey – Part 1. *ACM Transactions on Programming Languages and Systems*, **3**(4), 431–483

Arora, R. K. and Sharma, N. K., Guarded procedure: a distributed programming concept. *Information Processing Letters*, **13**(4,5), 171–176

Ash, W. L., Mxec: parallel processing with an advanced macro facility. *Communications of the ACM*, **24**(8), 502–510

Badal, D. Z., Concurrency control overhead or closer look at blocking versus nonblocking concurrency control mechanisms. Report 81-005, Naval Postgraduate School, Monterey, California, USA, June

Barlow, R. H., Evans, D. J. and Shanehchi, J., A parallel merging algorithm. *Information Processing Letters*, **13**(3), 103–106

Barnes, G. H. and Lundstrom, S. F., Design and validation of a connection network for many-processor multiprocessor systems. *IEEE Computer*, **14**(12)

Ben-Ari, M., Cheap concurrent programming. *Software Practice and Experience*, **11**(12), 1261–1264

Bergstra, J. A. and Tucker, J. V., Algebraically specified programming systems and Hoare's Logic. In *Lecture Notes in Computer Science*, **115**, Springer-Verlag, Berlin, pp. 348–362

Bernstein, P. A. and Goodman, N., Concurrency control in distributed database systems. *ACM Computing Surveys*, **13**(3), 185–221

Bernstein, P. A., Goodman, N., Wong, E., Reeve C. L. and Rothnie, J. B., Query processing in a system for distributed databases (SDD-1), *ACM Transactions on Database Systems*, **6**(4), 602–625, December

Boral, H. and De Witt, D. J., Processor allocation strategies for multiprocessor database machines. *ACM Transactions on Database Systems*, **6**(2), 227–254

Boszormenyi, L., Development of multi-task systems in a high-level language. *Tanulmanyok Magy. Tud. Akad. Szamitastech. & Autom. Kut. Intez. (Hungary)*, **128**, 7–160

Broy, M., Are fairness assumptions fair? *Proceedings of the 2nd International Conference on Distributed Computing Systems*, Paris, France, April, pp. 116–125

Burton, W. and Sleep, R., The zero assignment parallel processor (ZAPP) project. *Symposium on Functional Programming Languages and Computer Architecture*, Wentworth by the Sea, Portsmouth, New Hampshire, USA, October

Casanova, M. A., The concurrency control problem for database systems. In *Lecture Notes in Computer Science*, **116**, Springer-Verlag, Berlin

Ceri, S. and Pelagatti, G., An upper bond on the number of execution nodes for a distributed joint. *Information Processing Letters*, **12**(1), 46–48

Chandy, K. M. and Misra, J., Asynchronous distributed simulation via a sequence of parallel computations. *Communications of the ACM*, **24**(4), 198–205

Chen, P.-Y., Lawrie, D. H., Padua, D. A. and Yew, P.-C., Interconnection networks using shuffles. *IEEE Computer*, **14**(12)

Chuang-qi, Z. and Ren-Ben, S., Alignment network used for connecting a prime number of memory blocks with a power of 2 of processing elements. In *8th Annual Symposium on Computer Architecture Conference Proceedings*, ACM, New York, pp. 495

Clark, G. M., Use of polya distributions in approximate solutions to nonstationary M/M/s queues. *Communications of the ACM*, **24**(4), 206–217

Clark, K. L. and Gregory, S., A relational language for parallel programming. Report 81/16, Department of Computing, Imperial College of Science and Technology, London, July

Clark, K. L. and Gregory, S., A relational language for parallel programming. *Symposium on Functional Programming Languages and Computer Architecture*, October

Coffmann, E. G. Jr., Gelenbe, E. and Plateau, B., Optimization of the number of copies in a distributed data base. *IEEE Transactions on Software Engineering*, **7**(1), 78–84

Cohen, J., Garbage collection of linked data structures. *ACM Computing Surveys*, **13**(3), 341–367

Cohler, E. U. and Storer, J. E., Functionally parallel architecture for array processors. *IEEE Computer*, **14**(9)

Darlington, J. and Reeve, M., ALICE – a multi-processor reduction machine for the parallel evaluation of applicative languages. *Symposium on Functional Programming Languages and Computer Architecture*, October

Davenport, R. A., Design of distributed data base systems. *BCS Computer Journal*, **24**(1), 31–41

Decitre, P., A concurrency control algorithm in a distributed environment. In *AFIPS National Computer Conference Proceedings*, Chicago, Illinois, USA, AFIPS Press, Montvale, New Jersey, pp. 473–480

Denning, D. E. and Sacco, G. M., Technical note: timestamps in key distribution protocols. *Communications of the ACM*, **24**(8)

Dias, D. M. and Jump, R. J., Packet switching interconnection networks for modular systems. *IEEE Computer*, **14**(12)

Dratman, R. and Lapin, S., PL/MT: a minimal multitasking Pascal. *Proceedings of MICRO-DELCON '81*, Newark, Delaware, USA, pp. 103–108

Ehrenfeucht, A. and Rozenberg, G., On the subword complexity of D0L languages with a constant distribution. *Information Processing Letters*, **13**(3), 108–113

Ekanadam, K. and Mahjoub, A., Microcomputer networks. *BCS Computer Journal*, **24**(1), 17–24

Eswaran, K. P., Hamacher, V. C. and Shedler, G. S., Collision-free access control for computer communications bus networks. *IEEE Transactions on Software Engineering*, **7**(6), 574–582

Ewusi-Mensah, K., Computer network usage control through peak load pricing. *BCS Computer Journal*, **24**(1), 71–77

Feng, T., A survey of interconnection networks. *IEEE Computer*, **14**(12)

Galbiati, G. and Fischer, M. J., On the complexity of 2-output Boolean networks. *Theoretical Computer Science*, **16**, 177–185

Galil, Z., On the theoretical efficiency of various network flow algorithms. *Theoretical Computer Science*, **14**, 103–111

Georgiadis, P. I., Papazoglou, M. P. and Maritsas, D. G., Towards a parallel simula machine. In *8th Annual Symposium on Computer Architecture Conference Proceedings*, ACM, New York, p. 263

Gilou, W. K. and Behr, P., An IPC protocol and its hardware realization for a high-speed distributed multicomputer system. In *8th Annual Symposium on Computer Architecture Conference Proceedings*, ACM, New York, p. 481

Glasner, I. D. and Hayes, P. J., Automatic correction of explanation networks for a cooperative user interface, Report Department of Computer Science, Carnegie-Mellon University, Pittsburgh, Pennsylvania, USA, November

Goldstein, I., Integrating a network-structured database into an object-oriented programming language. *ACM SIGPLAN Notices*, **16**(1), 124–125

Greif, I. and Meyer, A. R., Specifying the semantics of while programs: a tutorial and critique of a paper by Hoare and Lauer. *ACM Transactions on Programming Languages and Systems*, **3**(4), 484–507

Gupta, S., Architectures and algorithms for parallel updates of raster scan displays. Report, Department of Computer Science, Carnegie-Mellon University, Pittsburgh, Pennsylvania, USA, December

Hankley, W. J., McBride, R. A. and Wallentine, V. E., Discrete simulation with a concurrent language. In *Proceedings of the 1981 Summer Computer Simulation Conference*, AFIPS Press, Montvale, New Jersey, July, pp. 13–18

Harland, D. M., Concurrency in a language employing messages, *Information Processing Letters*, **12**(2), 59–62

Harrison, P. G., Applications of queuing network transient analysis. Report 81/15, Department of Computing, Imperial College of Science and Technology, London, UK, March

Harrison, P. G., Approximate analysis and prediction of time delay distributions in networks of queues. Report 81/11, Department of Computing, Imperial College of Science and Technology, London, UK, June

Hasegawa, M., Nakamura, T. and Shigei, Y., Distributed communicating media – a multitrack bus – capable of concurrent data exchanging. In *8th Annual Symposium on Computer Architecture Conference Proceedings*, ACM, New York, p. 367

Hassin, R., Maximum flow in (s,t) planar networks. *Information Processing Letters*, **13**(3), 107

Hoare, C. A. R., A calculus of total correctness for communicating processes. *Science of Computer Programming*, **1**, 49–72

Hoare, C. A. R., A model for communicating sequential processes. Report PRG-22, Oxford University Computing Laboratory Programming Research Group, Oxford, UK, June

Hockney, R. W., Characterization of parallel algorithms. Report RCS 152, Department of Computer Science, University of Reading, Reading, UK, February

Hockney, R. W., Characterization of parallel computers and algorithms. Report RCS 158, Deparment of Computer Science, University of Reading, Reading, UK, March

Jenevien, R., DeGroot, D. and Lipovski, G. J., A hardware support mechanism for scheduling resources in a parallel machine environment. In *8th Annual Symposium on Computer Architecture Conference Proceedings*, ACM, New York, p. 57

Juelich, O. C. and Foulk, C. R., Compilation of acyclic smooth programs for parallel execution. *ACM Transactions on Programming Languages and Systems*, **3**(1), 24–48

Kessels, J. L. W., The Soma: a programming construct for distributed processing. *IEEE Transactions on Software Engineering*, **7**(5), 502–509

Kim, K. H., Approaches to mechanization of the conversation scheme based on monitors. *Proceedings of a Symposium on Reliability in Distributed Software and Database Systems*, Carnegie-Mellon University, Pittsburgh, Pennsylvania, USA, pp. 70–77, July

Kodres, U. R., Paccassi, J. G. and Wicke, C. E., A function-descriptive language for concurrent processing. *International Journal of Mini and Microcomputers*, **3**(2), 19–24

Kohler, W. H., A survey of techniques for synchronization and recovery in decentralized computer systems. *ACM Computing Surveys*, **13**(3), 149–183

Kollias, J. G. and Hatzopoulos, M., Criteria to aid in solving the problems of allocating copies of a file in a network. *BCS Computer Journal*, **24**(1), 29–30

Konstam, A. H., A method for controlling parallelism in programming languages. *ACM SIGPLAN Notices*, **16**(9), 60–65

Kornfeld, W. A. and Hewitt, C. E., The scientific community metaphore. *IEEE Transactions on Systems Man and Cybernetics*, **11**(1), 24–33

Kramer, J., Magee, J. and Sloman, M. Intertask communication primitives for distributed control systems. Department of Computing, Imperial College of Science and Technology, London, UK, April

Kramer, J., Magee, J. and Sloman, M. A software architecture for distributed computer control systems. Report 81/18, Department of Computing, Imperial College of Science and Technology, London, UK, August

Kung, H. T. and Robinson, J. T., On optimistic methods for concurrency control. *ACM Transactions on Database Systems*, **6**(2), 213–226

Lamport, L., Technical note: password authentication with insecure communication. *Communications of the ACM*, **24**(11), 770–771

Lampson, B. W., Paul, M. and Siegert, H. J., Distributed systems – architecture and implementation. *Lecture Notes in Computer Science*, **105**, Springer-Verlag, Berlin

Lauer, P. E., Synchronisation of concurrent processes without globality assumptions. *ACM SIGPLAN Notices*, **16**(9), 66–80

Lauer, P. E. and Shields, M. W., Interpreted COSY programs: programming and verification. *Proceedings of the 2nd International Conference on Distributed Computing Systems*, Paris, France, April, pp. 137–148

Le Lann, G., A distributed system for real-time transaction processing. *IEEE Computer*, **14**(2)

Lehmann, D., Pnueli, A. and Stavi, J., Impartiality, justice and fairness: the ethics of concurrent termination. In *Lecture Notes in Computer Science*, **115**, Springer-Verlag, Berlin, pp. 264–277

Letham, P. L. and Yao, S. B., Efficient locking for concurrent operations on B-trees. *ACM Transactions on Database Systems*, **6**(4), 650–670

Levin, G. M. and Gries, D., A proof technique for communicating sequential processes. *Acta Informatica*, **15**, 281–302

Lewis, G. N., Boynton, N. J. and Burton, F. W. Expected complexity of fast search with uniformly distributed data. *Information Processing Letters*, **13**(1), 4–7

Liskov, B., Report on the workshop on fundamental issues in distributed computing. *ACM SIGPLAN Notices*, **16**(10), 20–49

Lynch, N. A. and Fischer, M. J., On describing the behaviour and implementation of distributed systems. *Theoretical Computer Science*, **13**, 17–43

Maggiolo-Schettini, Wedde, A. H. and Winkowski, J., Modelling a solution for a control problem in distributed systems by restrictions. *Theoretical Computer Science*, **13**, 61–83

McLean, G., Comments on SDD-1 concurrency control mechanisms. *ACM Transactions on Database Systems*, **6**(2), 347–350

McMillen, R. J. and Siegel, H. J., Dynamic rerouting tag schemes for the augmented data manipulator network. In *8th Annual Symposium on Computer Architecture Conference Proceedings*, ACM, New York, p. 505

Misra, J. and Chandy, K. M., Proofs of networks of processes. *IEEE Transactions on Software Engineering*, **7**(4), 417–426

Morven, W., Message passing between sequential processes: the reply primitive and the administrator concept. *Software Practice and Experience*, **11**, 435–466

Moss, J. E., Nested transaction and reliable distributed computing. *2nd Symposium on Reliability in Distributed Software and Database Systems*, Carnegie-Mellon University, Pittsburgh, Pennsylvania, USA, July

Nakamura, A. and Aizawa, K., Acceptors for isometric parallel context-free array languages. *Information Processing Letters*, **13**(4,5), 182–186

Nivat, M., Foreword to special issue on semantics of concurrent computation. *Theoretical Computer Science*, **13**, p. 1

Overman, W. T., Crocker, S. D. and Kini, V., A multiprocessor descriptive language. In *Proceedings of AFIPS Conference 50*, Arlington, Virginia, USA, AFIPS Press, Montvale, New Jersey, May, pp. 19–25

Pechura, M. A., Microcomputers as remote nodes of a distributed system. *Communications of the ACM*, **24**(11), 734–738

Perros, H. G., A symmetrical exponential open queue network with blocking and feedback. *IEEE Transactions on Software Engineering*, **7**(4), 395–402

Pneuli, A., The temporal semantics of concurrent programs. *Theoretical Computer Science*, **13**, 45–60

Preparata, F. P. and Vuillemin, J., The cube-connected cycles: a versatile network for parallel computation. *Communications of the ACM*, **24**(5), 300–309

Preparata, F. P. and Vuillemin, J. E., Area-time optimal VLSI networks for computing integer multiplication and discrete Fourier transform. In *Lecture Notes in Computer Science*, **115**, Springer-Verlag, Berlin, pp. 29–40

Rashid, R. F. and Robertson, G. G., Accent: a communication oriented network operating system kernel. Report CMU-CS-81-123, Department of Computer Science, Carnegie-Mellon University, Pittsburgh, Pennsylvania, USA, April

Reif, J. H., Minimum S-T cut of a planar undirected network in O(n log $\char"005E$ 2 n) time. In *Lecture Notes in Computer Science*, Springer-Verlag, Berlin, 115, pp. 56–67

Ricart, G. and Agrawala, A. K., Corrigendum: an optimal algorithm for mutual exclusion in computer networks. *Communications of the ACM*, 24(9), 578

Ricart, G. and Agrawala, A. K., An optimal algorithm for mutual exclusion in computer networks. *Communications of the ACM*, 24(1), 9–17

Schlageter, B., Optimistic methods for concurrency control in distributed database systems. In *Proceedings of the International Conference on Very Large Databases*, IEEE, Cannes, France September, IEEE, New York

Sequin, C. H., Doubly twisted Torus networks for VLSI processing arrays. In *8th Annual Symposium on Computer Architecture Conference Proceedings*, ACM, New York, pp. 471

Sevcik, K. C. and Mitrani, I., The distribution of queuing network states at input and output instants. *Journal of the ACM*, 28(2), 358–371

Sheperd, W. D., Ancilla – A server for the Cambridge model distributed system. *Software Practice and Experience*, 11(11), 1185–1196

Shrivastava, S. K., Structuring distributed systems for recoverability and crash resistance. *IEEE Transactions on Software Engineering*, 7(4), 436–446

Siegel, H. J. and McMillen, R. J., The multistage cube: a versatile interconnection network. *IEEE Computer*, 14(12)

Siegel, H. J. and McMillen R. J., Using the augmented data manipulator network in PASM. *IEEE Computer*, 14(2)

Silverschatz, A., A note on the distributed program component cell. *ACM SIGPLAN Notices*, 16(7)

Slana, M. F. and Lehman, H. R., Tutorial Series-8: Data communication using the telecommunication network. *IEEE Computer*, 14(5)

Smoliar, S. W., Operational requirements accommodation in distributed system design. *IEEE Transactions on Software Engineering*, 7(6), 531–536

Soderlund, L., Concurrent data base reorganization – assessment of a powerful technique through modeling. In *Proceedings of the International Conference on Very Large Databases*, Cannes, France, September IEEE, New York

Sowa, M., Real-time multi-microprocessor system introduced concept of data-driven. *IFAC–IFIP Workshop on Real-Time Programming*, Kyoto, Japan, pp. 115–120

Srinivasan, B. and Sankar, B., Algorithms to distribute a database for parallel searching. *IEEE Transactions on Software Engineering*, 7(1), 112

Steinberg, D. and Rodeh, M., A layout for the shuffle-exchange network with O($n \char"005E 2$/log n) area. *Information Processing Letters*, 12(2), 83–88

Tanenbaum, A. S., Network protocols. *ACM Computing Surveys*, 13(4), 453–489

Thanos, C. and Carlesi, C., Performance evaluation of two concurrency control mechanisms in a distributed database system. In *Trends in Information Processing Systems* (eds A. J. W. Duijvestijn and P. C. Lockemann), Proceedings of the 3rd Conference of European Cooperation in Informatica, Springer-Verlag, Berlin, October, pp. 266–279

Thurber, K. J., A pragmatic view on distributed processing systems (abstract only). In *8th Annual Symposium on Computer Architecture Conference Proceedings*, ACM, New York, P. 1

Tsukamoto, M., Language structures and management method in a distributed real-time environment. In *Distributed Computer Control Systems* (ed. W. E. Miller), 3rd IFAC Workshop on Distributed Computer Control Systems, Beijing, China, August, pp. 103–113

Valiant, L. G., Addendum (see also 'Computing multivariate polynomials in parallel', *IP Letters* 11(1) (1980) 44–45). *Information Processing Letters*, 12(1) 54

Van Oost, E. M. J. C., Multi-processor description and simulation using structured multi-programming languages. *Computer Architecture News*, 9(2), 16–32

Wah, B. W. and Ma, Y. W., MANIP – A parallel computer system for implementing branch and bound algorithms. In *8th Annual Symposium on Computer Architecture Conference Proceedings*, ACM, New York, p. 239

Watson, W., Configuration-dependent performance of a prioritized CSMA broadcast network. *Computer*, **14**(2)

Weinberg, R., Parallel processing image synthesis and anti-aliasing. *Computer Graphics*, **15**(3), 55–62

Wettstein, H., Locking operations for maximum concurrency. *BCS Computer Journal*, **24**(3), 243–248

Williams, A., A proposal for parallel language constructs. Report RCS 161, Department of Computer Science, University of Reading, Reading, UK, May

Wirth, N. and Schindler, M., Modula-2 adds concurrency to structured programming. *Electronic Design*, **29**(15), 117–122

Wood, G. K. and Larmouth, J., Distributing viewdata and teletext services to a user community. *Software Practice and Experience*, **11**(10), 1009–1018

Wu, C., Interconnection networks: guest editor's introduction. *IEEE Computer*, **14**(12)

Yau, S. S., Yang, C.-C. and Shatz, S. M., An approach to distributed computing system software design. *IEEE Transactions on Software Engineering*, **7**(4), 427–435

1982

Agrawal, D. P., Testing and fault tolerance of multistage interconnection networks. *Computer*, **15**(4)

Ahmed, H. M., Delosme, J.-M. and Morf, M., Highly concurrent computing structures for matrix arithmetic and signal processing. *IEEE Computer*, **15**(1)

Alshawi, H., A clustering technique for semantic network processing. Report 25, University of Cambridge, Computer Laboratory, Cambridge, UK, May

Andrews, G. R., The distributed programming language SR – mechanisms, design and implementation. *Software Practice and Experience*, **12**(8), 719–754

Andrews, G. R. and Schneider, F. B., Concepts and notations for concurrent programming. Report TR 82-520, Department of Computer Science, Cornell University, Ithaca, New York, USA, September

Babb, E., Joined normal form: a storage encoding for relational databases. *ACM Transactions on Database Systems*, **7**(4), 588–614

Balsamo, S. and Iazeolla, G., An extension of Norton's theorem for queuing networks. *IEEE Transactions on Software Engineering*, **8**(4), 298–305

Barlow, R. H., Evans, D. J. and Shanehchi, J., Parallel multisection for the determination of the eigenvalues of symmetric quindiagonal matrices. *Information Processing Letters*, **14**(3), 117

Barlow, R. H. and Evans, D. J., Parallel algorithms for the interative solution to linear systems. *BCS Computer Journal*, **25**(1), 56–60

Baroody, A. J. Jr. and DeWitt, D. J., The impact of run-time schema interpretation in a network data model DBMS. *IEEE Transactions on Software Engineering*, **8**(2), 123–136

Berg, H. K., Guest Editor's introduction: distributed system testbeds – experimentation with distributed systems. *IEEE Computer*, **15**(10)

Bernstein, P. A. and Goodman, N., A sophisticate's introduction to distributed database concurrency control, (invited paper). In *Proceedings of the 8th International Conference on Very Large Data Bases*, Mexico City, Mexico, September

Bhargava, B., Guest editorial: reliability in distributed systems. *IEEE Transactions on Software Engineering*, **8**(3), 165–166

Bhat, K. V. S., Algorithms for finding diagnosability level and t-diagnosis in a network of processors. Report 82-01, Department of Computer Science, University of Iowa, Iowa City, Iowa, USA, February

Birrell, A. D., Levin, R., Needham, R. M. and Schroeder, M. D., Grapevine: an exercise in distributed computing. *Communications of the ACM*, **25**(4), 260–273

Boari, M., MML: a programming line for multiple-microprocessors systems. *Proceedings of the 3rd International Conference on Distributed Computing Systems*, Washington, USA, October, pp. 680–688

Boyle, B. J. and Stanton, P. B., NOVON (a distributed resource network). *Proceedings of the International Conference on Cybernetics and Society*, IEEE, New York, October, pp. 501–505

Bozyigit, M. and Paker, Y., A topology reconfiguration mechanism for distributed computer systems. *BCS Computer Journal*, **25**(1), 87–92

Brayer, K. and Lafleur, V. A testbed approach to the design of a computer communication network. *IEEE Computer*, **15**(10)

Brown, J. W., Controlling the complexity of menu networks. *Communications of the ACM*, **25**(7), 412–418

Carrol, J. A., An island parsing interpreter for augmented transition networks. Report 33, University of Cambridge Computer Laboratory, Cambridge, UK, October

Carvalho, O. S. F. and Roucairol, G., On the distribution of an assertion. *ACM SIGACT-SIGOPS Symposium on Principles of Distributed Computing*, pp. 121–131

Casey, M., Packet switched data networks: an international review. *Information Technology: Research and Development*, **1**(3), 217

Castan, M. and Organick, E. I., u3L: an HLL-RISC processor for parallel execution of FP-language programs. In *9th Annual Symposium on Computer Architecture Conference Proceedings* ACM, New York, p. 239

Ceri, S. and Pelagatti, G. A solution method for the non-additive resource allocation problem in distributed system design. *Information Processing Letters*, **15**(4), 174

Chan, T. C. K. and Abraham, J. A., Load balancing of distributed systems. *IEEE Transactions on Software Engineering*, **8**(4), 401–411

Chandi, K. M. and Neuse, D., Linearizer: a heuristic algorithm for queuing network models of computing systems. *Communications of the ACM*, **25**(2), 126–133

Chandy, M. K. and Misra, J., Distribution computation on graphs: shortest path algorithms. *Communications of the ACM*, **25**(11), 833

Chang, E. J. H., Echo algorithms: depth parallel operations on general graphs. *IEEE Transactions on Software Engineering*, **8**(4), 391–400

Cheemalavagu, S. and Malek, M., Analysis and simulation of Banyan interconnection networks with 2×2, 4×4 and 8×8 switching elements. In *Proceedings of the IEEE Real-Time Systems Symposium*, Los Angeles, California, IEEE, New York, pp. 83–90

Chin, F. Y., Lam, J. and Chen, I-N., Efficient parallel algorithms for some graph problems. *Communications of the ACM*, **25**(9), 659

Choo, Y., Hierarchical nets a structured petri net approach to concurrency. Report 5044:82, California Institute of Technology, Pasadena, California, USA, November

Clemmensen, G. B., *A Formal Model of Distributed Ada Tasking*, AdaTEC Tutorial and Conference on ADA, Arlington, Virginia, USA, October 4–8

Cohen, J., Hickey, J. and Katcoff, J., Upper bounds for speedup in parallel parsing. *Journal of the ACM*, **29**(2), 408–428

Cohen, N. H., Parallel quicksort: an exploration of concurrent programming in Ada. *Ada Letters*, **2**(2), 61–68

Dalal, Y. K., Use of multiple networks in the Xerox network system. *IEEE Computer*, **15**(10)

Daley, S., Probability distributions. University of York 3rd year project, York, UK

Dannenberg, R. B., Resource sharing in a network of personal computers. Report CMU-CS-82-152, Department of Computer Science, Carnegie-Mellon University, Pittsburgh, Pennsylvania, USA, December

Dellar, C. N. R., A file server for a network of low cost personal microcomputers. *Software Practice and Experience*, **12**(11), 1051–1068

Dowdy, L. W. and Foster, D. V., Comparative models of the file assignment problem. *Computing Surveys*, **14**(2), 287–313

Dunnan, B. R., Schach, S. R. and Wood, P. T., A mainframe implementation of Concurrent Pascal. *Software Practice and Experience*, **12**(1), 85–90

Efe, K., Heuristic models of task assignment scheduling in distributed systems. *IEEE Computer*, **15**(6)

Elmqvist, H. and Matsson, S. E., Implementation of real-time facilities in Pascal. In *Proceedings of the 3rd IFAC–IFIP Symposium on Software for Computer Control*, Pergamon Press, Oxford, pp. 77–82

Elrad, T. and Francez, N., Decomposition of distributed programs into communication-closed layers. *Science of Computer Programming*, **2**, 155–173

Ericson, L. W., DPL-82: a language for distributed processing. Report, Department of Computer Science, Carnegie-Mellon University, Pittsburgh, Pennsylvania, USA, 26 July

Finkel, R. A. and Fishburn, J. P., Parallelism in alpha-beta search. *Artificial Intelligence*, **19**(1), 89–106

Fischer, M. J., Griffeth, N. D. and Lynch, N. A., Global states of a distributed system. *IEEE Transactions on Software Engineering*, **8**(3), 198–202

Forth, H. K., Deadlock freedom using edge locks. *ACM Transactions on Database Systems*, **7**(4) 632–652

Francez, N. and Rodeh, M., Achieving distributed termination without freezing. *IEEE Transactions on Software Engineering*, **8**(3), 287–292

Franklin, M. and Wann, D., Asynchronous and clocked control structures for VLSI based interconnection networks In *9th Annual Symposium on Computer Architecture Conference Proceedings*, ACM, New York, pp. 50

Franta, W. R., Berg, H. K. and Wood, W. T., Issues and approaches to distributed testbed instrumentation. *IEEE Computer*, **15**(10)

Garcia-Molina, H. and Wiederhold, G., Read-only transactions in a distributed database. *ACM Transactions on Database Systems*, **7**(2), 209–324

Goldschlager, L. M., A universal interconnection pattern for parallel computers. *Journal of the ACM*, **29**(4), 1073–1086

Gommaa, H., The design and calibration of a simulation model of a star computer network. *Software Practice and Experience*, **12**(7), 599–610

Goswami, A. K. and Patnaik, L. M., A bit flow processor module for distributed computing systems. In *IEEE International Conference on the Circuits and Computers*, IEEE, New York, pp. 71–74

Gottlieb, A., Grishman, R., Kriskal, C. P., McAuliffe, K. P. Rudolph, L. and Snir, M., The NYU ultracomputer – designing a MIMD, shared-memory parallel machine. In *9th Annual Symposium on Computer Architecture Conference Proceedings*, ACM, New York, p. 27

Gottlieb, A. and Schwartz, J. T., Networks and algorithms for very-large-scale parallel computation. *IEEE Computer*, **15**(1)

Greenberg, A. C., Ladner, A. C., Paterson, M. S. and Galil, Z., Efficient parallel algorithms for linear recurrence computation. *Information Processing Letters*, **15**(1), 31

Griffith, R. L., Three principles of representation for semantic networks. *ACM Transactions on Database Systems*, **7**(3), 417–422

Hailpern, B. T., Verifying concurrent processes using temporal logic. In *Lecture Notes in Computer Science*, **129**, Springer-Verlag, Berlin

Hart, J. M., Permutation inversions and multidimensional cumulative distribution functions. *Information Processing Letters*, **14**(5), 218

Havel, I. and Liebl, P., A relational DBMS in Concurrent Pascal. *Tanulmanyok Magy. TUD. Akad. Szamitastech. & Autom. Kut. Intez (Hungary)*, **133**, 99–110

Haynes, L. S., Highly parallel computing: Guest Editor's introduction. *IEEE Computer*, **15**(1)

Haynes, L. S., Lau, R. L., Siewiorek, D. P. and Mizell, D. W., A survey of highly parallel computing. *IEEE Computer*, **15**(1)

Holt, R. C., A short introduction to Concurrent Euclid. *ACM SIGPLAN Notices*, **17**(5), 60–79

Hudak, P. and Keller, R. M., Garbage collection and task deletion in distributed applicative processing systems. In *ACM Symposium on LISP and Functional Programming*, Pittsburgh, Pennsylvania, ACM, New York, August, pp. 168–178

Hunter, J. A. and Hall, N. F., A network screen editor implementation. *Software Practice and Experience*, **12**(9), 845–856

Hwang, Kai, Croft, W. J., Goble, G. H., Wah, B. W., Briggs, F. A., Simmons, W. R. and Coates, C. L., A Unix-based local computer network with load balancing. *IEEE Computer*, **15**(4)

Irani, K. B. and Wu, W. S. F., A data mapping methodology for enhancing the capability of a class of multistage interconnection networks. *Proceedings of the IEEE Real-Time Systems Symposium*, Los Angeles, California, IEEE, New York, pp. 101–112

Ito, T. and Nishitani, Y., On universality of concurrent expressions with synchronization primitives (note). *Theoretical Computer Science*, **19**, 105–115

Jacobson, P. A. and Lazowska, E. D., Analyzing queuing networks with simultaneous resource possession. *Communications of the ACM*, **25**(2)

Jessop, W. H., Ada packages and distributed systems. *ACM SIGPLAN Notices*, **17**(2), 28–36

Katz, F. M., Time and tuples: concurrency control in LOGIX. *USENIX Association Conference Proceedings*, Boston, New Jersey, USA, p. 29, Summer

Kerridge, J. M., A Fortran implementation of Concurrent Pascal. *Software Practice and Experience*, **12**(1), 45–56

Kerschberg, L., Ting, P. D. and Yao, S. B., Query optimization in star computer networks. *ACM Transactions on Database Systems*, **7**(4), 678–711

Kieburtz, R. and Silberschatz, A., On the static access-control mechanism in Concurrent Pascal. *BCS Computer Journal*, **25**(1), 17–21

Kim, K. H., Abou-El-Naga, A., Heu, S. and Yang, S. M., Process scheduling and prevention of communication deadlocks in an experimental microcomputer network. *Proceedings of the IEEE Real-Time Systems Symposium*, Los Angeles, California, IEEE, New York, pp. 124–132

Korczynski, W. and Winkowski, J., A communication concept for distributed systems. *Information Processing Letters*, **15**(3), 111

Kruijer, H. S. M., A multi-user operating system for transaction programming, written in Concurrent Pascal. *Software Practice and Experience*, **12**(5), 445–454

Kucera, L., Parallel computation and conflicts in memory access. *Information Processing Letters*, **14**(2), 93

Ku, J., A formal model for maximum concurrency in transactions systems with predeclared writesets. *Proceedings of the 8th International Conference on Very Large Data Bases*, Mexico City, Mexico, September

Kwong, Y.-S. and Wood, D., A new method for concurrency in B-Trees. *IEEE Transactions on Software Engineering*, **8**(3), 211–222

Lamport, L., An assertional correctness proof of a distributed algorithm. *Science of Computer Programming*, **2**, 175–206

Lamport, L. and Schneider, F. B., The 'Hoare Logic' of CSP, and all that. Report, TR-82-490, Department of Computer Science, Cornell University, Ithaca, New York, USA

Lamport, L., Shostak, R., and Pease, M., The Byzantine generals' problem. *Transactions on Programing Languages and Systems*, **4**(3), 382–401

Lam, S. S., Dynamic scaling and growth behavior of queuing network normalization constants. *Journal of the ACM*, **29**(2), 492–513

Langer, A. M. and Shum, A. W., Technical note: the distribution of granule accesses made by database transactions. *Communications of the ACM*, **25**(11), 831

Lemmens, W. J. M., PAP preprocessor: a precompilier for a language for concurrent processing on a multiprocessor system. Report EUT-82-E-130, Eindhoven University of Technology, The Netherlands, October

Lengauer, C. and Hehner, E. C. R., A methodology for programming with concurrency: an informal presentation. *Science of Computer Programming*, **2**, 1–18

Lengauer, C., A methodology for programming with concurrency: the formalism. *Science of Computer Programming*, **2**, 19–52

Levitan, S. P. and Foster, C. C., Finding an extremum in a network. In *9th Annual Symposium on Computer Architecture Conference Proceedings*, ACM, New York, p. 321

Liskov, B., The Argus language and system. In *Lecture Notes in Computer Science*, **190**, Springer-Verlag, Berlin, pp. 344–430

Liskov, B., On linguistic support for distributed programs. *IEEE Transactions on Software Engineering*, **8**(3), 203–210

Litvin, Y., Parallel evolution programming language for data flow machines. *ACM SIGPLAN Notices*, **17**(11)

Mackie, P. H., Multitasking-Pascal extensions solve concurrency problems. *EDN (USA)*, **27**(19), 145–149

Mahjoub, A., A distributed operating system for a local area network. *Proceedings of the 9th Australian Computer Conference*, August, pp. 633–647

Marovac, N., The rotating bus as a basis for interprocess communication in distributed systems. *BCS Computer Journal*, **25**(1), 22–31

Marsland, T. A. and Campbell, M., Parallel search of strongly ordered game trees. *ACM Computing Surveys*, **14**(4), 533–551

McCulloch, C. M., QUICKSHUNT – a distributive sorting algorithm. *BCS Computer Journal*, **25**(1), 102–104

McDonald, W. C. and Smith, R. W., A flexible distributed testbed for real-time applications. *IEEE Computer*, **15**(10)

McGraw, J. R. and Skedzielewski, S. K., Streams and iteration in VAL: additions to a data flow language. *Proceedings of the 3rd International Conference on Distributed Computing Systems*, Washington, USA, October, pp. 730–739

McGregor, D. R. and Malone, J. R., The fact database: a system using generic associative networks. *Information Technology: Research and Development*, **1**(1), 55

McMillen, R. J. and Siegel, H. J., Performance and fault tolerance improvements in the inverse augmented data manipulator network. In *9th Annual Symposium on Computer Architecture Conference Proceedings*, ACM, New York, p. 63

Miller, L. J., A heterogeneous multiprocessor design and the distributed scheduling of its task group workload. In *9th Annual Symposium on Computer Architecture Conference Proceedings*, ACM, New York, p. 283

Minoura, T. and Wiederhold, G., Resilient extended true-copy token scheme for a distributed database system. *IEEE Transactions on Software Engineering*, **8**(3), 173–188

Misra, J. and Chandy, K. M., A distributed graph algorithm: knot detection. *ACM Transactions on Programming Languages and Systems*, **4**(4), 678–686

Mitchell, J. G. and Dion, J., A comparison of two network-based file servers. *Communications of the ACM*, **25**(4), 233–245

Mohan, J., A study in parallel computation – the traveling salesman problem. Report CMU-CS-82-136, Department of Computer Science, Carnegie-Mellon University, Pittsburgh, Pennsylvania, USA, 18 August

Moor, I. W., An applicative compiler for a parallel machine. *ACM SIGPLAN Notices*, **17**(6), 284–293

Moret, B. M. E., Decision trees and diagrams. *ACM Computing Surveys*, **14**(4), 593–623

Munro, A. and Dagless, E. L., Real-time control including concurrency, II. Implementation. *Software & Microsystems*, **1**(4), 99–107

Nassimi, D. and Sahni, S., Parallel permutation and sorting algorithms and a new generalized connection network. *Journal of the ACM*, **29**(3), 642–667

Nath, D. and Maheshwari, S. N., Parallel algorithms for the connected components and minimal spanning tree problems. *Information Processing Letters*, **14**(1), 7

Obermarck, R., Distributed deadlock detection algorithm. *ACM Transactions on Database Systems*, **7**(2), 187–208

Opper, E. and Malek, M., Real-time diagnosis of Banyan networks. *Proceedings of the IEEE Real-Time Systems Symposium*, Los Angeles, California, USA, pp. 27–36

Ossefort, M., Corrigendum to 'Proofs of networks of processes', *IEEE Transactions on Software Engineering*, **8**(2), 160

Owicki, S. and Lamport, L., Proving liveness properties of concurrent programs. *Transactions on Programming Languages and Systems*, **4**(3), 455–495

Papadimitriou, C. H., A theorem in database concurrency control. *Journal of the ACM*, **29**(4), 998–1006

Parker, D. S. and Raghavendra, C. S., The gamma network: a multiprocessor interconnnection network with redundant paths. In *9th Annual Symposium on Computer Architecture Conference Proceedings*, ACM, New York, p. 73

Purser, M., The Euronet Diane Network for information retrieval. *Information Technology: Research and Development*, **1**(3), 197

Ravn, A. P., Pointer variables in Concurrent Pascal. *Software Practice and Experience*, **12**(3), 211–222

Reddy, P. G., Bhalla, S. and Prasad, B. E., A method of concurrency control in distributed database systems. *Information Processing Letters*, **14**(5), 208

Reddy, G., Bhalla, P. S. and Prasad, B. E., Robust, centralized certifier based concurrency control for distributed databases. *Information Processing Letters*, **15**(3), 105

Reif, J. H., On the power of probabilistic choice in synchronous parallel computations. In *Lecture Notes in Computer Science*, **140**, Springer-Verlag, Berlin, pp. 442–450

Reynolds, P. F. Jr., A shared resource algorithm for distributed simulation. In *9th Annual Symposium on Computer Architecture Conference Proceedings*, ACM, New York, p. 259

Ries, D. R. and Smith, G. C., Nested transactions in distributed systems. *IEEE Transactions on Software Engineering*, **8**(3), 167–172

Robinson, J. T., Design of concurrency controls for transactions processing systems. Report, Department of Computer Science, Carnegie-Mellon University, Pittsburgh, Pennsylvania, USA, 2 April

Rowe, L. A. and Birman, K. P., A local network based on the UNIX operating system. *IEEE Transactions on Software Engineering*, **8**(2), 137–146

Samelson, C. L. and Bulgren, W. G., A note on product form solution for queuing networks with poisson arrivals and general service time distributions with finite means. *Journal of the ACM*, **29**(3), 830–840

Schmidt, E. E., Controlling large software development projects in a distributed environment. Report, CSL-82-7, Palo Alto Research Centers, Xerox, Palo Alto, California, USA, December

Schneider, F. B., Synchronization in distributed systems. *Transactions on Programming Languages and Systems*, **4**(2), 125–148

Shanthikumar, J. G., A recursive algorithm to generate joint probablity distribution of arrivals from exponential sources during a random time interval. *Information Processing Letters*, **14**(5), 214

Shoch, J. F., Dalal, Y. K., Redell, D. D. and Crane, R. D., Evolution of the Ethernet local computer network. *IEEE Computer*, **15**(8)

Shoch, J. F. and Hupp, J. A., The 'Worm' programs – early experience with a distributed computation. *Communications of the ACM*, **25**(3), 172–180

Shoja, G. C., Some experiences of implementing the Ada concurrency facilities on a distributed multiprocessor computer system. *Software & Microsystems* , **1**(6), 147–152

Silberschatz, A., Priority and queuing specification in distributed processes. *BCS Computer Journal*, **25**(1), 34–36

Simmons, R. F. and Chester, D., Relating sentences and semantic networks with procedural logic. *Communication of the ACM*, **25**(8), 527

Snodgrass, R., Monitoring distributed systems: a relational approach. Report CMU-CS-82-154, Department of Computer Science, Carnegie-Mellon University, Pittsburgh, Pennsylvania, USA, December

Snyder, L., Introduction to the configurable, highly parallel computer. *IEEE Computer*, **15**(1)

Spector, A. Z., Performing remote operations efficiently on a local computer network. *Communications of the ACM*, **25**(4), 246–259

Stotts, P. D. Jr., A comparative study of concurrent programming languages. *ACM SIGPLAN Notices*, **17**(10), 50–61

Szenes, K., An application of a parallel systems planning language in decision support-production scheduling. In *Proceedings of the IFIP WG 5.7 Working Conference*, (eds G. Doumeingts and W. A. Carter), August, pp. 241–249

Takamizawa, K., Nishizeki, T. and Saito, N., Linear time computability of combinatorial problems and series parallel graphs. *Journal of the ACM*, **29**(3), 623–641

Taylor, R. and Wilson, P., Process-oriented language meets demands of distributed processing. *Electronics*, **55**(24), 89–95

Thomas, R. C. and Burns, A., The case for distributed decision making systems. *BCS Computer Journal*, **25**(1), 148–152

Tobagi, F. A., Distributions of packet delay and interdeparture time in slotted ALOHA and carrier sense multiple access. *Journal of the ACM*, **29**(4),907–927

Traiger, I. L., Gray, J., Galtieri, C. A. and Lindsay, B. G., Transactions and consistency in distributed database systems. *ACM Transactions on Database Systems*, **7**(3), 323–342, September

Van Tilborg, A. M. and Wittie, L. D., Packet switching in the MICRONET network computer. *IEEE Transactions on Communications*, **30**(10), 1426–1433

Wallach, Y., Alternating sequential/parallel processing. In *Lecture Notes in Computer Science*, **127**, Springer-Verlag, Berlin

Weding, R. G. and Flynn, M. J., Concurrency detection in language-oriented processing systems. *Proceedings of the 3rd International Conference on Distributed Computing Systems*, Washington, USA, October, pp. 805–810

Welch, H. O. and Moquin, W. A., An analysis of a multicache shared memory ring interconnection. *Proceedings of the IEEE Real-Time Systems Symposium*, Los Angeles, California, IEEE, New York, pp. 91–100

Wise, M. J., A parallel Prolog: the construction of a data-driven model. *ACM Symposium on LISP and Functional Programming*, Pittsburgh, Pennsylvania, USA, August, pp. 55–66

Yao, A. C. C., On parallel computation for the knapsack problem. *Journal of the ACM*, **29**(3), 898–903

Yemini, S., *On the Suitability of Ada Multitasking for Expressing Parallel Algorithms*, AdaTEC Tutorial and Conference on Ada, Arlington, Virginia, USA, October 4–8

Zahorjan, J., Sevick, K. C., Eager, D. L. and Galler, B., Balanced job bound analysis of queuing networks. *Communications of the ACM*, **25**(2), 134–141

1983

Agrawal, D. P., and Kaur, D., Fault tolerant capabilities of redundant multistage interconnection networks. *Proceedings of the IEEE Real-Time Systems Symposium*, Arlington, Virginia, USA, pp. 119–130

Ando, M., Tsujino, Y., Araki, T. and Tokura, N., Concurrent C: a programming language for distributed microprocessor systems. *Transactions of the Information Processing Society of Japan*, **24**(1), 30–38

Andrews, G. R. and Schneider, F. B., Concepts and notation for concurrent programming. *ACM Computing Surveys*, **15**(1), 3–43

Anon., *Reference Manual for the ADA Programming Language*, United States Department of Defence, ANSI/MIL-SID 1815A, Washington DC, January

Anon., Programming environments: deriving language dependent tools from structured denotation semantics. *International Computer Symposium*, **83**, Nuremburg, March

Anon., Local area networks: an advanced course. Proceedings 1983, In *Lecture Notes in Computer Science*, **184**, Springer-Verlag, Berlin

Apers, P. M. G., Hevner, A. R. and Yao, S. B., Optimization alogrithms for distributed queries. *IEEE Transactions on Software Engineering*, **9**(1), 57–68

Arjomandi, E., Fischer, M. J. and Lynch, N. A., Efficiency of synchronous versus asynchronous distributed systems. *Journal of the ACM*, **30**(3), 448–56

Ayache, J. M., Coutiat, J. P. and Diaz, M., Protocol design and validation. application to the REBUS network. *Technology and Science of Informatics*, **1**(4), 249

Baiardi, F., De Francesco, N., Matteoli, E., Stefanini, S. and Vaglini, G., Development of a debugger for a concurrent language. *ACM SIGPLAN Notices*, **18**(8), 98–106

Barlow, R. H., Evans, D. J. and Shanehchi, J., Parallel multisection applied to the eigenvalue problem. *BCS Computer Journal*, **26**(1), 6–9

Barter, C. J., Communication policy for composite processes. *Australian Computer Journal*, **15**(1), 9–16

Bates, P. and Wileden, J. C., An approach to high-level debugging of distributed systems. *ACM SIGPLAN Notices*, **18**(8), 107–111

Bernard, G., Interconnection of local computer networks: modeling and optimization problems. *IEEE Transactions on Software Engineering*, **9**(4), 463–469

Bernstein, P. A., Goodman, N. and Lai, M-Y., Analysing concurrency control algorithms when user and system operations differ. *IEEE Transactions on Software Engineering*, **9**(3), 233–239

Bernstein, P. A. and Goodman, N., Multiversion concurrency control – theory and algorithms. *ACM Transactions on Database Systems*, **8**(4), 465–483

Bhargava, B. and Hua, C. T., A casual model for analyzing distributed concurrency control algorithms. *IEEE Transactions on Software Engineering*, **9**(4), 470–486

Birman, K. P., Skeen, D., Abbadi, A. El., Dietrich, W. C. and Raeuchle, T., ISIS: an environment for constructive fault-tolerant distributed systems. Report TR 83-552, Department of Computer Science, Cornell University, Ithaca, New York, USA, May

Bitton, D., Boral, H., DeWitt, D. J. and Wilkinson, W. K., Parallel algorithms for the execution of relational database operations. *ACM Transactions on Database Systems*, **8**(3), 323–353

Blum, N., A note on the 'parallel computation thesis'. *Information Processing Letters*, **17**(4), 203

Boari, M., Concurrent programming features in CHILL language. *Proceedings of MELECON*, 83, 2 Vols., Mediterranean Electrotechnical Conference. Athens, Greece, May

Bracha, G. and Toueg, S., A distributed algorithm for generalized deadlock detection. Report TR 83-558, Department of Computer Science, Cornell University, Ithaca, New York, USA, June

Brachman, R. J., What IS-A is and isn't: an analysis of taxonomic links in semantic networks. *IEEE Computer*, **16**(10)

Brady, M., Parallelsim in vision, (correspondent's report). *Artificial Intelligence*, **21**, 271

Brookes, S. D., On the relationship of CCS and CSP. Report CMU-CS-83-111, Department of Computer Science, Carnegie-Mellon University, Pittsburgh, Pennsylvania, USA, March

Brookes, S. D., On the relationship of CCS and CSP. In *Lecture Notes in Computer Science*, **154**, Springer-Verlag, Berlin, p. 83–96

Broomell, G. and Heath, J. R., Classification categories and historical development of circuit switching technologies. *ACM Computing Surveys*, **15**(2), 95–133

Brunet, P., Surface representation from irregularly distributed data points. *Technology of Science and Informatics*, **2**(2), 97

Buckley, G. N. and Silberschatz, A., An effective implementation for the generalized input-output construct of CSP. *Transactions on Programming Languages and Systems*, **5**(2), 223–235

Burr, W. E., An overview of the proposed American national standard for local distributed data interfaces. *Communications of the ACM*, **26**(8), 554–561

Bux, W., Meister, B. and Wong, J. W., Bridges for interconnection of ring networks–a simulation study. *IFIP Congress*, Paris, pp. 181–186

Cahn, D. U. and Yen, A. C., A device-independent network graphics System. *Computer Graphics*, **17**(3), 167–174

Campbell, R. H. and Randell, B., Error recovery in asynchronous systems. Report UIUCDCS-R-83-1148, Department of Computer Science, University of Illinois at Urbana-Champaign, USA, December

Cardenas, A. F., Alavian, F. and Avizienis, A., Performance of recovery architectures in parallel associative database processors. *ACM Transactions on Database Systems*, **8**(3), 291–323

Ceri, S., Navathe, S. and Wiederhold, G., Distribution design of logical database schemas. *IEEE Transactions on Software Engineering*, **9**(4), 487–503

Ceri, S. and Pelagatti, G., Correctness of query execution strategies in distributed databases. *ACM Transactions on Database System*, **8**(4), 577–607

Chandy, K. M., Haas, L. M. and Misra, J., Distributed deadlock detection. *Transactions on Computer System*, **1**(2), 144–156

Chandy, K. M. and Martin, A. J., A characterization of product-form queuing networks. *Journal of the ACM*, **30**(2), 286–299

Chen, B-S. and Yeh, R. T., Formal specification and verification of distributed systems. *IEEE Transactions on Software Engineering*, **9**(6), 710–721

Chen, M. C., A semantics for general concurrent systems and an algebra for linear systems. *Proceedings of the IEEE Workshop on Languages for Automation*, IEEE Computer Society Press, Silver Spring, Maryland, USA, November

Chesnais, A., Gelenbe, E. and Mitrani, I., On the modeling of parallel access to shared data. *Communications of the ACM*, **26**(3), 196–202

Cheung, T-Y., Graph traversal techniques and the maximum flow problem in distribution computation. *IEEE Transactions on Software Engineering*, **9**(4), 504–511

Ciepielewski, A. and Haridi, S., A formal model for Or-Parallel execution of logic programs. *IFIP Congress*, Paris, pp. 299–306

Clarke, E. M., Emerson, E. A. and Sistla, A. P., Automatic verification of finite-state concurrent systems using temporal logic specifications: a practical approach. In *10th Annual Symposium on Principles of Programming Languages*, Austin, Texas, ACM, New York, pp. 117–126

Cohen, S., Lehmann, D. and Pnueli, A., Symmetric and economical solutions to the mutual exclusion problem in a distributed system. In *Lecture Notes in Computer Science*, **154**, Springer-Verlag, Berlin, pp. 128–136

Cole, R. and Lloyd, P., A flexible architecture for protocol studies in a multi-network environment. *IFIP Congress*, Paris, 401–406

Comer, D., A computer science research network CSNET: a history and status report. *Communications of the ACM*, **26**(10), 747–753

Cornhill, D., A survivable distributed computing system for embedded application programs written in Ada. *Ada Letters*, **3**(3), 79–86

Darondeau, P and Kott, L., On the observational semantics of fair parallelism. In *Lecture Notes in Computer Science*, **154**, Springer-Verlag, Berlin, pp. 147–159

Dasgupta, P. and Kemdem, Z. M., A non-two-phase locking protocol for concurrency control in general databases. In *Proceedings of the 9th International Conference on Very Large Databases*, Florence, Italy, IEEE, New York, October

Davis, R. and Smith, R. G., Negotiation as a metaphor for distributed problem solving. *Artificial Intelligence*, **20**, 63

de Bakker, J. W., Processes and the denotational semantics of concurrency. *Information and Control*, **54**(1–2), 70–120

Dekel, E. and Sahni, S., Parallel generation of postfix and tree forms. *Transactions on Programming Languages and Systems*, **5**(3), 300–317

Derniame, J. C. and Berger, P., Network standards at EDF-GDF. RETINA, Reseau Tele-Informatique National (National Teledata Network): an Interview with V. Lesaout. *Technology and Science of Informatics*, **1**(6), 411

Dijkstra, E. W., Reprint: solution of a problem in concurrent programming control. *Communications of the ACM*, **26**(1), 21–22

Dijkstra, E. W., Feigen, W. H. J. and van Gasteren, A. J. M., Derivation of a termination algorithm for distributed computations. *Information Processing Letters*, **16**(5), 217

Dix, T. I., Exceptions and interrupts in CSP. *Science of Computer Programming*, **3**, 189–204

Eager, D. L. and Sevcik, K. C., Achieving robustness in distributed database systems. *ACM Transactions on Database Systems*, **8**(3), 354–381

Eager, D. L. and Sevcik, K. C., Performance bound hierarchies for queuing networks. *ACM Transactions on Computer Systems*, **1**(2), 99–115

Eichholz, S., Optimal networks for distributing nonsequential programs, *Information Processing Letters*, **16**(2), 71–74

Er, M. C., A parallel computation approach to topological sorting. *BCS Computer Journal*, **26**(4), 293–295

Faasch, H., Haarslev, V. and Nagel, H-H., Ada on a minicomputer-network for image sequence analysis: an investigative implementation. *Ada Letters*, **2**(4), 92–96

Fernandez, C. and Martinez, J. A., Concurrent Pascal as a simulation language. *Microprocessors & Microprograms*, **12**(3–4), 245–248

Fidge, C. J. and Pascoe, R. S. V., A comparison of concurrency constructs and module facilities of CHILL and Ada. *Australian Computer Journal*, **15**(1), 17–27

Finance, J. P. and Ouerghi, M. S., On the algebraic specification of concurrency and communication. In *Proceedings of 1983 International Conference on Parallel Processing*, Bellaire, Michigan, USA, IEEE Computer Society Press, Silver Spring, Maryland, August

Fiume, E., Fournier, A. and Rudolph, L., A parallel scan conversion algorithm with anti-aliasing for a general purpose ultracomputer. *Computer Graphics*, **17**(3), 141–150

Freeman, H. A., Guest Editor's introduction: network interconnection. *IEEE Computer*, **16**(9)

Fuchs, W. K., Abraham, J. A. and Huang, K-H., Concurrent error detection in VLSI interconnection networks. In *10th Annual Symposium on Computer Architecture Conference Proceedings*, ACM, New York, p. 309

Fushimi, M. Tezuka, S., The k-distribution of generalized feedback shift-register pseudorandom numbers. *Communications of the ACM*, **26**(7), 516–524

Gaillat, G., The design of a parallel processor for image processing on-board satellites: an application oriented approach. In *10th Annual Symposium on Computer Architecture Conference Proceedings*, ACM, New York, p. 379

Galil, Z. and Wolfgang, J. P., An efficient general-purpose parallel computer. *Journal of the ACM*, **30**(2), 360–387

Gallager, R. G., Humblet, P. A. and Spira, P. M., A distributed algorithm for minimum-weight spanning trees. *ACM Transactions on Programming Languages and Systems*, **5**(1), 66–77

Garcia-Molina, H. Using semantic knowledge for transaction processing in a distributed database. *ACM Transactions on Database Systems*, **8**(2), 186–213

Garetti, P., Laface, P. and Riviora, S., Multiprocessor implementations of tasking facilities in Ada. *IFAC-IFIP Workshop on Real-Time Programming*, Hatfield, UK, pp. 97–102

Gilbert, B. K., Schwaab, D. J. and Kinter, T. M., Design and fabrication of ring networks for high-speed communications between computers. *Proceedings of the IEEE Real-Time Systems Symposium*, Arlington, Virginia, USA, pp. 190–202

Giloi, W. K. and Behr, P., Hierarchical function distribution – a design principle for advanced multicomputer architectures. In *10th Annual Symposium on Computer Architecture Conference Proceedings*, ACM, New York, p. 318

Gligor, V. D. and Luckenbaugh, G. L., An assessment of the real-time requirements for programming environments and languages. *Proceedings of the real-time Systems Symposium*, IEEE Computer Society Press, Silver Spring, Maryland, pp. 3–19

Goeman, H. J. M., Groenwegen, L. P. J., Kleijn, H. C. M. and Rozenberg, G., Constrained Petri nets. *Ann. Soc. Math. Pol. Ser. IV: Fundam. Inf.*, **6**(1), 81–125

Gross, T., Distributed debugging – summary. *ACM SIGPLAN Notices*, **18**(8), 96–97

Grumberg, O., Francez, N. and Katz, S., A complete proof rule for strong equifair termination. In *Lecture Notes in Computer Science: Logics of Programs*, Springer-Verlag, Berlin, pp. 257–278

Gupta, N. C., System analysis and design considerations for large integrated computer networks in developing countries – a case study. *IFIP Congress*, Paris, pp. 833–838

Gupta, P. and Bhattacharjee, G. P., Parallel generation of permuations. *BCS Computer Journal*, **26**(2), 97–105

Gusfield, D., Parametric combinatorial computing and a problem of program module distribution. *Journal of the ACM*, **30**(3), 551–63

Guzaitis, J., Concurrent CP/M. *Byte*, **8**(11), 257–268

Hajek, B., The proof of a folk theorem on queuing delay with applications to routing in networks. *Journal of the ACM*, **30**(4), 834–51

Hansen, J. V., Audit considerations in distributed processing systems. *Communications of the ACM*, **26**(8), 562–569

Hart, S. and Sharir, M., Concurrent probabilistic program or: how to schedule if you must. In *Lecture Notes in Computer Science*, **154**, Springer-Verlag, Berlin, pp. 304–318

Hart, S., Sharir, M. and Pneuli, A., Termination of probabilistic concurrent programs. *Transactions on Programming Languages and Systems*, **5**(3)

Hennesy, M. and Milner, R., Algebraic laws for nondeterminism and concurrency. Report CSR-133-83, Department of Computer Science, University of Edinburgh, Edinburgh, UK, June

Hinden, R., Haverty, J. and Sheltzer, A., The DARPA internet: interconnecting heterogeneous computer networks with gateways. *IEEE Computer*, **16**(9)

Holt, R. C., Mendel, M. P. and Perlegut, S. G., TUNIS: a portable, UNIX compatible kernel written in Concurrent Euclid. *USENIX Association Conference Proceedings*, Toronto, Ontario, Canada, Summer, pp. 61–74

Hoppe, J., MAGNET: a local network for Lilith computers. ETH Institut für Informatik Report 57, Zürich, Switzerland

Hughes, J. W. and Powell, M. S., DTL: a language for the design and implementation of concurrent programs as structured networks. *Software Practice and Experience*, **13**(12), 1099–1112

IEEE Computer Society, Special Section on the Fifth Berkeley Workshop on Distributed Data Management and Computer Networks. *IEEE Transactions on Software Engineering*, **9**(3), 218–246

Ilushin, A. I., Myamlin, A. N. and Shtarkman, V. S., Computer network software design based on abstract objects. *IFIP Congress*, Paris, pp. 23–28

Inverardi, P., Levi, G., Montanari, U. and Vallario, G. N., A distributed KAPSE architecture. *Ada Letters*, **3**(2), 55–61

Jagannathan, J. R. and Vasudevan, R., Comments on 'Protocols for deadlock detection in distributed database systems'. *IEEE Transactions on Software Engineering*, **9**(3), 371

Jajodia, S., Liu, J. and Ng, P. A., A scheme of parallel processing for MIMD systems. *IEEE Transactions on Software Engineering*, **9**(4), 436–445

Jensen, E. D., Sha, L., Rashid, R. F. and Northcutt, J. D., Distributed cooperating processes and transactions. *ACM SIGCOMM Symposium*, Waterloo, Canada

Jones, C. B., Specification and design of (parallel) programs. *IFIP Congress*, Paris pp. 321–332

Joseph, M. and Moitra, A., Cooperative recovery from faults in distributed programs. *IFIP Congress*, Paris, pp. 481–486

Julliand, J., Algebraic specification of communication between parallel processes. *Technology of Science and Informatics*, **2**(4), 243

Kak, S. C., Guest Editor's introduction: Data security in computer networks. *IEEE Computer*, **16**(2)

King, A., Locking expressions for increased database concurrency. *Journal of the ACM*, **30**(1), 36–54

King, R. M., Research on the synthesis of concurrent computing systems. In *10th Annual Symposium on Computer Architecture Conference Proceedings*, ACM, New York, p. 39

Kishi, M., Yasuhara, H. and Kawamura, Y., DDDP: a distributed data driven processor. In *10th Annual Symposium on Computer Architecture Conference Proceedings*, ACM, New York, p. 236

Kluge, W. E., Concurrent reduction machines. *IEEE Transactions on Computers*, **32**(11), 1002–1012

Koymans, R., Vytopil, J. and de Roever, W. P., Real-time programming and asynchronous message passing. *Proceedings of the 2nd Annual ACM Symposium on Principles of Distributed Computing*, ACM, New York, August, pp. 187–197

Kucera, L., Parallel computation and conflicts in memory access, (erratum), *Information Processing Letters*, **17**(2), 107

Kuchcinski, K. and Wiszniewski, B., A man-machine intercommunication facility in well-structured concurrent systems. *IFAC–IFIP Workshop on Real-Time Programming*, Hatfield, UK, pp. 63–67

Kumar, M., Dias, D. M. and Jump, J. R., Switching strategies in a class of packet switching networks. In *10th Annual Symposium on Computer Architecture Conference Proceedings*, ACM, New York, pp. 284

Lamport, L., Specifying concurrent program modules. *Transactions on Programming Languages and Systems*, 5(2), 190–222

Lampson, B. W. and Schmidt, E. E., Organising software in a distributed environment. *ACM SIGPLAN Notices*, 18(6), 1–13

Lam, S. S. and Lien, Y. L., A tree convoluted algorithm for the solution of queuing networks. *Communications of the ACM*, 26(3), 203–215

Larson, J. A., Bridging the gap between network and relational database management systems. *IEEE Computer*, 16(9)

Le Lann, G., On real-time distributed computing. *IFIP Congress*, Paris, pp. 741–754

LeBlanc, T. J. and Cook, R. P., An analysis of language models for high-performance communication in local-area networks. *ACM SIGPLAN Notices*, 18(6), 65–72

Lel'chuk, T. I. and Marchuk, A. G., Polyar, a parallel asynchronous programming language. *Programming and Computer Software*, 9(4), 203–210

Lenfant, J., Parallel memories and interconnection networks. *Technology and Science of Informatics*, 1(2), 103

Lester, L. N., Accuracy of approximating queuing network departure processes with independent renewal processes. *Information Processing Letters*, 16(1), 43

Letichevsky, A., Algebra of algorithms, data structures and parallel computation. *IFIP Congress*, Paris, pp. 859–864

Lindgard, A., Oxenboll, J. and Sorensen, E., Hierarchical multi-level computer network for laboratory automation. *Software Practice and Experience*, 13(3), 227–240

Liskov, B. and Scheifler, R., Guardians and actions: linguistic support for robust, distributed programs. *Transactions on Programming Languages and Systems*, 5(3), 381–404

Lynch, N. A., Multilevel atomicity – a new correctness criterion for database concurrency control. *ACM Transactions on Database Systems*, 8(4), 484–502

Madadevan, S. and Shyamasundar, R. K., Correctness preserving transformations for distributed programs. *IFIP Congress*, Paris, pp. 307–314

Mai, S. and Evans, D. J., A parallel algorithm for the fast Fourier transform. Report 205, Department of Computer Studies, University of Technology, Loughborough, UK, December

Marie, R. A. and Pellaumail, J., Steady-state probabilities for a queue with a general service distribution and state-dependant arrivals. *IEEE Transactions on Software Engineering*, 9(1), 109–112

McCurley, R. and Schneider, F. B., Derivation of a distributed algorithm for finding paths in directed networks. Report TR 83-586, Department of Computer Science, Cornell University, Ithaca, New York, USA, December

Matinez, J., Chase, R. P. Jr. and Silva, M., A language for the description of concurrent systems modelled by coloured Petri nets: application to control of flexible manufacturing systems. *IEEE Workshop on Languages for Automation*, IEEE Computer Society Press, Silver Spring, Maryland, pp. 72–77

Megiddo, N., Applying parallel computation algorithms in the design on serial algorithms. *Journal of the ACM*, 30(4), 852–866

Metcalfe, R. M. and Boggs, D. R., Reprint: Ethernet: distributed packet switching for local computer networks. *Communications of the ACM*, 26(1), 90–95

Metcalfe, R. M., Local networking of personal computers. *IFIP Congress*, Paris, pp. 525–532

Mickunas, D. and Jalote, P., The delay/re-read protocol for concurrency control in databases. Report 83-1723, Department of Computer Science, University of Illionis, Urbana-Champaign, Illinois, USA, March

Milne, G. J., CIRCAL and the representation of communication concurrency and time. Report CSR-151-83, Department of Computer Science, University of Edinburgh, Edinburgh, UK, November 1983, updated October 1984

Murtagh, T. P., A data abstraction language for concurrent programming. Report TR 83-540, Department of Computer Science, Cornell University, Ithaca, New York, January

Neel, L., Bailly, M. and Tondeur, D., Microprocessor controlled equipment for measuring plate efficiency in distrillation. *IFIP Congress*, Paris, pp. 579–582

Nelson, P. A., Haibt, L. M. and Sheridan, P. B., Casting Petri net into programs. *IEEE Transactions on Software Engineering*, **9**(5), 590–602

Nevalainen, O. and Ernvall, J., Implementation of a distributive sorting algorithm. *Technology of Science and Informatics*, **2**(1), 33

Nicholson, P. D. and Tsang, C. P., A multiprocessor implementation of CSP. *Australian Computer Science Communication Proceedings of the 6th Australian Computer Science Conference*, February, pp. 57–64

Nikolaou, C. N., A methodology for verifying request processing protocols. *Computer Communication Review SIGCOMM '83*, Symposium on Communicational Architectures and Protocols, March, pp. 76–83

Nishimura, H., Ohno, H., Kawata, T., Chirakawa, I. and Omura, K., LINKS-1: a parallel pipelined multimicrocomputer system for image creation. In *10th Annual Symposium on Computer Architecture Conference Proceedings*, ACM, New York, pp. 387

Nowitz, D. A. and Lesk, M. E., A dial-up network of UNIX systems. In *UNIX Programmer's Manual, Seventh Edition*, Bell Telephone Laboratories Inc. Holt, Rinehart and Winston, Murray Hill, New Jersey, pp. 569–576

Opper, E. and Lipovski, G. J., Fault diagnosis in non-rectangular interconnection networks. *Proceedings of the IEEE Real-Time Systems Symposium*, Arlington, Virginia, USA, pp. 141–149

Parker, D. S. Jr., Popek, G. J., Rudisin, G., Stoughton, A., Walker, B. J., Walton, E., Chow, J. M., Edwards, D., Kiser, S. and Kline, C., Detection of mutual inconsistency in distributed systems. *IEEE Transactions on Software Engineering*, **9**(3), 240–246

Paul, W., Vishkin, U. and Wagener, H., Parallel dictionaries on 2-3 trees. In *Lecture Notes in Computer Science*, **154**, Springer-Verlag, Berlin, 597–609

Peinl, P. and Reuter, A., Empirical comparison of database concurrency control schemes. *Proceedings of the 9th International Conference on Very Large Databases*, IEEE, Florence, Italy, October

Peterson, G. L., Concurrent reading while writing. *Transactions on Programming Languages and Systems*, **5**(1), 46–55

Peterson, G. L., A new solution to Lamport's concurrent programming problem using small shared variables. *Transactions on Programming Languages and Systems*, **5**(1), 56–65

Philipson, L., Nilsson, B. and Breidegard, B., A communication structure for a multiprocessor computer with distributed global memory. In *10th Annual Symposium on Computer Architecture Conference Proceedings*, ACM, New York, p 334

Potter, J. L., Image processing on the massively parallel processor. *IEEE Computer*, **16**(1)

Priese, L. Automata and concurrency. *Theoretical Computer Science*, **25**(3), 221–265

Pyrwes, N., Szymanski, B. and Shi, Y., Nonprocedural-dataflow specification of concurrent programs. *Proceedings of COMPSAC '83*, IEEE Computer Society Press, Silver Spring, Maryland, November

Quirk, W. J., The problems of concurrent programs. In *Computer Systems for Safety and Control*, Oyez Scientific and Technical Services, London, UK

Rajlich, V., Determinism in parallel systems (note). *Theoretical Computer Science*, **26**(1,2) 225–231

Ramakrishnan, I. V. and Browne, J. C., A paradigm for the design of parallel algorithms with applications. *IEEE Transactions on Software Engineering*, **9**(4), 411–414

Ramamritham, K., Specification of synchronizing processes, SYSL specification language. *IEEE Transactions on Software Engineering*, **9**(6), 722–733

Rana, S. P., A distributed solution of the distributed termination problem. *Information Processing Letters*, **17**(1)

Reeves, C. M., Free store distribution under random fit allocation: Part 3. *BCS Computer Journal*, **26**(1), 25–35

Reif, J. and Sistla, A. P., A multiprocess network logic with temporal and spatial modalities. In *Lecture Notes in Computer Science*, **154**, Springer-Verlag, Berlin, pp. 629–639

Reimer, M., Solving the phantom problem by predicative optimistic concurrency control. *Proceedings of the 9th International Conference on Very Large Databases*, IEEE, Florence, Italy, October

Richards, R. C., Shape distribution of height-balanced trees. *Information Processing Letters*, **17**(1), 17

Ritchie, G. D. and Hanna, F. K., Semantic networks – a general definition and a survey. *Information Technology: Research and Development*, **2**(4), 187

Rosenfeld, A., Parallel image processing using cellular arrays. *IEEE Computer*, **16**(1)

Rudolph, L., *A Robust Sorting Network*. Report, Carnegie-Mellon University, Pittsburgh, Pennsylvania, USA, August 1983

Rushby, J. and Randell, B., A distributed secure system. *IEEE Computer*, **16**(7)

Salter, R., Concurrent applicative implementations of nondeterministic algorithms, *Computer Languages*, **8**(2), 61–68

Satyanarayanan, M., A methodology for modelling storage systems and its application to a network file system. Report CMU-CS-83-109, Department of Computer Science, Carnegie-Mellon University, Pittsburgh, Pennsylvania, USA, March

Sauer, C. H., Computational algorithms for state-dependent queuing networks. *Transactions on Computer Systems*, **1**(1), 67–92

Schagen, I. P., Contouring from spatially distributed categorical data. Report 206, Department of Computer Studies, University of Technology, Loughborough, UK, December

Schmittgen, C. and Kluge, W., A system architecture for the concurrent evaluation of applicative program expressions. *Proceedings of the 10th Annual International Conference on Computer Architecture*, Piazza, Italy, June, pp. 356–362

Schneidewind, N., Interconnecting local networks to long-distance networks. *IEEE Computer*, **16**(9)

Schoor, A., Physical parallel devices are not much faster than sequential ones. *Information Processing Letters*, **17**(2), 103

Selinger, P. G., State-of-the-art issues in distributed databases. *IEEE Transactions on Software Engineering*, **9**(3), 218

Sevcik, K. C., Comparison of concurrency control methods using analytic models. *IFIP Congress*, Paris, pp. 847–858

Shapiro, E. and Takeuchi, A., Object oriented programming in Concurrent Prolog. *New Generation Computing*, **1**(1), 25–48

Sheilds, M. W. and Wray, M. J., A CCS specification of the OSI network service. Report CSR-136-83, Department of Computer Science, University of Edinburgh, Edinburgh, UK, August

Silberschatz, A., Extending CSP to allow dynamic resource management. *IEEE Transactions on Software Engineering*, **9**(4), 527–530

Sistla, A. P., Theoretical issues in the design and verification of distributed systems. Report, Department of Computer Science, Carnegie-Mellon University, Pittsburgh, Pennsylvania, USA, August

Skeen, D. and Stonebraker, M., A formal method of crash recovery in a distributed system. *IEEE Transactions on Software Engineering*, **9**(3), 219–227

Smedema, C. H., CHILL: facilities for concurrency. In *Proceedings of COMPSAC '83*, IEEE Computer Society Press, Silver Spring, Maryland, November, pp. 148–159

Soundararajan, N., Correctness proofs of CSP programs. *Theoretical Computer Science*, **24**(2), 131–141

Sovis, F., Uniform theory of the shuffle-exchange type permutation networks. In *10th Annual Symposium on Computer Architecture Conference Proceedings*, ACM, New York, p. 185

Spector, A. Z. and Schwartz, P. M., Transactions: a construct for reliable distributed computing. Report CMU-CS-82-143, Department of Computer Science, Carnegie-Mellon University, Pittsburgh, Pennsylvania, USA, 4 January

Strom, R. E. and Yemini, S., NIL: an integrated language and system for distributed programming. *ACM SIGPLAN Notices*, **18**(6), 73–82

Stuck, B. W., Calculating the maximum mean data rate in local area networks. *IEEE Computer*, **16**(5)

Sugimoto, S. and Agusa, K., A multi-microprocessor system for concurrent LISP-language oriented system architecture. In *Proceedings of COMPCON '83*, IEEE Computer Society Press, Silver Spring, Maryland

Sugimoto, S. and Agusa, K., A multi-microprocessor system for concurrent LISP. *Proceedings of the 1983 International Conference on Parallel Processing*, Bellaire, Michigan, USA, August, pp. 135–143

Suri, R., Robustness of queuing network formulas. *Journal of the ACM*, **30**(3), 564–594

Sussenguth, E. H., Progress in computer networks. *IFIP Congress*, Paris, pp. 883–890

Swift, S. G., Using distributed microprocessors systems in marine applications. *Proceedings OCEANS '83*, Poland, September, pp. 150–154

Tanimoto, S. L., A pyramidal approach to parallel processing. In *10th Annual Symposium on Computer Architecture Conference Proceedings*, ACM, New York, p. 372

Taylor, R. N., A general purpose algorithm for analysing concurrent programs. *Communications of the ACM*, **26**(5), 362–376

Thanawastien, S. and Nelson, V. P., Distributed path testing in a shuffle/exchange network based on a write/verify approach. *Proceedings of the IEEE Real-Time Systems Symposium*, Arlington, Virginia, pp. 131–140

Thornton, J. E. and Christensen, G. S., Hyperchannel network links. *IEEE Computer*, **16**(9)

Tirri, H. R., Simulation, reduction and preservation of correctness properties of parallel systems. *Information Processing Letters*, **17**(1), 21

Tomita, S., Shibayama, K., Kitamura, T., Nakata, T. and Hagiwara, H., A user-microprogrammable, local host computer with low-level parallelism. In *10th Annual Symposium on Computer Architecture Conference Proceedings*, ACM, New York, p. 151

Tsay, D-P. and Liu, M. T., MIKE: a network operating system for the distributed double-loop computer network. *IEEE Transactions on Software Engineering*, **9**(2), 143–154

Tsujino, Y., Ando, M., Araki, T. and Tokura, N., The concurrent facility implemented by C library. *Transactions of the Information Processing Society of Japan*, **24**(1), 89–97

Umeyama, S. and Tamura, K., A parallel execution model of logic programs. In *10th Annual Symposium on Computer Architecture Conference Proceedings*, ACM, New York, p. 349

van Rumste, M., The iAPX432, a next generation microprocessor. *Microprocessing & Microprogramming*, **11**(2), 69–106

van Tilburg, A. M. and Wittie, L. D., Operating systems for the micronet network computer. *IEEE Micro*, **3**(2)

Voydock, V. L. and Kent, S. T., Security mechanisms in high-level network protocols. *ACM Computing Surveys*, **15**(2), 135–171

Wagner, B., Using the local area network magnet. Report 58a, ETH Institut für Informatik, Zürich, Switzerland

Wah, B. W., A comparative study of distributed resource sharing on multiprocessors. In *10th Annual Symposium on Computer Architecture Conference Proceedings*, ACM, New York, p. 301

Weber, J. C., Interactive debugging of concurrent programs. *ACM SIGPLAN Notices*, **18**(8), 112–113

Wedde, H., An iterative and starvation-free solution for a general class of distributed control problems based on interaction primitives. *Theoretical Computer Science*, **24**(1), 1–20

Wegner, P. and Smolka, S. A., Processes, tasks, and monitors: a comparative study of concurrent programming primitives. *IEEE Transactions on Software Engineering*, **9**(4), 446–462

Weiser, M., Reconstructing sequential behavior from parallel behavior projections. *Information Processing Letters*, **17**(3), 129

Wensley, J. H., Fault tolerance in a local area network used for industrial control. *Proceedings of the IEEE Real-Time Systems Symposium*, Arlington, Virginia, USA, pp. 113–118

Wilson, P., Language-based architecture eases system design. II. *Computer Design*, **22**(14), 109–120

Winskel, G., A representation of completely distributive algebraic lattices. Report CMU-CS-83-154, Department of Computer Science, Carnegie-Mellon University, Pittsburgh, Pennsylvania, USA, October

Wolper, P., Temporal logic can be more expressive. *Information and Control*, **56**(1–2), 72–99

Wong, E., Dynamic rematerialization: processing distributed queries using redundant data. *IEEE Transactions on Software Engineering*, **9**(3), pp. 228–232

Yamashita, M., An analysis of concurrent processing systems consisting of straight line processes, using synchronized production system-independent k-left linear, SPS and SPS languages. *Transactions of the Institute of Electronic and Communications Engineering of Japan*, Part D, **J66D**(11), 1286–1293

Yau, S. S. and Caglayan, M. U., Distributed software system design representation using modified Petri nets. *IEEE Transactions on Software Engineering*, **9**(6), 733–745

Yeh, P. C. C., Patel, J. H. and Davidson, E. S., Performance of a shared cache for parallel-pipelined computer systems. In *10th Annual Symposium on Computer Architecture Conference Proceedings*, ACM, New York, p. 117

Zheng, Z.-J., The duodirun merging algorithm: a new fast algorithm for parallel merging. *Information Processing Letters*, **17**(3), 167

1984

Amamiya, M. and Hasegawa, R., Dataflow computing and eager and lazy evaluations *New Generation Computing*, **2**(2), 105–129

Anon., Broadcasting sequential processes (BSP). *IEEE Transactions on Software Engineering*, **10**(4), 343–351

Anon., Mathematical foundations of computer science. Proceedings 1984. In *Lecture Notes in Computer Science*, **176**, Springer-Verlag, Berlin

Anon., *OCCAM Programming Manual*, Prentice-Hall, Englewood Cliffs, New Jersey

Anon., Seminar on concurrency. Proceedings 1984. *Lecture Notes in Computer Science*, **197**, Springer-Verlag, Berlin

Anon., Ada software tools interfaces. Proceedings 1983. In *Lecture Notes in Computer Science*, **180**, Springer-Verlag, Berlin

Antrim, W. and G. Baird Ltd., Word processor – phototypesetter network. Report CS 050, Department of Computer Science, The Queen's University of Belfast, Belfast, N. Ireland, December

Apt, K. R. and Francez, N., Modeling the distributed termination convention of CSP. *ACM Transactions on Programming Languages and Systems*, **6**(3), 370–379

Ardo, A. and Philipson, L., Implementation of a Pascal based parallel language for a multiprocessor computer. *Software Practice and Experience*, **14**(7), 643–658

Astesiano, E. and Costa, G., Distributive semantics for nondeterministic typed lambda-calculi. *Theoretical Computer Science*, **32**(1,2), 121–156

Atallah, M. J., Parallel strong orientation of an undirected graph. *Information Processing Letters*, **18**(1), 37

Babb, II R. G., Parallel processing with large-grain data flow techniques. *IEEE Computer*, **17**(7), 55–61

Baiardi, F., Ricci, L., Tomasi, A. and Vanneschi, M., Structuring processes for a cooperative approach to fault-tolerant distributed software. In *Proceedings of the 4th Symposium on Reliability in Distributed Software and Database Systems* (eds V. D. Gligor and P. A. B. Ng), IEEE Computer Society Press, Silver Spring, Maryland, pp. 218–231

Baiardi, F., Ricci, L. and Vanneschi, M., Static checking of interprocess communication in ECSP. *ACM SIGPLAN Notices*, **19**(6), 290–299

Barringer, H., Now you may compose temporal logic specifications. *Advanced NATO Study Institute on Logics and Models for Verification and Specification of Concurrent Systems*, Centre de Rocquencourt, Le Chesnay, France, October, pp. 376–404

Berkowitz, S. J., On computing the determinant in small parallel time using a small number of processors. *Information Processing Letters*, **18**(3), 147

Bernstein, P. A. and Goodman, N., An algorithm for concurrency control and recovery in replicated distributed databases. *ACM Transactions on Database Systems*, **9**(4), 596–615

Birman, K. P., Joseph, T. A. and Rauchle, T., Extending resilient objects efficiently. In *Fault-Tolerant Computing Systems* (eds K.-E. Grosspietsch and M. Dal Cin), Springer-Verlag, Berlin

Birman, K., Joseph, T. A. and Rauchle, T., Concurrency control in resilient objects. Report 84–622. Department of Computer Science, Cornell University, Ithaca, New York, USA, July

Birman, K. P. and Joseph, T. A., Low cost management of replicated data in fault-tolerant distributed systems. Report 84–644, Department of Computer Science, Cornell University, Ithaca, New York, USA, October

Birman, K. P., Joseph, T. A., Rauchle, T. and El Abbadi, A., Implementing fault-tolerant distributed objects. Report TR 84–594, Department of Computer Science, Cornell University, Ithaca, New York, USA, March

Bitton, D., DeWitt, D. J., Hsaio, D. K. and Menon, J., A taxonomy of parallel sorting. *ACM Computing Surveys*, **16**(3), 287–318

Blum, N., A Boolean function requiring 3n network size (note). *Theoretical Computer Science*, **28**(3), 337–345

Borgwardt, P., Parallel Prolog using stack segments on shared-memory multiprocessors. *Proceedings of the International Symposium on Logic Programming*, Atlantic City, New Jersey, USA, pp. 2–11

Brain, S., Writing parallel program in Occam. *Electronic Production Design*, **5**(9), 47–54

Brookes, S. D., Hoare, C. A. R. and Roscoe, A. W., A theory of communicating sequential processes. *Journal of the ACM*, **31**(3), 560–599

Browne, J. C. and Almasi, G., University, industry, and government collaboration workshop: research in parallel computing. *IEEE Computer*, **17**(7), 92–93

Broy, M. and Bauer, F. L., A systematic approach to language constructs for concurrent programs. *Science of Computer Programming*, **4**(2)

Buchanan, J. R., Fennell, R. D. and Samet, H., A database management system for the Federal Courts. *ACM Transactions on Database Systems*, **9**(1), 72–88

Carey, M. J. and Stonebraker, M. R., The performance of concurrency control algorithms for DBMSs. In *Proceedings of the 10th International Conference on Very Large Databases* (eds Seng U Dayal, G. Schlateger and Lim Huat), Singapore, August

Carpenter, B. E. and Caillau, R., Experience with remote procedure calls in a real-time control system. *Software Practice and Experience*, **14**(9), 901–907

Cheng, R. F., Naming and addressing in interconnected computer networks. Report 84-1702, University of Illinois, Department of Computer Science, Urbana-Champaign, Illinois, USA, January

Cheriton, D. R., The V Kernel: a software base for distributed systems. *IEEE Software*, **1**(2)

Chin, C.-Y. and Hwang, K., Connection principles for multipath switching networks. In *11th Annual Symposium on Computer Architecture Conference Proceedings*, ACM, New York, pp. 99

Ciciani, B., Analysis and comparison of two distributed procedures for the process termination in ECSP environment. *International Journal of Mini & Microcomputers*, **6**(3), 44–48

Clarke, E. M., Automatic verification of finite state concurrent systems using temporal logic specifications: a practical approach. In *Advanced NATO Study Institute on Logics and Models for Verification and Specification of Concurrent Systems*, Centre de Rocquencourt, Le Chesnay, France, October, pp. 241–262

Clarke, E. M. and Emerson, E. A., Design and synthesis of synchronization skeletons using branching time temporal logic. In *Advanced NATO Study Institute on Logics and Models for Verification and Specification of Concurrent Systems*, Centre de Rocquencourt, Le Chesnay, France, October, pp. 173–239

Clarke, S., Extending BCPL to support concurrency. University of York 3rd Year Project, York, UK

Clemente, G., Congui, S. and Moro, M., A language for concurrent process control in industrial automation. In *Engineering Software for Microcomputers* (eds B. A. Schrefler, R. W. Lewis and S. A. Odorizzi), Pineridge Press, Swansea, UK

Colbourn, C. J. and Proskurowski, A., Concurrent transmissions in broadcast networks. In *Lecture Notes in Computer Science*, **172**, Springer-Verlag, Berlin, pp. 128–136

Congui, S., Clemente, G. and Moro, M., A concurrent Pascal language for a multi-processor cross support system. *Proceedings of the Digital Equipment Computer Users Society Europe*, Paris, France, September, pp. 270–291

Cook, R. L., Porter, T. and Carpenter, L., Distributed ray tracing. *Computer Graphics*, **18**(3), 137–148

Cowan, D. D., Boswell, F. D. and Grove, T. R., A distributed file server for a personal computer network. Report CS-84-54, Computer Science Department, University of Waterloo, Waterloo, Ontario, Canada, December

Cox, P. T. and Pietrzykowski, T., Concurrent editing and executing a PROGRAPH on graphical microcomputers. *International Journal of Mini & Microcomputers*, **6**(1), 1–3

Crookes, D. and Elder, J. W. G., An experiment in language design for distributed systems. *Software Practice and Experience*, **14**(8), 957–971

Culik, K., Systolic tree acceptors. *RAIRO Informatique Theorique*, **18**(1), 53–69

Curry, B. J., Language-based architecture eases system design. III. Occam. *Computer Design*, **23**(1), 127–136

Curtis, R. and Wittie, L., Global naming in distributed systems. *IEEE Software*, **1**(3), 76–80

Darondeau, P., Infinitary languages and fully abstract models of fair asynchrony. *Advanced NATO Study Institute on Logics and Models for Verification and Specification of Concurrent Systems*, Centre de Rocquencourt, Le Chesnay, France, October, pp. 675–718

Davidson, S. B., Garcia-Molina, H. and Skeen, D., Consistency in a partitioned network: a survey. Report TR 84-617, Department of Computer Science, Cornell University, Ithaca, New York, USA, June

Davidson, S. B., Optimism and consistency in partitioned distributed database systems. *ACM Transactions on Database Systems*, **9**(3), 456–482

de Nicola, R. and Hennessy, M. C. B., Testing equivalences for processes concurrent programming. *Theoretical Computer Science*, **34**(1–2), 83–133

DeTreville, J., Phoan: an intelligent system for distributed control synthesis. *ACM SIGPLAN Notices*, **19**(5), 96–103

Dippe, M. and Swenson, J., An adaptive subdivision algorithm and parallel architecture for realistic image synthesis. *Computer Graphics*, **18**(3), 149–158

El Abbadi, A. and Rauchle, T., Resilient communication structures for local area networks. Report 84-653, Department of Computer Science, Cornell University, Ithaca, New York, USA, December

Elrad, T., A practical software development for dynamic testing of distributed programs. *Proceedings of the 1984 International Conference on Parallel Processing*, Bellaire, Michigan, USA, IEEE Computer Society Press, Silver Spring, Maryland, August, pp. 388–391

Emerson, E. A. and Chin, L. L., Model checking under generalized fairness constraints. Report TR-84-20, University of Texas at Austin, USA, June

Epstein, S. S., A restricted English query language for large database applications. In *Proceedings of the 1st Conference on Artificial Intelligence Applications*, pp. 424–431, IEEE Computer Society Press, Silver Spring, Maryland, December

Fisher, J. A., Ellis, J. R., Ruttenberg, J. C. and Nicolau, A., Parallel processing: a smart compiler and a dumb machine. *ACM SIGPLAN Notices*, **19**(6), 37–47

Francez, N., Lehmann, D. and Pnueli, A., A linear-history semantics for languages for distributed programming. *Theoretical Computer Science*, **32**(1,2), 25–46

Francez, N., Script: a communication abstraction mechanism and its verification. *Advanced NATO Study Institute on Logics and Models for Verification and Specification of Concurrent Systems*, Centre de Rocquencourt, Le Chesnay, France, October, pp. 629–674

Franta, W. R. and Heath, J. R., Hyperchannel local network interconnection through satellite links. *Computer*, **17**(5)

Fritzson, P., Preliminary experience from the DICE system, a distributed incremental compiling environment. *ACM SIGPLAN Notices*, **19**(5), 113–123

Fritz, T. E., Hefner, J. E. and Raleigh, T. M., A network of computers running the UNIX system. *AT & T Bell Laboratories Technical Journal*, **63**(8 part 2), 1877–1896

Gajski, D., Kim, W. and Fushimi, S., A parallel pipelined relational query processor: an architectural overview. In *11th Annual Symposium on Computer Architecture Conference Proceedings*, ACM, New York, p. 134

Garcia-Molina, H., Germano, F. Jr. and Kohler, W. H., Debugging a distributed computing system. *IEEE Transactions on Software Engineering*, **10**(2)

Gehani, N. and Cargill, T. A., Concurrent programming in the Ada language: the polling bias. *Software Practice and Experience*, **14**(5), 413–427

Gerth, R. and de Roever, W. P., A proof system for concurrent Ada programs. *Science of Computer Programming*, **4**, 159–204

Giordana, A., A concurrent language for describing network of frames for interpreting real-world data. In *Proceedings of the 7th International Conference on Pattern Recognition*, IEEE Computer Society Press, Silver Spring, Maryland, pp. 1191–1193

Goto, A., Tanaka, H. and Moto-oka, T., Highly parallel inference engine PIE -- goal rewriting model and machine architecture. *New Generation Computing*, **2**(1)

Gottlieb, A. and Kruskal, C. P., Complexity rules for computing data and other computations on parallel processors. *Journal of the ACM*, **31**(2), 193–209

Graube, M. and Mulder, M. C., Local area networks. *IEEE Computer*, **17**(10), 242–247

Gupta, A., Parallelism in production systems: the sources and the expected speed-up. Report, Department of Computer Science, Carnegie-Mellon University, Pittsburgh, Pennsylvania, USA, December

Hajek, B., The proof of a folk theorem on queuing delay with applications to routing in networks. *Journal of the ACM*, **31**(4), 834–851

Harrison, P. G., The distribution of cycle times in tree-like networks of queues. *BCS Computer Journal*, **27**(1), 27–36

Haugdahl, J. S., Local-area networks for the IBM PC. *Byte*, **9**(13)

Heine, P. and Kaiser, F., An economical implementation of the high level real-time language PEARL on microcomputers: Intel RMX86-PEARL. *Software Practice and Experience*, **14**(4), 377–382

Hellerstein, L., Implementing parallel algorithms in Concurrent Prolog: the Maxflow experience. *Proceedings of the International Symposium on Logic Programming*, Atlantic City, New Jersey, USA, pp. 99–115

Hinton, G. E., Sejnowski, T. J. and Ackley, D. H., Boltzmann machines: constraint satisfaction networks that learn. Report, Carnegie-Mellon University, Pittsburgh, Pennsylvania, USA, May

Holenderski, L., A note on specifying and verifying concurrent processes. *Information Processing Letters*, **18**(2), 77

Hoover, H. J., Klawe, M. M. and Pippenger, N. J., Bounding fan-out in logical networks. *Journal of the ACM*, **31**(1), 13–18

Hornig, D. A., Automatic partitioning and scheduling on a network of personal computers. Report CMU-CS-84-165, Department of Computer Science, Carnegie-Mellon University, Pittsburgh, Pennsylvania, USA, December

Hromada, W., The language of the 'transputer'. Occam-a simple computer language for complex problems. *Elektronikschau*, **60**, 48–60

Hsieh, W.-N. and Gitman, I., Routing strategies in computer networks. *Computer*, **17**(6)

Hughes, J. W. and Powell, M. S., Developing concurrent systems with DTL. In *Distributed Computing Systems Program*, (ed. D. A. Duce), Peter Peregrinus, Stevenage, pp. 154–168

Hull, M. E. C. and McKeag, R. M., Communicating sequential processes for centralised and distributed operating system design. *Transactions on Programming Languages and Systems*, **6**(2), 175–191

Hull, M. E. C. and McKeag, R. M., A general approach to queuing in CSP. *Software Practice and Experience*, **14**(8), 769–773

Hull, M. E. C. and McKeag, R. M., Concurrency in the design of data processing systems. *BCS Computer Journal*, **27**(4), 289–293

Hull, M. E. C., A parallel view of stable marriages. *Information Processing Letters*, **18**(2), 63

Ja'Ja', J. and Kumar, V. K. P., Information transfer in distributed computing with applications to VLSI. *Journal of the ACM*, **31**(1), 150–62

Kurose, J. F., Schwartz, M. and Yeimini, Y., Multiple-access protocols and time-constrained communication. *ACM Computing Surveys*, **16**(1), 43–70

Janicki, R., A method for developing concurrent systems. In *International Symposium on Programming 6th Colloquium* (eds M. Paul and B. Robinet), Springer-Verlag, Berlin, pp. 155–166

Jhon, C. S. and Kim, J. H., Towards applicative specification of concurrent digital systems. In *Proceedings of IEEE Workshop on Languages for Automation*, IEEE Computer Society Press, Silver Spring, Maryland, pp. 19–24

Johnson, J. L., Anatomy of an educational network database system. *Software Practice and Experience*, **14**(8), 739–754

Johnson, R. E. and Schneider, F. B., Symmetry and similarity in distributed systems. Report 85-677, Department of Computer Science, Cornell University, Ithaca, New York, USA

Jones, M. B., Rashid, R. F. and Thompson, M. R., Matchmaker: an interface specification language for distributed processing. Report CMU-CS-84-161, Department of Computer Science, Carnegie-Mellon University, Pittsburgh, Pennsylvania, USA, December

Joseph, M., Moitra, A. and Soundararajan, N., Proof rules for fault tolerant distributed programs. Report 84-643, Department of Computer Science, Cornell University, Ithaca, New York, USA, October

Joseph, T., Raeuchle, T. and Toueg, S., State machines and assertions (an integrated approach to modelling and of distributed systems). Report 84-652, Department of Computer Science, Cornell University, Ithaca, New York, USA, November

Kambayashi, Y. and Kondoh, S.-I., Global concurrency control mechanisms for a local network consisting of systems without concurrency control ability. *AFIPS National Computer Conference Proceedings*, Las Vegas, Nevada, USA, pp. 31–40

Kapauan, A., Field, J. T., Gannon, D. B. and Snyder, L., The Pringle parallel computer. In *11th Annual Symposium on Computer Architecture Conference Proceedings*, ACM, New York, p. 12

Kersten, M. L. and Tebra, H., Application of an optimistic concurrency control method. *Software Practice and Experience*, **14**(2), 153–168

Kim, Won., Gajski, D. and Kuck, D. J., A parallel pipelined relational relational query processor. *ACM Transactions on Database Systems*, **9**(2), 214–242

Kim, Won., Highly available systems for database applications. *ACM Computing Surveys*, **16**(1), 71–98

Korach, E., Rotem D., and Santoro, N., Distributed algorithms for finding centers and medians, in networks. *Transactions on Programming Languages and Systems*, **6**(3), 380–401

Kusalik, A. J., Serialization of process reduction in Concurrent Prolog. *New Generation Computing*, **2**(3)

Kusalik, A. J., Bounded-wait merge in Shapiro's Concurrent Prolog. *New Generation Computing*, **2**(2), 157–169

Lai, T.-H. and Sahni, S., Anomalies in parallel branch-and-bound algorithms. *Communications of the ACM*, **27**(6), 594–602

Lamport, L., Using time instead of timeout for fault-tolerant distributed systems. *ACM Transactions on Programming Languages and Systems*, **6**(2), 254–280

LeBlanc, T. J., Gerber, R. H. and Cook, R. P., The StarMod distributed programming kernel. *Software Practice and Experience*, **14**(12), 1123–1140

Leblang, D. B., Computer-aided software engineering in a distributed workstation environment. *ACM SIGPLAN Notices*, **19**(5), 104–112

Lee, M., Chase, R. P. Jr., Wu, C.-L., Performance analysis of circuit switching baseline interconnection networks. In *11th Annual Symposium on Computer Architecture Conference Proceedings*, ACM, New York, p. 82

Leon, G., Gonzalez, F., de Miguel, T., Chase, R. P. Jr. and de la Cruz, P., GTL: a specification language for concurrent systems. *Proceedings of EUROCON '84*, Peter Peregrinus, Stevenage, pp. 276–280

Lewis, E. G., Spitz, K. R., Chase, R. P. Jr. and McKennye, P. E., An interleave principle for demonstrating concurrent programs. *IEEE Software*, **1**(4), 54–64

Lindsay, B. G., Haas, L. M., Mohan, C., Wilms, P. F., Chase, R. P. Jr. and Yost, R. A., Computation and communcation in R*: a distributed database manager. *Transactions on Computer Systems*, **2**(1), 24–38

Lindstrom, G., Chase, R. P. Jr. and Panangaden, P., Stream-based excution of logic programs. *Proceedings of the Internationl Symposium on Logic Programming*, Atlantic City, New Jersey, USA, pp. 168–176

Loka, R. R., A note on parallel parsing. *ACM SIGPLAN Notices*, **19**(7), 22–24

Lyngbaek, P., Chase, R. P. Jr. and McLeod, D., Object management in distributed information systems. *Transaction on Office Information Systems*, **2**(2), 96–122

Ma, R. P.-Yi, A model to solve timing-critical application problems in distributed computer systems. *IEEE Computer*, **17**(1)

Magott, J., Performance evaluation of concurrent systems using Petri nets. *Information Processing Letters*, **18**(1), 7

Mahjoub, A., On the static evaluation of distributed systems performance. *BCS Computer Journal*, **27**(3), 201–208

Mai, S., Chase, R. P. Jr. and Evans, D. J., A parallel algorithm for the enumeration of the spanning trees of a graph. Report 212, Department of Computer Studies, University of Technology, Loughborough, UK, July

Mai, S., Chase, R. P. Jr. and Evans, D. J., Two parallel algorithms for the convex hull problem in a 2-dimensional space. Report 211, Department of Computer Studies, University of Technology, Loughborough, UK, July

Manber, U., Chase, R. P. Jr. and Ladner, R. E., Concurrency control in a dynamic search structure. *ACM Transactions on Database Systems*, **9**(3), 439–455

Manna, Z., Chase, R. P. Jr. and Pnueli, A., Adequate proof principles for invariance and liveness properties of concurrent programs. *Science of Computer Programming*, **4**, 257–289

McKendry, M. S., Clouds: a fault-tolerant distributed operating system. In *Distributed Processing Technical Committee Newsletter*, IEEE, New York, (also issued as Clouds Technical Memo #42)

McKenna, J., Chase, R. P. Jr. and Mitra, D., Asymptotic expansions and integral representations of moments of queue lengths in closed Markovian networks. *Journal of the ACM*, **31**(2), 346–360

Matwin, S., Motion-picture debugging in a dataflow language. *Proceedings of graphics Interface '84*, Ottawa, Ontario, Canada, pp. 249–250, May

Megiddo, N., Applying parallel computation algorithms in the design of serial algorithms. *Journal of the ACM*, **31**(4), 852–866

Mehrotra, R., Chase, R. P. Jr. and Talukdar, S. N., Scheduling of tasks for distributed processors. In *11th Annual Symposium on Computer Architecture Conference Proceedings*, ACM, New York, p. 263

Milne, G. J., CIRCAL and representation of communication concurrency and time. Report CSR-151-83, Department of Computer Science, University of Edinburgh, Edinburgh, UK, November 1983, updated October 1984

Misra, J., Reasoning about networks of communicating processes. *Advanced NATO Study Institute on Logics and Models for Verification and Specification of Concurrent Systems*, Centre de Rocquencourt, Le Chesnay, France, pp. 1–29, October

Mohan, J., Performance of parallel programs: model and analysis. Report CMU-CS-84-141, Department of Computer Science Science, Carnegie-Mellon University, Pittsburgh, Pennsylvania, USA, July

Moitra, A., Automatic construction of CSP programs from sequential non-deterministic programs. Report TR 84-597, Department of Computer Science, Cornell University, Ithaca, New York, USA, March

Moitra, A., Chase, R. P. Jr. and Iyenngar, S., Derivation of a maximally parallel algorithm for balancing binary search trees. Report 84-638, Department of Computer Science, Cornell University, Ithaca, New York, USA, September

Mokhoff, N., Parellelism makes strong bid for next generation computers, *Computer Design*, **23**(10), 104–131

Moore, R. T., Geer, N. F., Chase, R. P. Jr. and Graf, H. A., Gridnet: an alternative large distributed network. *IEEE Computer*, **17**(4)

Naeini, R., A few statement types adapt C language to parallel processing. *Electronics*, **57**(13), 125–129

Nakamura, K., Associative concurrent evaluation of logic programs. *The Journal of Logic Programming*, **1**(4), 285–296

Ng K.-W., Chase, R. P. Jr. and Li W.-K, GDPL-A generalized distributed programming language. *Proceedings of the 4th International Conference on Distributed Computing Systems*, San Francisco, California, USA, IEEE Computer Society Press, Silver Spring, Maryland, USA, pp. 69–78

Nguyen, V., Gries, D., Chase, R. P. Jr. and Owicki, S., A model and temporal proof system for networks of processes. Report 84-651, Department of Computer Science, Cornell University, Ithaca, New York, USA, November

Niimi, H., Imai, Y., Murakami, M., Tomita, S., Chase, R. P. Jr. and Hagiwara, H., A parallel processor system for three-dimensional color graphics. *Computer Graphics*, **18**(3), 67–76

Nitta, K., Parallel Prolog. *Information Processing Society of Japan*, **25**(12), 1353–1359

Olderog, E.-R., Specification-oriented programming in TCSP. *Advanced NATO Study Institute on Logics and Models for Verification and Specification of Concurrent Systems*, Centre de Rocquencourt, Le Chesnay, France, pp. 715-760, October

Oxborrow, E. A., The Proteus distributed database system. Computing Laboratory Report 21, University of Kent at Canterbury, UK, July

Oxborrow, E. A., A microcomputer database system in distributed database environment. Computing Laboratory Report 25, University of Kent at Canterbury, UK, October

Padmanabhan, K., Fault tolerance and performance improvement in multiprocessor interconnection networks. Report 84-1715, Department of Computer Science, University of Illinois, Urbana-Champaign, Illinois, USA, May

Papadimitriou, C. H., Chase, R. P. Jr. and Kanellakis, P. C., On concurrency control by multiple versions. *ACM Transactions on Database Systems*, **9**(1), 89–99

Papazoglou, M. P., Georgiadis, P. I., Chase, R. P. Jr. and Maritsas, D. G., Architectural considerations of the parallel SIMULA machine. *BCS Computer Journal*, **27**(3), 254–259

Parimala, N., Prakash, N., Chase, R. P. Jr. and Balloju, N., Concurrency control in admin. *BCS Computer Journal*, **27**(1), 62–66

Pashtan, A., Chase, R. P. Jr. and Unger, E. A., Resource monitors: a design methodology for operating systems. *Software Practice and Experience*, **14**(8), 791–806

Patnaik, L. M., Bhattacharya, P., Chase, R. P. Jr. and Ganesh, R., DFL: a data flow language. *Computer Languages*, **9**(2), 97–106

Petermann, U., Interrupts – an alternative communication mechanism between concurrent processes. *Informatyka (Poland)*, **19**(11), 4–7

Peters, J., Chase, R. P. Jr. and Rudolph, L., Parallel approximation schemes for subset sum and knapsack problems, Department of Computer Science, Carnegie-Mellon University, Pittsburgh, Pennsylvania, USA, August

Philipson, L., VLSI based design principles for MIMD multiprocessor computers with distributed memory management. In *11th Annual Symposium on Computer Architecture Conference Proceedings*, ACM, New York, p. 319

Pong, Man-Chi., I-PIGS: a concurrent programming environment with interactive graphical support. Computing Laboratory Report, 26, University of Kent at Canterbury, UK, November

Pournelle, J., User's column: new machines, networks, and sundry software. *Byte*, **9**(3)

Prakash, N., Parimala, N., Chase, R. P. Jr. and Bolloju, N., Specifying integrity constraints in a network DBMS. *BCS Computer Journal*, **27**(3), 209–217

Pramanik, S., Chase, R. P. Jr. and Weinberg, B., The implementation kit with monitors. *ACM SIGPLAN Notices*, **19**(9), 30–33

Purser, M., Horn, C., Chase, R. P. Jr. and Sheehan, J., The PHS protocol. *Software Practice and Experience*, **14**(4), 299–310

Quinn, M. J., Chase, R. P. Jr. and Deo. N., Parallel graph algorithms. *ACM Computing Surveys*, **16**(3), 319–348

Raghavendra, C. S., Fault tolerance in regular network architectures. *IEEE Micro*, **4**(6)

Rammamritham, K., Chase, R. P. Jr. and Stankovic, J. A., Dynamic task scheduling in hard real-time distributed systems. *IEEE Software*, **1**(3), 65–75

Reif, J., Chase, R. P. Jr. and Spirakis, P., Probabilistic bidding gives optimal distributed resource allocation. In *Lecture Notes in Computer Science*, **172**, Springer-Verlag, Berlin, pp. 391–402

Reif, J., Chase, R. P. Jr. and Spirakis, P., Real-time synchronization of interprocess communications. *ACM Transactions on Programming Languages and Systems*, **6**(2)

Reisig, W., Partial order semantics versus interleaving semantics for CSP-like languages and its impact on fairness. In *Lecture Notes in Computer Science*, **172**, Springer-Verlag, Berlin, pp. 403–413

Robinson, J. T., Separating policy from correctness in concurrency control design. *Software Practice and Experience*, **14**(9), 827–844

Roman, G.-C., Chase, R. P. Jr. and Day, M. S., Multifaceted distributed systems specification using processes and event synchronization. *Proceedings of the 7th International Conference on Software Engineering*, Orlando, Florida, pp. 44–55, March

Rom, R., Ordering subscribers on cable networks. *Transactions on Computer Systems*, **2**(4), 322–334

Ron, D., Rosemberg, F., Chase, R. P. Jr. and Pnueli, A., A hardware implementation of the CSP primitives and its verification. In *Lecture Notes in Computer Science*, **172**, Springer-Verlag, Berlin, pp. 423–435

Rudolph, L., Chase, R. P. Jr. and Segall, Z., Dynamic decentralized cache schemes for MIMD parallel processors. Report CMU-CS-84-139, Department of Computer Science, Carnegie-Mellon University, Pittsburgh, Pennsylvania, USA

Rudolph, L., Chase, R. P. Jr. and Segall, Z., Dynamic decentralized cache schemes for MIMD parallel processors. In *11th Annual Symposium on Computer Architecture Conference Proceedings*, ACM, New York, p. 340

Saltzer, J. H., Reed, D. P. Chase, R. P. Jr. and Clark D. D., End-to-end arguments in systems design. *Transactions on Computer Systems*, **2**(4), 277–288

Samatham, M. R., Chase, R. P. Jr. and Pradham, D. K., A multiprocessor network suitable for single-chip VLSI implementation. In *11th Annual Symposium on Computer Architecture Conference Proceedings*, ACM, New York, p. 328

Schlichting, R. D., Chase, R. P. Jr. and Schneider, F. B., Using message passing for distributed programming: proof rules and disciplines. *ACM Transactions on Programming Languages and Systems*, **6**(3), 402–422

Schoeffler, J. D., Distributed computer systems for industrial process control. *Computer*, **17**(2)

Schroeder, M. D., Birrell, A. D. Chase, R. P. Jr. and Needham, R. M., Experience with Grapevine: the growth of a distributed system. *ACM Transactions on Computer Systems*, **2**(1), 3–23

Seitz, C. L., Concurrent VLSI architectures. *IEEE Transactions on Computers*, **33**(12)

Shah, A., Chase, R. P. Jr. and Toueg, S., Distributed snapshots in spite of failures. Report 84-624, Department of Computer Science, Cornell University, Ithaca, New York, USA, July, (revised December 1984)

Shapiro, E., Systems programming in Concurrent Prolog. *11th Annual Symposium on Principles of Programming Languages*, ACM, Salt Lake City, Utah, USA, January 15–18, pp. 93–105

Shapiro, E., Chase, R. P. Jr. and Mierowsky, C., Fair, biased, and self-balancing merge operators: their specification and implementation in Concurrent Prolog. *New Generation Computers*, **2**(3), 221–240

Shapiro, E., Chase, R. P. Jr. and Mierowsky, C., Fair, biased and self-balancing merge operators: their specification and implementation in Concurrent Prolog. *Proceedings of the International Symposium on Logic Programming*, Atlantic City, New Jersey, USA, pp. 83–90

Shatz, M., Communication mechanisms for programming distributed systems. *IEEE Computer*, **17**(6)

Silberschatz, A., Cell: a distributed computing modularization concept. *IEEE Transactions on Software Engineering*, **10**(2), 178–184

Sindhu, P. S., Distribution and Reliability in a Multiprocessor Operating System, Technical Report, Department of Computer Science, Carnegie-Mellon University, Pittsburgh, Pennsylvania, USA, April

Smolka, S. A., Polynomial-time analysis for a class of communicating processes, In *Lecture Notes in Computer Science*, **172**, Springer-Verlag, Berlin, pp. 251–262

Snyder, L., Parallel programming and the poker programming environment. *IEEE Computer*, **17**(7), 27–36

Soundararajan, N., A proof technique for parallel programs. *Theoretical Computer Science*, **31**(1,2), 13–29

Spector, A. Z., Butcher, J., Daniels, D. S., Duchamp, D. J., Eppinger, Fineman, Heddaya, A., Chase, R. P. Jr. and Schwartz, P. M., Support for distributed transactions in the TABS prototype. Report CMU-CS-84-132, Department of Computer Science, Carnegie-Mellon University, Pittsburgh, Pennsylvania, USA, July

Stallings, W. Local networks. *ACM Computing Surveys*, **16**(1), 3–41

Steusloff, H. U., Advanced real-time languages for distributed industrial process control. *IEEE Computer*, **17**(2)

Svobodova, L., Resilient distributed computing. *IEEE Transactions on Software Engineering*, **10**(3), 257–268

Svobodova, L., File servers for network-based distributed systems. *ACM Computing Surveys*, **16**(4), 353–398

Szenes, K., In *Proceedings of the IFIP WG 5.7 Working Conference* (eds G. Doumeingts, R. P. Chase Jr. and W. A. Carter), North-Holland, Publishing Company, Amsterdam, pp. 241–249

Tamura, N., Implementing parallel Prolog on a multiprocessor machine. *Proceedings of the International Symposium on Logic Programming*, Atlantic City, New Jersey, USA, pp. 42–48

Taylor, R., Signal processing with Occam and the transputer. *IEE Proc. F.*, **131**(6), 610–614

Terry, D. B., Chase, R. P. Jr. and Andler, S., The COSIE communication subsystem: support for distributed office applications. *ACM Transactions on Office Information Systems*, **2**(2), 79–95

Tiekenheinrich, J., A 4n-lower bound on the monotone network complexity of a one-output Boolean function. *Information Processing Letters*, **18**(4), 201

Topor, R. W., Termination detection for distributed computations. *Information Processing Letters*, **18**(1), 33

Tsujino, Y., Ando, M., Araki, T., Chase, R. P. Jr. and Tokura, N., Concurrent C: a programming language for distributed multiprocessor systems. *Software Practice and Experience*, **14**(11), 1061–1078

Upfal, E. Efficient schemes for parallel communication *Journal of the ACM*, **31**(3), 507–517

Urda, B. M. O., A mechanism for communication between concurrent processes. *Control Cibernetics and Automation*, **18**(2), 3–7

Urquhart, J. C. and Knight, J. I. A., On the implementation and use of Ada on fault-tolerant distributed systems. *Ada Letters*, **4**(3), 53–64

Van-Hung, D., Languages for synchronized concurrent systems. *Koezl. Magy. Tud. Akad. Szamitastech. & Autom. Kut. Intez* (**31**), 33–43

Visvalingam, M., Chase, R. P. Jr. and Kirby, G. H., Communications over a network: MMI issues in a Perq PNX (UNIX) environment. Report 84/3, University of Hull, Department of Computer Science, Hull, UK

Waggoner, C. N., Tucker, C. Chase, R. P. Jr. and Nelson, C. J., NOVA*GKS, a distributed implementation of the graphical kernel system. *Computer Graphics*, **18**(3) 275–282

Wah, B. W., File placement on distributed computer systems. *Computer*, **17**(1)

Weiser, M., Program slicing. *IEEE Transactions on Software Engineering*, **10**(4), 352–357

Williamson, R., Chase, R. P. Jr. and Horowitz, E., Concurrent communication and synchronization mechanism. *Software Practice and Experience*, **14**(2), 135–151

Winskel, G., Synchronization trees. *Theoretical Computer Science*, **34**(1–2), 33–82

Wong, F. S., Chase, R. P. Jr. and Ito, M. R., Parallel sorting on a re-circulating systolic sorter. *BCS Computer Journal*, **27**(3), 260–269

Yalamanchili, S., Chase, R. P. Jr. and Aggarwal, J. K., Workstations in a local area network environment. *Computer*, **17**(11), 74–86

Yasuhara, H., Chase, R. P. Jr. and Nitadori, K., ORBIT: a parallel computing model of Prolog. *New Generation Computing*, **2**(3)

Yu, C. T., Chase, R. P. Jr. and Chang, C. C., Distributed query processing. *ACM Computing Surveys*, **16**(4), 399–433

Zedan, H., A note on deadlock-free proofs of network of processes. *ACM SIGPLAN Notices*, **19**(10), 58–62

Zhang, C. N., Chase, R. P. Jr. and Yun, D. Y. Y., Multi-dimensional systolic networks for discrete-Fourier transform. In *11th Annual Symposium on Computer Architecture Conference Proceedings*, ACM, New York, p. 215

Zhang, T. Y., Chase, R. P. Jr. and Suen, C. Y., A fast parallel algorithm for thinning digital patterns. *Communications of the ACM*, **27**(3), 236–240

Zhou, B., Chase, R. P. Jr. and Yeh, R. T., An algebraic system for deadlock detection and its applications. In *Proceedings of the 4th Symposium on Reliability in Distributed Software and Database Systems*, IEEE Computer Society Press, Silver Spring, Maryland, October

1985

Abrams, M. D., Observations on operating a local area network. *Computer*, **18**(5), 51–65

Agha, G., Actors: a model of concurrent computation in distributed systems. PhD Thesis, University of Michigan, Michigan, USA

Agrawal, R. and DeWitt, D. J., Integrated concurrency control and recovery mechanisms: design and performance evaluation. *ACM Transactions on Database Systems*, **10**(4), 529–564

Alford, M., SREM at the age of eight: the distributed computing design system. *Computer*, **18**(4), 36–46

Alford, M. W., Ansart, J. P., Hommel, G., Lamport, L., Liskov, B., Mullery G. P. and Schneider, F. B., Distributed systems. In *Lecture Notes in Computer Science*, **190**, Springer-Verlag, Berlin

Almes, G. T., Black, A. P., Lazowska, E. D. and Noe, J. D., The Eden system: a technical review. *IEEE Transactions on Software Engineering*, **11**(1), 43–59

Anderson, T., Real-time applications of the iPSC concurrent computer. *IFAC–IFIP Workshop on Real-Time Programming*, Purdue, West Lafayette, Indiana, USA, pp. 55–62

Anon., Local area networks: an advanced course. Proceedings 1983. In *Lecture Notes in Computer Science*, **184**, Springer-Verlag, Berlin

Anon., The analysis of concurrent systems. In *Lecture Notes in Computer Science*, **207**, Springer-Verlag, Berlin

Anon., *Concurrent Language in Distributed Systems. Hardware supported implementation.* Proceedings of the IFIP WG 10.3, Bristol, UK, North-Holland, Amsterdam

Anon., Seminar on concurrency. Proceedings 1984. In *Lecture Notes in Computer Science*, **197**, Springer-Verlag, Berlin

Appelbe, W. F. and Hansen, K., A survey of systems programming languages: concepts and facilities. *Software Practice and Experience*, **15**(2), 169–190

Armitage, J. W. and Chelini, J. V., Ada software on distributed targets. *ACM Ada Letters*, **4**(4), 32–37

Astesiano, E., On the parameterized algebraic specification of concurrent systems. In *Proceedings of TAPSOFT*, **1**, Springer-Verlag, Berlin, pp. 342–358

Avrunin, G. S. and Wileden, J. C., Describing and analyzing distributed software system designs. *ACM Transactions on Programming Languages and Systems*, **7**(3), 380–403

Awerbuch, B., Complexity of network synchronization. *Journal of the ACM*, **32**(4), 804–823

Back, R. J. R. and Kurki-Suonio, R., Serializability in distributed systems with handshaking. Report, Department of Computer Science, Carnegie-Mellon University, Pittsburgh, Pennsylvania, USA, February

Bagchi, A. and Mahanti, A., Three approaches to heuristic search in networks. *Journal of the ACM*, **32**(1), 1–27

Barak, A. and Litman, A., MOS: a multicomputer distributed operating system. *Software Practice and Experience*, **15**(8), 725–738

Bar-On, I. and Vishkin, U., Optimal parallel generation of a computation tree form. *ACM Transactions on Programming Languages and Systems*, **7**(2), 348–357

Barringer, H., A survey of verification techniques for parallel programs. In *Lecture Notes in Computer Science*, **191**, Springer-Verlag, Berlin

Barton, D., Parallelism in simple algebra systems. *BCS Computer Journal*, **28**(2), 142–147

Bates, J. L. and Constable, R. L., Proofs as programs. *ACM Transactions on Programming Languages and Systems*, **7**(1), 113–136

Bergstra, J. A. and Tucker, J. V., Top-down design and the algebra of communicating processes. *Science of Computer Programming*, 171–199

Binding, C., Cheap concurrency in C. *ACM SIGPLAN Notices*, **20**(9), 21–26

Birrell, A. D., Secure communication using remote procedure calls. *Transactions on Computer Systems*, **3**(1), 1–14

Black, D. L., On the existence of delay-intensive fair arbiters: Trace theory and its limitations. Report 85–173, Department of Computer Science, Carnegie-Mellon University, Pittsburgh, Pennsylvania, USA, 31 October

Brachs, G., Randomized agreement protocols and distributed deadlock detection algorithm. PhD. Thesis 85-657, Department of Computer Science, Cornell University, Ithaca, New York, USA, January

Brookes, S. D. and Roscoe, A. W., Deadlock analysis in networks of communicating processes. Report, Department of Computer Science, Carnegie-Mellon University, Pittsburgh, Pennsylvania, USA, February

Brookes, S. D. and Roscoe, A. W., An improved failure model for communicating processes. Report, Department of Computer Science, Carnegie-Mellon University, Pittsburgh, Pennsylvania, USA, February

Brookes, S., On the axiomatic treatment of concurrency. Report, Department of Computer Science, Carnegie-Mellon University, Pittsburgh, Pennsylvania, USA, February

Broy, M., Specification and top down design of distributed systems. In *Proceedings of TAPSOFT*, **1**, Springer-Verlag, Berlin, pp. 4–28

Brzozowski, J. A. and Seger, C. J., A characterization of ternary simulation of gate networks. Report CS-85-37, Computer Science Department, University of Waterloo, Waterloo, Ontario, Canada, October

Brzozowski, J. A., Combinatorial static CMOS networks. Report CS-85-42, Computer Science Department, University of Waterloo, Waterloo, Ontario, Canada, December

Burkhard, H. D., An investigation of controls for concurrent systems based on abstract control languages. *Theoretical Computer Science*, **38**(2–3), 193–122

Bush, V. J. and Gurd, J. R., Transforming recursive programs for execution on parallel machines. *Lecture Notes in Computer Science*, **201**, Springer-Verlag, Berlin, pp. 350–367

Cattaneo, G., CHILL concurrency on Intel iAPX 432 architecture. *Microprocess and Microprogram*, **15**(5), 233–251

Chandy, K. M. and Lamport, L., Distributed snapshots: determining global states of distributed systems. *ACM Transactions on Computer Systems*, **3**(1), 68–75

Chang-lin, Z. and Gang, S., A new language feature for concurrent programming. *Proceedings of the International Symposium on New Directions in Computing*, Washington DC, USA, IEEE Computer Society Press, Silver Spring, Maryland, August, pp. 311–317

Chanson, S. T. and Ravindran, K., State inconsistency issues in local area network-based distribution kernels. Report TR-85-7B. Department of Computer Science, University of British Columbia, Vancouver, Canada, August 1985 (revised November 1985)

Chapman, R. and Durrani, T. S., Design strategies for implementing systolic and wave-front arrays using Occam. In *Proceedings for the ICASSP '85*, IEEE, New York, 292–295

Cheriton, D. R. and Zwaenepoel, W., Distributed process groups in the V kernel. *ACM Transactions on Computer Systems*, **3**(2), 77–107

Choo, Y., Concurrency algebra and Petri nets. Report 5190:85, California Institute of Technology, Pasadena, California, June

Clarke, S., Extending BCPL to support concurrency. University of York 3rd year Project, 1984-1985, York, UK

Compton, A. J., An algorithm for the even distribution of entities in one dimension. *BCS Computer Journal*, **28**(5), 530–537

Conery, J. S. and Kibler, D. F., AND parallelism and nondeterminism in logic programs. *New Generation Computing*, **3**(1)

Cunningham, W. H., Optimal attack and reinforcement of a network. *Journal of the ACM*, **32**(3), 549–561

Czeck, E. W., Siewiorek, D. P. and Segall, Z., Fault free performance validation of a fault-tolerant multiprocessor: baseline and synthetic workload measurements. Report 85-177, Department of Computer Science, Carnegie-Mellon University, Pittsburgh, Pennsylvania, USA, 21 November

Dadam, P., Lum, V., Praedel, U. and Schlageter, G., Selective deferred index maintenance and concurrency control in integrated information systems. In *Proceedings of the 11th International Conference on Very Large Data Bases* (eds A. Vassiliou and A. Pirotte), Stockholm, Sweden, August

Dakin, R. J., Lederer, B. R. and Parker, K. R., A large scale network storage facility. *Software Practice and Experience*, **15**(9), 889–900

Dasgupta, P., LeBlanc, R., Spafford, E., Lundstrom, S. F. and Lawrie, D. H., The Clouds project: design and implementation of a fault-tolerant distributed operating system. *IEEE Software*, **2**(3), 5–6

De Bruin, A. and Bohm, W., The denotational semantics of dynamic networks of processes. *ACM Transactions on Programming Languages and Systems*, **7**(4), 656–679

Deen, S. M., Amin, R. R., Ofori-Dwumfuo, G. O. and Taylor, M. C., The architecture of a generalised distributed database system – PRECI. *BCS Computer Journal*, **28**(3), 282–290

Degano, P., and Montanari, U., Distributed systems, partial orderings of events, and event structures. In *Control Flow and Data Flow: Concept of Distributed Programming* (ed. M. Broy), Springer-Verlag, Berlin, pp. 7–106

Degano, P. and Montanari, U., Specification languages for modeling concurrency. In *Integrated Technology for Parallel Image Processing* (ed. S. Levialdi), Academic Press, London, pp. 1–18

Delves, L. M. and Mawdsley, S. C., DAP-Algol: a development system for parallel algorithms. *BCS Computer Journal*, **28**(2), 148–153

Dettmer, R., Occam and the transputer. *Electronics and Power*, **31**(4), 283–287

Dubois, M., A cache-based multiprocessor with high efficiency. *IEEE Transactions on Computers*, **34**(10), 968–972

Ellis, C. S., Concurrency and linear hashing. Report 151, Department of Computer Science, University of Rochester, New York, USA, March

Eppinger, J. L. and Spector, A. Z., Virtual memory management for recoverable objects in the TABS prototype. Report 85-163, Department of Computer Science, Carnegie-Mellon University, Pittsburgh, Pennsylvania, USA, December

Faro, A., Mirabella, O. and Vita, L., A multimicrocomputer-based structure for computer networking. *IEEE Micro*, **5**(2)

Farrag, A. A. and Ozsu, M. T., A general concurrency control for database systems. *AFIPS National Computer Conference Proceedings*, Chicago, Illinois, pp. 567–574

Feng, T.-Y. and Young, W., Parallel control algorithms for the reduced Omega-Omega**-1 network. *AFIPS National Computer Conference Proceedings*, Chicago, Illinois, pp. 167–174

Fischer, M. J., Lynch, N. A. and Paterson, M. S., Impossibility of distributed consensus with one faulty process. *Journal of the ACM*, **32**(2), 374–382

Flavin, R. A. and Williford, J. D., The network application manager. *Byte*, **10**(13)

Ford, R., Jipping, M. J. and Schultz, R., On the performance of an optimistic concurrent tree algorithm. Report 85-07, Department of Computer Science, University of Iowa, Iowa City, Iowa, USA, September

Franaszek, P. and Robinson, J. T., Limitations on concurrency in transaction processing. *ACM Transactions on Database Systems*, **10**(1), 1–28

Francez, N. and Yemini, S. A., Symmetric intertask communication. *ACM Transactions on Programming Languages and Systems*, **7**(4), 622–636

Frank, A J., Wittie, L. D. and Bernstein, A. J., Multicast communication on network computers. *IEEE Software*, **2**(3), 49–61

Fridrich, M. and Older, W., Helix: the architecture of the XMS distributed file system. *IEEE Software*, **2**(3), 21–29

Fuchs, K. and Kafura, D., Memory-constrained task scheduling on a network of dual processors. *Journal of the ACM*, **32**(1), 102–129

Fung, K. T., An entropy approach to solving some network reliability problems. *BCS Computer Journal*, **28**(4), 353–356

Gait, J., A debugger for concurrent programs. *Software Practice and Experience*, **15**(6), 539–554

Gammage, N. and Casey, L., XMS: a rendezvous-based distributed system software architecture. *IEEE Software*, **2**(3), 9–19

Garcia-Molina, H. and Barbara, D., How to assign votes in a distributed system. *Journal of the ACM*, **32**(4), 841–860

Garratt, P. W. and Michaelson, G. G., Analysis and design for a standard transport protocol. *Software Practice and Experience*, **15**(5), 427–438

Gehani, N. H. and Roome, W. D., Concurrent C – an overview. *USENIX Association Conference Proceedings*, Dallas, Texas, USA, Winter, pp. 43–50

Gerber, A. J., The trouble with mutual recursion in Concurrent Euclid. *ACM SIGPLAN Notices*, **20**(8), 64–70

Gifford, D. and Spector, A., Case study: The CIRRUS banking network. *Communications of the ACM*, **28**(8), 797–807

Goldberg, B. and Hudak, P., Serial combinators: optimal grains of parallelism. In *Lecture Notes in Computer Science*, **201**, Springer-Verlag, Berlin, pp. 382–399

Gregoretti, F. and Segall, Z., Programming for observability support in a parallel programming environment. Report 85-176, Department of Computer Science, Carnegie-Mellon University, Pittsburgh, Pennsylvania, USA, November

Gregory, S. T. and Knight, J. C., A new linguistic approach to backward error recovery. *15th Annual International Symposium on Fault-Tolerant Computing (FTCS 15)*, pp. 404–409

Gupta, R., The efficiency of storage management schemes for Ada programs. *ACM SIGPLAN Notices*, **20**(11), 30–38

Hamada, T., Handa, K. and Miyauchi, H., Practical use of DPL. *Sesian Kankyu*, **37**(4), 135–138

Hansen, A. G., Programming insight: simulating the normal distribution. *Byte*, **10**(10)

Harland, D. M., Towards a language for concurrent processes. *Software Practice and Experience*, **15**(9), 839–888

Headington, M. R. and Oldehoeft, A. E., Open predicate path expressions and their implementation in highly parallel computing environments. In *Proceedings of the International Conference on Parallel Processing* (ed. D. Degroot), IEEE Computer Society Press, Washington DC, USA, August, pp. 239–246

Hennessy, M. and Milner, R., Algebraic laws for nondeterminism and concurrency. *Journal of the ACM*, **32**(1), 137–161

Herlihy, M., Atomicity versus availability: concurrency control for replicated data. Department of Computer Science, Carnegie-Mellon University, Pittsburgh, Pennsylvania, USA, February

Hinton, G. E., Learning in parallel networks. *Byte*, **10**,(4)

Hoare, C. A. R., In *Communicating Sequential Processes*, Series in Computer Science, Prentice-Hall International, Hemel Hempstead

Hughes, J., A distributed garbage collection algorithm. *Lecture Notes in Computer Science*, **201**, Springer-Verlag, Berlin, pp. 256–272

Ibbett, R. N., Edwards, D. A., Hopkins, T. P., Cadogan, C. K. and Train, D. A., Centrenet – a high performance local area network. *BCS Computer Journal*, **28**(3), 231–242

Isle, R. and Lohr, K.-P, Modelling concurrent modules. In *Proceedings of TAPSOFT*, (eds H. Ehrig, C. Floyd, M. Nivat and J. Thatcher), Springer-Verlag, Berlin, pp. 309–324

Ito, N., Shimizu, H., Kishi, M., Kuno, E. and Rokusawa, K., Data-flow based execution mechanisms of parallel and Concurrent Prolog. *New Generation Computing*, **3**(1), pp. 15–41

Davis, N. J. and Siegel, H. J., The PASM prototype interconnection network design. *AFIPS National Computer Conference Proceedings*, Chicago, Illinois, USA, pp. 183–190

Jalote, P., Atomic actions in concurrent systems. Report 85-1731, Department of Computer Science, University of Illinois, Urbana-Champaign, Illinois, USA, August

Jeffrey, X. X., Virtual time. *ACM Transactions on Programming Languages and Systems*, **7**(3), 404–425

Jonak, J. E., Pascal and Comms programming. *ACM SIGPLAN Notices*, **20**(4), 33–41

Kant, K. and Silberschatz, A., Error propagation and recovery in concurrent environments. *BCS Computer Journal*, **28**(5), 466–473

Karp, R. M. and Wigderson, A., A fast parallel algorithm for the maximal independent set problem. *Journal of the ACM*, **32**(4), 762–773

Katoh, N., Ibaraki, T. and Kameda, T., Cautious transaction schedulers with admission control. *ACM Transactions on Database Systems*, **10**(2), 205–229

Keeffe, D., Tomlinson, G. M., Wand, I. C. and Wellings, A. J., *PULSE: an Ada-based Distributed Operating System*. APIC Studies in Data Processing Series, Academic Press, London

Keller, R. M., Distributed computation by graph reduction, *Systems Research*, **2**(4) 285–295

King, R. M., Synthesis of efficient structures for concurrent computation. In VLSI: *Algorithms and Architecture* (eds P. Bertolazzi and F. Luccio) pp. 377–386

Kleinrock, L., Distributed systems. *Communications of the ACM*, **28**(11), 1200–1213

Koo, R. and Toueg, S., Checkpointing and rollback-recovery for distributed systems. Report 85-706, Department of Computer Science, Cornell University, Ithaca, New York, USA, October

Koymans, R., Shyamasundar, R. K., de Roever, W. P., Gerth, R. and Arun-Kumar, S., Compositional semantics for real-time distributed computing. Report 68, Sectie Informatica, Katholieke Universiteit, Nijmegen, The Netherlands, April

Kung, H. T., Memory requirements for balanced computer architectures. Report 85–158, Department of Computer Science, Carnegie-Mellon University, Pittsburgh, Pennsylvania, USA

Kung, S. Y., Whitehouse, H. J. and Kailath, T., (eds) *VLSI and Modern Signal Processing*, Prentice-Hall, Englewood Cliffs, New Jersey, pp. 224–240

LeBlanc, T. J. and Cook, R. P., High-level broadcast communication for local area networks. *IEEE Software*, **2**(3), 40–48

Lee, K. F., Incremental network generation in template based word recognition. Report 85–181, Department of Computer Science, Carnegie-Mellon University, Pittsburgh, Pennsylvania, USA, December

Lee, R. K. S. and Goebel, R., Concurrent Prolog in a multi-process environment. Report CS-85-09, Computer Science Department, University of Waterloo, Waterloo, Ontario, Canada, May

Lengauer, C. and Huang, C.-H., Automated deduction in programming language semantics: the mechanical certification of program transformations to derive concurrency. Report TR-85-04, University Texas at Austin, USA, January

Lengauer, C., On the role of automated theorem proving in the compile-time derivation of concurrency. *Journal of Automated Reasoning*, **1**(1), 75–101

Leung C. H. C. and Wolfenden, K., Analysis and optimisation of data currency and consistency in replicated distributed databases. *BCS Computer Journal*, **28**(5), 518–523

Levinson, D., Proposal for an environment for distributed systems development. Report 85/192/5, Department of Computer Science, University of Calgary, Calgary, Alberta, USA, April

Liew, C. K., Choi, U. J. and Liew, C. J., A data distortion by probability distribution. *ACM Transactions on Database Systems*, **10**(3), 395–411, September

Lin, K. J. and Gannon, J. D., Atomic remote procedure call. *IEEE Transactions on Software Engineering*, **11**(10), 1126–1135

Maekawa, M., A square root of N algorithm for mutual exclusion in decentralised systems. *ACM Transactions on Computer Systems*, **3**(2), 145–159

Martin, A. J., Distributed mutual exclusion on a ring of processes. *Science of Computer Programming*, **5**, 265–276

Mastropietro, L. and Tomasi, A., The MuTEAM testbed for distributed architectures. In *Mini and Microcomputers and their Applications* (ed. E. Luque). pp. 111–114

Mellier-Smith, P. M., Synchronizing clocks in the presence of faults % A. Leslie Lamport. *Journal of the ACM* **32**(1), 52–78

Milne, G. J., CIRCAL and the representation of communication, concurrency and time. *ACM Transactions on Programming Languages and Systems*, **7**(2), 270–298

Moitra, A., Automatic construction of CSP programs from sequential non-deterministic programs. *Science of Computer Programming*, **5**, 277–307

Mond, Y. and Raz, Y., Concurrency control in B+-trees databases using preparatory operations. In *Proceedings of the 11th International Conference on Very Large Data Bases* (eds A. Vassiliou and Y. Pirotte), Stockholm, Sweden, August

Muhlenbein, H. and Warhaut, S., Concurrent multi-grid methods in an object-oriented environment—a case study. In *Proceedings of the International Conference on Parallel Processing* (ed. D. Degroot), IEEE Computer Society Press, Washington, DC, August, pp. 143–146

Muir, S., Hutchison, D. and Shepherd, D., Arca: a local network file server, *BCS Computer Journal*, **28**(3), 243–249

Murakami, K., Kakuta, T., Onai, R. and Ito, N., Research on parallel machine architecture for fifth-generation computer systems. *Computer*, **18**(6), 76–92

Nakamura, T., Ikeda, K., Ebihara, Y. and Nishikawa, M., Network management in a local computer network. *Software Practice and Experience*, **15**(4), 343–358

Nielson, F., Program transformation in a denotational setting., *ACM Transactions on Programming Languages and Systems*, **7**(3), 359–379

O'Leary, D. P. and Stewart, G. W., Data-flow algorithms for parallel matrix computations. *Communications of the ACM*, **28**(8), 840–853

Onai, R., Aso, M., Shimizu, H., Masuda, K. and Matsumato, A., Architecture of a reduction-based parallel inference machine: PIM-R. *New Generation Computing*, **3**(2)

Padmanabham, K. and Lawrie, D. H., Performance analysis of redundant-path networks for multiprocessor systems. *ACM Transactions on Computer Systems*, **3**(2), 117–144

Papadimitriou, C. H., Correction to 'A theorem for database concurrency control'. *Journal of the ACM*, **32**(3), 750

Papazoglou, M. P., Multiprocessor interrupting and synchronizing concepts in the parallel SIMULA machine and their representation by Petri-nets. *Microprocessing and Microprogramming*, **15**(4), 179–190

Patton, C., Software opens the way to true concurrency for multiprocessing. *Electronic Design*, **33**(18), 83–90

Paulk, M. C., The ARC network: a case study. *IEEE Software*, **2**(3), 62–69

Petermann, U. and Szalas, A., A note on PCI: distributed processes communicating by interrupts. *ACM SIGPLAN Notices*, **20**(3)

Quammen, D., Kearns, J. P. and Soffa, M. L., Efficient storage management for temporary values in concurrent programming languages. *IEEE Transactions on Computers*, **34**(9), 832–840

Radhakrishnan, T. and Grossner, C. P., Cuenet – a distributed computing facility. *IEEE Micro*, **5**(1)

Rattner, J., Concurrent processing: a new direction in scientific computing. *AFIPS National Computer Conference Proceedings*, Chicago, Illinois, USA, pp. 157–166

Rodeheffer, T. L., Compiling ordinary programs for execution on an aschronous multiprocessor. Report 85–155, Department of Computer Science, Carnegie-Mellon University, Pittsburgh, Pennsylvania, USA

Roscoe, A. W., Deadlock analysis in networks of communicating processes % A. S. D. Brookes. Report, Department of Computer Science, Carnegie-Mellon University, Pittsburgh, Pennsylvania, USA, February

Said, O. M., Application of algebraic specification to the definition of the semantics on parallel programming languages. In *Proceedings of the 3rd International Workshop on Software Specification and Design*, IEEE Computer Society Press, Washington, DC, USA, August, pp. 207–211

Sakata, S. and Ueda, T., A distributed interoffice mail system. *Computer*, **18**(10), 106–116

Samson, W. B. and Bendell, A., Rank order distribution and secondary key indexing. *BCS Computer Journal*, **28**(3), 309–312

Santoro, N. and Khatib, R., Labelling and implicit routing in networks. *BCS Computer Journal*, **28**(1), 5–8

Saraswat, V. A., Problems with Concurrent Prolog. Report 86–100, Department of Computer Science, Carnegie-Mellon University, Pittsburgh, Pennsylvania, USA, May

Schevon, C. A. and Vitter, J. S., A parallel algorithm for recognizing unordered depth-first search. Report 85–21, Brown University, Department of Computer Science, Providence, Rhode Island, USA

Schmidt, D. A., Detecting global variables in denotational specifications. *ACM Transactions on Programming Languages and Systems*, **7**(2), 299–310

Schneck, P. B., Austin, B., Squires, S. L., Lehmann, J., Mizell, D. and Wallgren, K. Parallel processor programs in the Federal Government. *Computer*, **18**(6), 43–56

Sears, K. H. and Middleditch, A. E., Software concurrency in real-time control systems: a software nucleus. *Software Practice and Experience*, **15**(8), 739–760

Sheltzer, A., Nework transparency in an internet environment. Report CSD-850028, Computer Science Department, University of California, Los Angeles, USA, August

Shields, M. W., Concurrent machines. *BCS Computer Journal*, **28**(5), 449–465

Shuford, R. S., An introduction to fiber optics, Part 2: connections and networks. *Byte*, **10**(1)

Skeen, D., Determining the last process to fail. *ACM Transactions on Computer Systems*, **3**(1), 15–30

Srini, V. P., An architecture for doing concurrent systems research. *AFIPS National Computer Conference Proceedings*, Chicago, Illinois, USA, pp. 267–278

Stockton, R. G., Overload resolution in Ada+. Report 85–186, Department of Computer Science, Carnegie-Mellon University, Pittsburgh, Pennsylvania, USA, December

Strom, R. E. and Yemini, S., Optimistic recovery in distributed systems. *ACM Transactions on Computer Systems*, **3**(3), 204–226

Strom, R. and Yemini, S., The NIL distributed systems programming language: a status report. *ACM SIGPLAN Notices*, **20**(5), 36–44

Subieta, K., Semantics of query languages for network databases. *ACM Transactions on Database Systems*, **10**(3), 347–394

Suzuki, I. and Kasami, T., A distributed mutual exclusion algorithm. *ACM Transactions on Computer Systems*, **3**(4), 344–349

Suzuki, N., Concurrent Prolog as an efficient VLSI design language. *IEEE Computer*, **18**(2), 33–40

Szalas, A. and Szczepanska, D., Exception handling in parallel computations. *ACM SIGPLAN Notices*, **20**(10), 95–104

Takeuchi, A. and Furukawa, K., Bounded buffer communication in Concurrent Prolog. *New Generation Computers*, **3**(2), 145–155

Tanenbaum, A. S. and Van Renesse, R., Distributed operating systems. *Computing Surveys*, **17**(4)

Tantawi, A. N. and Towsley, D., Optimal static load balancing in distributed computer systems. *Journal of the ACM*, **32**(2), 445–465

Tay, Y. C., Goodman, N., and Suri, R., Locking performance in centralized databases. *ACM Transactions on Database Systems*, **10**(4), 415–463, December

Tay, Y. C. and Suri, R., Error bounds for performance prediction in queuing networks. *ACM Transactions on Computer Systems*, **3**(3), 227–254

Taylor, D. J., Concurrency and forward recovery in atomic actions. Report CS-85-19, University of Waterloo, Department Computer Science, Waterloo, Ontario, Canada, July

Theorelli, L.-E., A language for linking modules into systems. *Bit*, **25**(2), 358–378

Thomas, R. H., Forsdick, H. C., Crowley, T. R., Schaaf, R. W., Tomlinson, R. S., Travers, V. M. and Robertson, G. G., Diamond: a multimedia, message system built on a distributed architecture. *Computer*, **18**(12), 65–78

Thompson, M. R., Sanson, R. D., Jones, M. B. and Rashid, R. F., Sesame: the spice file system. Report 85–172, Department of Computer Science, Carnegie-Mellon University, Pittsburgh, Pennsylvania, USA, 11 December

Tomlinson, G. M., Keeffe, D., Wand, I. C. and Wellings, A. J., The PULSE distributed file system. *Software Practice and Experience*, **15**(11), 1087–1101

Ueda, K., Concurrent Prolog compiler on top of Prolog. In *Proceedings of the Symposium on Logic Programming*, IEEE Computer Society, Press, Washington, DC, 119–126

Unger, B., Dewar, A., Cleary, J. and Birtwistle, G., A distributed software prototyping and simulation environment: Jade. Report 85/216/29, Department of Computer Science, University of Calgary, Calgary, Alberta, USA, October

Van Gils, W. J., How to cope with faulty processors in a completely connected network of communicating processors. *Information Processing Letters* **20**, 207–213

Weil, W. and Liskov, B., Implications of resilient atomic data types. *ACM Transactions on Programming Languages and Systems*, **7**(2), 244–269

Witt, Bernard, I., Communication modules: a software design model for concurrent distributed systems. *Computer*, **18**(1), 67–77

Witt, B. I., Parallelism, pipelines and partitions: variations on communicating modules. *Computer*, **18**(2), 105–112

Wong, W. L., Font storage, compression and scaling networked professional workstations. Report 85–1712, Department of Computer Science, University of Illinois, Urbana-Champaign, Illinois, USA, April

Woodman, M. and Ince, D. C., Keeffe, D., Tomlinson, G. M., Wand, I. C. and Wellings, A. J., A software tool for the construction and maintenance of structured analysis notation. *Software Practice and Experience*, **15**(11), 1057–1072

Yalamanchili, S. and Aggarwal, J. K., Reconfiguration strategies for parallel architectures. *Computer*, **18**(12), 44–61

Yemini, S. and Berry, D. M., A modular verifiable exception-handling mechanism. *ACM Transactions on Programming Languages and Systems*, **7**(2), 214–243

Zave, P., A distributed alternative to finite-state-machine specifications. *ACM Transactions on Programming Languages and Systems*, **7**(1), 10–36

Zedan, H., Safety decomposition of distributed programs. *ACM SIGPLAN Notices*, **20**(8), 107–112

1986

Anantharaman, T. S., Clarke, E. M., Foster, M. J. and Mishra, B., Compiling path expressions into VLSI circuits. *Distributed Computing*, **1**(3), 150–166

Anderson, D. B., Experience with Flamingo: a distributed object-oriented user interface system. *ACM SIGPLAN Notices*, **21**(11), 177–185

Andrews, G. and Olsson, R., The evolution of the SR language. *Distributed Computing*, **1**(3), 133–149

Anon. Current trends in concurrency. Overviews and tutorials. In *Lecture Notes in Computer Science*, **224**, Springer-Verlag, Berlin

Jalote, P. and Campbell, R. H., Atomic actions for fault-tolerance using CSP. *IEEE Transactions on Software Engineering*, **12**(1), 59–68

Birtwistle, B. W., Unger, G. Cleary, J., Hill, D., Keenan, T., Rokne, J. Witten, I., andWvyill, B., Project Jade final report – an environment for the development of distributed software. Report 86/237–11, Department of Computer Science, University of Calgary, Calgary, Alberta, Canada, April

Babaoglu, O., On the reliability of fault-tolerant distributed computing systems. Report 86-738, Department of Computer Science, Cornell University, Ithaca, New York, February

Badal, D. Z., The distributed deadlock detection algorithm. *ACM Transactions on Computer Systems*, **4**(4), 320–337

Baiardi, F., De Francesco, N. and Vaglini, G., Development of a debugger for a concurrent language. *IEEE Transactions on Software Engineering*, **12**

Banatre, J. P., Banatre, M., Lapalme, G. and Ployette, F., The design and building of Enchere, a distributed electronic marketing system. *Communications of the ACM*, **29**(1), 19–29

Barbara, D. and Garcia-Molina, H., Mutual exclusion in partitioned distributed systems. *Distributed Computing*, **1**(2), 119–132

Bini, D. and Pan, V., A logarithmic Boolean time algorithm for parallel polynomial division. In *VLSI Algorithms and Architectures* (eds F. Makedon, K. Melhorn, T. Papatheodorou and P. Sprirakis) Springer-Verlag, Berlin, pp. 246–251

Birman, K. P., ISIS: a system for fault-tolerant distributed computing. Report 86–744, Department of Computer Science, Cornell University, Ithaca, New York, USA, April

Black, D., On the existence of delay-insensitive fair arbiters: trace theory and its limitations. *Distributed computing*, **1**(4), 205–225

Bornat, R., A protocol for generalised Occam. *Software Practice and Experience*, **16**(9), 783–799

Bricker, A., Lebeck, T. and Miller, B. P., Dregs: a distributed runtime environment for game support. Report ♯657, University of Wisconsin-Madison, USA, August

Browne, J. C., Framework for formulation and analysis of parallel computation structures. *Parallel Computing*, **3**, 1–9

Bruno, G. and Balsamo, A., Petri net-based object-oriented modelling of distributed systems. *ACM SIGPLAN Notices*, **21**(11), 284–293

Burke, M. and Cytron, R., Interprocedural dependence analysis and parallelisation. *ACM SIGPLAN Notices*, **21**(7), 162–175

Carey, M. J., DeWitt, D. J. and Graefe, G. Mechanisms for concurrency control and recovery in Prolog. pp. 271–291 In *Expert Database Systems; Proceedings From the First International Workshop*, (eds L. Kerschberg, B. Cummings), pp. 271–291

Carey, M. J. and Muhanna, W. A., The performance of multiversion concurrency control. *Transactions on Computer Systems*, **4**(4), 338–378

Chandy, K. M. and Misra, J., How processes learn. *Distributed Computing*, **1**(1), 40–52

Chandy, K. M. and Misra, J., Systolic algorithms as programs. *Distributed Computing*, **1**(3), 177–183

Chan, H. W., Routing, flow control and fairness in computer networks. Report CSD-860067, Computer Science Department, University of California, Los Angeles, USA, October

Dally, W. and Satz, C., The Torus routing chip. *Distributed Computing*, **1**(4), 187–196

Dasgupta, P. and Morsi, M., Kernel structures for a distributed operating system. *Proceedings of the Conference on Object Programming Systems Languages and Applications*, pp. 57–66, (also released as technical report GIT-ICS-86/16)

Dasgupta, P., A probe-based monitoring scheme for an object-oriented distributed operating system. *ACM SIGPLAN Notices*, **21**(11), 57–66

Decouchant, D., Design of a distributed object manager for the smalltalk-80 system. *ACM SIGPLAN Notices*, **21**(11), 444–452

Dijkstra, E. W., A belated proof of self-stabilization. *Distributed Computing*, **1**(1), 5–6

Dowsing, R. D. and Sanderson, M. T., Writing concurrent assemblers – a case study in Path Pascal. *Software Practice and Experience*, **16**(12), 1117–1135

Fantechi, A., Invarardi, P. and Lijtmaer, N., Using high-level languages for local computer network communication: a case study in Ada. *Software Practice and Experience*, **16**(8), 701–717

Finkel, R. A., Scott, M. L. and Kalsow, W. K., Experience with Chatlotte: simplicity versus function in a distributed operating system. Report #653, University of Wisconsin-Madison

Fisher, A. J., A multi-processor implementation of occam. *Software Practice and Experience*, **16**(10), 875–892

Fisher, D. A. and Weatherly, R. M., Issues in the design of a distributed operating system for Ada. *IEEE Computer*, **19**(5), 38–47

Fisher, M. J., Lynch, N. A. and Merritt, M., Easy impossibility proofs for distributed consensus problems. *Distributed Computing*, **1**(1), 26–39

Francez, N., Script: a communication abstraction mechanism and its verification. *Science of Computer Programming*, **6**(1), 35–88

Frenkel, K. A., Complexity and parallel processing: an interview with Richard M. Karp. *Communications of the ACM*, **29**(2), 112–117

Frenkel, K. A., Evaluating two massively parallel architectures. *Communications of the ACM*, **29**(8), 752–758

Gait, J., A probe effect in concurrent programs. *Software Practice and Experience*, **16**(3), 225–233

Gannon, J. D., Katz, E. E. and Basili, V. R., Metrics for Ada packages: an initial study. *Communications of the ACM*, **29**(7), 616–623

Gavish, B. and Segev, A., Set query optimisation in distributed database systems. *ACM Transactions on Database Systems*, **11**(3), 265–293

Gehani, N. H. and Roome, W. D., Concurrent C. *Software Practice and Experience*, **16**(9), 821–844

Gelernter, D., Guest Editor's introduction: domesticating parallelism. *Computer*, **19**(8), 12–16

Goldsby, M. E., Concurrent use of genetic types in Modula-2. *ACM SIGPLAN Notices*, **21**(6), 28–34

Hack, J. J., Peak versus sustained performance in highly concurrent vector machines. *Computer*, **19**(9), 11–19

Halstead, R. H. Jr., Parallel symbolic computing. *Computer*, **19**(8), 35–43

Hillis, W. D. and Steele, G. L., Data parallel algorithms. *Communications of the ACM*, **29**(12), 1170–1183

Hill, R. D., Supporting concurrency, communication and synchronization in human–computer interaction – the Sassafras UIMS. *ACM Transactions on Graphics*, **5**(3), 179–210

Hsu, M. and Yang, W. P., Concurrent operations in extendible hashing. In *Proceedings of the 12th International Conference on Very Large Data Bases* (ed. K. Yahiko) Kyoto, Japan, August

Hull, M. E. C., Implementation of the CSP notation for concurrent systems. *BCS Computer Journal*, **29**(6), 500–505

Hull, M. E. C. and Donnan, G., Contextually communicating sequential processes: a software engineering environment. *Software Practice and Experience*, **16**(9), 845–864

Ishiwkawa, Y. and Tokoro, M., A concurrent object-oriented knowledge representation language Orient 84/K: its features and implementations. *ACM SIGPLAN Notices*, **21**(11), 232–241

Iyer, K. V. and Patnaik, L. M., Performance study of a centralized concurrency control algorithm for distributed database systems using SIMULA. *BCS Computer Journal*, **29**(2), 118–126

Jarosz, J. and Jaworowski, J. R., Computer tree – the power of parallel computations. *BCS Computer Journal*, **29**(2), 103–108

Jones, C. B., In *Systematic Software Development Using VDM*, Prentice-Hall International, Hemel Hempstead

Jones, M. B. and Rashid, N. F., Mach and matchmaker: kernel and language support for object-oriented distributed systems. *ACM SIGPLAN Notices*, **21**(11), 67–77

Jones, M. B. and Rashid, R. F., Mach and matchmaker: kernel and language support for object-oriented distributed systems. Report CMU-CS-87-150, Department of Computer Science, Carnegie-Mellon University, Pittsburgh, Pennsylvania, USA

Joseph, T. A. and Birman, K. P., Low cost management of replicated data in fault-tolerant distributed sytems. *ACM Transactions on Computer Systems*, **4**(1), 54–70

Kahn, K., Tribble, E. D., Miller, M. S. and Bobrow, D. G., Objects in concurrent logic programming languages. *ACM SIGPLAN Notices*, **21**(10), 29–38

Kahn, K., Tribble, E. D., Miller, M. S. and Bobrow, D. G., Objects in Concurrent Logic programming languages. *ACM SIGPLAN Notices*, **21**(11), 242–257

Keller, R. and Panangaden, P., Semantics of digital networks containing indeterminate modules. *Distributed Computing*, **1**(4), 234–245

Kerridge, J. and Simpson, D., Communicating parallel processes. *Software Practice and Experience*, **16**(1), 63–86

Kronenberg, N. P., Levy, H. and Strecker, W. D., VAXclusters: a closely-coupled distributed system. *ACM Transactions on Computer Systems*, **4**(2), 130–146

Kung, H. T. and Web, J. H., Mapping image processing operations onto a linear systolic machine. *Distributed Computing*, **1**(4), 246–257

Lafortune, S. and Wong, E., A state transition model for distributed query processing. *ACM Transactions on Database Systems*, **11**(3), 294–322

Lamport, L., On interprocess communication Part I: Basic formalism. *Distributed Computing*, **1**(2), 77–85

Lamport, L., On interprocess communication Part II: Algorithms. *Distributed Computing*, **1**(2), 86–101

Landram, F. G., Cook, J. R., Johnston, M., Spreadsheet calculations of probablilites form the F, t, ×2, and normal distribution. *Communications of the ACM*, **29**(11), 1090–1092

Lea, R. M., VLSI and WSI associative string processors for cost-effective parallel processing. *BCS Computer Journal*, **29**(6), 486–494

Lermen, C. W. and Maurer, D., A protocol for distributed reference counting. In *ACM Conference on LISP and Functional Programming*, MIT Press, Cambridge, Massachusetts, pp. 343–350

Linton, A. and Panzieri, F., A communication system supporting large datagrams on a local area network. *Software Practice and Experience*, **16**(3), 277–289

Liskov, B. and Weihl, W., Specification of distributed programs. *Distributed Computing*, **1**(2), 102–118

Lu, H. E. and Wang, P. S. P., A comment on 'A fast parallel algorithm for thinning digital patterns'. *Communications of the ACM*, **29**(3), 239–242

Mahmoud, H. M., The expected distribution of degrees in random binary search trees. *BCS Computer Journal*, **29**(1), 36–37

Martin, A. J., Compiling communication processes into delay-insensitive VLSI circuits. *Distributed Computing*, **1**(4), 226–234

McCurley, R. and Schneider, F. B., Derivation of a distributed algorithm for finding paths in directed networks. *Science of Computer Programming*, **6**, 1–9

Meldal, S., An axiomatic semantics for nested concurrency. *Bit*, **26**, 164–174

Meldal, S., An axiomatic semantics for nested concurrency. *Bit*, **26**, 295–302

Misra, J., Distributed-discrete event simulation. *ACM Computing Surveys*, **18**(1), 39–65

Mohan, C., Lindsay, B. and Obermarck, R., Transaction management in the R* distributed database management system. *ACM Transactions on Database Systems*, **11**(4), 378–396

Morris, J. H., Satyanarayanan, M., Connery, M. H., Howard, J. H., Rosenthal, D. S. H. and Donelson Smith, F., Andrew: a distributed personal computing environment. *Communications of the ACM*, **29**(3), 184–201

Moses, Y. Doley, D. and Halpen, J. Y., Cheating husbands and other stories: A case study of knowledge action and communication. *Distributed Computing*, **1**(3), 167–176

Mundie, D. A. and Fisher, D. A., Parallel processing in Ada. *Computer*, **19**(8), 20–25

Natarajan, N., A distributed synchronisation scheme for communicating processes. *BCS Computer Journal*, **29**(2), 108–117

Nguyen, V., Demers, A., Gries, D., and Owicki, S., A model and temporal proof system for networks of processes. *Distributed Computing*, **1**(1), 7–25

Paker, Y. *et al* (eds) *Proceedings of NATO ASI on 'Distributed Operating Systems—Theory and Practice'*, Izmir, Turkey, August

Parberry, I. On the time required to sum *n* semigroup elements on a parallel machine with simultaneous writes. In *VLSI Algorithms and Architectures*, Springer-Verlag, Berlin, pp. 296–304

Pnueli, A. and Zuck, L., Verification of multiprocesses probabilistic protocols. *Distributed Computing*, **1**(1), 53–72

Quarterman, J. S. and Hoskins, J. C., Notable computer networks. *Communications of the ACM*, **29**(10), 932–971

Rudalics, M., Distributed copying garbage collection. In *ACM Conference on LISP and Functional Programming*, MIT, Cambridge, Massachusetts, USA, 264–372

Samwell, A., Experience with occam for simulating systolic and wavefront arrays. *Software Engineering Journal*, 196–204

Sarkar, V. and Hennessey, J., Compile-time partitioning and scheduling of parallel programs. *ACM SIGPLAN Notices*, **21**(7), 17–26

Sarkar, V. and Hennessy, J., Partitioning parallel programs for macro-dataflow. *ACM Conference on LISP and Functional Programming*, MIT, Cambridge, Massachusetts, USA, pp. 202–211

Schneider, F. B., Abstractions for fault tolerance in distributed systems. Report 86–745, Department of Computer Science, Cornell University, Ithaca, New York, USA, April

Seger, C. J. H., Ternary simulation of asynchronous gate networks. Report CS-86–19, Computer Science Department, University of Waterloo, Waterloo, Ontario, Canada, 1 June

Shapiro, E., Concurrent Prolog: a progress report. *IEEE Computer*, **19**(8), 44–58

Sherman, M. and Marks, A., Using low-cost workstations to investigate computer networks and distributed systems. *Computer*, **19**(6), 32–41

Silver, R., A Concurrent N < = 8 Queen's algorithm using Modcap. *ACM SIGPLAN Notices*, **21**(9), 63–76

Soisalon-Soininen, E. and Wood, D., AVL trees on- the- fly restructuring and concurrency. Report CS-86-52 (2 copies), Computer Science Department, University of Waterloo, Waterloo, Ontario, Canada, October

Srikanth, T. K., Designing fault-tolerant algorithms for distributed systems using communication primitives. Report 86-739, Department of Computer Science, Cornell University, Ithaca, New York, USA, February

Stanfill, C. and Kahle, B., Parallel free-text search on the connection machine system. *Communications of the ACM*, **29**(12), 1229–1239

Steele, G. L. Jr. and Hillis, W. D., Connection machine LISP: fine-grained parallel symbolic processing. In *ACM Conference on LISP and Functional Programming*, MIT, Cambridge, Massachusetts, USA, pp. 279–297

Tanaka, H., A parallel inference machine. *Computer*, **19**(5), 48–54

Terry, P. D., A Modula-2 kernel for supporting monitors. *Software Practice and Experience*, **16**(5), 457–472

Tokoro, M. and Ishikawa, Y., Concurrent programming in Orient84/K: an object-oriented knowledge representation language. *ACM SIGPLAN Notices*, **21**(10), 39–48

Triolet, R., Irigoin, F. and Feautrier, P., Direct parallelization of call statements. *ACM SIGPLAN Notices*, **21**(7), 176–185

Tuynman, F. and Hertzberger, L. O., A distributed real-time operating system. *Software Practice and Experience*, **16**(5), 425–441

Tyrell, A. and Holding, D. J., Design of reliable software in distributed systems using the conversation scheme. *IEEE Transactions on Software Engineering*, **12**(9), 921–928

Udding, J. T., A formal model for defining and classifying delay-insensitive circuits and networks and systems. *Distributed Computing*, **1**(4), 197–204

Vassiliades, S., Sayers, M. D. and Bacon, J. M., A monitor tool for a network based on the Cambridge Ring. *Software Practice and Experience*, **16**(7), 671–687

Vernon, M., Zahorjan, J. and Lazowska, E. D., A comparison of performance Petri nets and queuing network models. Report #669, University of Wisconsin-Madison, USA, September

Wiebe, D., A distributed repository for immutable persistent objects. *ACM SIGPLAN Notices*, **21**(11), 453–465

Woodcock, J., Structuring specifications. Oxford Report, PRG, Oxford University, UK, August

Yampell, R., Maildriver: a distributed campus-wide mail system. Report, 86-07, Department of Computer Science, Brown University, Providence, Rhode Island, USA, January

Yokote, Y. and Tokoro, M., The design and implementation of Concurrent Smalltalk. *ACM SIGPLAN Notices*, **21**(11), 331–340

Yonezawa, A., Briot, J.-P. and Shibayama, E., Object-oriented concurrent programming in ABCL/1. *ACM SIGPLAN Notices*, **21**(11), 258–268

Zang, X., A proposal for implementing the concurrent mechanisms of Ada. *ACM SIGPLAN Notices*, **21**(8), 71–79

1987

Aarts, E. H. L. and Korst, J. H. M., Boltzmann machines and their applications. In *Lecture Notes in Computer Science*, **258**, Springer-Verlag, Berlin, pp. 34–50

Adams, G. B. III., Agrawal, D. P. and Siegel, H. J., A survey and comparison of fault-tolerant multistage interconnection networks. *Computer*, **20**(6), 14–27

Agrawal, D., Bernstein, A. J., Gupta, P. and Sengupta, S., Distributed optimistic concurrency control with reduced rollback. *Distributed Computing*, **2**(1), pp. 45–59

Agrawal, R., Carey, M. J. and Liroy, M., Concurrency control performance modeling: alternatives and implications. *ACM Transactions on Database Systems*, **12**(4), 608–654

Ahamad, M., Ammar, M. H., Bernabeu, J. and Khalidi, M. Y. A., A multicast scheme for locating objects in a distributed operating system. Technical Report GIT-ICS-87/01, School of Information and Computer Science, Georgia Institute of Technology, Atlanta, USA, January

Akl, S. G., Adaptive and optimal parallel algorithms for enumerating permutations and combinations. *BCS Computer Journal*, **30**(5), 433–436

Anderson, P., Hankin, C., Kelly, P., Osmon, P. and Shute, M., COBWEB-2: structured specification of a wafer-scale supercomputer. In *Lecture Notes in Computer Science*, **258**, Springer-Verlag, Berlin, pp. 51–67

Annot, J. K. and van Twist, R. A. H., A novel deadlock free and starvation free packet switching communication processor. In *Lecture Notes in Computer Science*, **258**, Springer-Verlag, Berlin, pp. 68–85

Apt, K. R., Bouge, L. and Clermont, P., Two normal form theorems for CSP programs. Report R 8735, Centrum Voor Wiskunde en Informatica, Department of Computer Science; Amsterdam, The Netherlands

Arabnia, H. R. and Oliver, M. A., A transfer network for the arbitrary rotation of digitised images. *BCS Computer Journal*, **30**(5), 425–432

Arvind and Nikhil, R. S., Executing a program on the MIT tagged-token dataflow architecture. In *Lecture Notes in Computer Science*, **259**, Springer-Verlag, Berlin, pp. 1–29

Augusteijn, L., Garbage collection in a distributed environment. In *Lecture Notes in Computer Science*, **259**, Springer-Verlag, Berlin, pp. 75–93

Avizienis, A. and Ball, D. E., On the achievement of a highly dependable and fault-tolerant air traffic control system. *Computer*, **20**(2), 84–90

Baeten, J. C. M., Bergstra, J. A. and Klop, J. W., Decidability of bisimulation equivalence for process generating context-free languages. In *Lecture Notes in Computer Science*, **259**, Springer-Verlag, Berlin, pp. 94–111

Bailey, D. A. and Cuny, J. E., An approach to programming process interconnection structures: aggregate rewriting graph grammars. In *Lecture Notes in Computer Science*, **259**, Springer-Verlag, Berlin, pp. 112–123

Barbacci, M. R. and Wing, J. M., Specifying functional and timing behaviour for real-time applications. In *Lecture Notes in Computer Science*, **259**, Springer-Verlag, Berlin, pp. 124–140

Barendregt, H. P., Eekelen, M. C. J. D., Glauert, J. R. W., Kenneway, J. R., Plasmeijer, M. J. and Sleep, M. R., Term graph rewriting. In *Lecture Notes in Computer Science*, **259**, Springer-Verlag, Berlin, pp. 141–158

Barendregt, H. P., Eekelen, M. C. J. D., Glauert, J. R. W., Kenneway, J. R., Plasmeijer, M. J. and Sleep, M. R., Towards an intermediate language based on graph rewriting. In *Lecture Notes in Computer Science*, **259**, Springer-Verlag, Berlin, pp. 159–175

Basco, P. G., Giachin, E., Giandonato, G., Martinengo, G. and Rullent, C., A parallel architecture for signal understanding through interference on uncertain data. In *Lecture Notes in Computer Science*, **258**, Springer-Verlag, Berlin, pp. 86–102

Bastani, F., Hilal, W. and Iyengar, S. S., Efficient abstract data type components for distributed and parallel systems. *Computer*, **20**(10), 33–44

Basu, J., Patnaik, L. M. and Goswami, A. K., Ordered ports – a language concept for high-level distributed programming. *BCS Computer Journal* **30**(6), 487–497

Bellia, M., Bosco, P. G., Giovannetti, E., Levi, G., Moiso, C. and Palamidessi, C., A two-level approach to Logic Plus functional programming integration. In *Lecture Notes in Computer Science*, **258**, Springer-Verlag, Berlin, pp. 374–393

Bennet, J. K., The design and implementation of distributed Smalltalk. *ACM SIGPLAN Notices*, **22**(12), 318–330 (Object-Oriented Programming Languages and Application Systems Conference, December 1987, Orlando, Florida, USA)

Bernstein, P. A. and Goodman, N., A proof technique for concurrency control and recovery algorithms for replicated databases. *Distributed Computing*, **2**(1), 32–44

Bertino, E., An evaluation of precompilation and interpretation in distributed database management systems. *BCS Computer Journal*, **30**(6), 519–528

Bertsekas, D. and Gallager, R., *Data Networks*, Prentice-Hall, Englewood Cliffs, New Jersey

Bevan, D. I., Burn, G. L. and Karia, R. J., Overview of a parallel reduction machine project. In *Lecture Notes in Computer Science*, **258**, Springer-Verlag, Berlin, pp. 394–413

Bevan, D. I., Distributed garbage collection using reference counting. In *Lecture Notes in Computer Science*, **259**, Springer-Verlag, Berlin, pp. 176–187

Bhuyan, K. N., Guest Editor's introduction: interconnection networks for parallel and distributed processing. *Computer*, **20**(6), 9–12

Bisiani, R. and Forin, A., Architectural support for multilanguage parallel programming on heterogeneous systems. *ACM SIGPLAN Notices*, **22**(10), 21–30 (Second International Conference on Architectural Support for Programming Languages and Operating Systems)

Bisiani, R., Alleva, F., Correrini, F., Lecouat, F., Forin, A. and Lerner, R., Heterogeneous parallel processing: The Agora shared memory. Report CMU-CS-87-112, Department of Computer Science, Carnegie-Mellon University, Pittsburgh, Pennsylvania, USA, March

Bishop, J. M., Adams, S. R. and Pritchard, D. J., Distributing Concurrent Ada programs by source translation. *Software Practice and Experience*, **17**(12), 859–884

Black, U., *Computer Networks: Protocols, Standards, Interfaces*, Prentice-Hall, Englewood Cliffs, New Jersey

Booch, G., *Software Engineering with ADA*, Addison-Wesley, Wokingham

Boxma, O. J. and Kindervater, G. A. P., A queuing network model for anlayzing a class of branch and bound algorithms on a master–slave architecture. CWI. Department of Operations Research and System Theory; R 8717, Amsterdam (1987)

Broy, M., Semantics of finite and infinite networks of concurrent communicating agents. *Distributed Computing*, **2**(1), 13–31

Brzozowski, J. A. and Seger, C. J., A unified theory of asynchronous networks. Report CS-87-24, Computer Science Department, University of Waterloo, Waterloo, Ontario, Canada, March

Burn, G. L., Evaluation transformers – a model for the parallel evaluation of functional languages (extended abstract). *Lecture Notes in Computer Science*, **274**, Springer-Verlag, Berlin, pp. 446–470

Burton, F. W., Functional programming for concurrent and distributed computing. *BCS Computer Journal*, **30**(5), 437–450

Butler, G. and Kendall, M. J., The suitability for master/slave concurrency of Concurrent Euclid, Ada and Modula. *Software Practice and Experience*, **17**(2), 117–134

Caplinger, M., An information system based on distributed objects. *ACM SIGPLAN Notices*, **22**(12), 126–137 (Object-Oriented Programming Languages and Application Systems Conference December 1987, Orlando, Florida, USA)

Chang, H. Y., Dynamic scheduling algorithms for distributed soft real-time systems. TR 728, Computer Sciences Department, University of Wisconsin-Madison, USA, November

Cheese, A., Combinatory code and a parallel packet based computational model. *ACM SIGPLAN Notices*, **22**(4), 49–58

Chen, R. J., Parallel algorithms for a class of convex optimization problems. Report #731, University of Wisconsin-Madison, USA, December

Chen, R. J. and Meyer, R. R., Parallel optimization for traffic assignment. Report #732, University of Wisconsin-Madison, USA, December

Cheriton, D. R., UIO: a uniform I/O system interface to distributed systems. *Transactions on Computer Systems*, **5**(1), 12–46

Chiarulli, D. M., Melhem, R. G. and Levitan, S. P., Using coincident optical pulses for parallel memory addressing. *Computer*, **20**(12), 48–57

Clark, K. L., PARLOG: the language and its applications. In *Lecture Notes in Computer Science*, **259**, Springer-Verlag, Berlin, pp. 30–53

Clark, R. H., Meyer, R. R., LeBlang, D. B. and Chase, R. P. Jr., Multiprocessor algorithms for generalized network flows. *IEEE Software*, **4**(6), 28–35

Clark, R. H. and Meyer, R. R., Multiprocessor algorithms for generalized network flows. Report #739, University of Wisconsin-Madison, USA, December

Clocksin, W. F., Principles of the Delphi Parallel Inference Machine. *BCS Computer Journal*, **30**(5), 386–392

Cohrs, D. L., Miller, B. P. and Call, L. A., Distributed Upcalls: a mechanism for layering asynchronous abstractions. Report TR 729, Computer Sciences Department, University of Wisconsin-Madison, USA, November

Cole, R., A method for interconnecting heterogeneous computer networks. *Software Practice and Experience*, **17**(6), 387–397

Collado, M., Morales, R. and Moreno, J. J., A Modula-2 implementation of CSP. *ACM SIGPLAN Notices*, **22**(6), 25–38

Conery, S. J., *Parallel Execution of Logic Programs*, Kluwer Academic, Dordrecht

Coulson, A. F. W., Collins, J. F. and Lyall, A., Protein and nucleic acid sequence database searching: a suitable case for parallel processing. *BCS Computing Journal*, **30**(5), 420–424

Czeck, E. W., Segall, Z. Z. and Siewiorek, D. P., Software implemented fault insertion: an FTMP example. Report CMU-CS-87-101, Department of CS, ECE and Statistics, Carnegie-Mellon University, Pittsburgh, Pennsylvania, USA, January

Damm, W. and Döhmen, G., An axiomatic approach to the specification of distributed computer architecture. In *Lecture Notes in Computer Science*, **258**, Springer-Verlag, Berlin, pp. 103–120

Dasgupta, P., LeBlanc, R. J. and Wilkes, C. T., The design of a distributed debugger for action-based object-oriented programs. *Proceedings of the 6th Symposium on Reliability in Distributed Software and Database Systems*, pp. 115–125

Dawids, U. G. and Løvenfreen, H. H., Rigorous development of a distributed calendar system. In *Lecture Notes in Computer Science*, **259**, Springer-Verlag, Berlin, pp. 188–205

Dekkers, A. L. M. and de Haan, L., On a consistent estimate of the index of an extreme value distribution. Report 8710, Centrum voor Wiskunde en Informatica, Department of Mathematical Statistics, Amsterdam, The Netherlands

DeLeone, R. and Mangasarian, O. L., Serial and parallel solution of large scale linear programs by Augmented Lagrangian Successive Overrelaxation. Report #701, University of Wisconsin-Madison, USA, June

Delisle, N. and Schwartz, M., A programming environment for CSP. *ACM SIGPLAN Notices*, **22**(1), 34–41

Dhne, F., Sack, J.-R. and Santoro, N., Computing on a systolic screen: hulls, contours and applications. In *Lecture Notes in Computer Science*, **258**, Springer-Verlag, Berlin, pp. 121–133

Dias, D. Iyer, B., Robinson, J. and Yu, P., Design and analysis of integrated concurrency-coherency controls. *Proceedings of the 13th International Conference on Very Large Data Bases* (eds P. M. Stocker, W. Kent and P. Hammersley) September

Dongarra, J. J. and Grosse, E., Distribution of mathematical software via electronic mail. *Communications of the ACM*, **30**(5), 403–407

Drake, B. L., Luk, F. T., Speiser, J. M. and Symanksi, J. J., SLAPP: a systolic linear algebra parallel processor. *Computer*, **20**(7), 45–49

Eckart, J. D. and LeBlanc, R. J., Distributed garbage collection. *ACM SIGPLAN Notices*, **22**(7), 264–273

Ellis, C. S., Concurrency in linear hashing. *ACM Transactions on Database Systems*, **12**(2), 195–217

Ellis, J. R., Li, K. and Appel, A. W., Real-time concurrent collection on stock multiprocessors. Report 25, Digital Equipment Corporation, Palo Alto, California, 14 February

Felleisen, M. and Friedman, D. P., A reduction semantics for imperative higher-order languages. In *Lecture Notes in Computer Science*, **259**, Springer-Verlag, Berlin, pp. 206–223

Forrest, B. M., Roweth, D., Stroud, N., Wallace, D. J. and Wilson, G. V., Implementing neutral network models on parallel computers. *BCS Computer Journal*, **30**(5), 413–419

Gamble, A. B., Conn, A. R. and Pulleyblank, W. R., A network penalty method. Report CS-87-25, Computer Science Department, University of Waterloo, Waterloo, Ontario, Canada

Gammage, N. D., Kamel, R. F., Casey, L. M., Remote rendezvous. *Software Practice and Experience*, **17**(10), 741–755

Garlan, D., Extending IDL to support concurrent views. *ACM SIGPLAN Notices*, **22**(11), 95–110

Gaudiot, J. L. and Lee. L. T., Multiprocessor systems programming in a high-level data-flow language. In *Lecture Notes in Computer Science*, **258**, Springer-Verlag, Berlin, pp. 134–151

Gelernter, D., Jagannathan, S. and London, T., Parallelism, persistence and meta-cleanliness in the Symmetric Lisp Interpreter. *ACM SIGPLAN Notices*, **22**(7), 274–282

Glasgow, J. I. and MacEwen, G. H., A computations model for distributed systems using operator nets. In *Lecture Notes in Computer Science*, **259**, Springer-Verlag, Berlin, pp. 243–260

Goldsby, M. E., Solving the "N < = Queens" problem with CSP and Modula-2. *ACM SIGPLAN Notices*, **22**(2), 43–52

Gonzalez-Rubio, R., Rohmer, J. and Bradier, A., An overview of DDC: delta driven computer. In *Lecture Notes in Computer Science*, **258**, Springer-Verlag, Berlin, pp. 414–433

Green, R. F., A stochastic model of optimal foraging: systematic search for negative-binomially distributed prey. Report 87-2, University of Minnesota, Duluth, Minnesota, USA, February

Gribomont, E. P., Design and proof of communicating sequential processes. In *Lecture Notes in Computer Science*, **259**, Springer-Verlag, Berlin, pp. 261–276

Gupta, A., Forgy, C., Kalp, D., Newell, A. and Tambe, M., Results of parallel implementation of OPS5 on the Encore multiprocessor. Report CMU-CS-87-146, Department of Computer Science, Carnegie-Mellon University, Pittsburgh, Pennsylvania, USA, August

Gurevich, Y. and Morris, J. M., Algebraic operational semantics for Modula-2. Report CRL-TR-10-87, Computing Research Laboratory. University of Michigan, Ann Arbor, Michigan, USA

Hale, R. and Moszowski, B., Parallel programming in Temporal Logic. In *Lecture Notes in Computer Science*, **259**, Springer-Verlag, Berlin, pp. 277–296

Hansen, P. B., Joyce, – A programming language for distributed systems. *Software Practice and Experience*, **17**(1), 29–50

Hansen, P. B., A Joyce implementation. *Software Practice and Experience*, **17**(4), 267–276

Harrison, D., RUTH: a functional language for real-time programming. In *Lecture Notes in Computer Science*, **259**, Springer-Verlag, Berlin, 297–314

Harter, P. K. Jr. Response times in level-structured systems. *Transactions on Computer Systems*, **5**(3), 232–248

Herlihy, M. P., Concurrency versus availability atomicity mechanisms. *Transactions on Computer Systems*, **5**(3), 249–274

Herlihy, M. P. and Wing, J. M., Specifying graceful degradation in distributed systems. Report CMU-CS-87-120, Department of Computer Science, Carnegie-Mellon University, Pittsburgh, Pennsylvania, USA

Hilbers, P. A., J., Koopman, M. R. J. and van de Snepscheut, J. L. A., The twisted cube. In *Lecture Notes in Computer Science*, **258**, Springer-Verlag, Berlin, pp. 152–159

Hinton, G. E., Learning translation invariant recognition in massively parallel networks. In *Lecture Notes in Computer Science*, **258**, Springer-Verlag, Berlin, pp. 1–13

Hoare, C. A. R., An overview of some formal methods for program design. *Computer*, **20**(9), 85–91

Holt, C. M., Stewart, A., Clint, M. and Perrott, R. H., An improved parallel thinning algorithm. *Communications of the ACM*, **30**(2), 156–160

Honeyman, P. and Parseghian, P. E., Parsing ambiguous addresses for electronic services. *Software Practice and Experience*, **17**(1), 51–60

Hooman, J., A compositional proof theory for real-time distributed message passing. In *Lecture Notes in Computer Science*, **259**, Springer-Verlag, Berlin, pp. 315–332

Hopkins, R. P. and Koutny, M., A model for dynamically structured communicating systems, Technical Report 239, Computing Laboratory, Newcastle University, Newcastle-upon-Tyne, UK

Huang, C.-H. and Lengauer, C., An implemented method for incremental systolic design. In *Lecture Notes in Computer Science*, **258**, Springer-Verlag, Berlin, pp. 160–177

Hudak, P. and Anderson, S., Pomset interpretations of parallel functional programs. In *Lecture Notes in Computer Science*, **274**, Springer-Verlag, Berlin, pp. 234–256

Iliffe, J. K., The use of parallel functions in system design. In *Lecture Notes in Computer Science*, **258**, Springer-Verlag, Berlin, pp. 178–194

Jifeng, H. and Hoare, C. A. R., Algebraic specification and proof of a distributed recovery algorithm. *Distributed Computing*, **2**, 1–12

Jorrand, P., Design and implementation of a parallel inference machine for First Order Logic: an overview. In *Lecture Notes in Computer Science*, **258**, Springer-Verlag, Berlin, pp. 434–445

Kaldewaij, A., The translation of processes into circuits. In *Lecture Notes in Computer Science*, **258**, Springer-Verlag, Berlin, pp. 195–212

Karp, A. H., Programming for parallelism. *Computer*, **20**(5), 43–57

Kearns, P., Cipriani, C. and Freeman, M., CCAL: an interpreted language for experimentation in concurrent control. *ACM SIGPLAN Notices*, **22**(7)

Kirkman, W. W., An optimized contention protocol for broadband networks. *Transactions on Computer Systems*, **5**(3), 275–283

Kloos, C. D., STREAM: a scheme language for formally describing digital circuits. In *Lecture Notes in Computer Science*, **259**, Springer-Verlag, Berlin, pp. 335–350

Kok, J. N., A fully abstract semantics for data flow nets. In *Lecture Notes in Computer Science*, **259**, Springer-Verlag, Berlin, pp. 351–368

Kok, J. N. and Rutten, J. M., Contractions in comparing concurrency semantics. Report 8755. Department of Computer Science. Centrum voor Wiskunde en Informatica, Amsterdam

Kotuiski, L., About the semantic nested monitor calls. *ACM SIGPLAN Notices*, **22**(4), 80–82

Kourie, D. G., The design and use of a Prolog trace generator for CSP. *Software Practice and Experience*, **17**(7), 423–438

Kummerle, K., Limb, J. O. and Tobagi, F. A. *Advances in Local Area Networks*, IEEE Press, New York

Krämer, O. and Mühlenbein, H., Mapping strategies in message based multiprocessor systems. In *Lecture Notes in Computer Science*, **258**, Springer-Verlag, Berlin, pp. 213–225

Krueger, P. and Livny, M., Load balancing, load sharing and performance in distributed systems. Report #700, University of Wisconsin-Madison, USA, August

Kujun, S. and Zhongxiu, S., An object-oriented programming language for developing distributed software. *ACM SIGPLAN Notices*, **22**(8), 51–56

Kumar, V. P. and Reddy, S. M., Augmented shuffle-exchange multistage interconnection networks. *Computer*, **20**(6), 30–40

Lamport, L., Win and Sin: predicate transformers for concurrency. 17 (2 copies), Digital Equipment Corporation, Palo Alto, California, USA, 1 May

Lavington, S. H., Standring, M., Jiang, Y. J., Wang, C. J. and Waite, M. E., Hardware memory management for large knowledge bases. In *Lecture Notes in Computer Science*, **258**, Springer-Verlag, Berlin, pp. 226–241

Levinthal, A., Hanrahan, P., Paquette, M. and Lawson, J., Parallel computers for graphics applications. *ACM SIGPLAN Notices*, **22**(10), 193–198. (Second International Conference on Architectural Support for Programming Languages and Operating Systems)

Linton, M. A., Distributed management of a software database. *IEEE Software*, **4**(6), 70–76

Lirov, Y. and Daunov, N., An integrated data dictionary to facilitate automatic report generation in a network database. *Software Practice and Experience*, **17**(3), 187–195

Livny, M. and Manber, U., u – a system for simulating and implementing distributed and parallel algorithms. Report #737, University of Wisconsin-Madison, USA, December

Lucco, S. E., Parallel programming in a virtual object space. *ACM SIGPLAN Notices*, **22**(12), 26–34 (Object-Oriented Programming Languages and Application Systems Conference 87, Orlando, Florida, USA, December)

Luckham, D. C., Helmbold, D. P., Bryan, D. L. and Haberler, M. A., Task sequencing language for specifying distributed Ada systems. In *Lecture Notes in Computer Science*, **259**, Springer-Verlag, Berlin, pp. 444–463

Martin, A. R. and Tucker, J. V., The concurrent assignment representation of synchronous systems. *Lecture Notes in Computer Science*, **259**, Springer-Verlag, Berlin, pp. 369–386

Mattern, F., Algorithms for distributed termination detection. Report 20/87, Computer Science Department, Kaiserslautern University, West Germany, January

Mattern, F., Asychronous distributed termination – parallel and symmetric solutions with echo algorithms. Report 21/87, Computer Science Department, Kaiserslautern University, West Germany, January

McAulay, A. D., Spatial-Light_modulator interconnected computers. *Computer*, **20**(10), 45–57

McBurney, D. L. and Sleep, M. R., Transputer-based experiments with the ZAPP architecture. In *Lecture Notes in Computer Science*, **258**, Springer-Verlag, Berlin, pp. 242–259

McDonald, J. F., Greub, H. J., Steinvorth, R. H., Donlan, B. J. and Bergendahl, A. S., Wafer scale interconnections for GaAs packaging – applications to RISC architecture. *Computer*, **20**(4), 21–35

Mehring, P. and Aposporidis, E., Multi-level simulator for VLSI – an overview. In *Lecture Notes in Computer Science*, **258**, Springer-Verlag, Berlin, pp. 446–460

Miller, B. P., Presotto, D. L. and Powell, M. L., DEMOS/MP: the development of a distributed operating system. *Software Practice and Experience* **17**(4), 277–290

Mongenet, C. and Perrin, G.-R., Synthesis of systolic arrays for inductive problems. In *Lecture Notes in Computer Science*, **258**, Springer-Verlag, Berlin, pp. 260–277

Mudge, T. N., Hayes, J. P. and Winsor, D. C., Multiple bus architectures, *Computer*, **20**(6), 42–48

Mullender, S. J. and Vitanyi, P. M. B., Distributed match-making. Report R8750, Department of Computer Science, Centruum voor Wiskunde en Informatica, Amsterdam, The Netherlands

Musa, J., *Software Reliability: measurement, production, application*, McGraw-Hill, New York

Nance, R. E., Moose, R. L. Jr. and Foutz, R. V., A statistical technique for comparing heuristics: an example from capacity assignment strategies in computer network design. *Communications of the ACM*, **30**(5), 430–442

Nelson, G. A generalization of Dijkstra's Calculus. Research Report 16, System Research Center, DEC, Palo Alto, California

Nielson, H. R., A Hoare-like proof system for analysing the computation time of programs. *Science of Computer Programming*, **9**, 107–136

Noe, J. and Wagner, D., Measured performance of time interval concurrency control techniques. *Proceedings of the 13th International Conference on Very Large Data Bases* (eds P. M. Stocker, W. Kent and P. Hammersley) Brighton, UK, September

North, S. C. and Reppy, J. H., Concurrent garbage collection on stock hardware. *Lecture Notes in Computer Science*, **274**, Springer-Verlag, Berlin, pp. 113–133

Notkin, D., Hutchinson, N., Sanislo, I. and Schwartz, M., Heterogeneous computing environments, Report on the ACM SIGOPS Workshop on Accommodating Heterogeneity. *Communications of the ACM*, **30**(2), 132–140

Odijk, E. A. M., The DOOM system and its applications: a survey of ESPRIT 415 subproject A, Philips Research Laboratories. *Lecture Notes in Computer Science*, **258**, Springer-Verlag, Berlin, pp. 461–479

Oflazer, K., Partitioning in parallel processing. Report CMU-CS-87-114, Department of Computer Science, Carnegie-Mellon University, Pittsburgh, Pennsylvania, USA, March

Peyton Jones, S. L., Clack, C., Salkid, J. and Hardie, M. GRIP – a high-performance architecture for parallel graph reduction. *Lecture Notes in Computer Science*, **274**, Springer-Verlag, Berlin, pp. 98–112

Polychronopoulos, C. D. and Banerjee, U., Processor allocation for horizontal and vertical parallelism and related speedup bounds. *IEEE Transactions on Computers*, **36**(4)

Pritchard, D. J., Askew, C. R., Carpenter, D. B., Glendinning, I. Hey, A. J. G. and Nicole, D. A., Practical parallelism using transputer arrays. In *Lecture Notes in Computer Science*, **258**, Springer-Verlag, Berlin, pp. 278–294

Rajopadhye, S. V. and Fujimoto, R. M., Systolic array synthesis by static analysis of program dependencies. In *Lecture Notes in Computer Science*, **258**, Springer-Verlag, Berlin, pp. 295–310

Ramesh, S., A new and efficient implementation of multiprocess synchronization. In *Lecture Notes in Computer Science*, **259**, Springer-Verlag, Berlin, pp. 387–401

Reed, D. A. and Grunwald, D. C., The performance of multicomputer interconnection networks. *Computer*, **20**(6), 63–73

Rem, M., Trace theory and systolic computations. In *Lecture Notes in Computer Science*, **258**, Springer-Verlag, Berlin, pp. 14–33

Rizk, A. and Halsall, F., Design and implementation of a C-based language for distributed real-time systems. *ACM SIGPLAN Notices*, **22**(6), 83–100

Ruggiero, C. A. and Sargeant, J., Control of parallelism in the Manchester Dataflow Machine. *Lecture Notes in Computer Science*, **274**, Springer-Verlag, Berlin, pp. 1–15

Sanders, B. A., An information structure of distributed mutual exclusion algorithms. *ACM Transactions on Computer Systems*, **5**(3), 284–299

Satyanarayanan, M., Integrating security in a large scale distributed system. Report CMU-CS-87-179, Department of Computer Science, Carnegie-Mellon University, Pittsburgh, Pennsylvania, USA, November

Satyanarayanan, M., On the influence of scale in a distributed system. Report CMU-CS-87-162, Department of Computer Science, Carnegie-Mellon University, Pittsburgh, Pennsylvania, USA, September

Sawchuk, A. A., Jenkins, B. K., Raghavendra, C. S. and Varma, A., Optical crossbar networks. *Computer*, **20**(6), 50–60

Scaefer, P. and Schnoebelen, P., Specification of a pipelined event driven simulator using FP2. *Lecture Notes in Computer Science*, **258**, Springer-Verlag, Berlin, pp. 311–328

Schnoebelen, P., Rewriting techniques for the temporal analysis of communicating processes. *Lecture Notes in Computer Science*, **259**, Springer-Verlag, Berlin, pp. 402–419

Schwartz, M., *Telecommunications Network: Protocols, Modeling and Analysis*, Addison-Wesley, Reading, Masachusetts, USA

Sha, L. *et al.*, Priority inheritance protocols – An approach to real-time synchronization. Report CMU-CS-87-181, Department of Computer Science, Carnegie-Mellon University, Pittsburgh, Pennsylvania, USA, December

Shatz, S. M. and Wang, J. P., Introduction to distributed software engineering. *Computer*, **20**(10), 23–31

Shih, A.-C., Chen, G.-H. and Lee, R. C. T., Systolic algorithms to examine all pairs of elements. *Communications of the ACM*, **30**(2), 161–167

Srihari, S. N., Rapaport, W. J. and Kumar, D., On knowledge representation using semantic networks and Sanskrit. Report 87-03, Department of Computer Science, University of New York at Buffalo, USA, February

Stepney, S. and Lord, S. P., Formal specification of an access control system. *Software Practice and Experience*, **17**(9), 575–593

Stone, H. S., Parallel querying of large databases: a case study. *Computer*, **20**(10), 11–21

Strenström, P. and Philipson, L., A layered emulator for design evaluation of MIMD multiprocessors with shared memory. In *Lecture Notes in Computer Science*, **258**, Springer-Verlag, Berlin, pp. 329–344

Summers, C., *Software Quality Assurance, Reliability and Testing*, Technical Press

Szlanko, J., *Real-time programming*, Pergamon Press, Oxford

Tebra, H., Optimistic and-parallelism in Prolog. In *Lecture Notes in Computer Science*, **259**, Springer-Verlag, Berlin, pp. 420–431

Test, J. A., Myszewski, M. and Swift, R. C., The Alliant FX/series: a language driven architecture for parallel processing of Dusty Deck Fortran. In *Lecture Notes in Computer Science*, **258**, Springer-Verlag, Berlin, pp. 345–356

Thacker, C. P. and Stewart, L. C., Firefly: a multiprocessor workstation. *ACM SIGPLAN Notices*, **22**(10), 164–172 (Second International Conference on Architectural Support for Programming Languages and Operating Systems)

Thompson, K. M., A parallel asychronous successive overrelaxation algorithm for solving the linear complementarity problem. Report #705, University of Wisconsin-Madison, USA, July

Thompson, K. M., A parallel pivotal algorithm for solving the linear complementarity problem. Report #707, University of Wisconsin-Madison, USA, July

Turner, D., Functional programming and communicating processes. In *Lecture Notes in Computer Science*, **259**, Springer-Verlag, Berlin, pp. 54–74

van der Gaag, L. C., A network approach to the certainty factor model. Report 8757, Department of Computer Science, Centruum voor Wiskunde en Informatica, Amsterdam, The Netherlands

van Glabbeek, R. and Vaandrager, F., Petri net models for algebraic theories of concurrency. In *Lecture Notes in Computer Science*, **259**, Springer-Verlag, Berlin, pp. 224–242

Wallqvist, A., Berne, B. J. and Pangali, C., Exploiting physical parallelism using supercomputers: two examples from chemical physics. *Computer*, **20**(5), 9–21

Waters, R. C., Efficient interpretation of synchronizable series expressions. *ACM SIGPLAN Notices*, **22**(7), 74–85

Watson, P. and Watson, I., An efficient garbage collection scheme for parallel computer architectures. In *Lecture Notes in Computer Science*, **259**, Springer-Verlag, Berlin, pp. 432–443

Watt, D., **ada** *Language and Methodology*, Prentice Hall, Englewood Cliffs, New Jersey

Weaver, A. C. and Colvin, M. A., A real-time messaging system for token ring networks. *Software Practice and Experience*, **17**(12), 899–922

Weiss, S. and Smith, J. E., A study of scalar compilation techniques for pipelined supercomputers. *ACM SIGPLAN Notices*, **22**(10), 105–111 (Second International Conference on Architectural Support for Programming Languages and Operating Systems)

Welch, P. H., Emulating Digital Logic using transputer networks (very high parallelism = simplicity = performance). In *Lecture Notes in Computer Science*, **258**, Springer-Verlag, Berlin, pp. 357–373

Wolfson, O., The overhead of Locking (and Commit) protocols in distributed databases. *ACM Transactions on Database Systems*, **12**(3), 453–471

Yang, C. Q., A structured and automatic approach to the performance measurement of parallel and distributed programs. Report #713, University of Wisconsin-Madison, USA, August

Yokote, Y. and Tokoro, M., Experience and evolution of Concurrent Smalltalk, *ACM SIGPLAN Notices*, **22**(12), 406–415 (Object-Oriented Programming Languages and Application Systems Conference, 1987, Orlando, Florida, USA, December)

1988

Abdul-Reda, A. J. A. and Farrell, P. G., Simulation performance study of Aloha network. *Proceedings of the 7th Annual International Phoenix Conference on Computers and Communications*, Scottsdale, Arizona, USA, March, pp. 161–165

Agarwal, A., Hennessy, J. and Horowitz, M., Cache performance of operating system and multiprogramming workloads. *ACM Transactions on Computer Systems*, **6**(4), 393–431

Agha, G., The relation between problems in large-scale concurrent systems and distributed databases. *Proceedings of the International Symposium on Databases in Parallel and Distributed Systems*, Austin, Texas, USA, IEEE Computer Society Press, Washington, DC, USA, December 5–7

Aiken, A. and Nicolau, A., Optimal loop parallelization. *ACM SIGPLAN Notices*, **23**(7), 308–317, (Proceedings of the SIGPLAN '88 Conference on Programming Language Design and Implementation, Atlanta, Georgia, USA, July)

Akscyn, R. M., McCracken, D. L. and Yoder, E. A., KMS: a distributed hypermedia system for managing knowledge in organisations. *Communications of the ACM*, **31**(7), 820–835

Albanese, A. and Menendez, R. C., Loop distribution using coherent detection. *IEEE Journal on Selected Areas in Communications*, **6**(6), 959–973

Albert, E., Knobe, K., Lukas, J. D. and Steele, G. L., Compiling Fortran 8 × array features for the connection machine computer system. *ACM SIGPLAN Notices*, **23**(9), 42–56 (Proceedings of the ACM/SIGPLAN '88 Conference on Parallel Programming: Experience with Applications, Languages and Systems, New Haven, Connecticut, USA, July 19–21)

Allen, R. and Johnson, S., Compiling C for vectorization parallelization and inline expansion. *ACM SIGPLAN Notices*, **23**(7), 241–249 (Proceedings of the SIGPLAN '88 Conference on Programming Language Design and Implementation, Atlanta, Georgia, USA, July)

Anderson, D. P., A software architecture for network communication. *Proceedings of the 8th International Conference on Distributed Computing Systems*, San Jose, California, USA, June, pp. 376–383

Angelopoulos, S., Papadopoulos, S. G. and Koubias, S., *Proceedings of the Seventh Annual International Phoenix Conference on Computers and Communications*, Scottsdale, Arizona, USA, March

Anon., Architecture considerations for photonic switching networks. *IEEE Journal on Selected Areas in Communications*, **6**(7), 1209–1226

Anon., Communication network needs and technologies – a place for photonic switching. *IEEE Journal on Selected Areas in Communications*, **6**(7) pp. 1036–1043

Anon., Minimizing total completion time in the two-machine flow shop by Langrangian relaxation. Report 8808, Department of Operations Research and System Theory, Centruum voor Wiskende en Informatica, Amsterdam, The Netherlands

Anon., PCMAIL: A distributed mail system for personal computers. RFC1056. *Internet Request for Comments*, Network Information Center, SRI International, Menlo Park, California, USA, June

Anon., RPC: remote procedure call protocol specification version 2; RFC1058. *Internet Request for Comments*, Network Information Center, SRI International, Menlo Park, California, USA, June

Anthonisse, J. M., Lenstra, J. K. and Savelsbergh, M. W. P., Behind the screen: DSS from an OR point of view. *Report 8805, Department of Operations Research and System Theory, Centrum voor Wiskunde en Informatica, Amsterdam, The Netherlands*

Apers, P. M. G., Data allocation in distributed database systems. *ACM Transactions on Database Systems*, **13**(1)

Appel, A. W., Ellis, J. R. and Li, K., Real-time concurrent collection on stock multiprocessors. *ACM SIGPLAN Notices*, **23**(7), 11–20 (Proceedings of the SIGPLAN '88 Conference on Programming Language Design and Implementation, July)

Aral, A. and Gertner, I., "Non-Intrusive and Interactive Profiling in Parasight", *ACM SIGPLAN Notices*, **23**(9), 21–30 (Proceedings of the CM/SIGPLAN '88 Conference on Parallel Programming: Experience with Applications, Languages and Systems, New Haven, Connecticut, USA, July 19–21)

Ashany, R., Ferrari, D. and Pasquale, J., Application of AI techniques to adaptive routing in wide-area networks. *Proceedings of the Seventh Annual International Phoenix Conference on Computers and Communications*, Scottsdale, Arizona, USA, March, pp. 157–161

Aspens, J., Fekete, A., Lynch, N., Merritt, M. and Weihl, W., A theory of timestamp-based concurrency control for nested transactions. *Proceedings of the 14th International Conference on Very Large Data Bases*, (eds F. DeWitt and D. J. Bancilhon) Los Angeles, California, USA, August/September

Athas, W. C. and Seitz, C. L., Multicomputers: message-passing concurrent computers. *Computer*, **21**(8), 9–24

Atkins, M. S. and Olsson, R. A., Performance of multi-tasking and synchronization mechanisms in the programming language SR. *Software Practice and Experience* **18**(9), 879–895

Batsani, F. B., Iyengar, S. S. and Yen, I-L., Concurrent maintenance of data structures in a distributed enviornment. *BCS Computer Journal*, **31**(2), 165–174

Bates, P., Distributed debugging tools for heterogeneous distributed systems. *Proceedings of the 8th International Conference on Distributed Computing Systems*, San Jose, California, USA, June, pp. 308–315

Bensley, E. H., Brando, T. J. and Prelle, M. J., An execution model for distributed object-oriented computation. *ACM SIGPLAN Notices*, **23**(11), 316–322 (Object-Oriented Programming Systems, Languages and Application Conference '88, San Diego, California, USA, November)

Bershad, B. N., Lazowska, E. D., Levy, H. M. and Wagner, D. B., An open environment for building parallel programming systems. *ACM SIGPLAN Notices*, **23**(9), 1–9 (Proceedings of the ACM/SIGPLAN '88 Conference on Parallel Programming: Experience with Applications, Languages and Systems, New Haven, Connecticut, USA, July 19–21)

Bhargava, A., Kurose, J. F. and Towsley, D., A hybrid media access protocol for high-speed ring networks. *IEEE Journal on Selected Areas in Communications*, **6**(6), 924–933

Bhargava, A., Kurose, J. F., Towsley, D. and Van Leemput, G., Performance comparison of error control schemes in high-speed computer communication networks. *IEEE Journal on Selected Areas in Communications*, **6**(9), (Special Issue: Broadband Packet Communications), 1565–1575

Biocchi, A., Carosi, M., Listanti, M., Pacifici, G., Roveri, A. and Winkler, R., Isochronous and non-isochronous traffic handling policies in Infonet network. In *Proceedings of the 9th International Computer Communication*, Tel Aviv, Israel, October 30–November 4, Elsevier, Amsterdam, pp. 72–77

Boddy, D. E., SOS: A monitor-based operating system for instruction. *ACM SIGPLAN Notices*, **23**(12), 115–124

Boel, R. K. and van Schuppen, J. H., Distributed routing for load balancing. *Report 8820, Department of Operations Research and System Theory, Centrum voor Wiskunde en Informatica, Amsterdam, The Netherlands*

Bovpoulos, A. D. and Lazar, A. A., Decentralized network flow control. In *Proceedings of the International Conference on Computer Communication*, Tel Aviv, Israel, Elsevier, Amsterdam, October 30–November 4, pp. 139–143

Boxma, O. J., Groenendijk, W. P. and Weststrate, J. A., A pseudoconversation law for service systems with a polling table. Report 8813. Department of Operations Research and System Theory, Centruum voor Wiskunde en Informatica, Amsterdam, The Netherlands

Brady, P. T., Effects on response time performace using an edge-to-edge protocol in an X.25 Packet Network. *IEEE Network*, **2**(4), 45–54

Bruegge, B., Program development for a systolic array. *ACM SIGPLAN Notices*, **23**(9), 31–41 (Proceedings of the ACM/SIGPLAN '88 Conference on Parallel Programming: Experience with Applications, Languages and Systems, New Haven, Connecticut, USA, July 19–21)

Burke, M., Cyton, R., Ferrante, J., Hsieh, W., Sarkar, V. and Shields, D., Automatic discovery of parallelism: a tool and an experiment, (extended abstract). *ACM SIGPLAN Notices*, **23**(9), (Proceedings of the ACM/SIGPLAN '88 Conference on Parallel Programming: Experience with Applications, Languages and Systems, New Haven, Connecticut, USA, July 19–21)

Burns, A., Davies, G. L. and Wellings, A. J., A Modula-2 implementation of a real-time process abstraction. *ACM SIGPLAN Notices*, **23**(10), 49–58

Burns, A. and Davies, G., Pascal-FC: a language for teaching concurrent programming. *ACM SIGPLAN Notices*, **23**(1), 58–66

Byrne, W. J., Survivability of financial networks – a Canadian model. In *Proceedings of the 9th International Conference on Computer Communication*, Tel Aviv, Israel, Elsevier, Amsterdam, October 30–November 4, pp. 99–103

Campbell, S. S. and Palumbo, P. W., UBGCCS-88 Proceedings of the third annual UB graduate-conference on computer science. Technical Report 88-03, Department of Computer Science, New York University at Buffalo, (SUNY), USA, March

Carey, M. J. and Livny, M., Distributed concurrency control performance: A study of algorithms, distribution, and replication. Technical Report 758, Department of Computer Sciences, University of Wisconsin-Madison, USA, March

Carey, M. and Livny, M., Distributed concurrency control performance: a study of algorithms, distribution and replication. *Proceedings of the 14th Intrnational Conference on Very Large Data Bases* (eds F. DeWitt and D. J. Bancilhon), Los Angeles, California, USA, August/September

Carpenter, G. A. and Grossberg, S., The ART of adaptive pattern recognition by a self-organizing neural network. *Computer*, **21**(3), 77–88

Carriero, N. and Gelernter, D., Applications experience with Linda. *ACM SIGPLAN Notices*, **23**(9), 173–187 (Proceedings of the ACM SIGPLAN '88 Conference on Parallel Programming: Experience with Applications, Languages and Systems, New Haven, Connecticut, USA, July 19–21)

Case, J., Fedor, M., Schoffstall, M. and Davin, J., A simple network management protocol. *Internet Request for Comments*, Network Information Center, SRI International, Menlo Park, California, USA, August

Chamberlain, R., Third conference on hypercube concurrent computers and applications. *Parallel Computing*, **7**(2), 257–258

Chao, H. J., Design of transmission and multiplexing systems for broadband packet networks. *IEEE Journal on Selected Areas in Communications* (Special Issue: Broadband Packet Communications), **6**(9), 1511–1520

Chiarawongse, J., Srinivasan, M. M. and Teorey, T. J., Performance analysis of a large interconnected network by decomposition. *IEEE Network*, **2**(4), 19–27

Chlamtac, I., Ganz, A. and Karmi, G., Circuit switching in multi-hop lightware networks. *Proceedings of ACM SIGCOMM 1988*, Stanford, California, USA, August, pp. 188–199

Chlamtac, I. and Ganz, A., A multibus train communication (AMTRAC) architecture for high-speed fiber optic networks. *IEEE Journal on Selected Areas in Communications*, **6**(6), 903–912

Choi, M. and Krishna, C. M., An adaptive algorithm to ensure differential service in a token ring network. *Proceedings of the 7th Annual International Phoenix Conference on Computers and Communications*, Scottsdale, Arizona, USA. March, pp. 324–329

Comer, D. and Yavatkar, R., A congestion filtering scheme for packet switched networks. Technical Report 758, Computer Science Department, Purdue University, West Lafayette, Indiana, USA, April 10

Cormack, G. V., Short communication: a micro-kernel for concurrency in C. *Software Practice and Experience*, **18**(5), 485–491

Crabb, D., Machinations: VLSI design and network help. *Byte*, **13**(13)

Crispin, M., Interactive mail access protocol – Version 2; RFC1064. *Internet Request for Comments*, Network Information Center, SRI International, Menlo Park, California, USA, July

Cupitt, J., Another new scheme for writing functional operating systems. Report 52, Department of Computer Science, University of Kent, Canterbury, UK, March

Currie, W. S., *LANs Explained: A guide to local area networks*, John Wiley, New York, Reviewed in *Computing Reviews*, **30**(4)

Daduna, H., Busy periods for subnetworks in stochastic networks: mean value analysis. *Journal of the ACM*, **35**(3), 668–674

Dasgupta, P., Leblanc, R. J. and Appelbe, W. F., The Clouds distributed operating system. *Proceedings of the 8th International Conference on Distributed Computing Systems*, San Jose, California, USA, June

Davis, G. R., Static priority queues with application to a computer network. *Proceedings of the 7th Annual International Phoenix Conference on Computers and Communications*, Scottsdale, Arizona, USA, March, pp. 335–339

Davis, H. and Hennessy, J., Characterizing the synchronization behaviour of parallel programs. *ACM SIGPLAN Notices*, **23**(9), 198–211, (Proceedings of the ACM/SIGPLAN 1988 Conference on Parallel Programming: Experience with Applications, Languages and Systems, New Haven, Connecticut, USA, July, 19–21)

de Bakker, J. W. and Kok, J. N., Uniform abstraction, atomicity and contractions in the comparative semantics of Concurrent Prolog. Report 8834, Department of Computer Science, Centruum voor Wiskunde en Informatica, Amsterdam, The Netherlands

de Bakker, J. W. and Meyer, J.-J. C., Metric semantics for concurrency. *Bit*, **28**(3), 504–529

de Waal, P. R., A sufficient condition for a product form distribution of a queuing network with controlled arrivals. Report 8803, Department of Operations Research and System Theory, Centruum voor Wiskunde en Informatica, Amsterdam, The Netherlands

Deen, S. M., Taylor, M. C., Ingram, P. A. and Rayner, K. W., A distributed directory database system for telecommunications. *BCS Computer Journal*, **31**(2), 175–181

Delp, G., Sethi, A. and Farber, D., An analysis of Memnet – an experiment in high speed memory mapped local networking. *Proceedings of ACM SIGCOMM 1988*, Stanford, California, USA, August, pp. 165–174

De-Pryker, M., Definition of network options for the Belgian ATM broadband experiment. *IEEE Journal on Selected Areas in Communications* (Special Issue: Broadband Packet Communications) **6**(9), 1538–1544

DeSchon, A. and Braden, B., Background file transfer program (BFTP); RFC 1068. *Internet Request for Comments*, Network Information Center, SRI International, Menlo Park, California, USA, August

Deutsch, M. S., Focusing real-time systems analysis on user operations. *IEEE Software*, **5**(5), 39–50

Dijkstra, E. W., *Predicate Calculus and Program Semantics*, Springer-Verlag, Berlin

Dubnicki, C., Madey, J. and Wygladala, W., Edison-N – an Edison implementation for a network of microcomputers. *Software Practice and Experience*, **18**(4), 349–363

Egyhazy, C. and Triantis, K., A query processing algorithm for distributed relational database systems. *BCS Computer Journal*, **31**(1), 34–40

Eich, M. H. and Wells, D. L., Database concurrency control using data flow graphs. *ACM Transactions on Database Systems*, **13**(2), 197–227

Eisenberg, M. and Mehravari, N., Performance of the multichannel multihop lightwave network under nonuniform traffic. *IEEE Journal on Selected Areas in Communications*, **6**(7), 1063–1078

Eng, K. Y., A photonic knockout switch for high speed packet networks. *IEEE Journal on Selected Areas in Communications*, **6**(7), 1107–1116

Esfahanian, A.-H. and Zimmerman, G., A distributed broadcast alogorithm for binary De Bruijn networks. *Proceedings of the 7th Annual International Phoenix Conference on Computers and Communications*, Scottsdale, Arizona, USA, March, pp. 318–323

Feldman, J. A., Fanty, M. A., Goddard, N. H., Computing with structured neural networks. *Computer*, **21**(3), 91–103

Fich, F. E. and Tompa, M., The parallel complexity of exponentiating polynomials over finite fields. *Journal of the ACM*, **35**(3), 651–637

Fidge, C. J., Lisp implementation of the model for communicating sequential processes. *Software Practice and Experience*, **18**(10), 923–943

Ford, R., Concurrent algorithms for real-time memory management. *IEEE Software*, **5**(5), 10–23

Fozdar, F. M., Network management on the OPSX MAN. *Proceedings of the 9th International Conference on Computer Communication*, Tel Aviv, Israel, October 30–November 4, Elsevier, Amsterdam, pp. 121–126

Francis, R. and Mathieson, I. Synchronized execution on shared memory multiprocessors. *Parallel Computing*, **8**(1–3), 165–175

Fukushima, K., A neural network for visual pattern recognition. *Computer*, **21**(3), 65–75

Garcia-Luna-Aceves, J. J., Routing management in very large-scale networks. *Future Generation Computing Systems*, **4**(2), 81–93. Reviewed in *Computing Reviews*, **30**

Garcia-Molina, H., Kogan, B. and Lynch, N., Reliable broadcast in networks with nonprogrammable servers. *Proceedings of the 8th International Conference on Distributed Computing Systems*, San Jose, California, USA, June, pp. 428–438

Gehani, N. and Gellnick A., *Concurrent Programming*, Addison-Wesley, Wokingham

Gehani, N. and Roome, W. D., Concurrent C++: concurrent programming with class(es). *Software Practice and Experience*, **18**(12), 1157–1177

Gelernter, D., Getting the job done. *Byte*, **13**(12)

Geller, J., A knowledge representation theory for natural language graphics. Technical Report, 88-15, Department of Computer Science, New York University at Buffalo (SUNY), USA, July

Gifford, D. K. and Glasser, N., Remote pipes and procedures for efficient distributed communication. *ACM Transactions on Computer Systems*, **6**(3), 258–283

Giuffrida, M., Big Brother: a network services expert. *Proceedings of 1988 Summer USENIX Conference*, San Francisco, California, USA, June 20–24 USENIX Assoc., pp. 393–398

Goldman, R. and Gabriel, R. P., Qlisp: experience and new directions. *ACM SIGPLAN Notices*, **23**(9), 111–123, (Proceedings of the ACM/SIGPLAN 1988 Conference on Parallel Programming: Experience with Applications, Languages and Systems, New Haven, Connecticut, July 19–21)

Goldsworthy, D. R. and Loader, R. J., An object oriented approach to the modelling of parallel systems. Report RCS 200, Department of Computer Science, University of Reading, Reading, UK, October

Gopalakrishnan, M. and Patnaik, L. M., Medium access control schemes for local area networks with multiple priority functions. *BCS Computer Journal*, **31**(3), pp. 209–219

Gora, W., Universal network monitoring based on FAN.1. *Proceedings of the 9th International Conference on Computer Communication*, Tel Aviv, Israel, October 30–November 4, Elsevier, Amsterdam, pp. 104–114

Graf, H. P., Jackel, L. D. and Hubbard, W. E., VLSI implementation of a neural network model. *Computer*, **21**(3), 41–49

Green, P. E., Evolution to all-optical networks. *Proceedings of the 9th International Conference on Computer Communication*, Tel Aviv, Israel, October 30–November 4, Elsevier, Amsterdam, pp. 144–148

Griffioen, J. and Yavatkar, R., Shadow editing: a distributed service for supercomputer access. *Proceedings of the 8th International Conference on Distributed Computing Systems*, San Jose, California, USA, June, pp. 215–223

Groenendijk, W. P., A conservation-law based approximation algorithm for waiting times in polling systems. Report 8816 CWI. Department of Operations Research and System Theory, Amsterdam, The Netherlands

Groenendijk, W. P., Waiting-time approximations for cyclic-service systems with mixed service strategies. Report 8802 CWI. Department of Operations Research and System Theory, Amsterdam, The Netherlands

Gupta, A. and Tucker, A., Exploiting variable grain parallelism at runtime. *ACM SIGPLAN Notices*, **23**(9), 212–221 (Proceedings of the ACM/SIGPLAN 1988 Conference on Parallel Programming: Experience with Applications, Languages and Systems, New Haven, Connecticut, USA, July 19–21)

Gupta, R. and Soffa, M. L., Compile-time techniques for efficient utilization of parallel memories. *ACM SIGPLAN Notices*, **23**(9), (Proceedings of the ACM/SIGPLAN 1988 Conference on Parallel Programming: Experience with Applications, Languages and Systems, New Haven, Connecticut, USA, July 19–21)

Hardt, S. L. and Shin, K. U., Interactive testing environment using connectionist network representation: the 16PF test as a case study. Report 88-11, Department of Computer Science, University of New York at Buffalo, (SUNY), USA, June

Hatley, J. D. and Pirbhai, I. A., *Strategies for Real-time System Specification*, John Wiley, Chichester

Hayes, E., J., *Machine Intelligence II: the logic and acquisition of knowledge*, Oxford University Press, Oxford

Heath, L. S., Rosenberg, A. L. and Smith, B. T., The physical mapping problem for parallel architectures. *Journal of the ACM*, **35**(3), 603–634

Hedrick, C., Routing information protocol; RFC1058. *Internet Request for Comments*, Network Information Center, SRI International, Menlo Park, California, USA, June

Helary, J. M., Plouzeau, N. and Raynal, M., A distributed algorithm for mutual exclusion in an arbitrary network. *Computer Journal*, **31**(4), 289–295

Hitson, B. L., Knowledge-based monitoring and control: an approach to understanding the behaviour of TCP/IP network protocols. *Proceedings of ACM SIGCOMM 1988*, Stanford, California, August, pp. 210–221

Hseush, W. and Kaiser, G. E., A network architecture for reliable distributed computing. *IEEE Network*, **2**(4), 28–45

Hui, J. Y., Resource allocation for broadband networks. *IEEE Journal on Selected Areas in Communications* (Special Issue: Broadband Packet Communications), **6**(9), 1598–1608

Hutchinson, J., Koch, C. and Lo, J., Computing motion using analog and binary resistive networks. *Computer*, **21**(3), 52–63

Jain, P., Mead, C. and Lam, S. S., Specification and verification of collision-free broadcast networks. *Proceedings of ACM SIGCOMM 1988*, Stanford, California, August, pp. 282–291

Kanakia, H., Mead, C. and Cheriton, D., The VMP network adaptor board (NAB): high-performance network communication for multiprocessors. *Proceedings of ACM SIGCOMM 1988*, Stanford, California, August, pp. 175–187

Karol, M. J., Optical interconnections using Shufflenet multihop networks in multiconnected ring topologies. *Proceedings of ACM SIGCOMM 1988*, Stanford, California, August, pp. 25–34

Katseff, H. P., Using data partitioning to implement a parallel assembler. *ACM SIGPLAN Notices*, **23**(9), 66–76, (Proceedings of the ACM/SIGPLAN 1988 Conference on Parallel Programming: Experience with Applications, Languages and Systems, New Haven, Connecticut, USA, July 19–21)

Katz, J. L., Mead, C. and Metcalf, B. D., SURVNET: a survivable network implementation. *IEEE Journal on Selected Areas in Communications*, **6**(6), 950–958

Kavehrad, M., Mead, C. and Habbab, I. M. I., A simple high-speed optical local area network based on flooding. *IEEE Journal on Selected Areas in Communications*, **6**(6), 944–949

Kent, C. A., Partridge, C., Mead, C. and McCloghrie, K., IP MTU discovery options; RFC1063. *Internet Request for Comments*, Network Information Center, SRI International, Menlo Park, California, USA

Kim, Y. K., Asynchronous DS-CDMA system for VSAT satellite communication networks. *Proceedings of the 7th Annual International Phoenix Conference on Computers and Communications*, Scottsdale, Arizona, USA, March, pp. 140–144

Kindseth, S., Internetworking between an ISDN and dedicated networks. In *Proceedings of the 9th International Conference on Computers Communication*, Tel Aviv, Israel, October 30–November 4, Elsevier, Amsterdam, pp. 16–20

King, C.-T., Gendreau, T. B., Mead, C. and Ni, L. M., Distributed election in computer networks. *Proceedings of the 7th Annual International Phoenix Conference on Computers and Communications*, Scottsdale, Arizona, USA, March, pp. 348–352

Kleyn, M. F., Mead, C. and Gingrich, P. C., GraphTrace – understanding object oriented systems using concurrently animated views. *ACM SIGPLAN Notices*, **23**(11), 191–205 (Object-Oriented Programming Systems, Languages and Application Conference 1988, San Diego, California, USA)

Kok, J. N., A compositional semantics for Concurrent PROLOG. Report 8809, Department of Computer Science, Centrum voor Wiskunde en Informatica, Amsterdam, The Netherlands

Koren, I., Mead, C. and Koren, Z., On the bandwidth of a multistage network in the presence of faulty components. *Proceedings of the 8th International Conference on Distributed Computing Systems*, San Jose, California, USA, June, pp. 26–32

Ganapathy, K., Machine segmentation and recognition of line drawings. Technical Report 88-18, Department of Computer Science, University of New York at Buffalo (SUNY), USA, August

Kwak, K. S., Mead, C. and Rao, R. R., Priority-based random access networks. *Proceedings of the 9th International Conference on Computer Communication*, Tel Aviv, Israel, October 30–November 4, Elsevier, Amsterdam, pp. 78–82

Laarhoven, P. J. M., Aarts, E. H. L., Mead, C. and Lenstra, J. K., Job shop scheduling by simulated annealing. Report 8809, Department of Operations Research and System Theory, Centruum voor Wiskunde en Informatica, Amsterdam, The Netherlands

Lamport, L., Concurrent reading and writing of clocks. Report 27, Digital Equipment Corporation Systems Research Center, 130 Lytton Avenue, Palo Alto, California, USA, April

Lamport, L., A theorem on atomicity in distributed algorithms. Report 28, Digital Equipment Corporation, Systems Research Center, 130 Lytton Avenue, Palo Alto, California, USA, May

Lane, A., Concurrent DOS 386. *Byte*, **13**(7)

Lang, G. R., Dharssi, M., Longstaff, F. M., Longstaff, P. S., Metford, A. S., Mead, C. and Rimmer, M. T., An optimum parallel architecture for high speed real-time digital signal processing. *IEEE Computer*, **21**(2), 47–57

LaQuey, T., *User's Directory of Computer Networks Accessible to the Texas Higher Education Network Member Institutions*, 2nd Edition, University of Texas System Office of Telecommunications Services, July

Larns, J. R., Mead, C. and Hilfinger, P. N., Restructuring Lisp programs for concurrent execution. *ACM SIGPLAN Notices*, **23**(9), 100–110, (Proceedings of the ACM/SIGPLAN '88 Conference on Parallel Programming: Experience with Applications, Languages and Systems, New Haven, Connecticut, USA, July 19–21)

LeBlanc, T. J., Scott, M. L., Mead, C. and Brown, C. M., Large-scale parallel programming: experience with the BBN butterfly parallel processor. *ACM SIGPLAN Notices*, **23**(9), 161–173, (Proceedings of the ACM/SIGPLAN 1988 Conference on Parallel Programming: Experience with Applications/Languages and Systems, New Haven, Connecticut, USA, July 19–21)

Le Riche, P. J., K6 – a protocol mode kernel for the iAPX286. *Software Practice and Experience*, **18**(12), 1109–1124

Lee, C.-C., Skedzielewski, S., Mead, C. and Feo, J., On the implementation of applicative languages on shared-memory, MIMD multiprocessors. *ACM SIGPLAN Notices*, **23**(9), 188–197 (Proceedings of the ACM/SIGPLAN 1988 Conference on Parallel Programming: Experience with Applications, Languages and Systems, New Haven, Connecticut, USA, July 19–21)

Lee, T. T., Nonblocking copy networks for multicast packet switching. *IEEE Journal on Selected Areas in Communications* (Special Issue: Broadband Packet Communications), **6**(9), 1455–1467

Lesser, V., Tutorial 2: distributed problem solving in knowledge/data environments. *Proceedings of the 2nd International Conference on Expert Database Systems*, April

Li, C., Concurrent programming language – LISPTALK. *ACM SIGPLAN Notices*, **23**(4), 71–80

Li, Y. P., A distributed knowledge model for multiple intelligent agents. In *Proceedings of the 2nd International Conference on Expert Database Systems*, April

Li, Z., Mead, C. and Yew, P.-C., Efficient interprocedural analysis for program parallelization and restructuring. *ACM SIGPLAN Notices*, **23**(9), 85–99 (Proceedings of the ACM/SIGPLAN 1988 Conference on Parallel Programming: Experience with Applications, Languages and Systems, New Haven, Connecticut, USA, July 19–21)

Linsker R., Self-organization in a perceptual network. *Computer*, **21**(3), 105–117

Liskov, B. and Guttag, J., *Abstraction and Specification in Program Development*, MIT Press, Cambridge

Liskov, B., Mead, C. and Shira, L., Promises: linguistic support for efficient asynchronous procedure cells in distributed systems. *ACM SIGPLAN Notices*, **23**(7), 260–267 (Proceedings of the SIGPLAN 1988 Conference on Programming Language Design and Implementation, Atlanta, Georgia, USA, July)

Maly, K., Overstreet, C., Qui, X., Mead, C. and Tang, D., *Proceedings of the ACM SIGCOMM 1988*, Stanford, California, USA, August, pp. 12–24

Mann, A., Mead, C. and Ruckert, J., A new distributed slot assignment protocol for packet radio networks. *Proceedings of the 9th International Conference on Computer Communication*, Tel Aviv, Israel, October 30–November 4, Elsevier, Amsterdam, pp. 83–88

Marques, J. A., Guedes, P., Guimaraes, N., Mead, C. and Cunha, A., The distributed operating system of the SMD Project. *Software Practice and Experience*, **18**(9), 859–877

Marshall, T., Real-world RISCs. *Byte*, **13**(5)

Martini, P., Spaniol. O., Mead, C. and Welzel, T., File transfer in high-speed token ring networks: performance evaluation by approximate analysis and simulation. *IEEE Journal on Selected Areas in Communications*, **6**(6), 987–996

Martin, J. and Chapman, K. K., *SNA: IBM's Networking Solution*, Prentice Hall, Englewood Cliffs, New Jersey. Reviewed in *Computing Reviews*, **30**(4)

Marzullo, K., Mead, C. and Schmuck, F., Supplying high availability with a standard network file system. *Proceedings of the 8th International Conference on Distributed Computing Systems*, San Jose, California, USA, June, pp. 447–455

Matsuoka, S., Mead, C. and Kawai, S., Using tuple space communication in distributed object-oriented languages. *ACM SIGPLAN Notices*, **23**(11), 276–284 (Object-Oriented Programming Systems, Languages and Application Conference, 1988, San Diego, California, USA)

Mazzei, U., Mazzetti, C., Mead, C. and Parodi, R., Planning large-size public packet networks with high throughput nodes. *Proceedings of the 9th International Conference on Computer Communication*, Tel Aviv, Israel, October 30–November 4, Elsevier, Amsterdam, pp. 162–166

McGettrick, D. A., *Program verification using ADA*, Cambridge University Press, Cambridge

Merteens, T. L. G. L., *Program Specification and Transformation*, North-Holland, Amsterdam

Midkiff, S. F., Link allocation in point-to-point multicomputer networks. *Proceedings of the 7th Annual International Conference on Computers and Communications*, Scottsdale, Arizona, USA, March, pp. 353–356

Miller, B. P., Mead, C. and Call, L. A., Distributed upcalls: a mechanism for layering asynchronous abstractions. *Proceedings of the 8th International Conference on Distributed Computing Systems*, San Jose, California, June, pp. 62–66

Miller, B. P., Mead, C. and Choi, J. D., A mechanism for efficient debugging of parallel programs. *ACM SIGPLAN Notices*, **23**(7), 135–144 (Proceedings of the SIGPLAN 1988 Conference on Programming Language Design and Implementation, Atlanta, Georgia, USA, July)

Mills, D., Network time protocol (Version 1): specification and implementation: RFC1059. *Internet Request for Comments*, Network Information Center, SRI International, Menlo Park, California, USA, July

Moss, E., Liskov, B., Yonezawa, A., Thomas, D. A., Mead, C. and Hewitt, C., Panel discussion: object-oriented concurrency. *ACM SIGPLAN Notices*, **23**(5), 119–127 (Addendum to Proceedings of Object-Oriented Programming Systems, Languages and Applications Conference '87, Orlando, Florida, USA)

Mukherjee, A., Landweber, L. H., Mead, C. and Strikwerda, J. C., Evaluation of retransmission strategies in a local area network environment. Technical Report 789, Computer Sciences Department, University of Wisconsin-Madison, USA, September

Muller, J., Mead, C. and Netwig, L., DAPHNE: support for distributed applications programming in heterogeneous computer networks. *Proceedings of the 8th International Conference on Distributed Computing Systems*, San Jose, California, USA, June, pp. 63–73

Mulley, G. P. C., Mead, C. and Loader, R. J., The application of a real-time systems simulation tool to protocol engine design. Report RCS 201, Department of Computer Science, University of Reading, Reading, UK, November

Murata, M., Mead, C. Takagi, H., Two-layer modeling for local area networks. *IEEE Transactions on Communications* (9)

Najjar, W., Mead, C. and Gaudiot, J. L., Network disconnection in distributed systems. *Proceedings of the 8th International Conference on distributed Computing Systems*, San Jose, California, USA, June, pp. 554–568

Newman, P., A fast packet switch for the integrated services backbone network. *IEEE Journal on Selected Areas in Communications* (Special Issue: Broadband Packet Communications), **6**(9), 1468–1479

Nichol, D. M., Parallel discrete-event simulation of FCFS stochastic queuing networks. *ACM SIGPLAN Notices*, **23**(9), 124–137 (Proceedings of the ACM/SIGPLAN 1988 Conference on Parallel Programming: Experience with Applications, Languages and Systems, New Haven, Connecticut, USA, July 19–21)

Nicholls, I., Data networks in air traffic services. *Proceedings of the 9th International Conference on Computer Communication*, Tel Aviv, Israel, October 30–November 4, Elsevier, Amsterdam, pp. 89–93

Nielsen, K. and Shumate, K., *Developing Large Real-time Systems with ADA*, McGraw-Hill, New York

Notkin, D., Snyder, L., Socha, D., Bailey, M. L., Forstall, B., Gates, K., Greenlaw, R., Griswold, W. G., Holman, T. J., Korry, R., Lasswell, G., Mitchell, R., Mead, C. and Nelson, P. A., Experiences with Poker. *ACM SIGPLAN Notices*, **23**(9), 10–20 (Proceedings of the ACM/SIGPLAN 1988 Conference on Parallel Programming: Experience with Applications, Languages and Systems, New Haven, Connecticut, USA, July 19–21)

Obermeier, K. K., Side by side. *Byte*, **13**(12)

Ohnishi, H., Okada, T., Mead, C. and Noguchi, K., Flow control schemes and delay-loss tradeoff in ATM networks. *IEEE Journal on Selected Areas in Communications* (Special Issue: Broadband Packet Communications), **6**(9), 1609–1616

Olson, S. M., Levine, P. H., Jones, S. H., Bodoff, S., Mead, C. and Bertrand, S. C., Concurrent access licensing. *USENIX Association Conference Proceedings*, San Francisco, California, pp. 287–294

Onions, J., Mead, C. and Rose, M., RFC 1086. *Internet Request for Comments*, Network Information Center, SRI International, Menlo Park, California, USA

Orda, A., Mead, C. and Rom, R., Routing with packet duplication and elimination in computer networks. *IEEE Transactions on Communications*, **36**(7)

Ousterhout, J. K., Cherenson, A. R., Douglis, F. *et al.*, The Sprite network operating system. *Computer*, **21**(2), 23–36

Parr, G. P., A distributed algorithm for mutual exclusion in an arbitrary network. *Computer Journal*, **31**(4), 296–303

Peters, J., A parallel algorithm for minimal cost network flow problems. Technical Report 762, Computer Sciences Department, University of Wisconsin-Madison, Wisconsin, April

Pleban, U. F., Mead, C. and Lee, P., An automatically generated realistic compiler for an imperative programming language. *ACM SIGPLAN Notices*, **23**(7), 222–232 (Proceedings of the SIGPLAN '88 Conference on Programming Language Design and Implementation, July)

Pontain, R., Parallelizing Prolog. *Byte*, **13**(12)

Pons, J., Mead, C. and Vilarem, J., Mixed concurrency control: dealing with heterogeneity in distributed database systems. *Proceedings of the 14th International Conference on Very Large Data Bases* (eds F. B. DeWitt, F. Bancilhon and J. David), Los Angeles, California, USA, August–September

Qian, X., Distribution design of integrity constraints. *Proceedings of the 2nd International Conference on Expert Database Systems*, April

Quinn, M. J., Hatcher, P. J., Mead, C. and Jourdenais, K. C., Compiling C* programs for a hypercube multicomputer. *ACM SIGPLAN Notices*, **23**(9), 57–65. (Proceedings of the ACM/SIGPLAN 1988 Conference on Parallel Programming: Experience with Applications, Languages and Systems, New Haven, Connecticut, USA, July 19–21)

Ramakrishnan, K. K., Mead, C. and Jain, R., An explicit binary feedback scheme for congestion avoidance in computer networks with a connectionless network layer. *Proceedings of ACM SIGCOMM 1988*, Stanford, California, USA, August, pp. 303–313

Rash, W. Jr., Down to business: do you reall need a LAN? *Byte*, **13**(13)

Rhee, W. T., Mead, C. and Talagrand, M., Some distributions that allow perfect packing. *Journal of the ACM*, **35**(3), 564–678

Rising, L., Tasking troubles and tips. *ACM SIGPLAN Notices*, **23**(8), 63–72

Romano, S., Stahl, M., Mead, C. and Recker, M., Internet numbers; RFC1062. *Internet Request for Comments*, Network Information Center, SRI International, Menlo Park, California, USA, July

Romkey, J., A nonstandard for transmission of IP datagrams over serial lines; SLIP, RFC1055. *Internet Request for Comments*, Network Information Center, SRI International, Menlo Park, California, USA, June

Rose, J., The parallel decomposition and implementation of an integrated circuit global router. *ACM SIGPLAN Notices*, **23**(9), 138–145, (Proceedings of the ACM/SIGPLAN 1988 Conference on Parallel Programming: Experience with Applications, Languages and Systems, New Haven, Connecticut, July 19–21)

Rose, M., ISO presentation services on top of TCP/IP-based internets; RFC 1085 *Internet Request for Comments*, Network Information Center, SRI International, Menlo Park, California, USA, December

Rose, M., Mead, C. and McCloghrie, K., Management information base for network management of TCP/IP-based internets. RFC 1066. *Internet Request for Comments*, Network Information Center, SRI International, Menlo Park, California, USA, August

Rose, M., Mead, C. and McCloghrie, K., Structure and identification of management information for TCP/IP-based internets. RFC 1065. *Internet Request for Comments*, Network Information Center, SRI International, Menlo Park, California, USA, August

Ross, M. J., Covo, A. A., Mead, C. and Hart, C. D. Jr., An AI-based network management system. *Proceedings of the 7th Annual International Phoenix Conference on Computers and Communications*, Scottsdale, Arizona, USA, March

Rubin, K. S., Jones, P. M., Mitchell, C. M., Mead, C. and Goldstein, T. C., A Smalltalk implementation of an intelligent operator's associate. *ACM SIGPLAN Notices*, **23**(11), 234–247 (Object-Oriented Programming Systems, Languages and Application Conference 1988, San Diego, California, USA, November)

Rumbaugh, J., Controlling propagation of operations using attributes on relations. *ACM SIGPLAN Notices*, **23**(11), 285–296 (Object-Oriented Programming Systems, Languages and Application Conference 1988, San Diego, California, USA, November)

Russo, V., Johnson, G., Mead, C. and Campbell, R., Process management and exception handling in multiprocessor operating systems using object-oriented design techniques. *ACM SIGPLAN Notices*, **23**(11), 248–258, (Object-Oriented Programming Systems, Languages and Application Conference 1988, San Diego, California, USA, November)

Rutten, J. J. M. M., Correctness and full abstraction of metric semantics for concurrency. Report 8831. Department of Computer Science, Centruum voor Wiskunde en Informatica, Amsterdam, The Netherlands

Schaffner, S. C., Mead, C., Borkan, M., Segue: support for distributed graphical interfaces. *Computer*, **21**(12), 42–55

Scholl, F. W., Mead, C. and Coden, M. H., Passive optical star systems for fiber optic local area networks. *IEEE Journal on Selected Areas in Communications*, **6**(6), 913–923

Schouten, F. A., van der Duyn, Mead, C. and Ronner, T., Calculation of the availability of a two-unit parallel system with cold standby: an illustration of the embedding technique. Report 8815. Department of Operations Research and System Theory, Wiskunde en Informatica, Amsterdam, The Netherlands

Schriver, A., Disjoint circuits of prescribed homotopies in a graph on a compact surface, Report 8812. Department of Operations Research and System Theory, Wiskunde en Informatica, Amsterdam, The Netherlands

Schriver, A., Homtopy and crossings of systems of curves on a surface, Report 8811. Department of Operations Research and System Theory, Wiskunde en Informatica, Amsterdam, The Netherlands

Schriver, A., The Klein bottle and multicommodity flows, Report 8810. Department of Operations Research and System Theory, Wiskunde en Informatica, Amsterdam, The Netherlands

Schumacher, J. M., Analytic methods for the modeling of flexible structures, Report 8804. Department of Operations Research and System Theory, Wiskunde en Informatica, Amsterdam, The Netherlands

Schumacher, J. M., State representations of linear systems with output constraints, Report 8807. Department of Operations Research and System Theory, Wiskunde en Informatica, Amsterdam, The Netherlands

Seo, K., Crowcroft, J., Spilling, P., Laws, J., Mead, C. and Leddy, J., Distributed testing and measurement across the atlantic packet satellite network (SATNET). *Proceedings of ACM SIGCOMM 1988*, August, 235–246

Seshadri, V., Wortman, D. B., Junkin, M. D., Weber, S., Yu, C. P., Mead, C. and Small, I., Semantic analysis in a concurrent compiler. *ACM SIGPLAN Notices*, **23**(7), 233–240 (Proceedings of the SIGPLAN 1988 Conference on Programming Language Design and Implementation, Altanta, Georgia, USA, July)

Shapiro, E., Applications only: real-world answers. *Byte*, **13**(1)

Shapiro, E., *Concurrent Prolog: Collected Papers*, MIT Press, Cambridge, Massachusetts

Sharifi, M. H., Mead, C. and Arozullah, M., A multiple access technique for centralized multiple satellite networking with on-board processing in the central node. *Proceedings of the 7th Annual International Phoenix Conference on Computers and Communications*, Scottsdale, Arizona, USA, March, pp. 145–151

Shasha, D., Mead, C. and Goodman, N., Concurrent Search Structure algorithms. *ACM Transactions on Database Systems*, **13**(1)

Shaw, A. C., Real-time systems = process + abstract data types. Report 88-12-07, Department of Computer Science, University of Washington, Seattle, USA, December

Shibayama, E., How to invent distributed implementation schemes of an object-based concurrent language: a transformational approach. *ACM SIGPLAN Notices*, **23**(11), 297–305 (Object-Oriented Programming Systems, Languages and Application Conference 1988, San Diego, California, USA, November)

Shumate, K., *Understanding Concurrency in ADA*, McGraw-Hill, Maidenhead

Signorile, R. P., LaTourrette, J., Mead, C. and Fleisch, M., MBRAM – a priority protocol for PC based local area networks. *IEEE Network*, **2**(4), 55–59

Smulders, S. A., Control of freeway traffic flow. Report 8817 Department of Operations Research and System Theory, Centruum voor Wiskunde en Informatica, Amsterdam, The Netherlands

Smulders, S. A., Filtering of freeway traffic flow. Report 8806 Department of Operations Research and System Theory, Centruum voor Wiskunde en Informatica, Amsterdam, The Netherlands

Smyth, C. J., Nonblocking photonic switch networks. *IEEE Journal on Selected Areas in Communications*, **6**(7), 1052–1062

Soundararajan, N., Mead, C. and Costello, R. L., Responsive sequential processes. *ACM SIGPLAN Notices* **23**(3), 53–62

Srihari, Sargur, N., The connectionist/PDP/neural-network approach to computation and its application to handwritten digit recognition. Technical Report 88–02, Department of Computer Science, University of New York, Buffalo (SUNY), USA, February

Stankovic, J. A., Misconceptions about real-time computing: a serious problem for next-generation systems. *Computer*, **21**(10), 10–19

Stone, J. M., Debugging concurrent processes: a case study. *ACM SIGPLAN Notices*, **23**(7), 145–153 (Proceedings of the SIGPLAN 1988 Conference on Programming Language Design and Implementation, Atlanta, Georgia, USA, July)

Stramm, B., Mead, C. and Berman, F., Communication-sensitive heuristics and algorithms for mapping compilers. *ACM SIGPLAN Notices*, **23**(9), 222–234 (Proceedings of the ACM/SIGPLAN 1988 Conference on Parallel Programming: Experience and Applications, Languages and Systems, New Haven, Connecticut, USA, July 19–21)

Tambe, M., Kalp, D., Gupta, A., Forgy, C., Milnes, B., Mead, C. and Newell, A., Soar/PSM-E: Investigating match parallelism in a learning production system. *ACM SIGPLAN Notices*, **23**(9), 146–160 (Proceedings of the ACM/SIGPLAN 1988 Conference on Parallel Programming: Experience with Applications, Languages and Systems, New Haven, Connecticut, USA, July 19–21)

Topkis, D. M., A k shortest path algorithm for adaptive routing in communications networks. *IEEE Transactions on Communications*, **36**(7), 855–859

Tsuchiya, P. F., The landmark hierarchy: a new hierarchy for routing in very large networks. *Proceedings of ACM SIGCOMM 1988*, Stanford, California, USA, August, pp. 35–42

Uematsu, H., Mead, C. and Watanabe, R., Architechture of a packet switched based on Banyan switching network with feedback loops. *IEEE Journal on Selected Areas in Communications* (Special Issue: Broadband Packet Communications), **6**(9), 1521–1528

van den Berg, J. L. and Boxma, O. J., Sojourn times in feedback and processor sharing queues. Report 8801, Department of Operations Research and System Theory, Centrum voor Wiskunde en Informatica, Amsterdam, The Netherlands

van Laarhoven, P. J. M., Aarts, E. H. L., Mead, C. and Lenstra, J. K., Job shop scheduling by simulated annealing. Report 8809, Department of Operations Research and System Theory, Centrum voor Wiskunde en Informatica, Amsterdam, The Netherlands

van de Velde, S. L., A simpler and faster algorithm for optimal total-work-content-power due date determination. Report 8814, Department for Operations Research and System Theory; Centrum voor Wiskunde en Informatica, Amsterdam, The Netherlands

Van de Voorde, M. T., Parallel compilation on a tightly coupled mutiprocessor. Report 26, Digital Equipment Corporation, Systems Research Center, 130 Lytton Avenue, Palo Alto, California, USA, 1 March

van der Woude, J. W., A graph theoretic characterization for the rank of the transfer matrix of a structured system. Report 8819, Department of Operations Research and System Theory, Centrum voor Wiskunde en Informatica, Amsterdam, The Netherlands

van der Woude, J. W., A note on pole placement by static output feedback for single-input systems. Report 8818, Department of Operations Research and System Theory, Centrum voor Wiskunde en Informatica, Amsterdam, The Netherlands

Vernon, M. K., Mead, C. and Manber Udi, Distributed round-robin and first-come first-serve protocols. Technical Report 745, Computer Sciences Department, University of Wisconsin-Madison, USA, February

Vianu, V., Mead, C. and Vossen, G., Conceptual level concurrency control of relational update transactions (extended abstract). In *ICDT '88: Proceedings of the 2nd International Conference on Database Theory*, Bruges, Belgium, August-September (eds M. Gucht, J. Gussens, and D. Van Paredaens). Lecture Notes in Computer Science Series, Springer-Verlag, Berlin

Vorstermans, J. P., Mead, C. and De Vleeschouwer, A. P., Layered ATM systems and architectural concepts for subsribers' premises networks. *IEEE Journal on Selected Areas in Communications* (Special Issue: Broadband Packet Communications), **6**(9), 1545–1555

Warrier, U., Relan, A., Berry, O., Mead, C. and Bannister, J., A network management language for OSI networks. *Proceedings ACM SIGCOMM 1988*, Stanford, California, USA, August, pp. 98–105

Wantanabe, T., Mead, C. and Yonezawa, A., Reflection in an object-oriented concurrent language. *ACM SIGPLAN Notices*, **23**(11), 306–315, (Object-Oriented Programming Systems, Languages and Application Conference '88, San Diego, California, USA, November)

Wilson, P., Parallel processing comes to PCs. *Byte*, **13**(12)

Wolfe, M., Multiprocessor synchronization for concurrent loops. *IEEE Software*, **5**(1), 34–42

Wolf, J. J., Mead, C. and Ghosh, B., Simulation and analysis of very large area networks (VLAN) using an information flow model. *IEEE Network*, **2**(4), 6–18

Wrench, K. L., CSP-i: An implementation of communicating sequential processes. *Software Practice and Experience*, **18**(6), 545–560

Zedan, H., Achieving atomicity in Occam. *Microprocessing and Microprogramming*, **23**, 261–266

Zedan, H., On the analysis of Occam real-time distributed computations. *Microprocessing and Microprogramming*, **24**, 491–500

1989

Anon., Ethics and the Internet. Internet Activities Board, Report 1087, *Internet Request for Comments*, Network Information Center, SRI International, Menlo Park, California, January

Axford, T., *Concurrent Programming: fundamental techniques for real-time and parallel programming*, John Wiley, Chichester

Acompora, A. S. and Karol, M. J., An overview of lightwave packet networks. *IEEE Network*, **3**(1), 29–41

Aguilar, L., NCMA, a management architecture that integrates enterprise network assets. In *Integrated Network Management*, Proceedings of the IFIP TC 6/WG 6.6 Symposium on Integrated Network Management, Boston Massachusetts, USA, May 14–17, North-Holland, Amsterdam, pp. 27–40

Aicardi, M., Davoli, F. and Giordano, A., Radio_ISA_Net: a single-hop centralized packet radio network for PC-to-mainframe interconnection. *IEEE Journal on Selected Areas in Communications*, **7**(2), 219–226

Anderson, D. P. Wahbe, R., A framework for multimedia communication in a general-purpose distributed system. *Technical Report 89/498*, Computer Science Division, University College, Berkeley, California, USA, March

Appelbe, W. and McDowell, C., Integrating tools for debugging and developing multitasking programs. *ACM SIGPLAN Notices*, **24**(1), 78–88, (Proceedings of the ACM SIGPLAN and SIGOPS Workshop on Parallel and Distributed Debugging, University of Wisconsin-Madison, USA, January)

Aral, X. and Gertner, I., High-level debugging in Parasight. *ACM SIGPLAN Notices*, **24**(1), 151–162, (Proceedings of the ACM SIGPLAN and SIGOPS Workshop on Parallel and Distributed Debugging, University of Wisconsin-Madison, USA, January)

Arbouw, P., Security in multiple, inter-enterprise and cascaded networks. *7th Worldwide Congress on Computer and Communications Security and Protection*, Paris, France, March 1–3

Arnould, E. A., Bitz, F. J., Cooper, E. C., Kung, H. T., Sansom, R. D. and Steenkiste, P. A., The design of Nectar: a network backplane for heterogeneous multicomputers. *Proceedings of the 3rd International Conference on Architectural Support for Programming Languages and Operating Systems*, Boston, Massachusetts, USA, April, ACM, New York, pp. 205–216

Bates, P., Debugging heterogeneous distributed systems using event-based models of behaviour. *ACM SIGPLAN Notices*, **24**(1), 11–22, (Proceedings of the ACM SIGPLAN and SIGOPS Workshop on Parallel and Distributed Debugging, University of Wisconsin-Madison, USA, January)

Ben-Artzi, A., Architecture for a multi-vendor network management system. *Integrated Network Management* (Proceedings of the IFIP TC 6/WG 6.6. Symposium on Integrated Network Management, Boston, Massachusetts, USA, May 14–17, North-Holland, Amsterdam, pp. 445–454)

Bergstra, A., Heering, J. J. and Klint, P., *Algebraic Specification*, Addison-Wesley, Wokingham

Bertsekas, P. D. and Gallager, R., *Data Networks*, Prentice-Hall, Inc., Englewood Cliffs, New Jersey

Bertsekas, P. D. and Tsitsiklis, J. N., *Parallel and Distributed Computation Numerical Methods*, Prentice-Hall, Inc., Englewood Cliffs, New Jersey

Bhargava, B. and Riedl, J., The raid distributed database system. *IEEE Transactions on Software Engineering*, **15**(6), 726–736

Bhuyan, L. N., Yang, Q. and Agrawal, D. P., Performance of multiprocessor interconnection networks. *IEEE Computer*, **22**(2), 25–37

Birman, K. P., How robust are distributed systems? Technical Report 89-1014, Department of Computer Science, Cornell University, Ithaca, New York, USA, June

Blackburn, M. R., Using expert systems to-construct formal specifications. *IEEE Expert*, **4**(1), 62–74

Black, D., Golub, D., Hauth, K., Tevanian, A. and Sanzi, R., The Mach exception handling facility. *ACM SIGPLAN Notices*, **24**(1), 45–56, (Proceedings of the ACM SIGPLAN and SIGOPS Workshop on Parallel and Distributed Debugging, University of Wisconsin-Madison, USA, January)

Boggs, D. R., Mogul, J. C. and Kent, C. A., Errata for 'Measured capacity of an Ethernet: myths and reality', *Computer Communication Review*, **19**(2), 10, ACM SIGCOMM, April

Bonn, G., Buegel, U., Kaiser, F. and Uslaender, Th., The management of an open, distributed and dependable computing system – Delta-4. In *Integrated Network Management*, Proceedings of the IFIP TC 6/WG 6.6. Symposium on Integrated Network Management, Boston, Massachusetts, USA, May 14–17, North-Holland, Amsterdam, pp. 573–584

Borchardt, R. L. and Ha, T. T., Packet communications in a multipath fading mobile radio network. In *Proceedings of the 8th International Phoenix Conference on Computers and Communications*, Scottsdale, Arizona, USA, IEEE, March 22–24, pp. 160–165

Bowen, J., POS – formal specification of a Unix tool. *IEE Software Engineering Journal*, **4**(1)

Braun, H.-W., Models of policy based routing. RFC 1104, *Internet Request for Comments*, Network Information Centre, SRI International, Menlo Park, California, USA, June

Braun, H.-W., The NSFNET routing architecture. RFC 1093, *Internet Request for Comments*, Network Information Centre, SRI International, Menlo Park, California, USA, February

Briot, J.-P. and de Ratuld, J., Design of a distributed implementation of ABC/I. *ACM SIGPLAN Notices*, **24**(4), 15–17, (Proceedings of the ACM SIGPLAN Workshop on Object-based Concurrent Programming '88, San Diego, California, USA, April)

Bruegge, B. and Gross, T., A program debugger for a systolic array: design and implementation. *ACM SIGPLAN Notices*, **24**(1), 174–182, (Proceedings of the ACM SIGPLAN and SIGOPS Workshop on Parallel and Distributed Debugging, University of Wisconsin-Madison, USA, January)

Brusil, P. and Stokesberry, D., Integrated network management. In *Integrated Network Management*, Proceedings of the IFIP TC 6/WG 6.6 Symposium on Integrated Network Management, Boston, Massachusetts, USA, May 14–17, North-Holland, Amsterdam, pp. 3–12

Buckley, D., The use of RSA public key encryption techniques for securing large EFT-POS networks, *7th Worldwide Congress Computer and Communications Security and Protection*, Paris, France, March 1–3

Burger, W., Networking of secure systems. *IEEE Journal on Selected Areas on Communications* **7**(2), 312–318

Burger, W. and Vasudevan, N., Networking of secure AIX and Xenix systems, *7th Worldwide Congress Computer and Communications Security and Protection*, Paris, France, March 1–3

Callahan, D. and Subhlok, J., Static analysis of low-level synchronization. *ACM SIGPLAN Notices*, **24**(1), 100–111, (Proceedings of the ACM SIGPLAN and SIGOPS Workshop on Parallel and Distributed Debugging, University of Wisconsin-Madison, USA, January)

Callon, R. and Braun, H. W., Guidelines for the use of Internet-IP addresses in the ISO connectionless-mode network protocol. RFC 1069, *Internet Request for Comments*, Network Information Center, SRI International, Menlo Park, California, USA, February

Camarda, P. and Gerla, M., Fault-tolerance in multichannel local area networks. *Proceedings of the 8th International Phoenix Conference on Computers and Communications*, Scottsdale, Arizona, USA, IEEE, March 22–24, pp. 133–137

Cameron, E. J. and Cohen, D., The IC* system for debugging parallel programs via interactive monitoring and control. *ACM SIGPLAN Notices*, **24**(1), 261–270, (Proceedings of the ACM SIGPLAN and SIGOPS Workshop on Parallel and Distributed Debugging, University of Wisconsin-Madison, USA, January)

Carey, M. J. and Livny M., Parallelism and concurrency control performance in distributed database machines. Technical Report 831, Computer Sciences Department, University of Wisconsin-Madison, USA, March

Carrieri, E., Fioretti, A., Rocchini, C. A. and Cole, M., OSI compatible architecture and management for integrated ultrawideband multichannel networks. In *Integrated Network Management*, Proceedings of the IFIP TC 6/WG 6.6. Symposium on Integrated Network Management, Boston, Massachusetts, USA, May 14–17, North-Holland, Amsterdam, pp. 455–466

Case, J., Fedor, M., Schoffstall, M. and Davin, C., A simple network management protocol (SNMP). RFC 1098, *Internet Requests for Comments*, Network Information Center, SRI International, Menlo Park, Califonia, USA, April

Chang, C. K., Chang, Y.-F., Yang, Lin, Chou, C.-R. and Jong-Jeng, C., Modeling a real-time multitasking system in a time PQ net. *IEEE Software*, **6**(2), 46–51

Chao, C. Y. and Ilyas, M., Fast reconfigurable communication networks. *Proceedings of the 8th International Phoenix Conference on Computers and Communications*, Scottsdale, Arizona, USA, IEEE, March 22–24, pp. 248–252

Chen, W.-T. and Huang, N.-F., The strongly connecting problem on multihop packet radio networks. *IEEE Transactions on Communications*, **37**(3), 293–294

Cheng, A. S. K. and Reynolds, T. J., An OR parallel logic programing language and its abstract machine. Report 121, Department of Computer Science, St Lucia, Queensland, Australia, June

Cheriton, D. R. and Williamson, C. L., VMTP as the transport layer for high-performance distributed systems. *IEEE Communications*, **27**(6), 37–44

Choudhary, A. N., Kohler, W. H., Stankovic, J. A. and Towsley, D., A modified priority based probe algorithm for distributed deadlock detection and resolution. *IEEE Software Engineering*, **15**(1), 10–17

Chowdhury, S., On message resequencing in computer networks. *Proceedings of the 8th International Phoenix Conference on Computers and Communications*, Scottsdale, Arizona, USA, IEEE, March 22–24, pp. 231–237

Chui, C. K. and Ron, A., On the convolution of a box spline with a compactly supported distribution: linear independence for the integer translates. Technical Report 812, Computer Sciences Department, University of Wisconsin-Madison, USA, January

Cieslak, R., Fawaz, A., Sachs, S., Varaiya, P., Walrand, J. and Li, A., The programmable network prototyping system. *Computer*, **22**(5), 67–76

Clark, D., Policy routing in internet protocols. RFC 1102. *Internet Request for Comments*, Network Information Center, SRI International, Menlo Park, California, USA, (May 1989)

Cohen, B., Justification of formal methods for systems specification. *IEE Software Engineering Journal*, **4**(1), 26–35

Cohen, B., A rejustification of formal notations. *IEE Software Engineering Journal*, **4**(1), 36–39

Cohrs, D. L. and Miller, B. P., Specification and verification of network managers for large internets. Technical Report 832, Computer Science Department, University of Wisconsin-Madison, USA, March

Conery, S. J., *Parallel Execution of Logic Programs*, Kluwer Academic, Dordrecht

Crawford, J., Graphics for network management: an interactive approach. In *Integrated Network Management*, Proceedings of the IFIP TC 6/WG 6.6. Symposium on Integrated Network Management, Boston, Massachusetts, USA, May 14-17, North-Holland, Amsterdam, pp. 197–210

Davies, J. I., An analysis of requirements for the management of distributed systems. In *Integrated Network Management*, Proceedings of the IFIP TC 6/WG 6.6. Symposium on Integrated Network Management, Boston, Massachusetts, USA, May 14-17, North-Holland, Amsterdam, pp. 519–530

de Bakker, J. W., de Roever, W. P. and Rozenberg, G., *Linear Time, Branching Time and Partial Order in Logics and Models for Concurrency*, Springer-Verlag, Berlin

Dupuy, A., Schwartz, J., Yemini, Y., Barzilai, G. and Cahana, A., Network fault management: a user's view. In *Integrated Network Management*, Proceedings of the IFIP TC 6/WG 6.6. Symposium on Integrated Network Management, Boston, Massachusetts, USA, May 14–17, North-Holland, Amsterdam, pp. 101–109

Elshoff, I., A distributed debugger for Amoeba. *ACM SIGPLAN Notices*, **24**(1), 1–10 (Proceedings of the ACM SIGPLAN and SIGOPS Workshop on Parallel and Distributed Debugging, University of Wisconsin-Madison, USA, January

Emrath, P. and Padua, D., Automatic detection of nondeterminacy in parallel programs. *ACM SIGPLAN Notices*, **24**(1), 89–99, (Proceedings of the ACM SIGPLAN and SIGOPS Workshop on Parallel and Distributed Debugging, University of Wisconsin-Madison, USA, January)

Enslow, P. H. Jr., Management of high speed and large networks. In *Integrated Network Management*, Proceedings of the IFIP TC 6/WG 6.6 Symposium on Integrated Network Management, Boston, Massachusetts, USA, North-Holland, Amsterdam, The Netherlands, May 14–17, pp. 383–386

Eu, J. H., A sampling approach to real-time performance monitoring of digital transmission systems. *Proceedings of the 8th International Phoenix Conference on Computers and Communications*, Scottsdale, Arizona, USA, IEEE, March 22–24, pp. 207–213

Felderman, R. E., Schooler, E. M. and Kleinrock, L., The Benevolent Bandit Laboratory: a testbed for distributed algorithms. *IEEE Journal on Selected Areas in Communications*, **7**(2), 303–311

Feldkhun, L., Integrated network management schemes – a global perspective on the issue. In *Integrated Network Management*, Proceedings of the IFIP TC 6/WG 6.6 Symposium on Integrated Network Management, Boston, Massachusetts, USA, North-Holland, Amsterdam, The Netherlands, May 14–17, pp. 279–304

Feldman, S. and Brown, C., IGOR: a system for programming debugging via reversible execution. *ACM SIGPLAN Notices*, **24**(1), 112–123, (Proceedings of the ACM SIGPLAN and SIGOPS Workshop on Parallel and Distributed Debugging, University of Wisconsin-Madison, USA, January)

Ferrari, D., Guaranteeing performance for real-time communications in wide-area networks. Technical Report 89/485, Computer Science University College, Berkeley, California, USA, January

Fidge, C., Partial orders for parallel debugging. *ACM SIGPLAN Notices*, **24**(1), 183–194, (Proceedings of the ACM SIGPLAN and SIGOPS Workshop on Parallel and Distributed Debugging, University of Wisconsin-Madison, USA, January)

Finkel, R. A., Scott, M. L., Artsy, Y. and Chang, H.-Y., Experience with Charlotte: simplicity and function in a distributed operating system. *IEEE Transactions on Software Engineering*, **15**(6), 676–685

Forin, A., Debugging of heterogeneous parallel systems. *ACM SIGPLAN Notices*, **24**(1), 131–140, (Proceedings of University of the ACM SIGPLAN and SIGOPS Workshop on Parallel and Distributed Debugging, University of Wisconsin-Madison, USA, January)

Fowler, R., LeBlanc, T. and Mellor-Crummey, J., An integrated approach to parallel program debugging and performance analysis on large-scale multiprocessors. *ACM SIGPLAN Notices*, **24**(1), 163–173, (Proceedings of the ACM SIGPLAN and SIGOPS Workshop on Parallel and Distributed Debugging, University of Wisconsin-Madison, USA, January)

Fratta, L. and Wozniak, J., PR-EXPRESS: collision-free access protocol for packet radio networks. *Computer Networks and ISDN Systems*, **16**(3), 229–242

Friedman, E. and Ziegler, C., Packet voice communications over PC-based local area networks. *IEEE Journal on Selected Areas in Communications*, **7**(2), 211–218

Gaitonde, S. S., Jacobson, D. W. and Pohm, A. V., Bounding delay on a token ring network with voice, data and facsimile applications: a simulation study. *Proceedings of the 8th International Phoenix Conference on Computers and Communications*, Scottsdale, Arizona, USA, IEEE, March 22–24, pp. 201–206

Goldberg, A. and Robson, D., *Smalltalk 80 – the language*, Addison-Wesley, Wokingham

Goldsmith, S., Enterprise network management. In *Integrated Network Management*, Proceedings of the IFIP TC 6/WG 6.6 Symposium on Integrated Network Management, Boston, Massachusetts, USA, North-Holland, Amsterdam, The Netherlands, May 14–17, pp. 541–554

Goldszmidt, G., Katz, S. and Yemini, S., Interactive blackbox debugging for concurrent languages. *ACM SIGPLAN Notices*, **24**(1), (Proceedings of the ACM SIGPLAN and SIGOPS Workshop on Parallel and Distributed Debugging, University of Wisconsin-Madison, USA, January)

Goodman, R., Miller, J., Smuth, P. and Latin, H., Real-time autonomous expert systems in network managment. In *Integrated Network Management*, Proceedings of the IFIP TC 6/WG 6.6 Symposium on Integrated Network Management, Boston, Massachusetts, USA, North-Holland, Amsterdam, The Netherlands, May 14–17, pp. 599–626

Ha, T. T., Personal computer communications via VSAT networks. *IEEE Journal on Selected Areas in Communications*, **7**(2), 235–245

Hagens, R., Hall, N. and Rose, M., Use of the internet as a subnetwork for experimentation with the OSI network layer. RFC 1070 *Internet Request for Comments*, Network Information Center, SRI International, Menlo Park, California, USA, February

Hall, J. and Turnbull, D. M., Accounting and resource management in an internet distributed operating system. In *Integrated Network Management*, Proceedings of the IFIP TC 6/WG 6.6 Symposium on Integrated Network Management, Boston, Massachusetts, USA, North-Holland, Amsterdam, The Netherlands, May 14–17, pp. 531–540

Hansen, P. B., The Joyce language report. *Software Practice and Experience*, **19**(6), 553–578

Hansen, P. B., A multiprocessor implementation of Joyce. *Software Practice and Experience*, **19**(6), 579–592

Hauser, S. E., Felsen, M. I., Gill, M. J. and Thoma, G. R., Networking AT-class computers for image distribution. *IEEE Journal on Selected Areas in Communications*, **7**(2), 268–276

Heatley, S. and Stokesberry, D., Analysis of transport measurements over a local area network. *IEEE Communications*, **27**(6), 16–22

Homan, P., Malizia, B. and Reisner, E., Tandem's distributed systems management. In *Integrated Network Management*, Proceedings of the IFIP TC 6/WG 6.6 Symposium on Integrated Network Management, Boston, Massachusetts, USA, North-Holland, Amsterdam, The Netherlands, May 14–17, pp. 555–564

Hong, P., Jeromnimon, J., Louit, G., Min, J. and Sen, P., Integrated fault management in interconnected networks. In *Integrated Network Management*, Proceedings of the IFIP TC 6/WG 6.6 Symposium on Integrated Network Management, Boston, Massachusetts, USA, North-Holland, Amsterdam, The Netherlands, May 14–17, pp. 333–344

Hough, A. and Cuny, J., Initial experiences with a pattern-oriented parallel debugger. *ACM SIGPLAN Notices*, **24**(1), 195–205, (Proceedings of the ACM SIGPLAN and SIGOPS Workshop on Parallel and Distributed Debugging, University of Wisconsin-Madison, USA, January)

Hseush, W. and Kaiser, G., Data path debugging: data oriented for a concurrent programming language. *ACM SIGPLAN Notices*, **24**(1), 236–247, (Proceedings of the ACM SIGPLAN and SIGOPS Workshop on Parallel and Distributed Debugging, University of Wisconsin-Madison, USA, January)

Hsu, M. and Tam, V.-O., Transaction synchronization in distributed shared virtual memory systems. Technical Report-05-89, Harvard University, Center for Research in Computing Technology, Cambridge, Massachusetts, USA, January

Hui, J. Y., Network, transport, and switching integration for Broadband. *IEEE Network*, **3**(2), 40–51

IAB Official Protocol Standards. RFC 1100, *Internet Request for Comments*, Network Information Center, SRI International, Menlo Park, California, April

Iturbide, J. A. V., Formalization of the control stack. *ACM SIGPLAN Notices*, **24**(3), 46–54

Jalote, P., Resilient objects in broadcast networks. *IEEE Software Engineering*, **15**(1), 68–71

Jo, C.-H., Fisher, D. D. and George, K. M., Abstraction and specfication of local area networks. *Proceedings of the 8th International Phoenix Conference on Computers and Communications*, Scottsdale, Arizona, USA, IEEE, March 22–24, pp. 337–343

Jul, E., Object mobility in a distributed object-oriented system. Report 88-12-06, Department of Computer Science, University of Washington, Seattle, USA

Kaminow, I. P., Non-coherent photonic frequency-multiplexed access networks. *IEEE Networks*, **3**(2), 4–12

Katz, D., A proposed standard for the transmission of IP datagrams over FDDI networks. RFC 1103, *Internet Request for Comments*, Network Information Center, SRI International, Menlo Park, California, USA, June

Kemmerer, R. A., Analyzing encryption protocols using formal verification techniques. *IEEE Journal on Selected Areas in Communications*, **7**(4), 448–457

Kessler, R. E. and Livny, M., An analysis of distributed shared memory algorithms. TR 825, Computer Sciences Department, University of Wisconsin-Madison, USA, February

Khasnabish, B., A bound of deception capability in multiuser computer networks. *IEEE Journal on Selected Areas in Communications*, **7**(4), 590–594

Kim, K. H., An approach to experimental evaluation of real-time fault-tolerant distributed computing schemes. *IEEE Transactions on Software Engineering*, **15**(6), 715–725

Kobayashi, Y., Standardization issues in integrated network management. In *Integrated Network Management*, Proceedings of the IFIP TC 6/WG 6.6 Symposium on Integrated Network Management, Boston, Massachusetts, USA, North-Holland, Amsterdam, The Netherlands, May 14–17, pp. 79–92

Kumar, A. and Stonebraker, M., Performance considerations for an operating system transaction manager. *IEEE Transactions on Software Engineering*, **15**(6), 705–714

Kumar, D., Systems whose distributed simulation requires low overhead. *Proceedings of the 8th International Phoenix Conference on Computers and Communications*, Scottsdale, Arizona, USA, IEEE, March 22–24, pp. 520–527

Lai, M.-Y., Wilkinson, K. and Lanin, V., On distributing JASMIN'S optimistic multiversioning page manager. *IEEE Transactions on Software Engineering*, **15**(6), 696–704

Lai, W.-S., Network and nodal architectures for the internetworking between frame relaying services. *Computer Communication Review*, **19**(1), 72–84

Lamden, Y., Iyer, B., Barzilai, G. and Cahana, A., Dialog manager for network management. In *Integrated Network Management*, Proceedings of the IFIP TC 6/WG 6.6 Symposium on Integrated Network Management, Boston, Massachusetts, USA, North-Holland, Amsterdam, The Netherlands, May 14–17, pp. 269–278

Lam, H.-K., Fragano, M., Maymon, G. and Yamarone, R., Unified primary-operations-state model for objects in the network-element database. In *Integrated Network Management*, Proceedings of the IFIP TC 6/WG 6.6 Symposium on Integrated Network Management, Boston, Massachusetts, USA, North-Holland, Amsterdam, The Netherlands, May 14–17, pp. 323–332

Lee, G. M., Integrating UNIX terminal services into a distributed operating system. *Proceedings of the 1989 Winter USENIX Technical Conference*, San Diego, California, USA, January 30–February 3, USENIX Association, pp. 29–42

Lee, I., King, R. B. and Paul, R. P., A predictable real-time kernel for distributed multisensor systems. *IEEE Computer*, **22**(6), 78–83

Leffler, S., McKusick, K., Karels, M. and Quarterman, J. S., *The Design and Implementation of the 4.3BSD UNIX Operating System*, Addison-Wesley, Massachusetts

LeGall, F., About loss probabilities for general routing policies in circuit-switched networks. *IEEE Transactions on Communications*, **37**(1), 57–59

Le-Roux, Y., Information security in a local area network integrating different worldwide networks – The security of DECWorld 1988. *7th Worldwide Congress Computer and Communications Security and Protection*, Paris, France, March 1–3

Levy, E. and Silberschatz, A., Distributed file systems. Technical Report 89-04, March

Lichtenstein, Y. and Shapiro, E., Concurrent algorithmic debugging. *ACM SIGPLAN Notices*, **24**(1), 248–260, (Proceedings of the ACM SIGPLAN and SIGOPS Workshop on Parallel and Distributed Debugging, University of Wisconsin-Madison, USA, January)

Lin, C. and LeBlanc, R., Event-based debugging of object/action programs. *ACM SIGPLAN Notices*, **24**(1), 23–34, (Proceedings of the ACM SIGPLAN and SIGOPS Workshop on Parallel and Distributed Debugging, University of Wisconsin-Madison, USA, January)

Linke, R. A., Frequency division multiplexed optical networks using heterodyne. *IEEE Network*, **3**(2), 13–21

Liu, J.-C. and Shin, K. G., Polynomial testing of packet switching networks. *IEEE Transactions on Computers*, **38**(2), 202–217

Lougheed, K. and Rekhter, Y., A border gateway protocol (BGP). RFC 1105, *Internet Request for Comments*, Network Information Center, SRI International, Menlo Park, California, USA, June

Magee, J., Kramer, J. and Sloman, M., Constructing distributed systems in Conic, *IEEE Transactions on Software Engineering*, **15**(6), 663–676

Mancini, L. V. and Shrivastava, S. K., Replication within atomic actions and conversations: a case study in fault-tolerance duality. Report 281, Computing Laboratory, University of Newcastle-upon-Tyne, UK, April

Marcy, G., Telnet X display location option. RFC 1096, *Internet Request for Comments*, Network Information Center, SRI International, Menlo Park, California, USA, March

Mazumdar, S. and Lazar, A., Knowledge-based monitoring of integrated networks. In *Integrated Network Management Proceedings of the IFIP TC 6/WG 6.6 Symposium on Integrated Network Management*, Boston, Massachusetts, USA, North-Holland, Amsterdam, The Netherlands, pp. 235–246

McKinley, P. and Liu, J. W. S., Multicast tree construction in bus-based networks. *Proceedings of the 8th International Phoenix Conference on Computers and Communications*, Scottsdale, Arizona, USA, IEEE March 22–24, pp. 171–177

McLaughlin, L., A standard for the transmission of IP datagrams over NetBIOS networks. RFC 1088, *Internet Request for Comments*, Network Information Center, SRI International, Menlo Park, California, USA, February

Menchi, C., The design of an OSI compatible network management. In *Integrated Network Management, Proceedings of the IFIP TC 6/WG 6.6 Symposium on Integrated Network Management*, Boston, Massachusetts, USA, May 14–17, North-Holland, Amsterdam, The Netherlands, pp. 305–314

Miller, B. and Choi, J.-D., A mechanism for efficient debugging of parallel programs. *ACM SIGPLAN Notices*, **24**(1), 141–150, (Proceedings of the ACM SIGPLAN and SIGOPS Workshop on Parallel and Distributed Debugging, University of Wisconsin-Madison, USA, January)

Miller, B. P., Lars, F. and So, B., An empirical study of the reliability of operating system utilities. Technical Report 830, Computer Sciences Department, University of Wisconsin-Madison, USA, March

Miller, B., Telnet subliminal-message option. RFC 1097, Network Information Center, SRI International, Menlo Park, California, USA, April

Minnich, R. G. and Farber, D. J., Mether: a distributed shared memory for SunOS 4.0. *Proceedings of the 1989 Summer USENIX Conference*, San Francisco, California, USA, June

Mitchell, T. L. and Nilsson, A. A., Analytical results for the error free spiral computer network topology. *Proceedings of the 8th International Phoenix Conference on Computers and Communications*, Scottsdale, Arizona, USA, IEEE, March 22–24, 219–223

Mockapetris, P. V., DNS encoding of network names and other types. RFC 1101, *Internet Request for Comments*, Network Information Center, SRI International, Menlo Park, California, USA, April

Needham, R. and Herbert, A., Report on the third European SIGOPS Workshop: Autonomy or interdependence in distributed systems. *Operating Systems review*, **23**(2), 3–19

Nelson, M. N., Welch, B. B. and Ousterhout, J. K., Caching in the Sprite network file system. *ACM Transactions on Computer Systems*, **6**(1), 134–154

Nowicki, W., Transport issues in the network file system. *Computer Communication Review*, **19**(2), 16–20

Okamoto, E. and Tanaka, K., Identity-based information security management system for personal computer networks. *IEEE Journal on Selected Areas in Communications*, **7**(2), 290–294

Okamoto, E. and Tanaka, K., Key distributed system based on identification information. *IEEE Journal on Selected Areas in Communications*, **7**(4), 481–485

Owen, S. A., An end-user network management model for ISDN. In *Integrated Network Management, Proceedings of the IFIP TC 6/WG 6.6 Symposium on Integrated Network Management*, Boston, Massachusetts, USA, May 14–17, North-Holland, Amsterdam, The Netherlands, pp. 387–396

Pan, D. and Linton, M., Supporting reverse execution for parallel programs. *ACM SIGPLAN Notices*, **24**(1), 124–129, (Proceedings of the ACM SIGPLAN and SIGOPS Workshop on Parallel and Distributed Debugging, University of Wisconsin-Madison, USA, January)

Partridge, C., Integrating network measurement agents into the OSI network management architecture. *Integrated Network Management, Proceedings of the IFIP TC 6/WG 6.6 Symposium on Integrated Network Management*, Boston, Massachusetts, USA, May 12–17, North-Holland, Amsterdam, The Netherlands

Parulkar, G. and Turner, J., Towards a framework for high speed communication in heterogeneous networking environment. *Proceedings of IEEE INFOCOM 1989*, Ottawa, Ontario, Canada, April 23–27

Patel, A., McDermott, G. and Mulvihill, C., Integrating network management and artificial intelligence. In *Integrated Network Management: Proceedings of the IFIP TC 6/WG 6.6 Symposium on Integrated Network Management*, Boston, Massachusetts, USA, May 14–17, North-Holland, Amsterdam, The Netherlands, pp. 647–662

Patt, Y. N., Guest Editor's Introduction: Real machines: design choices/engineering trade-offs. *IEEE Computer*, **22**(1), 8–10

Pileri, S. and Saracco, R., Towards the integrated network management of the Italian telecommunication network. *Integrated Network Management: Proceedings of the IFIP TC 6/WG 6.6 Symposium on Integrated Network Management*, Boston, Massachusetts, USA, May 14–17, North-Holland, Amsterdam, The Netherlands, pp. 409–422

Pimentel, J., Fieldbus network management: requirements and architectures. *Integrated Network Management: Proceedings of the IFIP TC 6/WG 6.6 Symposium on Integrated Network Management*, Boston, Massachusetts, USA, May 14–17, North-Holland, Amsterdam, The Netherlands, pp. 467–478

Pinkas, D., An access control model for distributed systems based on the use of trusted authorities. *7th Worldwide Congress on Computer and Communications Security and Protection*, Paris, France, March 1–3

Quarterman, J. S. *The Matrix: computer networks and conferencing systems worldwide*, Digital Press, Bedford, Massachusetts

Raeburn, K., Rochlis, J., Zanarotti, S. and Sommerfield, W., *Proceedings of the 1989 Winter USENIX Technical Conference*, San Diego, California, USA, January 30–February 3, USENIX Association

Rahuraman, V. and Sirisena, H. R., Dynamic entry-to-exit flow control for virtual circuit networks. *Proceedings of the 8th International Phoenix Conference on Computers and Communications*, Scottsdale, Arizona, USA, IEEE, March pp. 253–259

Ramakrishnan, K. K. and Emer, J. S., Performance analysis of mass storage service alternatives for distributed systems. *IEEE Transactions on Software Engineering*, **15**(2), 120–133

Raymond, K. and Mansfield, T., A comparison of LOTOS and Z for specifying distributed systems. Report 111, Department of Computer Science, St Lucia, Queensland, Australia, May

Raynal, M., *Networks and Distributed Computation: concepts, tools and algorithms*, MIT Press, Cambridge, Massachusetts

Redell, D., Experience with Topaz teledebugging. *ACM SIGPLAN Notices*, **24**(1), 35–44 (Proceedings of the ACM SIGPLAN and SIGOPS Workshop on Parallel and Distributed Debugging, University of Wisconsin-Madison, USA, January)

Rekhter, J., EGP and policy based routing in the new NSFNET backbone. RFC 1092, *Internet Request for Comments*, Network Information Center, SRI International, Menlo Park, California, USA, February

Richards, J. T., *Clausal Form Logic: an introduction to the logic of computer reasoning*, Addison-Wesley, Wokingham

Rider, M. J., Protocols for ATM access networks. *IEEE Network*, **3**(1), 17–22

Ron, A., On the convolution of a box spline with a compactly supported distribution: The exponential-polynomials in the linear span. Technical Report 813, Computer Sciences Department, University of Wisconsin-Madison, USA, January

Rosberg, Z. and Sidi, M., TDM policies in multistation packet radio networks. *IEEE Transactions on Communications*, **37**(1), 31–38

Rubin, R., Rudolph, L. and Zernik, D. Debugging parallel programs in parallel. *ACM SIGPLAN Notices*, **24**(1), 216–225 (Proceedings of the ACM SIGPLAN and SIGOPS Workshop on Parallel and Distributed Debugging, University of Wisconsin-Madison, USA, January)

Schneider, D. A. and DeWitt, D. J., A performance evaluation of four parallel join algorithms in a shared-nothing multiprocessor environment. Technical Report 836, Computer Sciences Department, University of Wisconsin-Madison, USA, April

Schneidewind, N. F., Distributed system software design paradigm with application to computer networks. *IEEE transactions on Software Engineering*, **15**(4), 402–412

Schoffstall, M., Davin, C., Fedor, M. and Case, J., SNMP over Ethernet. RFC 1089 *Internet Request for Comments*, Network Information Center, SRI International, Menlo Park, California, USA, February

Sevcik, P. J. and Korn, L., A network monitoring and control security architecture. In *Integrated Network Management: Proceedings of the IFIP TC 6/WG 6.6 Symposium on Integrated Network Management*, Boston, Massachusetts, USA, May 14–17, North Holland, Amsterdam, The Netherlands

Scharbach, P. N., *Formal Methods: theory and practice*, Blackwell Scientific, Oxford

Shein, B., Callahan, M. and Woodbury, P., NFSstone: a network file server performance benchmark. *Proceedings of the 1989 Summer USENIX Conference*, San Francisco, California, USA, June

Skov, M., Implementation of physical and media access protocols for high-speed networks. *IEEE Communications*, **27**(6), 45–53

Sloman, M. and Moffett, J., Domain management for distributed systems. In *Integrated Network Management: Proceedings of the IFIP TC 6/WG 6.6 Symposium on Integrated Network Management*, Boston, Massachusetts, USA, May 14–17, North-Holland, Amsterdam, The Netherlands, pp. 505–518

Socha, D., Bailey, M. and Notkin, D., Voyeur: graphical views of parallel programs. *ACM SIGPLAN Notices*, **24**(1), 206–215 (Proceedings of the ACM SIGPLAN and SIGOPS Workshop on Parallel and Distributed Debugging, University of Wisconsin-Madison, USA, January)

Spivey, J. M., An introduction to Z and formal specifications. *IEE Software Engineering Journal*, **4**(1), 40–50

Stone, J., A graphical representation of parallel processes. *ACM SIGPLAN Notices*, **24**(1), 226–235 (Proceedings of the ACM SIGPLAN and SIGOPS Workshop on Parallel and Distributed Debugging, University of Wisconsin-Madison, USA, January)

Stone, R. F. and Zedan, H., Designing time critical systems with TACT. In *Proceedings of the Euromicro workshop on Real-Time*, IEEE Computer Society Press, New York, 74–82

Stroustrup, B., *The C++ Programming Language*, Addison-Wesley, Wokingham, UK

Suda, T. and Bradley, T. T., Packetized voice/data integrated transmission on a token passing ring local area network. *IEEE Transactions on Communications*, **37**(3), 238–244

Sun Microsystems Inc., NFS: network file system protocol specification. RFC 1094. *Internet Request for Comments*, Network Information Center, SRI International, Menlo Park, California, USA, March

Sunderam, V. S., An experiment with network shared libraries. *Proceedings of the 1989 Summer USENIX Conference*, San Francisco, California, USA, June

Sy, K.-B. and Turcu, P. N., Network management of ISDN customer premises equipment. In *Integrated Network Management: Proceedings of the IFIP TC 6/WG 6.6 Symposium on Integrated Network Management*, Boston, Massachusetts, USA, May 14–17, North-Holland, Amsterdam, The Netherlands, pp. 397–408

Szlanko, J., *Real-time Programming*, Pergamon Press, Oxford

Tai, A. T., A study of the application of formal specification methods for fault-tolerant software. Report 880100, Computer Science Department, University of California, Los Angeles, USA, December

Tarouco, L., Intelligent network management. In *Integrated Network Management: Proceedings of the IFIP TC 6/WG 6.6 Symposium on Integrated Network Management*, Boston, Massachusetts, USA, May 14–17, North-Holland, Amsterdam, The Netherlands, pp. 141–158

Tcha, D.-W. and Jin, C.-Y., Link-by-link bandwidth allocation in an integrated voice/data network using the fuzzy set principle. *Computer Networks and ISDN Systems*, **16**(3), 217–228

Thrampoulidis, K. and Makios, V., Distributed reconfiguration algorithm for a unidirectional optimum bus local area network. *Proceedings of the 8th International Phoenix Conference on Computers and Communications*, Scottsdale, Arizona, USA, IEEE, pp. 127–132

Meertens, T. L. G. L., *Program Specification and Transformation*, North-Holland, Amsterdam, The Netherlands

Tokuda, H., Kotera, M. and Mercer, C., A real-time monitor for a distributed real-time operating system. *ACM SIGPLAN Notices*, **24**(1), 68–77 (Proceedings of the ACM SIGPLAN and SIGOPS Workshop on Parallel and Distributed Debugging, University of Wisconsin-Madison, USA, January)

Tripathi, A. R., Berge, E., and Aksit, M., An implementation of the object-oriented concurrent programming language SINA. *Software Practice and Experience*, **19**(3), 235–256

Tripathi, A. R., An overview of the Nexus distributed operating system design. *IEEE Transactions on Software Engineering*, **15**(6), 686–695

Tsai, C.-R., Gligor, V. D., Burger, W., Carson, M. E., Cheng, P.-C., Cugini, J. A., Hecht, M. S., Lo, S.-P., Malik, S. and Vasudevan, N., A trusted network architecture for AIX systems. *Proceedings of the 1989 Winter USENIX Technical Conference*, San Diego, California, USA, January 30–February 3, USENIX Association, pp. 457–471

Turman, B. and Rubin, R., Bell operating company packet interfaces between networks and subnets. *Computer Networks and ISDN Systems*, **16**(3), 187–196

Turski, M. W. and Maibaum, T. S. E., *The Specification of Computer Programs*, Addison-Wesley, Wokingham, UK

Ullmann, R., SMTP on X.25. RFC 1090, *Internet Request for Comments*, Network Information Center, SRI International, Menlo Park, California, USA, February

Van Bokkelen, J., Telnet terminal-type option. RFC 1091 *Internet Request for Comments*, Network Information Center, SRI International, Menlo Park, California, USA, February

Van Renesse, R., Van Staveren, H. and Tanenbaum, A. S., The performance of the Amoeba distributed operating system. *Software Practice and Experience*, **19**(3), 223–234

Vannucci, G., Combining frequency-division and code-division multiplexing in a high-capacity optical network. *IEEE Network*, **3**(2), 21–30

Verma, P. K., *Performance Estimation of Computer Communication Networks: A Structured Approach*, Computer Science Press, Rockville, Maryland

Vuong, S. T. and Ma, A. H. T., A low-cost and portable local area network for interconnecting PC's using electric power lines. *IEEE Journal on Selected Areas in Communications*, **7**(2), 192–201

Walpole, J., Blair, G. S., Malik, J. and Nicol, J. R., A unifying model for consistent distributed software development environments. *ACM SIGPLAN Notices*, **24**(2), 183–190 (Proceedings of the ACM SIGSOFT/SIGPLAN Software Engineering Symposium on Practical Software Development Environments, Boston, Massachusetts, USA, February)

Walshe, A., Formal methods for database language design and constraint handling. *IEE Software Engineering Journal*, **4**(1), 15–24

Wang, C. C., Cheng, U. and Yan, T.-Y., Novel network test-bed simulators. *Proceedings of the 8th International Phoenix Conference on Computers and Communications*, Scottsdale, Arizona, USA, IEEE March 22–24, pp. 166–170

Wang, Z., Model of network faults. In *Integrated Network Management: Proceedings of the IFIP TC 6/WG 6.6 Symposium on Integrated Network Management*, Boston, Massachusetts, USA, May 14–17, North-Holland, Amsterdam, The Netherlands, pp. 345–352

Warrier, U. and Besaw, L., The common management information services and protocol over TCP/IP (CMOT). Report RFC 1095 *Internet Request for Comments*, Network Information Center, SRI International, Menlo Park, California, USA, April

Warrier, U. and Sunshine, C., A platform for heterogeneous interconnection network management. In *Integrated Network Management: Proceedings of the IFIP TC 6/WG 6.6 Symposium on Integrated Network Management*, Boston, Massachusetts, USA, May 14–17, North-Holland, Amsterdam, The Netherlands

Welzel, T., FDDI and BWN backbone networks: a performance comparison based on simulation. *Proceedings of the 8th International Phoenix Conference on Computers and Communications*, Scottsdale, Arizona, USA, IEEE March 22–24, pp. 190–194

Wild, P. and C. Mitchell., One-stage one-sided rearrangeable switching networks. *IEEE Transactions on Communications*, **37**(1), 52–56

Wilson, D., A proposed approach for integrated network management in the army tactical command and control system. *Intergrated Network Management: Proceedings of the IFIP TC 6/WG 6.6 Symposium on Integrated Network Management*, Boston, Massachusetts, USA, May 14–17, North-Holland, Amsterdam, The Netherlands, pp. 435–444

Wittie, L., Debugging distributed C programs by real-time replay. *ACM SIGPLAN Notices*, **24**(1), 57–67, (Proceedings of the ACM SIGPLAN and SIGOPS Workshop on Parallel and Distributed Debugging, University of Wisconsin-Madison, USA, January)

Yakovlev, A. V., A relation-based approach to analysing semantics of asynchronous hardware specification. Report 286, Computing Laboratory, University of Newcastle-upon-Tyne, UK, June

Yamahira, T., Kiriha, Y. and Sakata, S., Unified fault management scheme for a network troubleshooting expert system. In *Integrated Network Management: Proceedings of the IFIP TC 6/WG 6.6 Symposium on Integrated Network Management*, Boston, Massachusetts, USA, May 14–17, North-Holland, Amsterdam, The Netherlands, pp. 637–646

Yeong, W., Schoffstall, M. L. and Fedor, M. S., A UNIX implementation of the simple network management protocol. *Proceedings of the 1989 Winter USENIX Technical Conference*, San Diego, California, USA, January 30–February 3, USENIX Association

Yu, C. T., Guh, K.-C., Brill, D. and Chen, A. L. P., Partition strategy for distributed query processing in fast local networks. *IEEE Transactions on Software Engineering*, **15**(6), 780–793

Zedan, H., Stone, R. F. and Simpson, D., PCHAN: a notion for dynamic resource management in distributed Occam systems. *Microprocessing and Microprograming*, **25**, 253–258

Zedan, H., Time closed layer: a design principle for time-critical applications. In *Proceedings of the Euromicro workshop on Real-Time*, IEEE Computer Society Press, New York, pp. 138–145

Zwiers, J., *Compositionality, Concurrency and Partial Correctness: proof theories for networks of processes, and their relationship*, Springer-Verlag, Berlin

Index

Italic page numbers refer to Figures